HE ROLLINGSTONES

A Visual Documentary by Miles

MW00490271

OMNIBUS PRESS
LONDON / NEW YORK / PARIS / SYDNEY

THE ROLLING STONES

Copyright © 1994 Omnibus Press.
(A division of Book Sales Limited)

Edited by Chris Charlesworth.
Cover & book designed by
Michael Bell Design.
Picture research by David Brolan.

ISBN 0.7119.3460.6
Order No. OP 47318

Exclusive Distributors:
Book Sales Limited
8 / 9 Frith Street, London W1V 5TZ, UK.

Music Sales Corporation
257 Park Avenue South, New York,
NY 10010, USA.

Music Sales Pty Limited
120 Rothschild Avenue, Rosebery,
NSW 2018, Australia.

To the Music Trade only:
Music Sales Limited
8 / 9 Frith Street, London W1V 5TZ, UK.

Front cover: London Features International;
Richie Aaron / Redferns: 97bl, 98x3, 99; Glenn
A. Baker / Redferns: 27t, 53br, 56tl&r; Dick
Barnatt / Redferns: 84; John Bellismo / Retna:
125c; Adrian Boot / Retna: 137tr; Dominick
Conde / Star File: 133x3, 135t; Fin Costello /
Redferns: 3bl, 71l, 73, 86, 88x3; Ian Dickson /
Redferns: 65b; Harry Goodwin: 3t, 5t&br, 6t, 7t,
10br, 13t, 14t, 15t, 26t&b, 37b, 45, 58t&b; Steve
Granitz / Retna: 129bl; Bob Gruen / Star File:
3br, 4bl, 71r, 85t, 90, 91t, 93t&b, 95t, 97br, 100t,
106t, 108tl&r, 113tr&bl, 115tr, 123b, 139b,
151br, 157tr&b; Jean Havilland / Retna: 137tl;
Malcolm Heywood / Retna: 121b, 152t; Bob
King / Redferns: 146, 148b; LFI: 4br, 5bl, 6br,
7br, 8t&b, 9t, 11tl, 12t, 14b, 16b, 20t, 21x3, 22tl,
25b, 28bl, 29b, 30bl&r, 34t, 36t&b, 37t, 47r,
52br, 53bl, 55br, 61b, 64, 72t, 75t, 79c&b, 81t,
85b, 89r, 91b, 94b, 96t, 100b, 112tl&r, 113br,
115tl&b, 116 / 117, 118tr, 119, 120c, 122x3,
125b, 127t&b, 128t, 129t&br, 131t&bl, 136t&b,
138t,bl&r, 139tl, 141x3, 143b, 145t&b, 147b,
149t&b, 150, 153x3, 155, 156b, 158b, 159b;
Jeffrey Mayer / Star File: 142; Gered
Mankowitz: 59l; Michael Melia / Retna: 147t;
Music Sales Archives: 4t, 12b, 18b, 22tr,
23t&b, 24b, 25tl&r, 27b, 28br, 30t, 31t&b, 32b,
33, 42b, 43t, 44r, 46t; Pictorial Press: 6bl, 10bl,
11tr&b, 13bx3, 16t, 17, 19x3, 22b, 24t, 34b,
39l&r, 40t&b, 41t&b, 42t, 44l, 46b, 47l, 48x3,
49x3, 50t&b, 51x3, 52t&bl, 54, 70; Barry
Plummer: 9bl, 57t&b, 68, 69t, 89l, 131, 159tr;
Neal Preston / Retna: 140b; Jonathan Postal /
Retna: 151t; Chuck Pulin / Star File: 7bl, 95t,
113tl, 151bl; Michael Putland / Retna: 66, 69b,
72b, 74l&r, 76, 77tr&b, 79t, 80t, 81b, 82t&b, 87,
101, 102, 110r, 124x3; David Redfern /
Redferns: 20b, 28t, 29t, 32t, 35t&b, 38x3, 67,
75b, 80b, 83; Redferns: 10t, 18t, 43b, 94t; Retna:
15b, 24c, 112b, 126, 134, 148t, 152b, 154t, 158t;
Ebet Roberts / Redferns: 9br, 97t, 103b,
104t&b, 105t, 106b, 108b, 109x3, 110l&c, 114,
tl&b, 120t&b, 122tr, 125tl, 128c, 130tl,tr&c,
135c&b, 138c, 140t&c, 154b; Tony Russel /
Redferns: 59r; Honey Salvadori / Retna: 130b;
Peter Sanders / Redferns: 55t, 56b; Joe Sia /
Star File: 60t, 61t, 62, 63t&b, 65t, 77tl; David
Seelig / Star File: 157tl; Gene Shaw / Star File:
159tl; Star File: 103t; Ray Stevenson / Retna:
55bl; Syndication International: 53t, 60t;
Rocky Widner / Retna: 107, 158l; Luciano Viti /
Retna: 128b, 156t; Scott Weiner / Retna: 131br;
Graham Wiltshire / Redferns: 78, 123t;
Frank Ziths / Star File: 121t; Vinnie Zuffante /
Star File: 92, 96b, 105t, 111, 137b, 139tr.

A catalogue record for this book is available
from the British Library.

Printed and bound in Italy.

MICHAEL PHILIP JAGGER

VOCALS

Born: 26 July, 1944, in Dartford, Kent. His father, Joe, was a physical education instructor and lecturer. His mother, Eva, stayed home to bring up Michael and his younger brother, Christopher. Mick went to Maypole Primary then to Wentworth County Primary School where he first met Keith Richards when he was six years old. Mick: "We lived on the same block for a while when we were kids. Another guy who lived on the block was the painter Peter Blake... it was a pretty rough block though. Keith and I went to the same school at one point and we walked home together. Then I met him later on and we really remembered each other."

Mick attended Dartford Grammar School where he formed a skiffle group when he was 15 but he quickly moved on to study the blues and R&B, ordering American blues and R&B records from the States, many of which were unknown in Britain.

He studied at the London School of Economics and was waiting for the train to go up to London from Dartford when he met his childhood friend Keith Richards and renewed a friendship which led to the formation of The Rolling Stones. They began to play together with an art college friend of Keith's called Dick Taylor, calling themselves Boy Blue and The Blue Boys. He and Keith felt isolated in their love of R&B until they attended a performance by Alexis Korner's Blues Incorporated at the Ealing Club and met Brian Jones who was sitting in with the band, playing slide guitar like Elmore James. Mick, Keith and Brian quickly became a team and Mick and Keith moved into Brian's flat in Edith Grove, Fulham, in order to practise their music together.

Mick was still receiving his college grant and dragged himself to the L.S.E. often enough to avoid being expelled.

MICKJAGGER

**Above: Mick in 1963.
Bottom left: On stage at Belle Vue, Manchester. Bottom right: Mick in New York to promote 'Wandering Spirit', February 1993.**

KEITH RICHARDS

GUITAR

Born: 18 December, 1943, in Dartford, Kent. His father, Bert, was an electrical engineer. His mother, Doris, demonstrated washing machines at the Dartford Co-op.

He was educated at Westhill Infants School, Wentworth County Primary School, where he first met Mick Jagger, and Dartford Technical School. Keith went through a Teddy boy period at Dartford Tech, wearing drainpipe trousers and lurid pink socks. He went on to do three years at Sidcup School of Art. Keith's grandfather was a country fiddler and before the war, his father ran a dance band. When he was 15, Keith's mother gave him a £10 guitar. His first public appearance was playing guitar with a Country and Western band made up of fellow art students.

He had a friend at Sidcup School of Art called Dick Taylor who together with Mick Jagger comprised the earliest line-up of The Rolling Stones. It was a tape of this trio that Jagger first sent to Alexis Korner, which helped get them their gig with Blues Incorporated. Taylor left when he was offered a place at the Royal College of Art.

[Keith dropped the 's' at the end of his surname for showbiz reasons when the Stones became successful. After 1977, he reassumed his proper name - with the 's'.]

KEITH RICHARDS

Above: Keith in his Isle of Man hotel room, August 13, 1964. Bottom: On stage in New York and with a guitar bought as a wedding present for him and Patti Hansen, December 1983.

LEWIS BRIAN HOPKINS-JONES

MULTI-INSTRUMENTALIST

Born: 28 February, 1942, in Cheltenham, Gloucestershire. Died 3 July, 1969. Brian's father, Lewis, worked at Dowty's aircraft works, the biggest engineering works in the area. His mother, Louisa, was a piano teacher. He was sent to Dean Close public school as a day boy and went from there to Cheltenham Grammar School. Even though he was suspended for a short spell for encouraging rebellion against the prefects, he passed nine 'O' levels and 2 'A' level GCE's, way above average.

Lewis was the organist at the local church and Brian sang in the choir. In 1958, Brian's interest in music led him to become membership secretary of the 66 Club, a local jazz club. He played saxophone in several local jazz bands including Bill Nile's Delta Jazz Band and joined The Ramrods, a loud Gloucester rock band that played local dances and art schools.

He became notorious in Cheltenham after getting several young girls pregnant and this led to his leaving school early and becoming estranged from his family. Instead of going on to University, he worked on the buses, as a coalman, in a record shop, but his only real interest was music.

When Alexis Korner played Cheltenham with the Chris Barber Jazz Band, Brian became friendly with him and thenceforth hitch-hiked to London to hear him play with Blues Incorporated. Here he met Charlie Watts who was already playing drums with Alexis.

One evening when he was playing a guest set with Blues Incorporated, Mick and Keith were in the audience and immediately recognised a fellow blues fanatic. Mick became one of Blues Incorporated's vocalists and Keith began to sit in. The inchoate Rolling Stones were born.

BRIAN JONES

Brian became the Stones' fashion plate.

BILLWYMAN

BILL WYMAN

BASS
Né Perks, Lord of the Manor of Gedding and Thormwoods

Born: 24 October, 1936, in Penge, Kent. His father, William, was a bricklayer and his mother, Kathleen was a bench worker in a local factory. He was one of five children: John, Paul, Judy, Anne and Bill. He went to Oakfield Junior School in Penge then to Beckenham Grammar School. His father played the piano accordion and Bill was in the church choir for ten years. He began piano lessons when he was four years old and by the time he was 14 he could play the piano, organ, and clarinet.

When he left school he worked as a bookmaker's clerk before doing his two years national service in the Royal Air Force, some of which he spent stationed in Germany. He worked in an engineering firm in Lewisham where he became an undermanager.

He met his first wife Diane at the Royston Ballroom, Beckenham, and they were married in October 1959. Not long afterwards he started his own group, The Cliftons. In 1962, he and Diane had a son, Stephen.

Above: Bill at Top Of The Pops, 1963. Bottom: Tuning up backstage the same year.

CHARLIE WATTS

DRUMS

Born: 2 June, 1941, in Wembley, Middlesex. His father, Charles, worked as a parcels lorry driver for British Rail at Kings Cross Station. When Charlie was 14, his father and mother, Lilly, gave him a £12 drum set. He played along with modern jazz records, and when he joined the Stones he listed Gil Evans and George Russell as his favourite composers.

He was educated at Tyler's Croft Secondary Modern School where he won prizes for Art and English. He then spent three years at Harrow School of Art. In 1961 he wrote and illustrated a small book on the life of saxophonist Charlie Parker which was first published in December 1964.

Charlie began playing in public with a group called Blues By Five at the Troubadour Club in Chelsea and later joined Alexis Korner's Blues Incorporated.

Charlie: "I met Alexis in a club somewhere and he asked me if I'd play drums for him. A friend of mine, Andy Webb, said I should join the band, but I had to go to Denmark to work in design, so I sort of lost touch with things. While I was away, Alexis formed his band, and I came back to England with Andy. I joined the band with Cyril Davies and Andy used to sing with us. We had some great guys in the band, like Jack Bruce. These guys knew what they were doing. We were playing at a club in Ealing and they, Brian, Mick and Keith, used to come along and sometimes sit in. It was a lot different then. People used to come up on the stand and have a go and the whole thing was great."

He joined The Rolling Stones in January 1963 but continued to work at Charles Hobson and Grey, a firm of advertising agents, until the group was able to turn professional. At an early Stones gig, he met Shirley Ann Shepherd and without telling the others, they were married on 14 October, 1964, at Bradford Register office in Yorkshire.

They lived in Paddington, in West London, then, when the Stones began to make money, bought the former home of Lord Shawcross in Lewes, Sussex, where Shirley was able to build a proper sculpture studio and Charlie to indulge his passion for American Civil War artefacts.

Above: Charlie at Top Of The Pops, 1963. Bottom left: Promoting his album 'From One Charlie' in New York, June 1991. Bottom right: Looking cool in 1966.

CHARLIE WATTS

MICK TAYLOR

MICK TAYLOR

GUITAR

Born: 17 January, 1948, Welwyn Garden City, Hertfordshire. His father, Lionel, was an aircraft worker and Mick had a sister, Marilyn, born in 1952. He went to Onslow Secondary Modern School but left at 15 and worked as a commercial artist for three months, then as a labourer in a paint factory. He taught himself to play the guitar and joined a local Welwyn Garden City band called The Gods. When Eric Clapton missed a gig with John Mayall's Bluesbreakers, Mick deputised for him and later, when Clapton left The Bluesbreakers, Taylor was called to be his replacement.

He was with Mayall for two years and appeared on the 'Crusade', 'Bare Wires' and 'Laurel Canyon' albums.

Above: Mick Taylor. Bottom: At his Stones début with the rest of the band in Hyde Park, London, July 5, 1969.

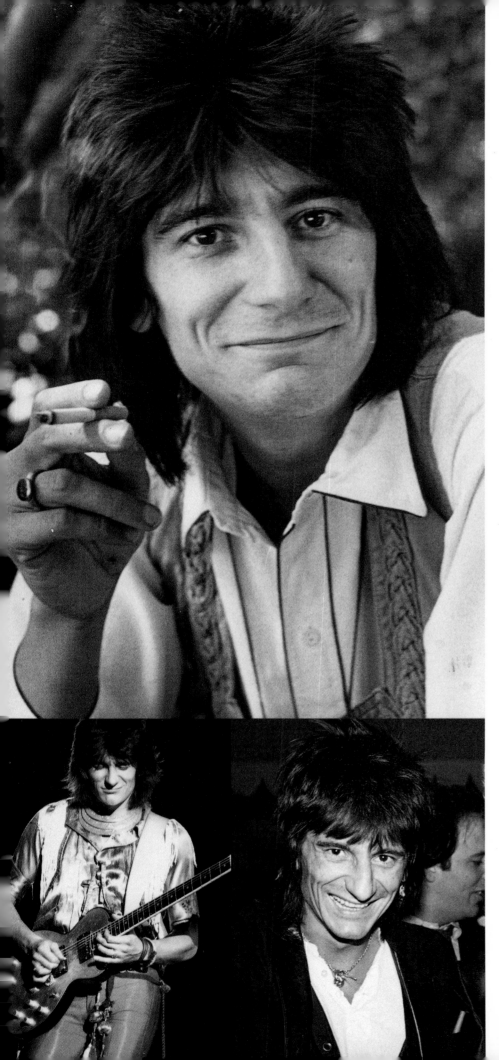

RON WOOD

GUITAR

Born: 1 June, 1947, Hillingdon, Middlesex. Ron's two older brothers, Art and Ted were both in bands, giving him valuable contacts and experience early in his career. When Ron was 12, Art was a vocalist with Alexis Korner's Blues Incorporated featuring Charlie Watts on drums. Art started his own band, The Artwoods, in 1963 and Ted was with The Temperance Seven.

Ron grew up learning to play the clarinet, horns, washboard, drums and guitar. He went to art college and when he was 16 he joined The Birds as a guitarist and played the Mod circuit around Acton, Shepherds Bush and Ealing. Ron: "I got my first break playing harmonica at the Crawdaddy Club with The Yardbirds. Keith Relf was ill and my friends all pushed me forward, 'Aw, c'mon! Play!' Eric [Clapton] took me back afterwards. We knew each other, kind of... He was good to me. He said, 'You really play harmonica well.' I said, 'Thank you very much. I also play guitar you know.' After that we used to swap ideas."

His next break came through Jeff Beck, also a former member of The Yardbirds, who asked Ron to join his solo group as a second guitarist, but when the bass player failed to show up at the first rehearsal, Ron switched to bass which he played throughout the group's stormy career. The Jeff Beck Band folded in mid-1969.

Meanwhile, Steve Marriott had decided to leave The Small Faces and they asked Ron to replace him, playing guitar. Ron brought along Rod Stewart from the Beck Band, as vocalist. The Faces prospered and by 1972, Ron was able to buy The Wick on Richmond Hill, Surrey, overlooking the Thames, the childhood home of Hayley Mills. He installed his own studio and began work on his first solo album. One of the people he invited to sit in as a guest was Keith Richards.

Keith: "I heard that he was starting work on his first album, and he was playing with Andy Newmark and Willie Weeks, so it sounded interesting. Then I got an invitation to come down and check it out, and if I wanted, to play on one track. I got there late that night... and I didn't get out of the house for three months." Keith moved into Ron's guest house. After this, it was inevitable that when Mick Taylor left the Stones at the end of 1974, Ron was regarded as the only possible replacement. Mick Jagger told him, "Either you join or we aren't doing the tour."

Above: Ron Wood. Bottom left: On stage at Knebworth Park, England, August 21, 1976. Bottom right: In 1983.

RONWOOD

Dates: Marquee Jazz Club [without Bill & Charlie] (12). The Stones also play one date at Ealing Jazz Club [without Bill & Charlie] [exact date unknown].

12
The Rolling Stones play their first gig. The day before *Jazz News* reported, "Mick Jagger, R&B vocalist, is taking a rhythm and blues group into the Marquee tomorrow (Thursday) while Blues Inc. is doing its Jazz Club gig. Called 'The Rolling Stones' ('I hope they don't think we're a rock'n'roll outfit,' says Mick), the line-up is: Jagger (vocal), Keith Richards, Elmo Lewis (guitars), Dick Taylor (bass), 'Stu' (piano), Mike Avery (drums). A second group under Long John Baldry will also be there." In those days the *Marquee* was at 165 Oxford Street.

AUGUST
Dates: The Stones play one date at the Ealing Jazz Club, London [without Bill & Charlie] [exact date unknown].

Mick: "I remember Tuesday nights at Ealing. Six people used to come. It was so cold we'd have to play with our coats on. Eric Clapton used to come and sing 'Roll Over Beethoven', he couldn't play guitar then - he couldn't..."

SEPTEMBER
Dates: The Stones [without Bill & Charlie] play three weekly dates at Ealing Jazz Club, London [exact dates unknown] and one date at the Marquee Jazz Club, London [exact date unknown].

Above: One of the earliest known group photographs, overlooking the Thames Embankment at Chelsea in early 1963. Below, left: On the set of Ready Steady Go! in 1963. Below, right: Mick perfecting his mic technique offstage the same year.

1960

OCTOBER
Late October, while taking the train from Dartford station to go up to LSE, Mick runs into Keith Richards, who is on his way to Sidcup Art College. Keith: "So I get on this train one morning and there's Jagger and under his arm he has four or five albums. I haven't seen him since the time I bought an ice cream off him and we haven't hung around since we were... five, six, ten years. We recognised each other straight off. 'Hi man,' I say. 'Where ya going?' he says. And under his arm he's got Chuck Berry and Little Walter, Muddy Waters. 'You're into Chuck Berry, man. Really? That's a coincidence...'."

1962

MARCH
17
Blues Incorporated play their first gig at the Marquee Club, London. The line-up is Alexis Korner on guitar, Charlie Watts on drums, Cyril Davies on harmonica, Dave Stevens on piano, Dick Heckstall-Smith on tenor saxophone and Andy Hoogenboom on bass.

31
Blues Incorporated play the Marquee. The line-up has changed, with Jack Bruce replacing Andy Hoogenboom on bass.

APRIL
7
Blues Incorporated play the Marquee. They have a guest guitar player who calls himself Elmo Lewis. In the audience are Mick and Keith. Keith told *Rolling Stone* magazine: "Alexis was packin' 'em in, man. Just playing blues. Very similar to Chicago stuff. Heavy atmosphere, workers and art students, kids who couldn't make the ballrooms with supposedly long hair then. Forget it, you couldn't go into those places. You gravitated to places where you wouldn't get hassled. And suddenly in '62, just when we were getting together, we read this little thing about a rhythm and blues club starting in Ealing. Everybody must have been trying to get one together, 'Let's go up to this place and find out what's happening,' There was this amazing old cat playing harp... Cyril Davies. Where did he come from? He turned out to be a panel beater from north London. He was a great cat Cyril. He didn't last long. I only knew him for about two years then he died.

"Alexis Korner really got this scene together. He'd been playin' in jazz clubs for ages and he knew all the connections for gigs. So we went up there. The first or second time Mick and I were sitting there, Alexis Korner gets up and says, 'We got a guest to play some guitar. He comes from Cheltenham. All the way up from Cheltenham just to play for you.' Suddenly it's *Elmore James*, this cat man. And it's Brian, man, he's sittin' on his little... he's bent over... da-da-da, da-da-da... I said, 'What? What the fuck?' playing bar slide guitar.

"We get into Brian after he finishes 'Dust My Broom'. He's really fantastic and a gas. We speak to Brian. He's been doin' the same as we'd been doin'... thinking he was the only cat in the world who was doin' it."

1963

Bill & Charlie] (4); Sidcup Art College, Sidcup, Kent [without Bill & Charlie] (12); The Youth Club, Church Hall, Putney, London [without Charlie] (15); Piccadilly Jazz Club, London [without Charlie] (21); Ealing Jazz Club, London [without Charlie] (22). The Stones [without Charlie] also played one date at the Red Lion pub, Sutton, Surrey [exact date unknown] and one date at South Oxhey, near Watford, Hertfordshire [exact date unknown].

5

Tony Chapman has told Bill Wyman that The Rolling Stones needed a bass player, and takes him to the Red Lion pub in Sutton where he is introduced to Ian Stewart, the Stones' pianist. Ian invites Bill to rehearsals.

7

Bill and Tony Chapman borrow Tony's dad's car and attend a Stones rehearsal in a back room of the Wetherby Arms pub in Chelsea. Ian Stewart introduces Bill to Mick, who is quite friendly, then to Brian and Keith who are at the bar and not interested in talking. Everything changes when Bill brings in his gear.

Keith: "We all turned up for rehearsals and in walks Bill with a huge speaker and a spare Vox AC30 amp, which was the biggest amp we'd seen in our lives! 'That's spare,' he said. 'You can put one of your guitars through there.' Whew! That put us up quite a few volts. He had the bass together already. He'd been playing in rock bands, knew how to play, but he didn't want to play with those shitty rock bands any more."

OCTOBER
Dates: Woodstock Hotel, North Cheam, Surrey (5). The Stones [without Bill & Charlie] also play two weekly dates at the Ealing Jazz Club, London [exact dates unknown] and one date at the Marquee Jazz Club, London [a Thursday, exact date unknown].

NOVEMBER
Dates: Piccadilly Jazz Club, London [without Bill & Charlie] (30). The Stones [without Bill & Charlie] also play two weekly dates at the Ealing Jazz Club, London [Saturdays, exact dates unknown], two weekly dates at the Flamingo Jazz Club [Mondays, exact dates unknown] and one date at the Red Lion pub, Sutton, Surrey [a Friday, exact date unknown].

DECEMBER
Dates: Ealing Jazz Club [without

JANUARY
Dates: Ealing Jazz Club, London [without Charlie] (5); Flamingo Jazz Club, London [without Charlie] (7); Red Lion pub, Sutton, Surrey [without Charlie] (9); Ricky Tick Club at the Star & Garter pub, Windsor, Berkshire (11); Flamingo Jazz Club, London (14); Marquee Jazz Club, London (17); Ealing Jazz Club, London (19); Flamingo Jazz Club, London (21); Red Lion pub, Sutton, Surrey (23); Marquee Jazz Club, London (24); Ricky Tick Club at the Star & Garter pub, Windsor, Berks (25); Ealing Jazz Club, London (26); Flamingo Jazz Club, London (28); Marquee Jazz Club, London (31).

9

Charlie Watts joins The Rolling Stones. Alexis Korner: "Then the Stones decided they wanted to get together and do things on their own. I didn't bug them because I thought, you know, 'They got things to do and they should go off and do them.' So they slid off, Mick, Keith, Brian and Ian Stewart on piano. I remember about a year later, Charlie Watts, who was still not blowing regularly with anybody, came up to my old lady and said, 'The Stones have asked me to join them, what do you think I should do?' And she said, 'Well, if you're not doing anything else, why don't you? What have you got to lose?' So Charlie joined the Stones."

28

28 - 2 FEBRUARY
The Stones record at IBC Studios, London, engineered by Glyn Johns. IBC own the tapes which have to be bought back by Eric Easton for £90 before the group can sign with Decca in May.

FEBRUARY
Dates: Ricky Tick Club at the Star & Garter pub, Windsor (1); Ealing Jazz Club, London (2); Ealing Jazz Club, London (5); Red Lion pub, Sutton (6); Harringay Jazz Club, Manor House pub, London (7); Ricky Tick Club at the Star & Garter pub, Windsor (8); Ealing Jazz Club, London (9); Ealing Jazz Club, London (12); Harringay Jazz Club, Manor House pub, London (14); Ealing Jazz Club, London (16); Ealing Jazz Club, London (19); Red Lion pub, Sutton (20); Ricky Tick Club at the Star & Garter pub, Windsor (22); Ealing Jazz Club, London (23); Station Hotel, Richmond (24); Harringay Jazz Club, Manor House pub, London (28).

7

The Stones have equal billing with Blues By Six, featuring Brian Knight, at the "Gala Opening Night" of Rhythm and Blues at the Harringay Jazz Club held at the Manor House pub, across from the Manor House tube station.

MARCH
Dates: Ealing Jazz Club, London (2); Studio 51, Ken Colyer Club, London / Station Hotel, Richmond (3); Red Lion pub, Sutton (6); Harringay Jazz Club at Manor House pub, London (7); Ricky Tick Club at the Star & Garter pub, Windsor (8); Wooden Bridge Hotel, Guildford, Surrey (9); Studio 51, Ken Colyer Club, London / Station Hotel, Richmond (10); Harringay Jazz Club at Manor House pub, London (14); Ricky Tick Club at the Star & Garter pub, Windsor (15); Studio 51, Ken Colyer Club, London / Station Hotel, Richmond (17); Red Lion pub, Sutton (20); Ricky Tick Club at the Star & Garter pub (22); Studio 51, Ken Colyer Club, London / Station Hotel, Richmond (24); Ricky Tick Club at the Star & Garter pub, Windsor (29); Wooden Bridge Hotel, Guildford, Surrey (30); Studio 51, Ken Colyer Club, London / Station Hotel, Richmond (31).

APRIL
Dates: Red Lion pub, Sutton (3); Studio 51, Ken Colyer Club, London / Station Hotel, Richmond (7); Studio 51, Ken Colyer Club, London / Crawdaddy Club at Station Hotel, Richmond (14); Wooden Bridge Hotel, Guildford (19); Crawdaddy Club at Station Hotel, Richmond (21); Eel Pie Island, Twickenham, Middlesex (24); Ricky Tick Club at the Star & Garter pub, Windsor (26); Studio 51, Ken Colyer Club, London / Crawdaddy Club at Station Hotel, Richmond (28).

The Stones record a soundtrack for a 20 minute documentary about themselves made by their manager Giorgio Gomelsky at R.G.Jones studio in London.

14

The Beatles visit the Stones at the Crawdaddy Club on their way back from recording *Thank Your Lucky Stars* at Twickenham. The two groups go back to Edith Grove to hang out and jam.

18

The Rolling Stones go backstage as The Beatles' guests at the Royal Albert Hall. They help The Beatles roadies carry out the gear and Brian is mistaken by fans for one of The Beatles. All the way home he tells manager Gomelsky, "Giorgio, that's what I want!"

Above left: Alexis Korner
Above right & below: On board HMS Discovery on the river Thames, 1963.

and the Stones sign an exclusive management agreement with Oldham and Eric Easton on this date. When Gomelsky returns, he finds he has been cut out of the deal completely. Within a week Oldham has secured a deal with Dick Rowe, A&R man at Decca Records, who is anxious to make up for missing out on signing The Beatles who went to EMI's Parlophone label.

10
The Stones record 'Come On', 'I Want To Be Loved', 'Love Potion No.9' and 'Pretty Thing' at Olympic Studios, Barnes, with Andrew Oldham and Eric Easton producing, Roger Savage engineering.

13
The Stones, minus Bill and Charlie, record an audition tape for BBC-Radio's Jazz Club. It is rejected.

JUNE
Dates: Studio 51, Ken Colyer Club, London / Crawdaddy Club at Station Hotel, Richmond (2); Studio 51, Ken Colyer Club, London (3); Eel Pie Island, Twickenham (5); Wooden Bridge Hotel, Guildford (7); Studio 51, Ken Colyer Club, London / Crawdaddy Club at Station Hotel, Richmond (9); Studio 51, Ken Colyer Club, London (10); Eel Pie Island, Twickenham (12); Ricky Tick Club at the Star & Garter pub, Windsor (14); Studio 51, Ken Colyer Club, London / Crawdaddy Club at Station Hotel, Richmond (16); Studio 51, Ken Colyer Club, London (17); Eel Pie Island, Twickenham (19); Scene Club, London (20); Ricky Tick Club at the Star & Garter pub, Windsor (21); Wooden Bridge Hotel, Guildford (22); Studio 51, Ken Colyer Club, London (23); Studio 51, Ken Colyer Club, London (24); Eel Pie Island, Twickenham (26); Scene Club, London (27); Ricky Tick Club at the Star & Garter pub, Windsor (28); Studio 51, Ken Colyer Club, London / Crawdaddy Club, Athletic Ground, Richmond (30).

7
The Stones first single, 'Come On' / 'I Wanna Be Loved', released on Decca. The 'A' side is a lesser known Chuck Berry song. It reaches No. 21 in the UK charts.

COME ON Berry /
I WANT TO BE LOVED
Dixon
S - Decca F 11675 (UK).
Released: June 1963.
Producer: Side A: Andrew Loog Oldham / Side B: Impact Sound (Andrew Loog Oldham).
Engineer: Roger Savage.
Studio: Olympic Sound, London May 10, 1963.

JULY
Dates: Studio 51, Ken Colyer Club, London (1); Eel Pie Island, Twickenham (3); Scene Club, London (4); Ricky Tick Club at the Star & Garter pub, Windsor (5); Studio 51, Ken Colyer Club, London (8); Eel Pie Island, Twickenham (10); Scene Club, London (11); Twickenham Design College, Eel Pie Island (12); Alcove Club, Middlesborough, Yorks(13); Studio 51, Ken Colyer Club, London / Crawdaddy Club, Athletic Ground, Richmond (14); Studio 51, Ken Colyer Club, London (15); Eel Pie Island, Twickenham (17); Corn Exchange, Wisbech, Cambridgeshire (20); Studio 51, Ken Colyer Club, London / Crawdaddy Club, Athletic Ground, Richmond (21); Studio 51, Ken Colyer Club, London (22); Eel Pie Island, Twickenham (24); Ricky Tick Club at Star & Garter pub, Windsor (26); California Ballroom, Dunstable, Beds (27); Studio 51, Ken Colyer Club, London / Crawdaddy Club, Athletic Ground, Richmond (28); Studio 51, Ken Colyer Club, London (29); Ricky Tick Club at Thames Hotel, Windsor (30); Eel Pie Island, Twickenham (31).

7
The Stones record a session for ATV's *Thank Your Lucky Stars* in Birmingham, performing 'Come On' in matching hound's tooth jackets.

13
The Stones session is broadcast on ATV's *Thank Your Lucky Stars*.

28
28 - 1 AUGUST
The Stones record at Decca Studios in West Hampstead.

AUGUST
Dates: Wooden Bridge Hotel, Guildford (2); St. Leonard's Hall, Horsham, Sussex (3), Studio 51, Ken Colyer Club, London / Crawdaddy Club, Athletic Ground, Richmond (4); Botwell House, Hayes, Middlesex (5); Ricky Tick Club at Thames Hotel, Windsor (6); Eel Pie Island, Twickenham (7); California Ballroom, Dunstable (9), Plaza Theatre, Handsworth, Birmingham / Plaza Theatre, Oldhill, Birmingham (10), Third National Jazz Festival, Richmond Athletic Association Grounds, Richmond (11), Studio 51, Ken Colyer Club, London (12); Town Hall, High Wycombe, Bucks (13); Eel Pie Island, Twickenham (14); Dreamland Ballroom, Margate, Kent (15), Winter Gardens, Banbury, Oxfordshire (16); Memorial Hall, Northwich, Cheshire (17); Studio 51, Ken Colyer Club, London / Crawdaddy Club, Athletic Ground, Richmond (18); Atlanta Ballroom, Woking, Surrey (19); Ricky Tick Club at Thames Hotel, Windsor (20); Eel Pie Island, Twickenham (21); Il Rondo Ballroom, Leicester (24); Studio 51, Ken Colyer Club, London / Crawdaddy Club, Athletic Ground, Richmond (25); Studio 51, Ken Colyer Club, London (26); Ricky Tick Club at Thames Hotel, Windsor (27); Eel Pie Island, Twickenham (28); Oasis Club, Manchester (30); Royal Lido Ballroom, Prestatyn, Wales (31).

28
The Stones appear on Associated Rediffusion TV's *Ready Steady Go!* in London.

29
The Stones appear on Granada TV's *Scene At 6.30* in Manchester.

Above: Until the Stones came along pop groups smiled for the camera, now they looked arrogant. Below: Mick demonstrates this week's dance craze.

28
Andrew Oldham, a 19-year-old former PR man for Brian Epstein's stable of Liverpool acts, sees the Stones for the first time in Richmond.

MAY
Dates: Eel Pie Island, Twickenham (1); Ricky Tick Club at the Star & Garter pub, Windsor, (3); *News Of The World* Charity Gala, Battersea Park, London (4); Studio 51, Ken Colyer Club, London / Crawdaddy Club at Station Hotel, Richmond (5); Eel Pie Island, Twickenham (8); Studio 51, Ken Colyer Club, London / Crawdaddy Club at Station Hotel, Richmond (12); Eel Pie Island, Twickenham (15); Wooden Bridge Hotel, Guildford (17); Studio 51, Ken Colyer Club, London / Crawdaddy Club at Station Hotel, Richmond (19); Eel Pie Island, Twickenham (22); Ricky Tick Club at the Star & Garter pub, Windsor (24); Studio 51, Ken Colyer Club, London / Crawdaddy Club at Station Hotel, Richmond (26); Eel Pie Island, Twickenham (29); Ricky Tick Club at the Star & Garter pub, Windsor (31).

3
The Stones' manager Giorgio Gomelsky's father died in the middle of April and he has to fly to Switzerland to make arrangements for the funeral and be with his family. While he is away, Andrew Oldham muscles his way on to the scene

SEPTEMBER

Dates: Studio 51, Ken Colyer Club, London / Crawdaddy Club, Athletic Ground, Richmond (1); Studio 51, Ken Colyer Club, London (2); Ricky Tick Club at Thames Hotel, Windsor (3); Eel Pie Island, Twickenham (4); Strand Palace Theatre, Walmer, Kent (5); Grand Hotel Ballroom, Lowestoft, Suffolk (6); Kings Hall, Aberystwyth, Wales (7); Studio 51, Ken Colyer Club, London (9); Ricky Tick Club at Thames Hotel, Windsor(10); Eel Pie Island, Twickenham (11); Cellar Club, Kingston-upon-Thames, Surrey (12); California Ballroom, Dunstable, Beds (13); Ritz Ballroom, King's Heath, Birmingham / Plaza Theatre, Oldhill, Birmingham (14); Great Pop Prom, Royal Albert Hall, London / Crawdaddy Club, Athletic Ground, Richmond (15); Studio 51, Ken Colyer Club, London (16); British Legion Hall, Harrow-on-the-Hill, London (17); Eel Pie Island, Twickenham (18); St. John's Hall, Watford, Herts (19); Savoy Ballroom, Southsea, Hants (20); Corn Exchange, Peterborough, Northants (21); Studio 51, Ken Colyer Club, London / Crawdaddy Club, Athletic Ground, Richmond (22); Studio 51, Ken Colyer Club, London (23); Ricky Tick Club at Thames Hotel, Windsor (24); Eel Pie Island, Twickenham (25); Floral Hall, Morecambe, Lancs (27); Assembly Hall, Walthamstow, London (28); New Victoria Theatre, London (29); Ballroom, Cambridge, Cambridgeshire (30).

The Stones record at Kingsway Studios on dates throughout September. Among the titles they record is 'I Wanna Be Your Man', a previously unrecorded Lennon / McCartney song written on the spot for them at a nearby club after a chance meeting in London's Denmark Street. In 1963, an unrecorded Beatles song was a passport to the charts.

POISON IVY Leiber, Stoller / FORTUNE TELLER
A. Toussaint
S - Decca F 11742 (UK).
Released: September 1963.
Not officially released but a few copies did enter circulation.
This is the rarest Stones record for collectors.
Producer: Side A: Impact Sound (Michael Barclay) / Side B: [unknown].
Studio: Decca, London.
Early August, 1963.

8

The Stones appear on *ATV's Thank Your Lucky Stars* in Birmingham.

14 - 15

The Stones record 'You Better Move On', 'Money' and 'Bye Bye Johnny' at Kingsway Studios, all three of which appear on their first EP, 'The Rolling Stones' the next year.

23

Bill, Brian and Charlie provide the backing for Bo Diddley on a recording for BBC-Radio's *Saturday Club*.

29

The Stones begin their first big British tour with Bo Diddley and The Everly Brothers.

OCTOBER

Dates: The Odeon, Streatham, London (1); Regal Theatre, Edmonton, London (2); The Odeon, Southend, Essex (3); The Odeon, Guildford (4); The Gaumont, Watford (5); Capitol Theatre, Cardiff, South Wales (6); The Odeon, Cheltenham, Gloucs (8); The Gaumont, Worcester (9); The Gaumont, Wolverhampton, Staffs (10); The Gaumont, Derby (11); The Gaumont, Doncaster, Yorks (12); The Odeon, Liverpool (13); Majestic Ballroom, Kingston-upon-Hull, Yorks (15); The Odeon, Manchester (16); The Odeon, Glasgow (17); The Odeon, Newcastle-upon-Tyne (18); The Gaumont, Bradford, Yorks (19); The Gaumont, Hanley, Staffs (20); The Gaumont, Sheffield, Yorks (22); The Odeon, Nottingham (23); The Odeon, Birmingham (24); The Gaumont, Taunton, Somerset (25); The Gaumont, Bournemouth, Hants (26); The Gaumont, Salisbury, Wilts (27); The Gaumont, Southampton, Hants (29); The Odeon, St. Albans, Herts (30); The Odeon, Lewisham, London (31).

5

Little Richard joins the tour at the Watford concert.

BBC-Radio transmits the Bo Diddley tape with some of the Stones backing on *Saturday Club*.

16

After playing a concert in Manchester, the Stones drive to Liverpool to visit the Cavern where The Big Three are recording. Mick: "We were really chuffed... We only went there to relax, not to perform, but as soon as the word got around that we were there, we were swamped with requests for autographs."

26

The Stones make their first appearance on BBC Radio *Saturday Club*.

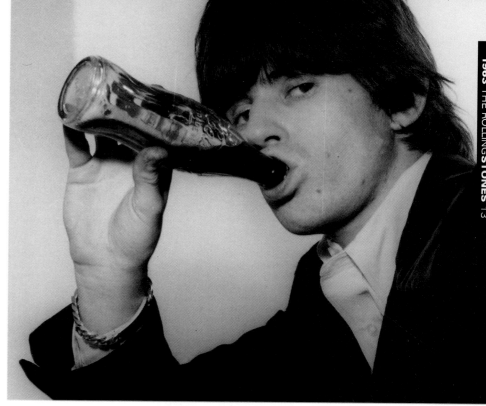

Above: Keith guzzles Coke backstage at Top Of the Pops, 1963. Below: In the dressing room at Thank Your Lucky Stars, Birmingham, September 8, 1963.

NOVEMBER

Dates: The Odeon, Rochester, Kent (1); The Gaumont, Ipswich, Suffolk (2); The Odeon, Hammersmith, London (3); Top Rank Ballroom, Preston, Lancs (4); The Cavern Club, Liverpool (5); Queen's Hall, Leeds, Yorks (6); Club A-Go-Go, Newcastle-upon-Tyne (8); Club A-Go-Go, Whitley Bay, Northumberland (9); Town Hall, Crewe, Cheshire (10); Pavilion Ballroom, Bath, Somerset (11); Town Hall, High Wycombe, Bucks (12); City Hall, Sheffield, Yorks (13); Co-op Ballroom, Nuneaton, Warwickshire (15); Matrix Ballroom, Coventry (16); State Ballroom, Kilburn, London (19); Chiswick Polytechnic Dance, Athletic Club, Richmond (20); McIlroy's Ballroom, Swindon, Wilts (21); Town Hall, Greenwich, London (22); The Baths, Leyton, London / Chez Don Club, Dalston, London (23); Studio 51, Ken Colyer Club, London / Majestic Ballroom, Luton, Beds (24); Ballroom, Warrington, Lancs (25); Ballroom, Altrincham, Cheshire (26); Ballroom, Wigan, Lancs / Memorial Hall, Northwich, Cheshire (27); The Baths, Urmston, Lancs (29); King's Hall, Stoke-on-Trent, Staffs (30).

1

'I Wanna Be Your Man' / 'Stoned' released on Decca. It enters the charts at No. 30 and reaches No. 9. The 'A'-side is a Lennon-McCartney composition given to the group after they bumped into The Beatles near Denmark Street in London's West End and Andrew Oldham casually asked if they'd any songs to spare.

I WANNA BE YOUR MAN
Lennon, McCartney /
STONED Nanker, Phelge
S - Decca F 11764 (UK).
Released November 1963.
Released in USA in 1964 as London 9641 but withdrawn almost immediately from sale.
Producer: Impact Sound (Eric Easton).
Studio: Kingsway, London, October 7, 1963.

Notes: The first few hundred pressings spelt the 'B' Side as 'Stones'.

17

The Stones record a session for ATV's *Thank Your Lucky Stars* in Birmingham.

22

The Stones appear on Associated Rediffusion TV's *Ready Steady Go!* in London.

23

The Stones recording for *Thank Your Lucky Stars* is shown on ATV.

28

The *Daily Mirror* reports: 'Gene Pitney Meets The Rolling Stones. When I first saw them I didn't know whether to say hello or bark. But then I got to know them. They are something, really something.'

Two weeks later Pitney releases 'This Girl Belongs To Yesterday' written by Mick and Keith, produced by Andrew Oldham.

DECEMBER

Dates: Oasis Club, Manchester (1); Assembly Rooms, Tamworth, Staffs (2); Floral Hall, Southport, Lancs (3); The Baths, Doncaster, Yorks (4); The Theatre, Worcester (5); The Odeon, Romford, Essex (6); Fairfield Hall, Croydon (7); Olympia Ballroom, Reading, Berks / The Gaumont, Watford, Herts (8); Bradford Arts Ball, King and Queen Hall, Bradford (11); Locarno Ballroom, Liverpool (12); Ballroom, Hertford (13); The Baths, Epsom, Surrey (14); Civic Hall, Guildford (15); Town Hall, High Wycombe, Bucks (17); The Corn Exchange, Bristol (18); Lido Ballroom, Winchester, Hants (20); Kayser Bondor Ballroom, Baldock, Herts (21); St. Mary's Hall, Putney, London (22); Town Hall, Leek, Staffs (24); Selby's Restaurant, London (26); Town Hall, Reading (27); Club Noreik, Tottenham, London (28); Studio 51, Ken Colyer Club, London (30); Drill Hall, Lincoln, Lincs (31).

19

The Stones record a session for a BBC-TV pilot show which is never broadcast.

27

The Stones appear on Associated Rediffusion TV's *Ready Steady Go!* in London.

1964

JANUARY

Dates: Glenlyn Ballroom, Forest Hill, London (3); Town Hall, Oxford (4); Olympia Ballroom, Reading (5); Granada Theatre, Harrow-on-the-Hill, London (6); The Adelphi Theatre, Slough, Bucks (7); Granada Theatre, Maidstone, Kent (8); Granada Theatre, Kettering, Northants (9); Granada Theatre, Walthamstow (10); The Baths, Epsom, Surrey (11); Granada Theatre, Tooting, London (12); Barrowlands Ballroom, Glasgow (13); Granada Theatre, Mansfield, Notts (14); Granada Theatre, Bedford, Beds (15); McIlroy's Ballroom, Swindon, Wilts (16); City Hall, Salisbury, Wilts (17); Pier Ballroom, Hastings, Sussex (18); The Theatre, Coventry (19); Granada Theatre, Woolwich, London (20); Granada Theatre, Aylesbury, Bucks (21); Granada Theatre, Shrewsbury, Shropshire (22); The Pavilion, Lowestoft, Suffolk (23); The Palais, Wimbledon, London (24); California Ballroom, Dunstable, Beds (25); De Montfort Hall, Leicester (26); Colston Hall, Bristol, Gloucs (27); Public Hall, Preston, Lancs (31).

The Stones are at Regent Sound Studio in London from late January until February recording the songs which make up their first album. Phil Spector is present on some sessions as are Gene Pitney, Graham Nash and Allan Clarke. Keith: "We did our early records on a two-track Revox in a room insulated with egg cartons at Regent Sound. It was a little demo studio in 'Tin Pan Alley', as it used to be called, Denmark Street in Soho. It was all done on a two-track Revox that he had on the wall. We used to think, 'Oh, this is a recording studio, huh? This is what they're like.' A tiny little back room. Under those primitive conditions it was easy to make the kind of sound we got on our first album and the early singles but hard to make a much better one."

READY, STEADY, GO!
Compilation

A- Decca LK 4577 (UK).
Released: January 1964.
Titles of Stones tracks: Come On (Berry) I Wanna Be Your Man (Lennon, McCartney). Origin of Stones tracks: 'A' sides of first two singles. Other artists appearing on compilation: The Big Three - I'm With You / The Chucks - The HitchHiker / Bern Elliott - Money / Jet Harris & Tony Meehan - Applejack / Heinz - Country Boy / Peter Jay & The Jaywalkers - Kansas City / Kathy Kirby - Secret Love / Peter Maclaine- Yes, I Do / The Mojos - Forever / Brian Poole - Do You Love Me? / Brian Poole - Twist and Shout / The Rockin' Berries - Itty Bitty Pieces / The Tornadoes - Dragonfly.

SATURDAY CLUB
Compilation

A - Decca LK 4583 (UK).
Released: January 1964.
Titles of Stones tracks: 1. Poison Ivy (Leiber, Stoller) / 2. Fortune Teller (Neville).
Recorded: Summer 1963.
Origin of Stones tracks: Originally scheduled for release as Decca single F 11742 in September 1963 but cancelled. Decca producer M. Barclay was assigned to handle the sessions.

Other artists appearing on compilation - Dave Berry - Memphis, Tennessee / The Chimes - Say It Again / Karl Denver - I Forgot What It Was Like / Lorne Gibson Trio - Go Easy On My Heart / Jet Harris and Tony Meehan - Applejack / Ted Heath Music - Saturday Club / Kathy Kirby - Bye Bye Birdie / Kathy Kirby - Dance On / The Marauders - Greenback Dollar / Brian Poole - Do You Love Me / Brian Poole - Twenty Miles / Doug Sheldon - Mickey's Monkey / The Tornadoes - Telstar / The Vernon Girls - Do You Know What I Mean?

Note: This is a different take of track 1 than the one that appeared on EP 'The Rolling Stones'.

1

The Stones record a session for BBC-TV's *Top Of The Pops* in Manchester.

2

The Stones recording is shown on *Top Of The Pops*.

6

The Stones begin their second British tour, ending on the 27th. Also on the bill are The Ronettes, Marty Wilde, Dave Berry and The Cruisers, The Swinging Blue Jeans, Al Paige and The Cheynes.

7

Cyril Davies dies of leukaemia in London.

10

'To Know Him Is To Love Him' (Spector) / 'There Are But Five Rolling Stones' (Leander, Oldham) by Cleo released on Decca. Produced by Andrew Oldham, all of the Stones play on the 'A' side.

17

'The Rolling Stones' [EP] released on Decca: 'Bye Bye Johnny' / 'Money' / 'You Better Move On' / 'Poison Ivy'. It enters the charts at No. 28 and reaches No. 15.

THE ROLLING STONES

EP- Decca DFE 8560 (UK).
Released: January 1964.
Producer: Impact Sound (Eric Easton).
Recorded: November 1963.

Side 1: 1. Bye Bye Johnny (Berry) / 2. Money (Gordy Jr., Bradford).

Side 2: 3. You Better Move On (Alexander) / 4. Poison Ivy (Leiber, Stoller).

Notes: Track 4 is a different mix or version from the withdrawn single. This earlier cut appears on the compilation album 'Saturday Club' (Matrix XDR 31643).

24

The Stones appear on BBC TV's *Go Man Go*.

29

The Stones record a session for BBC-TV's *Top Of The Pops* in Manchester.

30

BBC-TV screens the Stones session on *Top Of The Pops*.

The Stones record a session in London for BBC-TV's *Town and Around* which is shown in February.

FEBRUARY

Dates: Valentine Cherry Pop Show, Royal Albert Hall, London (1); The Country Club, Hampstead, London (2); Ballroom, Willenhall, Staffs (5); The Regal, Edmonton, London / "All Night Rave" at Club Noreik, Tottenham, London (8); De Montfort Hall, Leicester (9); The Odeon, Cheltenham, Gloucs (10); Granada Theatre, Rugby, Warwickshire (11); The Odeon, Guildford (12); Granada Theatre, Kingston-upon-Thames, Surrey (13); The Gaumont, Watford, Herts (14); The Odeon, Rochester, Kent (15); The Guildhall, Portsmouth, Hants (16); Granada Theatre, Greenford, Middlesex (17); Rank Cinema, Colchester, Essex (18); Rank, Stockton-on-Tees, Durham (19); Rank, Sunderland (20); The Gaumont, Hanley, Staffs (21); The Winter Gardens, Bournemouth, Hants (22); The Hippodrome, Birmingham (23); The Odeon, Southend, Essex (24); The Odeon, Romford, Essex (25); The Rialto, York (26); City Hall, Sheffield, Yorks (27); Sophia Gardens, Cardiff, Wales (28); The Hippodrome, Brighton, Sussex (29).

'365 Rolling Stones (One For Each Day Of The Year)' (Oldham, Leander) / 'Oh I Do Like To See Me On The 'B' Side' (Oldham, Watts, Wyman) by the Andrew Loog Oldham Orchestra is released on Decca. Judging by the composing credit, Charlie and Bill provide the rhythm section for this one.

3

The Stones record a session for BBC-Radio's *Saturday Club*.

7

The Stones record a session for ATV's *Arthur Haynes Show* at Elstree Studios.

8

ATV shows the *Arthur Haynes Show* in which the Stones appear.

The Stones appear on BBC Radio *Saturday Club*.

The Stones begin a third British tour which lasts until March 7. Also on the bill are John Leyton, Mike Berry, Jet Harris, The Innocents, Don Spencer, Billie Davies, The LeRoys and Billy Doyle.

14

The Stones appear on Associated Rediffusion TV's *Ready Steady Go!* in London.

18

The Stones February 8 tape is played on BBC-Radio's *Saturday Club*. The Stones appear on BBC Radio's *Pop Inn*.

21

'Not Fade Away' / 'Little By Little' is released on Decca. It enters the charts at No. 10 and reaches No. 3.

NOT FADE AWAY
Petty, Hardin /
LITTLE BY LITTLE
Nanker, Phelge, Spector

S - Decca F 11845 (UK).
Released: February 1964.
Producer: Side A: Andrew Loog Oldham / Side B: Impact Sound (Andrew Loog Oldham).
Studio: Regent Sound, London, February 1964.

Notes: Phil Spector plays maracas. Also in the studio were Gene Pitney whom Andrew Oldham had asked to stop by, and Allan Clarke and Graham Nash of The Hollies. Gene Pitney plays piano on 'Little By Little'.

22

The Stones record a session for BBC-TV's *Top Of The Pops* in Weymouth.

23

The Stones record a session for ATV's *Thank Your Lucky Stars* in Manchester.

29

ATV screens the Stones' appearance on *Thank Your Lucky Stars*.

MARCH

Dates: Empire Theatre, Liverpool (1); Albert Hall, Nottingham (2); Opera House, Blackpool, Lancs (3); The Gaumont, Bradford, Yorks (4); The Odeon, Blackburn, Lancs (5); The Gaumont, Wolverhampton, Staffs (6); The Winter Gardens, Morecambe, Lancs (7); Invicta Ballroom, Chatham, Kent (15); Assembly Hall, Tunbridge Wells, Kent (17); City Hall, Salisbury, Wilts (18); Whitehall, East Grinstead, Sussex (21); The Pavilion, Ryde, Isle-of-Wight, Hants (22); Guildhall, Southampton, Hants (23); Town Hall, Birmingham (25); Town Hall, Kidderminster, Worcestershire (26); Ex-Servicemen's Club, Windsor (27); Wilton Hall, Bletchley, Bucks / Club Noreik, Tottenham, London (28); Ricky Tick Club, Plaza Ballroom, Guildford / Olympia Ballroom, Reading, Berks (30); West Cliff Hall, Ramsgate, Kent (31).

'Not Fade Away' / 'I Wanna Be Your Man' released in the USA. It struggles into the charts at No. 98 and reaches No. 48.

NOT FADE AWAY
Petty, Hardin /
I WANNA BE YOUR MAN
Lennon, McCartney

S - London 9657 (USA).
Released: March 1964.
Producer: Side A: Andrew Loog Oldham / Side B: Impact Sound (Eric Easton).
Studio: Side A: Regent Sound, London. February 1964 / Side B: Kingsway Studios, London, October 7, 1963.

4

The Stones record a session for BBC-TV's *Top Of The Pops* in Manchester. The same day they record a session in Manchester for Granada TV's *Scene At 6.30* which is shown a few days later.

5

BBC shows the Stones' recording on *Top Of The Pops*.

Above: Bill endures a BBC canteen lamb chop. Below: Keith tunes his new Harmony 12-string, 1964.

13

The Stones, Georgie Fame & The Blue Flames and Long John Baldry record *Blues In Rhythm* for BBC Radio, to be broadcast May 9.

18

Radio Luxembourg records a number of Stones tracks for future editions of the *Nestlés' Top Swinging Groups* show.

19

The Stones tape a session for BBC Radio's *1st Stereo Show* in London.

APRIL

Dates: Locarno Ballroom, Stevenage, Herts (1); The Palais, Wimbledon, London (3); Leas Cliff Hall, Folkstone, Kent (4); The Gaumont, Ipswich, Suffolk (5); Royal Hotel Ballroom, Lowestoft, Suffolk (6); Mod Ball, Empire Pool, Wembley (8); McIlroy's Ballroom, Swindon, Wilts (9); The Baths, Leyton, London (10); Pier Ballroom, Hastings, Sussex (11); Fairfield Hall, Croydon (12); Cubi-Club, Rochdale, Lancs (16); Locarno Ballroom, Coventry (18); Carlton Ballroom, Slough, Bucks (22); The Gaumont, Norwich, Norfolk (24); The Odeon, Luton, Beds (25); *New Musical Express Poll Winners Concert*, Empire Pool, Wembley [afternoon] / Empire Pool Wembley [evening] (26); Pop Prom, Royal Albert Hall, London (27); Public Hall, Wallington, Surrey (28); Majestic Ballroom, Birkenhead, Cheshire (30).

3

The Stones appear on Associated Rediffusion TV's *Ready Steady Go!* in London.

8

The Stones play the *Mad Mod Ball* with Billy J. Kramer at the Wembley Empire Pool before 8,000 fans. Thirty people are arrested for riotous behaviour as police tackle a gang of rockers on motorbikes. The concert is recorded for a future *Ready Steady Go!* TV show.

BBC-TV's *Top Of The Pops* repeats the Stones film recorded on February 22.

10

The Stones make an appearance on BBC Radio's *Joe Loss Show*.

13

The Stones record a tape for BBC Radio's *Saturday Club* in London.

16

'The Rolling Stones', their first album, is released and jumps to No. 1 in the album charts after only eight days. It stays there for 11 weeks. The gig at the Cubi-Club, Rochdale has to be abandoned half way through when the audience riots.

17

Radio Luxembourg broadcasts the *Nestlés' Top Swinging Groups* show.

18

The Stones recording is on BBC Radio *Saturday Club*.

20-21

The Stones participate in the Golden Rose International Television Festival held annually in Montreux, Switzerland.

The Stones appear on Associated Rediffusion TV's *Ready Steady Go!* in Montreux, Switzerland.

24

Radio Luxembourg broadcasts the *Nestlés' Top Swinging Groups* show.

26

The Stones appear at the *New Musical Express Poll Winners' Concert* at Empire Pool, Wembley. Also on the bill are The Beatles and The Dave Clark Five. Two 90 minute films of the concert are shown on ABC-TV on May 3 and May 10. WINS Radio, New York also broadcasts a recording of the concert.

THE ROLLING STONES
A - Decca LK 4605 (UK).
Released: April 1964.
Producer: Impact Sound (Andrew Loog Oldham and Eric Easton).
Studio: Regent Sound, London.
Recorded on a two track Revox, February 1964.

Side 1: 1. Route 66 (Troup) / 2. I Just Want To Make Love To You (Dixon) / 3. Honest I Do (Reed) / 4. I Need You Baby (McDaniels) / 5. Now I've Got A Witness (Like Uncle Phil and Uncle Gene) (Phelge) / 6. Little By Little (Phelge, Spector).

Side 2: 7. I'm A King Bee (Moore) / 8. Carol (Berry) / 9. Tell Me (You're Coming Back) (Jagger, Richard) / 10. Can I Get A Witness (E&B Holland, Dozier) / 11. You Can Make It If You Try (Jarrett) / 12. Walking The Dog (Thomas).

Notes: Ian Stewart plays piano on 9 and 10. Ian Stewart plays organ on 5 and 11. Phil Spector plays maracas on 6. Gene Pitney plays piano on 6.

27

The Stones record for the upcoming BBC-TV show, *Top Beat Pop Prom* in London which is shown in May.

29

The Stones record a session for BBC-TV *Top Of The Pops* in Manchester.

30

BBC-TV's *Top Of The Pops* shows the Stones performance recorded the previous day.

MAY

Dates: Imperial Ballroom, Nelson, Lancs (1); Spa Royal Hall, Bridlington, Yorks (2); Palace Theatre, Manchester, Lancs (3); Savoy Ballroom, Southsea, Hants (7); Town Hall, Hove, Sussex (8); Savoy Ballroom, Catford, London (9); Colston Hall, Bristol, Gloucs (10); Winter Gardens, Bournemouth, Hants (11); City Hall, Newcastle-upon-Tyne (13); Trentham Gardens, Stoke-on-Trent, Staffs (15); The Regal, Edmonton, London (16); The Odeon, Folkestone, Kent (17); Chantingall Hotel, Hamilton, Lanarkshire (18); Capitol Theatre, Aberdeen (19); Caird Hall, Dundee (20); The Regal, Edinburgh (21); University of Leicester (23); The Theatre, Coventry (24); Granada Theatre, East Ham, London (25); Town Hall, Birmingham (26); Danilo Theatre, Cannock, Staffs (27); Essoldo Theatre, Stockport, Cheshire (28); City Hall, Sheffield, Yorks (29); Adelphi Theatre, Slough, Bucks (30); Pop Hit Parade, Empire Pool, Wembley [afternoon] / Empire Pool, Wembley [evening] (31).

'England's Newest Hit Makers - The Rolling Stones' is released in the USA and reaches No. 11 on the album charts.

ENGLAND'S NEWEST HIT MAKERS - THE ROLLING STONES
A - London PS 375 (USA).
Released: May 1964.
Producer: Impact Sound (Andrew Loog Oldham and Eric Easton).
Studio: Regent Sound, London.
Recorded on a two-track Revox, February 1964.

Side 1: 1. Not Fade Away (Petty Hardin) / 2. Route 66 (Troup) / 3. I Just Want To Make Love To You (Dixon) / 4. Honest I Do (Reed) / 5. Now I've Got A Witness (Like Uncle Phil and Uncle Gene) (Phelge) / 6. Little By Little (Phelge, Spector).

Side 2: 7. I'm A King Bee (Moore) / 8. Carol (Berry) / 9. Tell Me (You're Coming Back) (Jagger, Richard) / 10. Can I Get A Witness (E & B Holland, Dozier) / 11. You Can Make It If You Try (Jarrett) / 12. Walking The Dog (Thomas).

Notes: This first American album is essentially the same as the UK 'The Rolling Stones' except that 'I Need You Baby' is replaced with 'Not Fade Away'.

1
Radio Luxembourg broadcasts the Nestlés' Top Swinging Groups show.

3
ABC-TV screen the Stones performance at the NME Poll Winners Concert.

4
The Stones appear on Granada TV's Scene At 6.30 in Manchester.

6
The Stones record a session for Southern TV's Two Go Round in Southampton, which is shown later in the month.

8
Radio Luxembourg broadcasts their final Stones' track on the Nestlés' Top Swinging Groups show.

9
Blues In Rhythm, a half hour experimental stereo programme made by the Stones on March 13, broadcast by BBC radio.

The Stones record a session for BBC-TV's Open House in London for transmission later in the month.

10
The Stones are refused lunch at a hotel in Bristol because they are not wearing ties.

19
Police intervene when 4,000 fans, many with forged tickets, attempt to gatecrash the Stones gig in Aberdeen. A riot ensues.

FOURTEEN
Compilation
A - Decca LK 4695 (UK).
Released: May 1964.
Title of Stones track: 'Surprise Surprise' (Jagger, Richard) Origin of Stones track: Possibly a demo from their songwriting activities. Appears on third US album 'The Rolling Stones Now'. Other artists appearing on compilation: The Applejacks - Baby's In Black / The Bachelors - Maureen / Dave Berry - He's With You / Bern Elliott - Forget Her / Billy Fury - The Diamond Ring / The Johnny Howard Band - Tomboy / Tom Jones - Kiss, Kiss / Kathy Kirby - Soon I'll Wed My Love / Mike Leander Orchestra - Sandstorm / Lulu and The Luvvers - Just One Look / Them - Little Girl / Unit

Four Plus Two - Women From Liberia / The Zombies - Nothing's Changed.

Notes: All profits and all royalties from the artists were donated to The Lords Taverners National Playing Fields Association.

24
The Stones record a session for ABC-TV's Thank Your Lucky Stars in Birmingham.

25
The Stones record a Saturday Club appearance for BBC Radio in London

27
The Stones recording at Regent Sound studio.

29
The Daily Mirror reports, "They are called the ugliest group in Britain. They are not looked on very kindly by most parents or by adults in general. They are even used to the type of article that asks big brother if he would let his sister go out with one of them? But an awful lot of people love 'em - those five, shaggy-as-Shetland-ponies lads known as The Rolling Stones. One hundred and ten thousand people in Britain forked out nearly £200,000 across the record counters for their first LP - simply titled THE ROLLING STONES... Said 20 year old Mick Jagger, 'I never did like wearing a suit. Maybe I'll like a suit when I'm 25'."

30
ABC-TV shows the Stones on Thank Your Lucky Stars.

BBC Radio airs the Saturday Club tape recorded a week before.

JUNE

Dates: Swing Auditorium, San Bernardino, California. (5); "Teen Fair", San Antonio, Texas (6-7); Ballroom, Excelsior Fair, Minneapolis, Minnesota (12); Music Hall, Omaha, Nebraska (13); Olympia Stadium, Detroit, Michigan (14); Commemorative Ball, Magdalen College, Oxford (16); Westview Park, Pittsburgh, Pennsylvania (17); State Farm Arena, Harrisburg, Pennsylvania (19); Carnegie Hall, New York (20); "Welcome Home Stones", Alexandra Palace, London (26).

TELL ME Jagger, Richard / **I JUST WANT TO MAKE LOVE TO YOU** Dixon
S - London 9682 (USA).
Released: June 1964.
Producer: Impact Sound (Andrew Loog Oldham and Eric Easton).
Studio: Regent Sound, London. February 1964.

Notes: Taken from the first album.

1
The Stones fly to America to begin their first US tour. More than 500 fans are waiting for them at Kennedy Airport. Also on the tour bill are Bobby Vee, The Chiffons, Bobby Goldsboro and Bobby Comstock.

In New York the Stones are trapped in their Broadway hotel by fans wielding scissors, hoping to snip off a curl as a souvenir.

The Stones are interviewed for television news and radio, broadcast that same day across the USA. They are also interviewed on Murray the K's Swinging Soirée on WINS radio, New York.

Above: Manfred Mann wait their turn on the set of Ready Steady Go! Below: Mick with 'Terry' singer Twinkle, 1964.

2

The Stones appear on the *Les Crane Show*, a network TV talk show. Les Crane: "This is your first appearance on American television." Keith: "Yeah." Les Crane: "Isn't it exciting?" Keith: "Yeah, knocks me out." (much laughter from camera crew).

3

The Stones record a session for ABC-TV's *Hollywood Palace Show* where they are gratuitously insulted by the drunken host, Dean Martin: "Their hair is not long, it's just smaller foreheads and higher eyebrows." Commenting on a trampoline artist on the show, Martin says, "He's the father of The Rolling Stones, he's been trying to kill himself ever since."

6

Tell Me' / 'I Just Wanna Make Love To You' released in the States. It reaches No. 24 on the charts.

7

The Stones are interviewed on local radio in San Antonio, Texas.

10

The Stones are interviewed on the *Jack Eigen Show* on WMAQ Radio, Chicago.

10-11

The Stones record at Chess Studios in Chicago with Ron Malo at the control board. Muddy Waters and Willie Dixon welcome them in and Chuck Berry stops in to say hello. The tracks include their next single, 'It's All Over Now' and the material on the 'Five By Five' EP.

Keith: "Back in the old 'Five By Five' days, when we were recording in Chicago and Los Angeles, we used to go down to the local record stores, buy up a whole bunch of soul singles, sit down by the record player and learn 'em. Things like 'Oh Baby (We Got A Good Thing Goin')' and old Otis Redding stuff, and then we'd do 'em as quickly as possible."

The Stones record a session in Chicago for American network television, shown a few days later.

11

Police break up a press conference given by The Rolling Stones in the middle of South Michigan Avenue, Chicago, outside the Chess studios. The *Daily Telegraph* reports: "As shrieking fans surged around the five British singers, traffic was in danger of coming to a standstill.

"A senior police chief shouted angrily, 'Get out of here or we'll lock up the whole bunch'." The Stones move to the pavement.

The Stones appear on a TV newsreel, shown the same day on network TV and are interviewed on local radio.

12

The Stones are interviewed on local radio in Minneapolis.

13

The Hollywood Palace TV show is transmitted.

The Stones record a TV interview in Omaha, Nebraska.

14

The Stones are interviewed on local radio in Detroit.

16

A year ago, when the group was virtually unknown, the Stones were booked to play the Oxford Commem for a fee of £100. They fly back from the States especially to play the gig, returning the next morning. The cost of their air-tickets is £1,500.

17

The Stones are interviewed on local radio in Pittsburgh.

18

The Stones record TV and radio interviews in Cleveland, Ohio. They also appear on the *Mike Douglas Show* from Radio WHK Cleveland.

19

The Stones record TV and radio interviews in Harrisburg, Pennsylvania.

MICK JAGGER · CHARLIE WATTS · BRIAN JONES · KEITH RICHARD · BILL WYMAN

20

The Stones appear on WPIX-TV's *Clay Cole Show* in New York.

23

Waiting Stones fans riot as the group flies into London.

The Stones are interviewed for national television news at the airport.

24

The Stones receive *Record Mirror's* Pop Poll 'Best British Vocal Group' award and Jagger the 'Most Popular Individual Group Member' award at a presentation at the Savoy Hotel, London.

26

'It's All Over Now' / 'Good Times, Bad Times' released. It enters the charts at No. 7 and goes to No. 1. Jagger says: "I don't care a damn if our new record has reached number one… What's it matter anyway? 'It's All Over Now' has reached the top, that's great. But I can tell you, none of us has been worrying about it."

The Stones appear on Associated Rediffusion TV's *Ready Steady Go!* in London.

IT'S ALL OVER NOW
B & S Womack /
GOOD TIMES, BAD TIMES
Jagger, Richard
S - Decca F 11934 (UK).
Released: June 1964.
Released in USA in July 1964 as London 9687.
Producer: Impact Sound (Andrew Loog Oldham).
Engineer: Ron Malo.
Studio: Chess, Chicago, June 10, 1964.

Notes: Both tracks appear on the second US album '12 X 12' in a reprocessed form.

27

The Stones record an appearance for BBC-TV's *Juke Box Jury* and BBC-TV's *Top Of The Pops* in London.

JULY

Dates: Spa Royal Hall, Bridlington, Yorks (11); Queen's Hall, Leeds, Yorks (12); Beat City Club, London

(18); Hippodrome, Brighton, Sussex (19); Empress Ballroom, Blackpool, Lancs (24); Imperial Ballroom, Nelson, Lancs (25); De Montfort Hall, Leicester (26); Boom Boom Room, Ulster Hall, Belfast / Flamingo Ballroom, Ballymena, Northern Ireland (31)

'It's All Over Now' / 'Good Times, Bad Times' released in the USA. It enters the charts at No. 100 and climbs to No. 26.

1

The Stones' appearance on *Top of the Pops* is screened.

4

The Stones edition of *Juke Box Jury* is screened.

Above: In Hyde Park, 1965. Centre: on the set of Juke Box Jury, June 27, 1964. Below: partying with Andrew Oldham and Gene Pitney, 1964.

6

Brian is interviewed on Associated Rediffusion TV's *Ready Steady Win* in London.

8

Brian Jones, Keith Richard and Bill Wyman all attend the première of The Beatles' film *A Hard Day's Night* and the celebration party afterwards at the Dorchester Hotel, London.

12

A special on The Rolling Stones called *This Is Their Life* is broadcast on Radio Luxembourg.

15

The Stones record BBC-TV's *Top Of The Pops* in Manchester.

16

The BBC show the Stones on *Top Of The Pops*.

The Stones record a session for Radio Luxembourg's *Teen and Twenty Disc Club* in London.

17

The Stones play the *Joe Loss Pop Show* on the BBC Radio Light Programme. The same day, they record a session for BBC Radio's *Top Gear* show.

23

The Stones recording appears on BBC Radio *Top Gear*.

24

The Stones have to flee the stage for safety after a riot breaks out in the audience at the Empress Ballroom, Blackpool after Keith lashes out at a troublemaker who spits at Brian Jones. Two policemen and 30 fans are injured. Damage is estimated at £4,000 and four fans appear in court charged with assault. Jagger comments: "Some people in the audience obviously didn't like us. We just had enough."

26

Bill, Keith and Charlie are in the audience for *The Man They Call Genius* in Croydon, and appear in the film of the event made by Associated Rediffusion-TV.

28

The Stones record a session for ABC-TV's *Thank Your Lucky Stars* in Teddington.

31

The Stones' Belfast concert is stopped after 12 minutes for causing mass hysteria in the audience. Girls are carried out in strait-jackets.

The Stones appear on BBC-TV's *Six Ten* in Belfast.

AUGUST

Dates: Pier Ballroom, Hastings, Sussex (1); Longleat House, Warminster, Wilts (2); The Kurhaus, Scheveningen, The Hague, Netherlands (8); New Elizabethan Ballroom, Bellvue, Manchester (9); The Tower Ballroom, New Brighton, Cheshire (10); Palace Ballroom, Douglas, Isle of Man (13); The Palais, Wimbledon, London (14); St. George's Hall, New Theatre Ballroom, Guernsey, Channel Islands (18-20); Springfield Hall, St Helier, Jersey, Channel Islands (21-22), The Gaumont, Bournemouth, Hants (23); The Gaumont, Weymouth, Dorset (24); The Odeon, Weston-super-Mare, Somerset (25); ABC Theatre, Exeter, Devon (26); ABC Theatre, Plymouth, Devon (27); The Gaumont, Taunton, Somerset (28); Town Hall, Torquay, Devon (29); The Gaumont, Bournemouth, Hants (30).

2

The stage for the third annual pop concert at Longleat House is the imposing flight of steps at the main entrance. When the Stones take the stage, row after row of fans in the front row are pressed against the crush barriers. Over 200 faint. The Marquis of Bath sums up: "A delightful day... So few hospital cases - the fans were wonderful."

The Stones are interviewed by television news at Longleat House.

5

The Stones record a session for the *Red Skelton Hour* on US television.

7

The Stones appear on Associated Rediffusion TV's *Ready Steady Go!* in London.

8

Two girls have their clothes ripped off when the fans riot at the Stones concert in the Hague. Fans unable to get seats do more than £1000 worth of damage to the hall.

The Stones do two interviews for Dutch television in the Hague.

The Stones session for *Thank Your Lucky Stars* is transmitted.

10

Mick Jagger is fined £32 in court in Liverpool for driving without insurance, failing to produce his driving licence and speeding.

13

The Stones do television and radio interviews in Douglas, Isle of Man.

14

'Five-by-Five' EP released on Decca. 'If You Need Me' / 'Empty Heart' / '2120 South Michigan Avenue' / 'Confessin' The Blues' / 'Around And Around'. It enters the charts at No.13 and reaches No.7.

FIVE BY FIVE
EP - Decca DFE 8590 (UK).
Released: August 1964.
Producers: Impact Sound (Andrew Loog Oldham).
Engineer: Ron Malo.
Studio: Chess, Chicago, June 11, 1964.

Side 1: If You Need Me (Pickett, Bateman, Sanders) / Empty Heart (Nanker, Phelge) / 2120 South Michigan Avenue (Nanker, Phelge).

Side 2: Confessin' The Blues (Brown McShann) / Around And Around (Berry).

15

Mick and Keith are among the guests at a London party for Brian Epstein.

20

The Stones do a television interview in Guernsey, Channel Islands.

24

TWW-TV interview the Stones in Dorchester.

25

The Stones appear on TWW-TV's *Here Today* at Weston-super-Mare.

Above: En route to Paris.
Opposite: On the streets of Paris.

26

Bill, Keith and Charlie are in audience shots of Associated Rediffusion TV's film *The Man They Call Genius*.

SEPTEMBER

Dates: Astoria Theatre, Finsbury Park, London (5); The Odeon, Leicester (6), The Odeon, Colchester, Essex (8); The Odeon, Luton, Beds (9); The Odeon, Cheltenham, Gloucs (I0); Capitol Theatre, Cardiff, Wales (11); The Odeon, Sheffield, Yorks (12); ABC Theatre, Chester, Cheshire (14); The Odeon, Manchester (15); ABC Theatre, Wigan, Lancs (16), ABC Theatre, Carlisle, Cumberland (I7); The Odeon, Newcastle-upon-Tyne (18); Usher Hall, Edinburgh (19); The Globe Theatre, Stockton-on-Tees, Durham (20); ABC Theatre, Hull, Yorks (21); ABC Theatre, Lincoln (22); The Gaumont, Doncaster, Yorks (24); The Gaumont, Hanley, Staffs (25); The Odeon, Bradford, Yorks (26); Hippodrome, Birmingham (27); The Odeon, Guildford, Surrey (29).

TIME IS ON MY SIDE
Meade, Norman /
CONGRATULATIONS
Jagger, Richard
S - London 9708.
Released: September 1964.
Producer: Andrew Loog Oldham.
Engineer: Ron Malo.
Studio: Chess, Chicago.

Notes: Taken from the US album '12 X 5'. Side 'A' appears on the second UK album 'Rolling Stones No. 2' / Side 'B' appears on the Decca compilation 'No Stone Unturned'.

2

The *Red Skelton Hour*, TV show featuring the Stones is filmed for transmission in the USA. 40 Stones fans are used as extras.

5

The Stones begin a British tour. Also on the bill are Inez and Charlie Foxx, Mike Berry, The Mojos, Simon Scott, The LeRoys, Billie Davis.

16

Andrew Loog Oldham, 20, marries Sheila Klein, 18, in Glasgow.

17

The Stones are interviewed by Border-TV in Carlisle.

19

Fans force the Stones to make their departure from the Usher Hall, Edinburgh, in the back of an armoured payroll van.

20

The concert in Hull is filmed by a full camera team from ABC Pathé resulting in a 12-minute colour film.

21

Despitè a row of two dozen rugby-players, hired as a human crash-barrier in front of the stage, one girl manages to get through and knock Jagger flat on his back. As he tries to get up he falls three feet into the empty orchestra pit. The rugby players are almost submerged beneath a wave of screaming girls.

22

The session recorded for the *Red Skelton Show* is shown on US network television to an audience of five million.

25

'Time Is On My Side' / 'Congratulations' released in the USA. It enters the charts at No. 80. The Stones record an interview for the North Staffs Hospital Broadcasting Service in Hanley, Staffordshire.

28

The Stones' hospital interview is transmitted for the first time over the Staffordshire hospital service.

OCTOBER

Dates: Colston Hall, Bristol, Gloucs (1); The Odeon, Exeter, Devon (2); Regal, Edmonton, London (3); The Gaumont, Southampton, Hants (4); The Gaumont, Wolverhampton (5); The Gaumont, Watford, Herts (6); The Odeon, Lewisham, London (8); The Gaumont, Ipswich, Suffolk (9); The Odeon, Southend, Essex (10); Hippodrome, Brighton, Sussex (11); The Olympia, Paris (20); Academy of Music, New York City (24); Memorial Auditorium, Sacramento, California (26); The Tami Show, Civic Auditorium, Santa Monica, California (28-29); Swing Auditorium, San Bernardino, California (31).

'12 X 5' released in the USA and climbs to No. 3 on the album charts. '16 Hip Hits' by the Andrew Loog Oldham Orchestra released on Decca / Ace of Clubs. Produced by Andrew Oldham. Mick Jagger sings on 'Da Doo Ron Ron' which was later re-issued on the Decca compilation, 'Hard Up Heroes'.

12 X 5
A - London PS 402 (USA).
Released: October, 1964.
Producer: Andrew Loog Oldham.
Engineer: Ron Malo.
Studio: Chess, Chicago, 1964.

Side 1: 1. Around and Around (Berry) / 2. Confessin' The Blues (McShann, Brown) / 3. Empty Heart (Nanker, Phelge) / 4. Time Is On My Side (Meade) / 5. Good Times, Bad Times (Jagger, Richard) / 6. It's All Over Now (Womack).

Side 2: 7. 2120 South Michigan Avenue (Nanker, Phelge) / 8. Under The Boardwalk (Resnick, Young) / 9. Congratulations (Jagger, Richard) / 10. Grown Up Wrong (Jagger, Richard) / 11. If You Need Me (Bateman, Pickett, Sanders) / 12. Susie Q (Broadwater, Lewis, Hawkins).

Notes: Not released in the UK. Tracks 5 and 6 come from the single Decca F 11934, but have been reprocessed. Tracks 1, 2, 3, 7 and 11 come from the 'Five By Five' EP, Decca DFE 8590. Tracks 4, 8, 10 and 12 appeared in the UK three months later on the 'The Rolling Stones No. 2' album. Track 9 was not released in the UK until the Decca compilation 'No Stone Unturned' SKL 5173.

1

The Stones, in Bristol for a concert, are banned from the Strand Hotel because of the way they are dressed.

3

The Stones appear on ITV *Thank Your Lucky Stars*.

8

The Stones record a session in London for the BBC World Service programme *Rhythm and Blues*.

14

Charlie Watts marries Shirley Ann Shepherd in Bradford.

16 - 17

The Stones are in Berlin to record a TV appearance.

18

The Stones fly from Berlin to Brussels where 5,000 fans besiege them at the airport. They film a Belgian TV Special on stage at the American Theater in the World Fair grounds.

The *Daily Express* reported: "Chef Thomas Catsolidis put on something special for The Rolling Stones, Britain's long haired pop group, at a Brussels restaurant today. His menu: Cream of tomato soup; tomatoes stuffed with shrimps; and roast pork à la Greque with a special sauce. But the Stones asked for chips and a bottle of branded British sauce. Said the chef, 'I feel like committing suicide or murder. I worked hours of overtime preparing this special sauce for them'."

19

The Stones fly to Paris where they rehearse at the Olympia for the next day's show and make a colour film for the European Scopitone Juke Box company during the day.

20

150 fans are arrested and £1,400 worth of damage done by fans during the Stones first show at the Paris Olympia when 2000 fans riot and break seats and windows. The show is recorded by Europe No.1 Radio for future transmission.

The Stones are interviewed by French radio in Paris.

23

The Stones fly to New York to begin their second US tour. Crowds of fans jam Times Square and the surrounding streets as the Stones' Cadillacs try to reach the Hotel Astor. They approach their rooms by taking the tradesman's lift to the basement, then walking through the kitchens to reception. Pinkerton men keep the corridors clear of fans. It takes three attempts to get them out of the hotel to the *Ed Sullivan Show* for rehearsals of camera angles and positions. They visit Murray the K at WINS Radio and appear on his *Swinging Soirée* show. So many fans gather outside that they cannot leave until police and Pinkerton men make the area safe. They appear on the *Ed Rudy* radio show the same day.

'Blowin' In The Wind' (Dylan) / 'House Of The Rising Sun' by Marianne Faithfull is released on Decca featuring Keith Richard on acoustic guitar on side 'A'.

Above left: Keith runs from the Stones' armoured van at Belle Vue, Manchester, August 9, 1965. Above right: Leaving Vienna, September 18, 1965, photographed by 'Sixth Stone' Ian Stewart. Below: Keith, Mick and Brian with Honor Blackman, May 11, 1965. Opposite: With Andrew Oldham during the recording of 'The Last Time'.

24
The Stones play two shows to 8,000 people at the Academy of Music in New York.

In between sets, they record a session for WPIX-TV's *Clay Cole Show*.

25
The Stones appear on CBS-TV's *Ed Sullivan Show*. Fans in the audience riot and grim faced Sullivan tells the press: "I promise you they will never be back to our show… If things can't be handled, we'll stop the whole business. We won't book any more rock'n'roll groups and we'll ban teenagers from the theatre if we have to. Frankly, I didn't see the group until the day before the broadcast. They were recommended by my scouts in England. I was shocked when I saw them."

26
The Stones fly to Los Angeles, then on to Sacramento. They return to Los Angeles after the show and stay at the Hollywood Roosevelt.

27
Mick and Keith are interviewed on the *Gary Mack Show*, Radio KRLA, Los Angeles and many other radio shows.

28
Brian is interviewed for a Santa Monica radio station.

The Stones rehearse for the *TAMI Show* which is held the next day.

28 - 29
The Stones film for the *TAMI (Teen Age Music International)* TV Show in Los Angeles before a live audience. Also on the show are The Beach Boys, Chuck Berry, James Brown, Marvin Gaye, Smokey Robinson & The Miracles, The Supremes, Gerry & The Pacemakers, Jan & Dean, Lesley Gore and Billy J. Kramer & The Dakotas.

31
BBC World Service broadcasts 'Dust My Pyramids' on the *Rhythm and Blues* show. This song, co-written with Keith, is the only writing credit Brian Jones has in the entire Stones catalogue.

WPIX-TV screens the *Clay Cole Show* which features the Stones.

NOVEMBER
Dates: Civic Auditorium, Long Beach Arena, California [afternoon] / Balboa Park Bowl, San Diego, California [evening] (1); Public Hall, Cleveland, Ohio (3); Loews Theater, Providence, Rhode Island (4), Auditorium, Milwaukee, Wisconsin (11) Coliseum, Fort Wayne, Indiana (12); Hara Arena, Dayton, Ohio (13); Memorial Auditorium, Louisville, Kentucky (14); Arie Crown Theater, McCormick Place, Chicago, Illinois (15); Glad Rag Ball, Empire Pool, Wembley (20).

2
Jack Good films the Stones for his TV show *Shindig*.

That evening the Stones make their first recordings at RCA Studios, Hollywood. They recorded five numbers, of which three were retained.

Their co-manager Eric Easton is taken ill in New York and has to fly back to London with pneumonia.

3
A 17-year old girl falls from the balcony at the Stones concert and the Mayor of Cleveland bans all future pop concerts. Before the show the mayor goes on the radio and advises parents that the Stones' performance is immoral and that no teenagers should be allowed to see it.

4
The Stones fly to Rhode Island. They miss the first plane because fans block the entrances of the hotel.

5
The Stones fly to Milwaukee, then to Chicago to record.

5 - 8
Recording at Chess Studios, Chicago, Illinois.

10
The *Red Skelton Hour* repeats the Stones session recorded in August.

12
The Stones are interviewed live before an audience on WANE-TV in Fort Wayne, Indiana. Brian begins complaining that he doesn't feel well.

13
'Little Red Rooster' / 'Off The Hook' released. There are advance orders of 300,000 copies and it goes straight to number one in the British charts.

Keith Richard: "Releasing 'Little Red Rooster' was our distinction. The only way we could set ourselves apart from everything else that was going on."

Back in Chicago, Brian collapses and is admitted to Passvant Hospital

with a temperature of 105°F and delirious. He has to be fed intravenously but soon recovers. Doctors diagnose bronchitis and extreme exhaustion. He misses the shows in Dayton, Louisville and Chicago.

The Stones drive to Dayton, Ohio and arrive at the Biltmore Hotel in the early hours.

LITTLE RED ROOSTER
Dixon / **OFF THE HOOK**
Nanker, Phelge
S - Decca F 12014 (UK).
Released: November 1964.
Producer: Impact Sound (Andrew Loog Oldham).
Engineer: Ron Malo.
Studio: Chess, Chicago.

14
The Stones leave Dayton and drive 400 miles to Louisville, Kentucky. They are too exhausted to drive back to Chicago that night so send the equipment on and stay over.

15
The Stones fly to Chicago from Kentucky.

16
The Stones fly to New York for a photo session for the cover of *Billboard* because their new album is selling so fast.

20
The Stones appear on Associated Rediffusion TV's *Ready Steady Go!* in London.

The Stones record a session for Associated Rediffusion TV's *Glad Rag Ball* at Wembley.

22
The Stones appear on BBC Radio *Teen Scene*.

23
BBC bans the Stones from appearing after they failed to show up to record sessions for *Saturday Club*, *Top Gear* and the *Joe Loss Show*. Jagger said, "I understand that the bookings were made on our behalf but we never consented to them. That is partly the reason we didn't turn up." The bookings were cancelled by Andrew Oldham.

That same day, BBC Radio records an interview with Bill for *Pop Inn*.

24
The interview with Bill is transmitted on BBC Radio's *Pop Inn*.

27
Mick Jagger's solicitor, Dale Parkinson, appears on his behalf in court at Tettenhall, Staffs, to answer three driving charges. He tells the court, "The Duke of Marlborough had longer hair than my client and he won some famous battles. His hair was powdered, I think because of fleas. My client has no fleas." His client is fined £16.

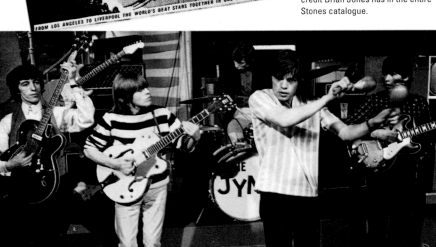

29
The Stones record a session for ABC-TV's *Thank Your Lucky Stars* in Birmingham.

DECEMBER
Date: Fairfield Hall, Croydon, Surrey (4).

'Heart of Stone' / 'What A Shame' released in the USA.

**HEART OF STONE
Jagger, Richard /
WHAT A SHAME
Jagger, Richard**
S - London 9725 (USA).
Released: December 1964.
Producer: Andrew Loog Oldham.
Studio: Chess, Chicago and RCA, Hollywood.

Notes: Side 'A' was not available in the UK until the 'Out Of Our Heads' album was released ten months later / Side 'B' appeared in the UK on the 'The Rolling Stones No. 2' album.

5
The Stones' recording for ABC-TV's *Thank Your Lucky Stars* is shown.

12
Brian Jones denies rumours in the pop press that he is leaving the Stones.

15
The Stones record two shows for Jack Good's US TV show *Shindig* at Halliford Studios, Shepperton.

18
Brian is interviewed on Radio Luxembourg.

31
The Stones appear on Associated Rediffusion TV's *Ready Steady Go!* in London.

1965

JANUARY
Dates: ABC Theatre, Belfast, Northern Ireland (6); The Adelphi Theatre, Dublin, Eire (7); Savoy Theatre, Cork, Ireland (8); The Commodore, Hammersmith, London (10); Manufacturers' Auditorium, Agricultural Hall, Sydney, Australia (22-23); City Hall, Brisbane, Australia (25-26); Manufacturers' Auditorium, Agricultural Hall, Sydney, Australia (27); Palais Theatre, St Kilda, Melbourne, Australia (28-29).

'All I Want Is My Baby' backed with 'Each And Every Day', both Jagger- Richard compositions recorded by Bobby Jameson is released on Decca. The record is produced by Andrew Oldham with musical direction by Keith Richard,

and is the first fruits of Oldham's insistence that Mick and Keith start writing their own material.

'What A Guy' by Bobbie Miller, a Bill Wyman production, is released on Decca.

6
The Stones arrive in Ireland and appear on BBC-TV's *Six Five* in Belfast. BBC Radio also tapes an interview.

9
The Stones return to London.

11-12
The Stones recording at Regent Sound Studio, Denmark Street, London.

13
The Stones record a session for ABC-TV's *Thank Your Lucky Stars* in Teddington.

15
'The Rolling Stones No. 2' released. It enters the British album charts at No.1.

The Stones appear on Associated Rediffusion TV's *Ready Steady Go!* in London.

**THE ROLLING STONES
No. 2**
*A - Decca LK 4661 (UK).
Released: January, 1965.
Producer: Impact Sound (Andrew Loog Oldham).
Engineers: Chess: Ron Malo.
RCA: Dave Hassinger.
Studios: Chess Chicago, RCA Hollywood, Impact Sound, London.*

Side 1: 1. Everybody Needs Somebody To Love (Russell, Burke, Wexler) / 2. Down Home Girl (Leiber, Butler) / 3. You Can't Catch Me

(Berry) / 4. Time Is On My Side (Meade, Norman) / 5. What A Shame (Richard, Jagger) / 6. Grown Up Wrong.

Side 2: 7. Down The Road Apiece (Raye) / 8. Under The Boardwalk (Resnick, Young) / 9. I Can't Be Satisfied (Waters) / 10. Pain In My Heart (Redding, Walden) / 11. Off The Hook (Nanker, Phelge / 12. Susie-Q (Broadwater, Lewis, Hawkins).

Notes: On the third US album, 'The Rolling Stones Now', the version of 'Everybody Needs Somebody To Love' is a studio run-through that was issued by mistake. Jack Nitzsche plays piano on 2. Jack Nitzsche plays Nitzsche-phone on 10. Ian Stewart plays piano on 1 and 5. Ian Stewart plays organ on 4.

17
The Stones fly to Los Angeles on their way to their first Australian tour. Also on the bill are Roy Orbison, Dionne Warwick and Rolf Harris.

In Los Angeles they record 'The Last Time' at RCA Studios.

18
The Stones buy a lot of clothes at

Beau Gentry's and Devo's and in the evening do the rounds of the Los Angeles clubs.

19
The Stones fly to Sydney, refuelling at Honolulu and Fiji. The flight lasts 18 hours.

21
3,000 fans riot at Sydney airport when the Stones arrive. 300 girls tear through a chain wire fence then smash their way into the quarantine area. The group stays at the Cheveron Hilton where they have a whole floor to themselves with a fabulous view of Sydney Harbour.

The Stones record two interviews for Australian TV in Sydney and radio interviews, including one with Radio 2UE Sydney.

Above left: With Andrew Oldham and an unusually friendly US cop, captured on film by Ian Stewart. Below: Brian and Cathy McGowan miming to Sonny and Cher's 'I Got You Babe' on the set of Ready Steady Go!, while Keith accompanies them on sousaphone.

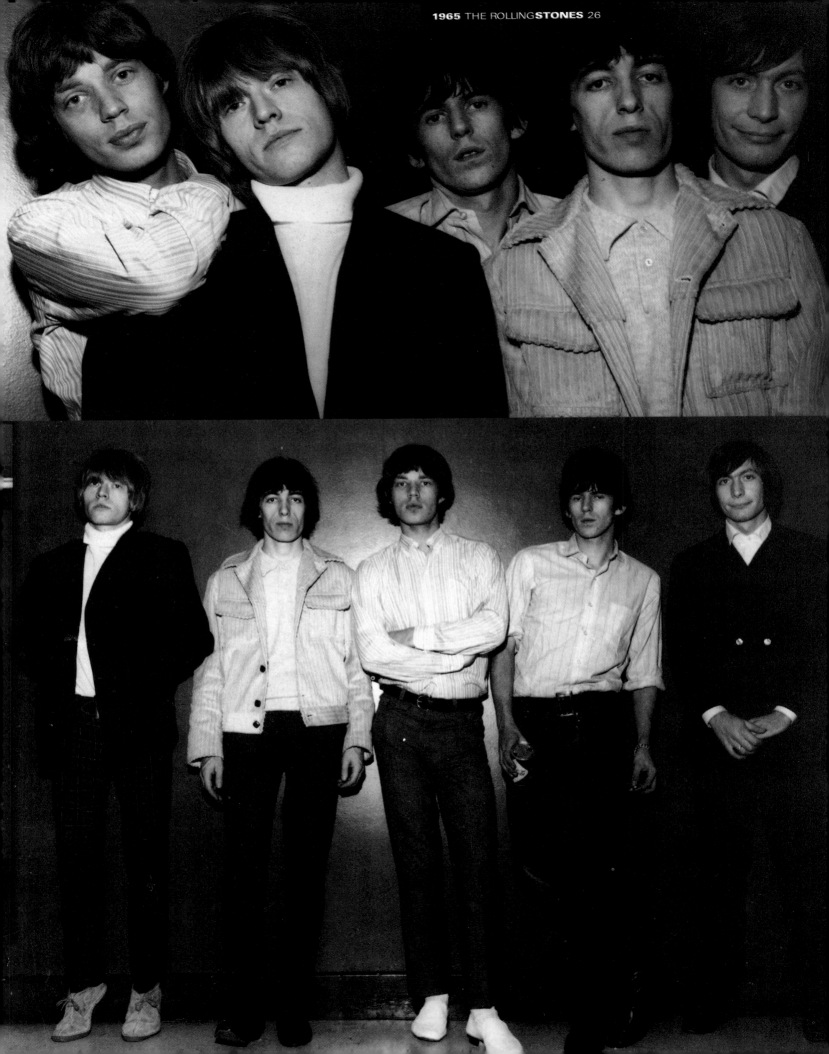

22

Ode To A High Flying Bird by Charlie Watts published by Beat publications, publishers of the official Rolling Stones monthly fan magazine. It is the life of legendary saxophonist Charlie Parker written as an illustrated children's story. Charlie wrote the book in 1961: "It doesn't matter if you don't know anything about Charlie Parker, because it's just about this little bird. In fact, it's the kind of book you can buy for a kid."

The Stones spend the day in a private house backing on to Sydney Harbour owned by a relative of their promoter and are able to recover from their trip. The press gather in boats at the water's edge and the Stones stage a water fight for their benefit. That evening they play two sold-out concerts in Sydney to 5,200 people in each house.

23

The Stones take a sightseeing trip around the harbour before playing three more shows.

24

The Stones fly to Brisbane where they stay at Lennon's Hotel (no relation).

25

40 fans storm the stage at Brisbane Town Hall. Mick Jagger: "I almost got torn to pieces and Keith's shirt was torn so much that it looks as though he has been living in it on a desert island for two years."

The Stones record local press and TV interviews.

26

The Stones hire two cars and drive 50 miles to Surfer's Paradise on Paradise Island, a major surfing centre. They spend the day relaxing before returning to Brisbane for the two shows that evening. On the way back, they are involved in a potentially dangerous road accident when Andrew Oldham swerves out of the path of a speeding local and brakes. Keith bangs his head on the windscreen.

27

The Stones return to Sydney and the Cheveron Hilton.

28

The Stones fly to Melbourne and record interviews with local television and radio. Police ban fans from the airport but about 1,000 manage to get in. Police escort the Stones to the John Batman Motor Inn. They spend the afternoon round the pool of the house of a local lawyer, arranged by their promoter Harry Miller.

29

The Stones record a TV show, *The Rolling Stones Special* for ATVO, Melbourne. They spend the afternoon at their lawyer's house, relaxing.

'Down And Out' backed with 'Stop Running Around', both songs written and produced by Bill and recorded by The Cheynes, released on Columbia.

30

The Stones appearance recorded for *Thank Your Lucky Stars* is shown.

In Melbourne the Stones record TV ads and plugs for their concerts in New Zealand and meet staff from Radio 3KZ which has been plugging their records.

31

The Stones fly to New Zealand on Teal Airlines. Everyone who flies Teal gets given a lucky charm. They do local radio interviews in Christchurch on arrival.

FEBRUARY

Dates: Theatre Royal, Christchurch, New Zealand (1); Civic Theatre Invercargill, New Zealand (2); Town Hall, Dunedin, New Zealand (3); Town Hall, Auckland, New Zealand (6); Wellington, New Zealand (8); Palais Theatre, St. Kilda, Melbourne, Australia (10); Centennial Hall, Adelaide, Australia (12); Capitol Theatre, Perth, Australia (13); Badminton Stadium, Singapore (16), Hong Kong (17).

'The Rolling Stones Now' released in the USA. It reaches No. 5 in the album charts.

THE ROLLING STONES NOW

A - London PS 420 (USA). Released: February 1965. Producer: Andrew Loog Oldham.

Side 1: 1. Everybody Needs Somebody To Love (Russell, Burke, Wexler) / 2. Down Home Girl (Leiber, Butler) / 3. You Can't Catch Me (Berry) / 4. Heart Of Stone (Jagger, Richard) / 5. What A Shame (Jagger, Richard) / 6. I Need You Baby (Mona) (McDaniels).

Side 2: 7. Down the Road Apiece (Raye) / 8. Off The Hook (Nanker, Phelge) / 9. Pain In My Heart (Neville) / 10. Oh Baby (We Got A Good Thing Goin') (Ozen) / 11. Little Red Rooster (Dixon) / 12. Surprise, Surprise (Jagger, Richard).

Notes: Track 1: This version was released by mistake. It is a studio run-through. The correct version appears on the UK 'The Rolling Stones No. 2' which is where tracks 2, 3, 5, 7, 8 and 9 also appear. Track 4 was previously released in the USA as a single coupled with track 5. Track 6 was on the first UK album 'The Rolling Stones' but left off the US version. Track 10 didn't appear in the UK for another seven months when it was included on the UK 'Out Of Our Heads' album. Track 11 was UK single Decca F 12014. Track 12 was on the Decca compilation 'Fourteen' in the UK.

1

The Stones spend the day on the beach before their two evening shows.

2

The Stones book into the Grand Hotel.

3

The Stones fly to Dunedin, the most southerly point of New Zealand.

4

The Stones fly to Auckland, arriving late and finding that the hotel they are booked into will not let them stay. Other accommodation is found.

5

The Stones visit the famous hot springs for a dip. Bill visits the mud baths at Rotorua. In the afternoon they go horse riding.

Below: Brian at Munich Airport, September, 1965, photographed by Ian Stewart.

8

The Stones fly to Wellington. The Midland Hotel refuses to allow them to stay so they fly back to their original hotel in Christchurch. The owner of the Black Cat restaurant opens up at 2:00am and gives them steaks all round.

9

The Stones fly back to Melbourne, Australia, and their old hotel, the John Batman Motor Inn. The local lawyers, Mr. & Mrs. Ham, throw a big barbecue party for them.

11

The Stones fly into Adelaide and check into the Akabar Motel.

12

The Stones make the 4½ hour flight to Perth, check into the Adelphi Hotel, then drive to the beach for a swim.

ATVO, Melbourne, screens its *Rolling Stones Special.*

14

The Stones hire two cars and drive 30 miles up the coast to find a deserted beach. A crowd gathers within an hour.

15

The Stones fly from Perth to Singapore for two concerts. They arrive after dark and check into the Singapura Hotel. The press conference is an odd experience for them as Eastern etiquette dictates that reporters must never shout or get angry since that would be "losing face". For the first time in their career, the conference is conducted in quiet, polite tones.

16

The Stones have lunch with the High Commissioner of Singapore and his family at Government House. After a 2½ hour meal of Chinese dishes, they are given a tour of the gardens before a visit to China Town for a shopping expedition.

17

The Stones fly to Hong Kong then to Los Angeles via Tokyo and Honolulu, gaining a day by crossing the dateline. During the stop-over in Tokyo, they are interviewed by Japanese TV news and Japanese radio. When they finally reach Los Angeles they put up at the Ambassador Hotel.

18

Mick re-records the vocal track of 'The Last Time' at RCA Studios, Hollywood.

21

Charlie is met by his wife, Shirley, in Los Angeles and they fly to Miami for a vacation. Mick and Bill return to London. Stu, Keith and Andrew Oldham fly to New York for business talks before Keith and Oldham fly on to Paris.

25

Brian flies back to London from Hollywood where he has been staying with Joey Paige, the former guitarist with The Everly Brothers.

26

'The Last Time' / 'Play With Fire' is released on Decca. It enters the British charts at No. 8 rising to No. 1 where it stays for four weeks.

Mick Jagger injures his ankle when fans mob the Stones during a live appearance on Associated Rediffusion TV's *Ready Steady Go!.* Mick says: "I thudded down on the floor and a mass of girls smothered me, I was stamped on by scores of stiletto heels."

THE LAST TIME
Jagger, Richard /
PLAY WITH FIRE
Nanker, Phelge
S - Decca F 12104 (UK) and London 9741 (USA).
Released: February 1965 (UK)
March 1965 (USA).
Producer: Impact Sound (Andrew Loog Oldham).
Engineer: Dave Hassinger.
Studio: RCA, Hollywood.

Notes: Phil Spector plays acoustic guitar on 'Play With Fire'.

28

Brian Jones celebrates his 22nd birthday with the Stones live on ABC-TV's *Eamonn Andrews Show.*

Keith Richard and Andrew Oldham go to Paris for a short holiday.

MARCH

Dates: Regal Theatre, Edmonton, London (5); Empire Theatre, Liverpool, Lancs (6); Palace Theatre, Manchester, Lancs (7); The Futurist, Scarborough, Yorks (8); The Odeon, Sunderland, Durham (9); ABC Theatre, Huddersfield, Yorks (10); City Hall, Sheffield, Yorks (11); The Trocadero, Leicester (12); Granada Theatre, Rugby, Warwickshire (13), The Odeon, Rochester, Kent (14); The Odeon, Guildford (15); Granada Theatre, Greenford, Middlesex (16); The Odeon, Southend, Essex (17); ABC Theatre, Romford, Essex (18); Fyns Forum, Odense, Denmark (26); Koncert Sal, Tivoli Gardens, Copenhagen, Denmark (28, 30); Masshallen, Gothenburg, Sweden (31).

Below, right: Brian and Keith at Double Bay, Sydney, Australia, January 1965.

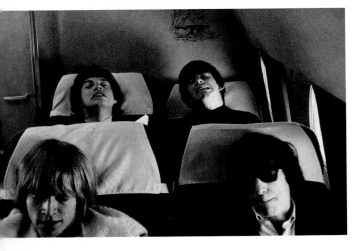

1

The Stones record a session for BBC Radio's *Top Gear*.

2

Some of the Stones appear on BBC Radio's *Pop Inn*.

4

The Stones record for BBC-TV's *Top Of The Pops* in Manchester.

5

The Stones UK tour begins. Also on the bill are The Hollies, Dave Berry and The Cruisers, The Checkmates, Goldie and The Gingerbreads, The Konrads, Johnny Ball.

6

The Stones' tape is broadcast on BBC Radio's *Top Gear*.

7

The *Daily Mirror* reports: A screaming teenage girl fan fell 15 feet from the dress circle... The girl, waving her arms in ecstasy leaned too far over the rail at the front of the circle as The Rolling Stones played at the Palace Theatre, Manchester." She landed on the people below and broke several teeth but was otherwise uninjured.

10

'The Last Time' / 'Play With Fire' is released in the USA. It enters the charts at No. 79 and climbs to No. 9.

11

The Stones record a session for ABC-TV's *Big Beat 65* in Wembley, Brian is interviewed by the BBC World Service for a programme called *Sights and Sounds of London*, then they travel to Granada TV's Manchester studios where they record segments for the *Scene At 6:30* and *In The North* shows before going on to play Sheffield City Hall.

BBC-TV screens their recording for *Top of the Pops*.

12

The Stones have the No. 1 single and the No. 1 album in the British charts.

14

The guard on the stage door at Rochester will not let the Stones into the theatre. When a gang of fans spots them and charges towards the group, Keith knocks the man to the ground so they can reach safety.

16

Brian is interviewed in Greenford, Middlesex for BBC Radio's *Melody Fair*.

18

Returning to London from the final date of the British tour at the ABC Romford, the Stones stop at a filling station in the Romford Road, West Ham but are denied the use of a lavatory. Bill Wyman, Brian Jones and Mick Jagger use a wall in the station forecourt instead, leading to a celebrated court case.

BBC-TV's *Top Of The Pops* repeats the Stones' recording made on March 4th.

21

The Stones make a recording for ABC-TV's *Thank Your Lucky Stars* in Birmingham.

23

The Stones record another session for BBC-TV's *Top Of The Pops* in London.

24

The Stones fly to Denmark to begin a Scandinavian tour.

25

BBC-TV's *Top Of The Pops* shows their new Stones recording. The Stones are interviewed by Danish TV in Copenhagen.

26

Bill Wyman receives a 220 volt shock and is knocked unconscious on stage in Odense, Denmark, but recovers in time for the second night.

28

The Stones see Ella Fitzgerald and Oscar Peterson in concert in Copenhagen. They also attend a party arranged by the Danish Rolling Stones fan club.

APRIL

Dates: Kungliga Tennishallen, Stockholm, Sweden (1-2); Open air concert in Helsinki, Finland (3); *New Musical Express* Poll Winner Concert, Empire Pool, Wembley (11); The Olympia, Paris (16-18); Maurice Richard Arena, Montreal, Canada (23); YMCA Auditorium, Ottawa, Canada (24); Maple Leaf Gardens, Toronto, Canada (25); Treasure Island Gardens, London, Ontario (26); Palace Theater, Albany, New York (29); Auditorium, Worcester, Massachusetts (30).

2

The Stones record a *TV Special* for Swedish television.

3

Bill Wyman is in hospital for treatment for a severe eye infection.

8

Swedish TV shows *The Rolling Stones Special* recorded the week before.

9

The Stones appear live on TV *Ready Steady Go!* in London.

13 - 16

The Stones play several concerts in West Germany and record a session for German television.

16

The Stones travel to Paris for three concerts at the Olympia. The first show is recorded by Radio Europe No. 1 for future transmission.

18

ABC-TV shows the Stones' recording on *Big Beat 65*.

19

The Stones fly back to London and refuse to appear on the family TV variety show *Sunday Night At The London Palladium*.

22

The Stones fly to Montreal to begin their third North American tour. They are interviewed on arrival by local television news and radio.

25

The Stones play to an audience of 16,000 at the Maple Leaf Gardens.

The Stones are interviewed by a Toronto TV station and local radio.

26

The police turn off the power and turn on the house lights in an attempt to stop the concert in London, Ontario. The Stones do their best to continue: Mick singing and playing maracas, Charlie drumming, Brian playing tambourine and Keith and Bill hand-clapping but no-one can hear. The police refuse to allow the concert to continue and the Stones apologise to the audience before leaving the stage.

A London Ontario TV station interviews the group and they also do local radio interviews.

29

Radio WTRY Albany, New York interviews the group.

30

Radio WDIC Hartford, Connecticut, interviews the group.

MAY

Dates: Academy of Music, New York [afternoon] / Convention Hall, Philadelphia, Pennsylvania (I); Georgia Southern College Auditorium, Statesboro, Georgia (4); Jack Russell Stadium, Clearwater, Florida (6); Legion Field Stadium, Birmingham, Alabama (7); Coliseum, Jacksonville, Florida (8); Arie Crown Theater, McCormick Place, Chicago, Illinois. (9); New Civic Auditorium, San Francisco, California (14); Swing Auditorium, San Bernardino, California (15); Civic Auditorium, Long Beach, California (16); Community Concourse, Convention Hall, San Diego, California (17); Civic Auditorium, San Jose, California (21); Radcliff Convention Hall, Fresno, California / Municipal Auditorium, Sacramento, California (22); (23); Academy of Music, New York (29).

2

The Stones appear on CBS-TV's *Ed Sullivan Show*. He appears not to have banned rock'n'roll bands after all. The Stones pre-record four numbers behind locked doors. That evening London Records hold a party in their honour.

Above: Brian with low slung Gibson Thunderbird.

3

The Stones record for the *Clay Cole Show* in New York.

4

Police are called after motorists complain of topless women exposing themselves at a hotel but all they find are only the Stones sunbathing.

7

The Stones play Birmingham, Alabama with The Beach Boys and The Righteous Brothers.

8

Brian Jones breaks two ribs while doing karate exercises by the pool at the Stones' hotel in Jacksonville, Florida.

9

The BBC World Service transmits the interview with Brian which was done for the show *Sights And Sounds of London*.

11

The Stones are interviewed by Radio KHJ, Los Angeles.

10 - 11

The Stones record four tracks in 17 hours at Chess Studios, Chicago, Illinois. They fly to Los Angeles on the evening of the 11th.

12 - 13

Marathon recording sessions at RCA Studios, Hollywood, result in three more tracks. On the 13th the Stones finish working on '(I Can't Get No) Satisfaction'.

15

The Stones record a session for the US TV show *Hollywood A-Go-Go*.

They are interviewed on Radio KMEN, San Bernardino.

16

The Stones play Long Beach with The Byrds. Fans swarm over their limo as they leave and cave in the roof by standing on it. The Stones attempt to hold up the roof while their driver pulls away with fans still hanging all over the vehicle.

The Stones record an appearance for the TV show *Shivaree*.

20

The Stones film an appearance for Jack Good's ABC-TV show *Shindig* in Los Angeles.

25

The Stones fly to New York City and check into the Gotham Hotel.

27

'(I Can't Get No) Satisfaction)' / 'Under Assistant West Coast Promotion Man' released in the USA. It enters the US charts at No. 67 and becomes their first US No.1.

(I CAN'T GET NO) SATISFACTION Jagger, Richard / **THE UNDER ASSISTANT WEST COAST PROMOTION MAN** Nanker, Phelge
S- London 9766 (USA).
Released: May 1965.
Producer: Andrew Loog Oldham.
Engineers: Chess: Ron Malo / RCA: Dave Hassinger.
Studio: Chess, Chicago, May 10, 1965, and RCA, Hollywood, May 12.

Notes: The UK version had a different 'B' Side. The 'B' Side here is a different version of the same title which appears on the 'Out Of Our Heads' album.

29

The Stones record six numbers for the *Clay Pole TV Show*.

The Rolling Stones take a short break: Mick and Keith take a driving holiday through the Sonora Desert in Arizona; Charlie Watts, a scholar of American history, goes to Gettysburg to further his studies; Brian and Bill return to Los Angeles to party.

JUNE

Dates: The Odeon, Glasgow, Scotland (15); Usher Hall, Edinburgh, Scotland (16); Capitol Theatre, Aberdeen, Scotland (17); Caird Hall, Dundee, Scotland (18); Messhallen, Oslo, Norway (24); Yyteri Beach, Pori, Finland (25); Copenhagen, Denmark (26); Baltiska Hallen, Mälmo, Sweden (29).

The Stones return to London early in the month.

4

The Stones appear live on Associated Rediffusion TV's *Ready Steady Go!es Live* at Wembley.

6

The Stones record a session for ABC-TV's *Thank Your Lucky Stars* in Birmingham.

10

The Stones appear on BBC-TV's *Top Of The Pops* from Manchester and also on BBC-Radio's *Top Gear*.

11

'Got Live If You Want It' EP released on Decca. It enters UK charts at No. 13 and reaches No. 7.

GOT LIVE IF YOU WANT IT
EP - Decca DFE 8620 (UK).
Released: June 1965.
Producer: Impact Sound (Andrew Loog Oldham).
Studio: Recorded live by Glyn Johns at the Regal, Edmonton, March 5, 1965. The Empire, Liverpool, March 6, 1965. The Palace Manchester March 7, 1965. (The first three dates of the March tour).

Side 1: 1. We Want The Stones (Nanker, Phelge) / 2. Everybody Needs Somebody To Love (Russell, Burke, Wexler) / 3. Pain In My Heart (Redding, Walden) / 4. (Get Your Kicks On) Route 66 (Troup).

Side 2: 5. I'm Moving On (Snow) / 6. I'm Alright (Nanker, Phelge).

Notes: The first track consists entirely of the audience chanting: 'We Want The Stones!', on which the Stones claimed the publishing royalties by listing it as a separate track. The US album of the same name contains an entirely different recording of different songs recorded at a later concert.

Above: Keith and Mick in their hotel room on the Isle of Man, August 13, 1964. Below, left: Running from fans.

12

The Stones appear on ITV *Thank Your Lucky Stars* taped the week before.

17

In the course of the Stones' short Scottish tour, 40 girls faint at their concert in Dundee.

21

The Stones appear on BBC Radio's *Teen Scene* and record a session for BBC Radio's *Woman's Hour*.

23

The Stones fly to Oslo, Norway to begin another Scandinavian tour. They are interviewed by Norwegian TV news.

24

Baton-wielding police battle with rioting fans as an audience of 3,000 goes berserk during the Stones' first visit to Norway. One girl reaches the stage, kisses Charlie Watts and faints dead away.

27

The Stones record an interview with the pirate radio SYD in Denmark.

29

Charlie is interviewed by Swedish Radio in Malmö.

JULY

Dates: The Odeon, Exeter, Devon (16); Guildhall, Portsmouth, Hants (17); Gaumont Theatre, Bournemouth, Hants (18); ABC Theatre, Great Yarmouth, Norfolk (25); Leicester (26).

'Out Of Our Heads' album released in the USA. It reaches No. 1 on the album charts on August 21st.

OUT OF OUR HEADS

A - London PS 429 (USA). Released: July 1965. Producer: Andrew Loog Oldham. Studio: Chess, Chicago and RCA, Hollywood. May 10, 1965 onwards.

Side 1: 1. Mercy, Mercy (Covay, Miller) / 2. Hitch Hike (Gaye, Stevenson, Paul) / 3. The Last Time (Jagger, Richard) / 4. That's How Strong My Love Is (Jamison) / 5. Good Times (Cooke) / 6. I'm All Right (Nanker, Phelge).

Side 2: 7. (I Can't Get No) Satisfaction (Jagger, Richard) / 8. Cry To Me (Russell) / 9. The Under Assistant West Coast Promotion Man (Nanker, Phelge) / 10. Play With Fire (Nanker, Phelge) / 11. The Spider And The Fly (Nanker, Phelge) / 12. One More Try (Jagger, Richard).

Notes: Though the UK and USA editions have the same title there are many differences: tracks 6, 7, 10, 11 and 12 do not appear on the UK version. Track 12 was not released in the UK until 1971 when it appeared on the Decca compilation 'Stone Age'.

1

The Stones fly back to London.

7

The Stones fly to Los Angeles to mix their next album, 'Out Of Our Heads' and make other recordings.

13

The Stones return to London. They appear on BBC-TV's *The World of Jimmy Savile*.

22

Three Rolling Stones fined in Romford, Essex. The *Daily Express* reports the next day: "Three of The Rolling Stones were fined £5 each yesterday for insulting behaviour and were rebuked for not setting a higher moral standard for their fans... The court heard of the night a Daimler car pulled into a petrol station in Romford Road, West Ham.

Mr. Kenneth Richardson, prosecuting, said that eight or nine boys and girls got out and Wyman asked if he could go to the lavatory but was refused. A mechanic, Mr. Charles Keeley, asked Jagger to get the group off the forecourt of the garage. He brushed him aside, saying, "We will piss anywhere, man". This was taken up by a group in a chant as one of them danced. Wyman, Jagger and Jones were seen to urinate on a wall of the garage. The car drove off with people inside sticking their hands through the windows in a well known gesture."

The magistrate tells them, "Just because you have reached an exalted height in your profession, it does not mean you can behave in this manner."

25

The Crawdaddy Club in Richmond closes its doors.

26

The Stones record for ABC-TV's *Thank Your Lucky Stars* in Birmingham.

28

The Stones two sessions for the US ABC-TV show *Shindig* at Twickenham Studios.

29

The press reports that Charlie Watts has bought a sixteenth century mansion near Lewes, Sussex, from Lord Shawcross, the former British Attorney General. Charlie's father, a parcels truck driver at Kings Cross railway station, comments in the *Evening News* on August 10th: "We are proud of Charlie, but we can't understand why he prefers an old place like this to something modern which is what I would have liked myself."

Above: On the set of Ready Steady Go! in 1966.

AUGUST

Dates: London Palladium (1); The Futurist, Scarborough, Yorks (22).

Bill's production of 'Hole In My Soul' by The Preachers released by Columbia.

1

The Stones do two shows at the Palladium supported by Steam Packet, The Walker Brothers, The Moody Blues, The Quiet Five, The Fourmost and Julia Grant. After the show, the Stones go on vacation. Mick and Brian go to Tangier with Brian taking his girlfriend, 18-year old Linda Lawrence. Bill goes to Germany. Keith goes to the South of France.

ABC-TV shows the Stones session on *Thank Your Lucky Stars*.

4

Andrew Oldham launches his own record label: Immediate Records.

9

The first of the *Shindig* specials is shown in the USA.

14

Mick, Keith and manager Andrew Oldham fly to New York. Jagger is quoted in the press as saying, "The whole British music scene is dead boring now. There hasn't been anything new or exciting for ages. First there was The Beatles, then us, now there's nothing."

Linda Lawrence brings a court order against Brian Jones to get official recognition of their one-year old son, Julian Brian. She and Brian are still together in Tangier.

15

Mick and Keith in the audience to see The Beatles play Shea Stadium, New York City. That evening they visit The Beatles at their hotel.

16

The second of the *Shindig* specials is shown in the USA.

18

Mick is back in London from New York to attend the wedding of photographer David Bailey and Catherine Deneuve.

19

The Stones record a session for BBC-TV's *Top Of The Pops* in London.

20

'Satisfaction' / 'Spider And The Fly' released. It enters the charts at No. 3 and goes to No. 1 for three weeks.

The Stones appear on BBC *Top Of The Pops*. They also record a session for the BBC Radio August Bank Holiday Special called *Yeh! Yeh!* and the BBC Radio show *Saturday Club*.

Decca releases 'The Rolling Stones Songbook' by the Andrew Oldham Orchestra. Keith Richard plays on the album.

(I CAN'T GET NO) SATISFACTION
Jagger, Richard /
THE SPIDER AND THE FLY
Nanker, Phelge
S - Decca F 12220.
Released: August 1965.
Producer: Impact Sound (Andrew Loog Oldham).
Studio: Chess, Chicago, Original track May 10 until 5am May 11, 1965. RCA, Hollywood, May 12 until 2.30am May 13, 1965.

23

Security guards spray 200 screaming teenagers with a fire hose when they break through a barrier at Granada TV's Manchester television studios while waiting for the group to arrive. Security guard, Mr. Harry Oldham, aged 49, says: "The fans went wild. I had to turn on the hose. I tried to control the water..." The Stones are there to appear on Granada-TV's *Scene At 6.30*.

24

The Stones hold business meetings with Allen Klein at the Hilton Hotel. He promises to make them millionaires but finishes up owning all their early copyrights.

27

The Stones play live on TV *Ready Steady Go!* in Wembley.

28

The London *Evening Standard* reports that the Stones have appointed Tito Burns as their British agent; that Allen Klein - previously their American accountant - is now co-managing them with Andrew Oldham; and that they have signed a new five-year contract with Decca for a massive advance.

29

The *Daily Express* reports that the Stones have signed a new contract with London Records in the USA. Andrew Oldham is quoted as saying, "Under the terms of a deal concluded with our American business manager, Mr. Allen Klein, the Stones are guaranteed three million dollars over the next five years."

The Stones record a session for ABC-TV's *Lucky Stars Summer Spin* in Birmingham.

30

The Stones' August 20 recording is played on the BBC Radio Bank Holiday Special, *Yeh! Yeh!*.

SEPTEMBER

Dates: Adelphi Theatre, Dublin, Eire (3); ABC Theatre, Belfast, Northern Ireland (4); Palace Theatre, Douglas, Isle of Man (8); Munsterland Halle, Münster, Germany (11); Grugahalle, Essen, Germany (12); Ernst Merckhalle, Hamburg, Germany (13); Circus-Krone-Bau, Munich, Germany (14); Waldbühne Halle, Berlin, Germany (15); Wiener Stadthalle, Vienna, Austria (17); Astoria Theatre, Finsbury Park, London (24); Gaumont Theatre, Southampton, Hants (25); Colston Hall, Bristol, Gloucs (26); The Odeon, Cheltenham, Gloucs (27); Capitol Theatre, Cardiff, Wales (28); Granada Theatre, Shrewsbury, Shropshire (29); Gaumont Theatre, Hanley, Staffs (30).

Brian Jones tells the press that the Stones have no plans to move to the United States. "I think this got started because I've bought a house in Los Angeles. It's purely a business investment and neither I nor any of the others have plans to settle out there."

'Get Off Of My Cloud' / 'I'm Free' released in the USA. It was recorded in Hollywood during the 6th and 7th of the month and released immediately. It enters the US charts at No. 64 and spends two weeks at No.1.

GET OFF OF MY CLOUD
Jagger, Richard /
I'M FREE
Jagger, Richard
S - London 9792 (USA).
Released: September 1965.
Producer: Andrew Loog Oldham.
Engineer: Dave Hassinger.
Studio: RCA, Hollywood, September 5-6, 1965.
Notes: The UK release the next month had a different 'B' side.

2

The Stones August 19 recording is shown on BBC-TV's *Top Of The Pops*.

The Stones record a TV special for Associated Rediffusion TV's *Ready Steady Go!* in Wembley.

3

During the second of their two shows in Dublin, the audience riots and 30 youths manage to get on stage. *Melody Maker* reports: "The youths swarmed all over the stage. Mick Jagger was dragged to the floor. Brian Jones was wrestling with three punching teenagers and Bill Wyman was forced back against a piano at the side of the stage. Keith Richard managed to escape off stage, and implacable Charlie Watts carried on playing stone faced as bedlam raged around him."

4

Eighty seats are smashed and thrown at the stage as fans run riot at the Stones' Belfast concert. Two people have serious leg injuries.

The Stones perform on TV *Lucky Stars Summer Spin*.

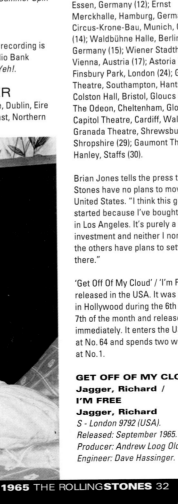

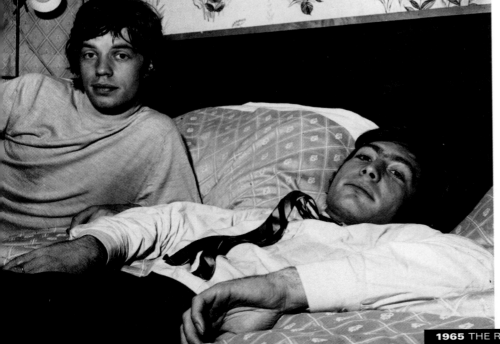

Below: Mick and Charlie in the Isle of Man, August, 1964.

5

The Stones fly to Los Angeles directly after their Dublin show. Jagger says: "We are recording in the US solely because we believe we can produce our best work there. We can record right through from 6 o'clock in the morning over there without so much as a tea break, and the engineers are first class."

6 - 7

The Stones record at RCA Studios, Hollywood.

8

The Stones fly directly to the Isle of Man for a concert.

9

BBC-TV's *Top Of The Pops* shows a repeat of the Stones' August 19 recording.

10

The Stones Associated Rediffusion TV special *Ready Steady Go! - The Rolling Stones Special Show* is shown.

11

The Stones fly to Düsseldorf to begin a tour of Germany and Austria. Thousands of fans riot at Düsseldorf airport, 200 of whom break through a police cordon, smash the doors to the airport lounge and attack the police. None of the main hotels in Düsseldorf will allow the Stones to stay.

13

2000 fans riot at the concert in Hamburg.

15

Fifty rows of seats are damaged during the Stones Berlin concert. 400 police armed with rubber truncheons battle it out with fans after the concert. 32 fans and six policemen are detained in hospital. Later, fans smashed up railway carriages and attacked the conductor.

16

BBC-TV's *Top Of The Pops* shows a repeat of the Stones' August 19th recording.

18

BBC Radio *Saturday Club* plays the tape recorded on August 20.

23

The Stones appear on BBC TV's *Top Of The Pops* in London.

The Stones choose to rehearse for their British tour at the Ken Colyer Club off Leicester Square. The last time they played there was Christmas 1963.

24

The Rolling Stones begin another British tour. Also on the bill are The Spencer Davis Group, Unit 4 + 2, The Checkmates, Charles Dickens, The Habit, The End and compère Ray Cameron, the Canadian comedian. For some concerts,

The Moody Blues replace Unit 4 Plus 2.

'Out Of Our Heads' released. It enters the album charts at No. 3, peaking at No. 2.

OUT OF OUR HEADS
A - Decca LK 4733.
Released: September 1965.
Producer: Andrew Loog Oldham.
Studios: Chess Chicago. RCA, Hollywood, May 10, 1965 onwards.

Side 1: 1. She Said Yeah (Jackson, Christy) / 2. Mercy, Mercy (Covay, Miller) / 3. Hitch Hike (Gaye, Stevenson, Paul) / 4. That's How Strong My Love Is (Jamison) / 5. Good Times (Cooke) / 6. Gotta Get Away (Jagger, Richard).
Side 2: 7. Talkin' 'Bout You (Berry) / 8. Cry To Me (Russell) / 9. Oh Baby (We Got A Good Thing Going) (Ozen) / 10. Heart Of Stone (Jagger, Richard) / 11. The Under Assistant West Coast Promotion Man

(Nanker, Phelge) / 12. I'm Free (Jagger, Richard).

Notes: A different take of track 11 was released as the US 'B'-side of 'Satisfaction'. Matrix number XDR 35802 it came from the same May 10-13 sessions in Chicago and Hollywood. Ian Stewart plays piano and organ on some tracks. Jack Nitzsche plays piano and organ on some tracks. Ian Stewart plays marimbas on some tracks. Jack Nitzsche plays percussion on some tracks. J.W. Alexander plays percussion on some tracks. Tracks 4 and 11 were recorded in Chicago, engineered by Ron Malo.

30

BBC-TV's *Top Of The Pops* shows a third repeat of the Stones' August 19 recording.

OCTOBER

Dates: ABC Theatre, Chester, Cheshire (1); ABC Theatre, Wigan, Lancs (2); The Odeon, Manchester, Lancs (3); Gaumont Theatre, Bradford, Yorks (4); ABC Theatre, Carlisle, Cumberland (5); The Odeon, Glasgow (6); City Hall, Newcastle-on-Tyne (7); ABC Theatre, Stockton-on-Tees, Durham (8); The Odeon, Leeds, Yorks (9); The Empire, Liverpool (10); Gaumont Theatre,

Sheffield, Yorks (11); The Odeon, Doncaster, Yorks (12); De Montfort Hall, Leicester (13); The Odeon, Birmingham (14); ABC Theatre, Cambridge (l5); ABC Theatre, Northampton (16); Granada, Tooting, London (17); The Forum, Montreal, Canada (29); Barton Hall, Cornell University, Ithica, New York [afternoon] / War Memorial Hall, Syracuse, New York (30); Maple Leaf Gardens, Toronto, Canada (31).

Bill's production of 'Every Beat Of My Heart' by Bobbie Miller is released by Decca.

3

Seats are smashed at the Stones' Manchester concert and Keith Richard is knocked unconscious for five minutes by flying debris. He is carried off stage but soon recovers. Mick Jagger is cut near his eye but carries on singing.

14

BBC-TV shows a clip from 'Charlie Is My Darling' on *Top Of The Pops*.

Left: Andrew Oldham with Charlie and Keith on the Ready Steady Go! set.

18
The Stones record radio promos for Radio KHJ, Los Angeles in the London studio.

19
The Stones record a session for BBC-TV's *Top Of The Pops*.

21
The Stones appear on BBC TV *Top Of The Pops*.

22
The Stones appear on Associated Rediffusion TV's *Ready Steady Go!* in Wembley.

'Get Off Of My Cloud' / 'The Singer Not The Song' is released on Decca. It enters the charts at No. 3 and spends three weeks at No. 1.

Bill's production of 'I Can't Get Any Joy' by The End is released on Philips.

GET OFF OF MY CLOUD
Jagger, Richard /
THE SINGER NOT THE SONG Jagger, Richard
*S - Decca F 12263 (UK).
Released: October 1965.
Producer: Andrew Loog Oldham.
Engineer: Dave Hassinger.
Studio: RCA, Hollywood,
September 6-7, 1965.*

25
Andrew Oldham flies to New York to make the final arrangements for the Stones' upcoming US tour.

27
The Stones fly into New York City to begin their North American tour. They take over two floors of the Warwick Hotel at 65 West 54th Street as their HQ and travel between concerts in a private plane.

28
The Stones give an interview to US television news and local radio.

29
In Montreal, 440 fans rush the stage and forty girls need treatment in hospital. Charlie's jacket is torn to pieces as he leaves the stage and Brian receives a cut on the forehead. Mick and Keith are trapped on stage for twenty minutes surrounded by security before they can leave.

30
The Stones hold a press conference at the New York Hilton. They are transported in the freight elevator, still inside their limousine. Hilton security officers said: "They were the only personalities to be taken inside the hotel in a car, save for the late President Kennedy who visited the hotel in mid-1963."

Bob Dylan visits Brian Jones at the Warwick Hotel.

NOVEMBER
Dates: Memorial Auditorium, Rochester, New York (1); Auditorium, Providence, Rhode Island (3); Arena, New Haven, Connecticut (4), Boston Gardens, Boston, Massachusetts (5); Academy of Music, New York [afternoon] / Convention Hall, Philadelphia, Pennsylvania (6); Mosque Theater, Newark, New Jersey (7); Reynolds Coliseum, Raleigh, North Carolina (10); War Memorial Auditorium, Greensboro, North Carolina (12); Coliseum, Washington DC [afternoon] / Civic Center, Baltimore, Maryland (13); Civic Coliseum, Knoxville, Tennessee (14); Coliseum, Charlotte, North Carolina (15); Municipal Auditorium, Nashville, Tennessee (16); Mid South Coliseum, Memphis, Tennessee (17); State Fair Youth Center, Shreveport, Louisiana (20); Will Rogers Stadium, Fort Worth, Texas [afternoon] / Memorial Auditorium, Dallas, Texas (21); Assembly Hall, Tulsa, Oklahoma(23); Civic Arena, Pittsburgh, Pennsylvania (24); Municipal Arena, Milwaukee, Wisconsin (25); Cobo Hall, Detroit,

Michigan (26); Hara Arena, Dayton, Ohio [afternoon] / The Gardens, Cincinnati, Ohio (27); Arie Crown Theater, McCormick Place, Chicago, Illinois (28); Coliseum, Denver, Colorado (29); Veterans Memorial Coliseum, Phoenix, Arizona (30).

'December's Children' album released in the USA. It reaches No. 2 in the album charts.

DECEMBER'S CHILDREN
A - London PS 451 (USA).

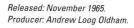

*Released: November 1965.
Producer: Andrew Loog Oldham.*

Side 1: 1. She Said Yeah (Roderick, Christy, Jackson) / 2. Talkin' 'Bout You (Berry) / 3. You Better Move On (Alexander) / 4. Look What You've Done (Margonfield) / 5. The Singer Not The Song (Jagger, Richard) / 6. Route 66 (Troup).

Side 2: 7. Get Off Of My Cloud (Jagger, Richard) / 8. I'm Free (Jagger, Richard) / 9. As Tears Go By (Jagger, Richard, Oldham) / 10. Gotta Get Away (Jagger, Richard) / 11. Blue Turns To Grey (Jagger, Richard) / 12. I'm Moving On (Snow).

Notes: Tracks 4 and 11 were not released in the UK until Decca released the 'Stone Age' compilation album in 1971.

THE ROLLING STONES
*EP - Decca SDE 7503 (UK).
Released: Late 1965 [November?].
Producer: Andrew Loog Oldham.*

Side 1: 1. She Said Yeah (Roderick, Christy, Jackson) / 2. Gotta Get Away (Jagger, Richard).

Side 2: 3. Talkin' 'Bout You (Berry) / 4. The Singer Not The Song (Jagger, Richard).

1
In New York, the Stones record promos for a Boston radio station.

4
BBC-TV shows their new recording of The Rolling Stones on *Top Of The Pops*.

6
The Stones are interviewed for US TV news in Philadelphia.

11
The Stones pre-record a session for the TV show *Hullaballoo* in New York City.

BBC-TV repeats its film of the Stones on *Top Of The Pops*.

15
The Stones recording made for *Hullabaloo* is transmitted on US TV.

18
BBC-TV's *Top Of The Pops* repeats their October 19 Stones recording.

19
'Farlowe In The Midnight Hour', an EP by Chris Farlowe is released by Immediate Records. It is the first product of We Three Producers, a new production company formed by Mick Jagger, Keith Richard and Andrew Oldham.

Above: Brian on the set of Thank Your Lucky Stars.

26

The Stones are invited by Berry Gordy to visit his Tamla-Motown Recording Studios and watch a session.

DECEMBER

Dates: Agrodrome, Vancouver, Canada (1); Coliseum, Seattle, Washington (2); Memorial Auditorium, Sacramento, California (3); Civic Auditorium, San Jose, California (4); Convention Hall, San Diego, California [afternoon] / Sports Arena, Los Angeles, California (5).

'As Tears Go By' / 'Gotta Get Away' released in the US. It enters the charts at No. 79 reaching No. 6.

AS TEARS GO BY
Jagger, Richard, Oldham /
GOTTA GET AWAY
Jagger, Richard
S- London 9808 (USA).
Released: December 1965.
Producer: Andrew Loog Oldham.
Engineer: Dave Hassinger.
Studio: RCA, Hollywood.

3

Keith is knocked unconscious by an electric shock on stage in Sacramento.

5

The Stones play to 14,000 fans at the LA Sports Arena. Brian Jones' girlfriend Anita Pallenberg flies out from London to join him and see the final show.

6-10

The Stones record ten new tracks at RCA Studios in Hollywood.

11

The May 16 recording for *Shivaree* is repeated on US TV.

22

Keith flies to London from New York to spend Christmas with his family.

23

BBC-TV show a recording of the Stones on *Top Of The Pops*.

24

Mick flies to London from New York to spend Christmas with his parents. He gives his brother Chris a Mini-Cooper car for Christmas.

25

Brian Jones and Anita spend Christmas in the Virgin Islands where Brian is laid low by a tropical virus. Bill and Charlie return two weeks before Christmas to work on their new houses. Mick spends Christmas in Jamaica.

The BBC show a repeat of a Stones recording on their *Top Of The Pops Christmas Show*.

26

The BBC repeats their Christmas Day *Top Of The Pops Christmas Show*.

27

Brian and Anita return to London.

30

BBC-TV's *Top Of The Pops* repeats the recording made on October 19.

Some of the Stones are interviewed in London for Granada-TV's *Man Alive*.

31

The Stones appear on Associated Rediffusion TV's *The New Year Starts Here* [*Ready Steady Go!* by another name].

1966

JANUARY

Mick flies to Paris to buy clothes. Brian visits Copenhagen.

Chris Farlowe's single, 'Think', by Jagger and Richards released on Immediate, produced by Mick, Keith and Andrew Oldham.

1

Keith takes delivery of a dark blue Bentley Continental. He has not yet passed his driving test.

The Stones are featured on the New Year's Day edition of Associated Rediffusion-TV's *Ready Steady Go!*

FEBRUARY

Dates: Commemoration Auditorium, Showgrounds, Sydney, Australia (18-19); City Hall, Brisbane, Australia (21); Centennial Hall, Adelaide, Australia (22); Palais Theatre, St Kilda, Melbourne, Australia (23-26); Town Hall, Wellington, New Zealand (28).

Another of Andrew Oldham's kitsch masterpieces, 'Today's Pop Symphony: The Aranbee Pop Symphony Orchestra Under The Direction Of Keith Richard' released on Immediate. Produced by Keith Richard, it includes four Jagger / Richard compositions, 'Play With Fire', 'Mother's Little Helper', 'Take It Or Leave It' and 'Sittin' On A Fence' as well as several tracks by The Beatles.

3

The Stones record a session for BBC-TV's *Top Of The Pops* in London.

Above: Brian playing sitar on 'Paint It Black' on Ready Steady Go!, May 1966.

4

'19th Nervous Breakdown' / 'As Tears Go By' released. It enters the charts at No. 2 and quickly reaches No. 1. '19th Nervous Breakdown' / 'Sad Day' released in the USA. It enters the US charts at No. 46 and reaches No. 1.

19TH NERVOUS BREAKDOWN Jagger, Richard / **AS TEARS GO BY** Jagger, Richard, Oldham
S - Decca F 12331 (UK).
Released: February 1966.
Producer: Andrew Loog Oldham.
Engineer: Dave Hassinger.
Studio: RCA, Hollywood.

19TH NERVOUS BREAKDOWN Jagger, Richard / **SAD DAY** Jagger, Richard
S - London 9823.
Released: February.
Producer: Andrew Loog Oldham.
Engineer: Dave Hassinger.
Studio: RCA, Hollywood.

6

The Stones appear on the TV Eamonn Andrews Show.

8

Keith fails his driving test in Dartford, Kent. His chauffeur Patrick retains his job. Bill takes his test this month and passes.

10

BBC-TV screens their latest Stones recording on Top Of The Pops.

12

The Stones fly to New York.

13

The Stones appear on CBS-TV's Ed Sullivan Show again.

14

The Stones fly to Sydney, via Los Angeles to begin a tour of Australia and New Zealand

16

The Stones are interviewed by Australian radio and TV in Sydney.

17

BBC-TV's Top Of The Pops repeats its February 3 recording of the Stones.

20

The Stones fly into Brisbane where 5,000 fans are waiting. It is a brilliant sunny day, in contrast to the previous five days in Sydney when it has rained non-stop.

22

The Stones record a session for BBC-TV's Top Of The Pops in Brisbane.

23

The Stones fly to Melbourne. Radio 3UZ Melbourne, records that night's show for broadcast.

24

At the Stones concert in Melbourne,

fans attack the stage resulting in Keith visiting hospital for treatment to a cut eye.

28

The Stones have to finish their act 15 minutes early in Wellington because police could not hold back the crowds.

MARCH

Dates: Civic Centre, Auckland, New Zealand (1); Capitol Theatre, Perth, Australia (2); Brabanthall Danbosche, Amsterdam, Netherlands (26); Palais des Sports, Brussels, Belgium (27); The Olympia Theatre, Paris, Musicorama, Salle Vallier, Marseilles, France (30); Palais d'Hivers, Lyon, France (31).

'Big Hits (High Tide & Green Grass)', the first Stones compilation LP, released in the USA. It spends almost two years in the charts and reaches No. 2.

BIG HITS (HIGH TIDE AND GREEN GRASS) Compilation
A - London NPS 1.
Released: March 1966.

Side 1: 1. The Last Time (Jagger, Richard) / 2. As Tears Go By (Jagger, Richard, Oldham) / 3. Time Is On My Side (Meade, Norman) / 4. It's All Over Now (Womack) / 5. Tell Me (Jagger, Richard) / 6. 19th Nervous Breakdown (Jagger, Richard).

Side 2: 7. Heart of Stone (Jagger, Richard) / 8. Get Off Of My Cloud (Jagger, Richard) / 9. Not Fade Away (Petty, Hardin) / 10. Good Times Bad Times (Jagger, Richard) / 11. Play With Fire (Nanker, Phelge).

Notes: This American greatest hits compilation has different tracks to the one issued in the UK. Confusingly Decca kept the same title when they released theirs eight months later.

1

The Stones fly to Los Angeles, gaining a day by crossing the International Date Line. Keith, Mick and Charlie stop over for three days in Fiji, bathing and diving off the Coral Reef. Brian and Bill go straight to Los Angeles and check out the club scene.

3

BBC-TV's Top Of The Pops shows the Stones track they recorded in Brisbane.

3-12

The Stones record 21 new songs at RCA Studios, Hollywood.

4

'14 Things To Think' an album by Chris Farlowe, released on Immediate. It is produced by Mick, Keith and Andrew Oldham.

11

'Everywhere I Go' (Brown, Williams, Groom) by Bobbie Miller / 'Stu Ball' (Wyman, Stewart) by Ian Stewart and The Railroaders released on Decca. Produced by Bill Wyman. The Railroaders consist of Bill on bass, Keith on guitar, Ian Stewart on piano and Tony Meehan on drums.

26

The Stones fly to Amsterdam from London to begin a short European tour.

27

The Stones decide to fly to Paris a day earlier than planned.

28

The Stones appear on French TV from a Paris studio. In the evening they go to Castelles, the hottest club in Paris.

29

Charlie suffering from food poisoning but plays the Paris Olympia concert against doctor's orders. The show is transmitted live by Europe No. 1 Radio. At a party after the concert, held at the Georges V Hotel, the Stones meet Brigitte Bardot and Françoise Hardy.

30

Fifty seats are wrecked and 85 fans held overnight by police after 2,500 fans riot during the Stones concert in Marseilles. Mick is hit in the eye by a chair and goes to hospital to have eight stitches. Mick: "They were ripping the seats apart and beating up the gendarmes. The kids were going bonkers. Even hitting the police with their own truncheons. I kept out of it as much as possible. I don't like seeing police being thumped."

31

The Stones charter a plane to fly to Lyon after lunch. They take a sleeping car train back to Paris after the concert. Mick, Keith and Charlie continue on to London. Bill and Brian stay in Paris.

APRIL

Dates: Kungliga Tennishallen, Stockholm, Sweden (3); K.B. Hallen, Copenhagen, Denmark (5).

'Paint It Black' / 'Stupid Girl' released in the USA. It enters the US charts at No. 48 and goes to No. 1.

PAINT IT BLACK
Jagger, Richard /
STUPID GIRL
Jagger, Richard
S - London 901 (USA).
Released: April 1966.
Producer: Andrew Loog Oldham.
Engineer: Dave Hassinger.
Studio: RCA, Hollywood,
March 3 -12, 1966.

1

Brian and Bill are in the audience for a Ready Steady Go! recorded in Paris at La Locomotive by Associated Rediffusion. After the show Brian and Bill go to Castelles with the Ready Steady Go! crowd.

2

Brian and Bill fly to Stockholm from Paris.

3

Mick, Keith and Charlie arrive in Stockholm in the morning. The concert is held in the afternoon in a glass roofed tennis stadium.

5

The Stones fly to Copenhagen from Stockholm.

6

The Stones arrive back in London.

14

The Stones appear on BBC TV's Top Of The Pops in London. The recording is repeated a further three times.

15

'Aftermath' released. It enters the album charts at No. 2 and spends seven weeks at No. 1.

AFTERMATH
A - Decca SKL 4786.
Released: April 1966.
Producer: Andrew Loog Oldham.
Engineer: Dave Hassinger.
Studio: RCA, Hollywood.

Side 1: 1. Mother's Little Helper (Jagger, Richard) / 2. Stupid Girl (Jagger, Richard) / 3. Lady Jane (Jagger, Richard) / 4. Under My Thumb (Jagger, Richard) / 5. Doncha Bother Me (Jagger, Richard) / 6. Goin' Home (Jagger, Richard).

Side 2: 7. Flight 505 (Jagger, Richard) / 8. High And Dry (Jagger, Richard) / 9. Out Of Time (Jagger, Richard) / 10. It's Not Easy (Jagger, Richard) / 11. I Am Waiting (Jagger, Richard) / 12. Take It Or Leave It (Jagger Richard) / 13. Think (Jagger, Richard) / 14. What To Do (Jagger, Richard).

Notes: Jack Nitzsche plays percussion on some tracks. Jack Nitzsche plays piano on some tracks. Jack Nitzsche plays organ on some tracks. Ian Stewart plays piano on some tracks. Ian Stewart plays organ on some tracks.

19

The Stones April 14 recording for BBC-TV's Top Of The Pops is repeated.

26

Bob Dylan plays the Royal Albert Hall and "goes electric". The Stones take a box for the first night. They get together backstage and continue visiting until the early hours.

The Stones April 14 recording for BBC-TV's Top Of The Pops is repeated.

27

The Stones appear on Associated Rediffusion-TV's Ready Steady Go! from Wembley.

20

Mick and Chrissie Shrimpton holiday in Paris.

24

Brian and Anita Pallenberg are among the guests at the 21st birthday party for Guinness heir Tara Browne.

30

Mick and Brian spend a weekend at Tara Browne's mansion in Ireland.

MAY

Dates: New Musical Express Poll Winners Concert, Empire Pool, Wembley, Middlesex [afternoon] (1).

Keith Richard buys Redlands, a large Tudor house in West Wittering, West Sussex. "It's gorgeous" says Keith, "and has a moat around it."

Mick moves from his flat in Montagu Square, London, to 52 Harley House, Marylebone Road.

1

BBC-TV show the NME Poll Winners Concert Live from Wembley.

8

The Stones appear live on ABC-TV's Thank Your Lucky Stars from Birmingham.

12

The Stones April 14th recording for BBC-TV's Top Of The Pops is repeated.

Brian takes a week's holiday in Marbella, Spain, staying in a friend's villa.

13

'Paint It Black' / 'Long Long While' released on Decca . It enters the UK charts at No. 5 and reaches No. 1.

PAINT IT BLACK Jagger, Richard / **LONG LONG WHILE** Jagger, Richard
S - Decca F 12395 (UK).
Released: May 1966.
Producer: Andrew Loog Oldham.
Engineer: Dave Hassinger.
Studio: RCA, Hollywood,
March 3 -12, 1966.

19

The Stones April 14 recording for BBC-TV's Top Of The Pops is repeated.

26

29

Brian off to Marbella again for a short break.

JUNE

Dates: Manning Bowl, Lynn, Massachusetts (24); Cleveland, Ohio [afternoon] / Civic Arena, Pittsburgh, Pennsylvania (25); Coliseum, Washington DC [afternoon] / Civic Center, Baltimore, Maryland (26); Dillon Stadium, Hartford, Connecticut (27); Buffalo, New York (28); Maple Leaf Gardens, Toronto, Canada (29); The Forum, Montreal, Canada (30).

'Aftermath' released in the USA on London with a different track selection. It reaches No. 1.

AFTERMATH
A - London PS 476 (USA).
Released: June 1966.
Producer: Andrew Loog Oldham.
Engineer: Dave Hassinger.
Studio: RCA, Hollywood.

Side 1: 1. Paint It Black (Jagger, Richard) / 2. Stupid Girl (Jagger, Richard) / 3. Lady Jane (Jagger, Richard) / 4. Under My Thumb (Jagger, Richard) / 5. Doncha Bother Me (Jagger, Richard) / 6. Think (Jagger, Richard).

Side 2: 7. Flight 505 (Jagger, Richard) / 8. High And Dry (Jagger, Richard) / 9. It's Not Easy (Jagger, Richard) / 10. I Am Waiting (Jagger, Richard) / 11. Goin' Home (Jagger, Richard).

Notes: Released two months after the UK version, the US version lacks a number of tracks: 'Mother's Little Helper', 'Out Of Time', 'Take It Or Leave It' and 'What To Do' are all missing, however 'Paint It Black', their current US single is included which is not on the UK version.

The double 'A' side: 'Mother's Little Helper' / 'Lady Jane' is released in the USA. 'Mother's Little Helper' enters the charts at No. 70 and goes to No. 8. 'Lady Jane' enters at No. 83 and gets to No. 24.

MOTHER'S LITTLE HELPER
Jagger, Richard / **LADY JANE** Jagger, Richard
S - London 902 (USA).
Released: June 1966.
Producer: Andrew Loog Oldham.

14
Mick reported as collapsing from exhaustion at his new flat in Harley House, Marylebone Road by Regents Park. He recovers sufficiently to appear on TV the next day.

15
Mick is interviewed on BBC-TV's *A Whole Scene Going*.

17
Chris Farlowe's version of 'Out Of Time' by Mick and Keith, produced by Mick, is released on Immediate. It reaches No.1 in the UK charts.

21
The Stones file a £1,750,850 damages suit against 14 of New York's top hotels, alleging that they had injured their reputation by turning down their bookings. The Stones also claim that the refusal of bookings amounts to "discrimination on account of national origin"- violating New York's civil rights laws.

23
The Stones fly into New York to begin their US tour. They use the yacht *S.S.Sea Panther* as their floating HQ.

24
The Stones meet the press on board their yacht and cruise up and down the Hudson River. Linda Eastman gets the exclusive photographs of the group that launch her career as a rock photographer.

The tour opens in Lynn, Massachusetts that evening, but before their crew leaves New York,

their custom-built equipment is stolen, including the world's only electric dulcimer, used by Brian Jones.

30
The concert in Montreal is stopped because the audience riots.

JULY
Dates: Stadium, Atlantic City, New Jersey (l); Forest Hills Tennis Stadium, Queens, New York City (2); Asbury Park, New Jersey (3); Virginia Beach, Virginia (4); War Memorial Hall, Syracuse, New York (6); Cobo Hall, Detroit, Michigan (8); State Fairgrounds Coliseum, Indianapolis, Indiana (9); Arie Crown Theater, McCormick Place, Chicago, Illinois (10); Sam Houston Coliseum, Houston, Texas (1l); Kiel Convention Hall, St Louis, Missouri (12); Winnipeg, Canada (14); Civic Auditorium, Omaha, Nebraska (I5); P.N.E.Forum, Vancouver, Canada (19); Seattle, Washington (20); Memorial Coliseum, Portland, Oregon (21); Auditorium, Sacramento, California (22); The Lagoon, Salt Lake City, Utah [afternoon] / Phoenix, Arizona (23); Bakersfield, California (24); Hollywood Bowl, Los Angeles, California (25); San Francisco, California (26); International Sports Center, Honolulu, Hawaii (28).

7
Police at Syracuse, New York, investigate a report by a number of angry residents that a member of The Rolling Stones dragged an American flag along the floor of the War Memorial Hall. It happened

when the Stones were walking through the auditorium to the stage for a concert. According to witnesses, one of them snatched the flag from a chair where it had been spread to dry. During a brief scuffle it was grabbed by a member of staff. Police said the musician said he wanted the flag as a souvenir, and had apologised for the incident. The police retaliated by arresting the editor of the Syracuse University student newspaper, accusing him of disorderly conduct.

AUGUST
3 - 12
The Stones recording at RCA Studios in Hollywood.

10
The Stones appear on CBS-TV's *The Ed Sullivan Show*.

12
The Stones take a break. Mick flies to Mexico, Keith flies to New York, Bill and girlfriend Diane fly to Palm Springs, California, and Charlie flies to London.

13
Charlie arrives in London to meet up with Shirley and continue on for a holiday in Greece.

14
Brian flies into London from Los Angeles and continues on to Tangier.

25
Mick crashes his Aston Martin DB6 near his flat in Marylebone. Chrissie Shrimpton was with him but neither was hurt. Repairing the damage costs £700.

SEPTEMBER
Dates: Royal Albert Hall, London (23); The Odeon, Leeds, Yorkshire (24); The Empire, Liverpool, Lancashire (25); Apollo Theatre, Ardwick, Manchester, Lancashire (28); ABC Theatre, Stockton-on-Tees, Durham (29), The Odeon, Glasgow, Scotland (30).

2
The Stones record at IBC Studios in London with producer Mike Leander and an orchestra.

4
On holiday in Tangier, Brian falls while climbing in the Atlas Mountains,

breaking two small tendon bones in his left hand, and flies immediately to London to see a specialist.

7
Mick and Keith fly to Los Angeles to mix the Stones next single.

9
Mick and Keith fly to New York where the rest of the group is waiting for them. They make a recording for CBS-TV's *Ed Sullivan Show*.

10
The Stones appear pre-recorded on Associated Rediffusion-TV's *Ready, Steady, Go!* to plug their new single.

11
The Stones appear on the *Ed Sullivan Show*. They plug their next single, 'Have You Seen Your Mother, Baby, Standing In The Shadow?'

12
The Stones are filmed walking about New York for BBC-TV's *Top Of The Pops*.

16
The flamboyant Labour MP Tom Driberg is to ask the House of Commons to "deplore the action of a magistrate who called The Rolling Stones pop group 'complete morons' who wore 'filthy clothes'."

19
Mick and Keith are interviewed by Radio Luxembourg.

Above: Mick with Chris Farlowe during the recording of Farlowe's 'Out Of Time', 1966. Below: Brian in May, 1968.

22
The Stones appear on BBC-TV's *Top Of The Pops* walking about New York.

23
'Have You Seen Your Mother, Baby, Standing In The Shadow?' / 'Who's Driving Your Plane?' released in the UK and USA. It enters the UK charts at No. 10 and reaches No. 5. It enters the US charts at No. 40 and gets to No. 5.

The Stones begin another British tour. Also on the bill are The Ike and Tina Turner Revue, The Yardbirds, Peter Jay and The New Jaywalkers and Long John Baldry. The opening concert at the Royal Albert Hall is chaotic, with more than 50 girls taken to hospital after a stage invasion. Keith is knocked to the ground and fans nearly strangle Mick. Brian and Bill run off the stage, pursued by fans.

There is an after concert party at the nearby Kensington Hotel where the Stones receive a number of gold discs. BBC-TV films the event for use on *Top Of The Pops*.

HAVE YOU SEEN YOUR MOTHER, BABY, STANDING IN THE SHADOW?
Jagger, Richard /
WHO'S DRIVING YOUR PLANE Jagger, Richard
S - Decca F 12497 (UK) and London 903 (USA).
Released: September 1966.
Producer: Andrew Loog Oldham.
Engineer: Dave Hassinger.
Studio: RCA, Hollywood.

27
Mick is interviewed by BBC Radio.

29
BBC-TV's *Top Of The Pops* screens the Stones receiving gold discs a week before.

OCTOBER
Dates: City Hall, Newcastle-upon-Tyne (I), Gaumont Theatre, Ipswich, Suffolk (2); The Odeon, Birmingham (6); Colston Hall, Bristol, Gloucs (7); Capitol Theatre, Cardiff, Wales (8), Gaumont Theatre, Southampton, Hants (9).

'Ride On Baby' by Chris Farlowe, produced by Mick Jagger, released on Immediate.

4
The Stones record a session for Associated Rediffusion TV's *Ready Steady Go!*

7
The Stones' film is broadcast on Associated Rediffusion TV's *Ready Steady Go!* Meanwhile, Peter Whitehead's promo film for 'Have You Seen Your Mother...' is banned by BBC's *Top Of The Pops*.

9
The Stones finish their UK tour. Brian Jones comments: "A new generation came to see us on tour. Youngsters who had never seen us before, from the age of about 12 were turning up at the concerts. It was like three years ago when the excitement was all new."

Keith: "We were in danger of becoming respectable! But now the new wave has arrived, rushing the stage just like old times!"

14
Mick is interviewed on Associated Rediffusion TV's *David Frost Show.*

15
Mick Jagger appears in public for the first time with his future girlfriend, Marianne Faithfull, at the launch party for the underground newspaper *International Times* held at the Round House in Chalk Farm, London. Chrissie Shrimpton still lives with Jagger at 52 Harley House, Marylebone Road.

25
The Stones attend a party given for Bobby Darin who is in London.

NOVEMBER
BIG HITS (HIGH TIDE AND GREEN GRASS)
Compilation
A - Decca TXS 101.
Released: November 1966.
Producer: Andrew Loog Oldham.

Side 1: 1. Have You Seen Your Mother, Baby, Standing In The Shadow? (Jagger, Richard) / 2. Paint It Black (Jagger. Richard) / 3. It's All Over Now (B. Womack, S. Womack) / 4. The Last Time (Jagger, Richard) / 5. Heart Of Stone (Jagger, Richard) / 6. Not Fade Away (Petty, Hardin) / 7. Come On (Berry).

Side 2: 8. (I Can't Get No) Satisfaction (Jagger, Richard) / 9. Get Off Of My Cloud (Jagger, Richard) / 10. As Tears Go By (Jagger, Richard) / 11. 19th Nervous Breakdown (Jagger, Richard) / 12. Lady Jane (Jagger, Richard) / 13. Time Is On My Side (Meade, Norman) / 14. Little Red Rooster (Dixon).

GOT LIVE IF YOU WANT IT!
A - London PS 493.
Released: November 1966.
Producer: Andrew Loog Oldham.
Studio: Recorded live at the Royal Albert Hall by Glyn Johns, September 23, 1966.

Side 1: 1. Under My Thumb (Jagger, Richard) / 2. Get Off Of My Cloud (Jagger, Richard) / 3. Lady Jane (Jagger, Richard) / 4. Not Fade Away (Petty, Hardin) / 5. I've Been Loving You Too Long (To Stop Now) (Redding, Butler) / 6. Fortune Teller (Neville).

Side 2: 7. The Last Time (Jagger Richard) / 8. 19th Nervous Breakdown (Jagger, Richard) / 9. Time Is On My Side (Meade, Norman) / 10. I'm Alright (Nanker, Phelge) / 11. Have You Seen Your Mother, Baby, Standing In The Shadow? (Jagger, Richard) / 12. (I Can't Get No) Satisfaction (Jagger, Richard).

Notes: This is a totally different recording to that on the UK Extended Play of the same name. This album was never released in the UK though some tracks appeared on the Decca compilation 'Gimme Shelter' and a CD was issued in Europe, distributed in the UK, in 1987.

4
'Got Live If You Want It' album released in the USA and reaches No. 6 in the album charts.

In the UK, Decca released the compilation 'Big Hits (High Tide and Green Grass)' which enters the album charts at No. 6 and peaks at No. 4.

'Farlowe In The Midnight Hour' an EP by Chris Farlowe, produced by Mick, Keith and Andrew Oldham, is released. It includes Farlowe's cover of 'Satisfaction'. Farlowe's album, 'The Art Of Chris Farlowe', produced by Mick, is also released by Immediate.

7
Brian Jones attends a party at the Playboy Club.

10
The Stones record at Olympic Studios, Barnes.

11
At a party for The Four Tops, Keith, Charlie and Mick join John Lennon, George Harrison, Donovan and Eric Burdon in an all-star guest list.

25
The Stones recording at Olympic Studios.

DECEMBER
6
The Stones finish their recording sessions at Olympic.

13
Andrew Oldham flies to New York to complete the editing of tracks for a new album and single.

Brian and Keith fly to Los Angeles to spend Christmas there.

15
Mick and Chrissie Shrimpton should have been flying to Jamaica for their Christmas holidays but Mick cancels the tickets and spends the day with Marianne Faithfull having lunch in Knightsbridge, then buying presents at Harrods afterwards.

17
BBC-TV films the Stones for *Top Of The Pops* in London.

19
Mick finally tells Chrissie that their three-year romance is over and that he is in love with someone else. He later told the press, "Three years is a long time to be spent with somebody, but although we were unofficially engaged we hadn't set any date for a wedding."

Chrissie Shrimpton says: "We were very much in love but we argued all the time. As time goes on you begin to feel different about life and each other. There wasn't a row. We broke by mutual agreement." However, a few days after breaking up, Chrissie is admitted to the Greenway Nursing Home in London after attempting suicide. Mick refuses to pay the bill for her stay in the nursing home and sends it on to her.

23
Mick is interviewed on the final edition of Associated Rediffusion TV's *Ready Steady Go!* in Wembley.

24
Mick hires a removal company to collect all of Chrissie's belongings from Harley House.

26
December: BBC-TV's *Top Of The Pops* shows films of the Stones recorded on February 3 and April 14 in their round-up of the year.

Below: Brian enjoys the attention at the Royal Albert Hall, London, September 23, 1966.

1967

JANUARY

The Stones mix their new album 'Between The Buttons' at Olympic Studios in Barnes.

Chris Farlowe's 'My Way Of Giving', produced by Mick, released on Immediate. Nicky Scott's 'Backstreet Girl' (Jagger, Richard) produced by Mick Jagger and Andrew Oldham released on Immediate.

BETWEEN THE BUTTONS
A - London PS 499.
Released: January 1967.
Producer: Andrew Loog Oldham.
Studio: Olympic Studios, London.

Side 1: 1. Let's Spend The Night Together (Jagger, Richard) / 2. Yesterday's Papers (Jagger, Richard) / 3. Ruby Tuesday (Jagger, Richard) / 4. Connection (Jagger, Richard) / 5. She Smiled Sweetly (Jagger, Richard) / 6. Cool, Calm And Collected (Jagger, Richard).

Side 2: 7. All Sold Out (Jagger, Richard) / 8. My Obsession (Jagger, Richard) / 9. Who's Been Sleeping Here (Jagger, Richard) / 10. Complicated (Jagger, Richard) / 11. Miss Amanda Jones (Jagger, Richard) / 12. Something Happened To Me Yesterday (Jagger, Richard).

Notes: The US version lost 'Back Street Girl' and 'Please Go Home' but gained both sides of their latest single: tracks 1 and 3.

15

The Stones record a session for the Ed Sullivan Show. Jagger mumbles the words to 'Let's Spend The Night Together' rather than change them to "spend some time together" which Sullivan wanted. Naturally several US radio stations ban the record.

'Let's Spend The Night Together' / 'Ruby Tuesday' released in Britain and the USA. It is reported that when it was recorded at RCA Studios in Hollywood, two policemen went to investigate strange noises coming from the studio in the early morning and were persuaded to help out. One policeman is playing a drum with two truncheons [unless this is an Andrew Oldham press release].

In the UK 'Let's Spend The Night Together' enters the charts at No. 17 and climbs to No. 2. The 'B'-side 'Ruby Tuesday' enters at No. 29 and rises to No. 22.

In the USA the less controversial 'Ruby Tuesday' is made the 'A'-side. It enters the charts at No. 78 and gets to No. 1. 'Let's Spend The Night Together' enters the charts at No. 86 and reaches No. 55.

LET'S SPEND THE NIGHT TOGETHER Jagger, Richard / RUBY TUESDAY Jagger, Richard
S - Decca F 12546 (UK) and London 904 (USA).
Released: January 1967.
Producer: Andrew Loog Oldham.
Studio: Olympic, London.

Bottom: Marianne Faithfull in 1966.

20

'Between The Buttons' released in the UK. It enters the charts at No. 4 rising only one place to No. 3.

BETWEEN THE BUTTONS
A - Decca LK 4852.
Released: January 1967.
Producer: Andrew Loog Oldham.
Studio: Olympic Studios, London.

Side 1: 1. Yesterday's Papers (Jagger, Richard) / 2. My Obsession (Jagger, Richard) / 3. Back Street Girl (Jagger, Richard / 4. Connection (Jagger, Richard) / 5. She Smiles Sweetly (Jagger, Richard) / 6. Cool, Calm and Collected (Jagger, Richard).

Side 2: 7. All Sold Out (Jagger, Richard) / 8. Please Go Home (Jagger, Richard) / 9. Who's Been Sleeping Here (Jagger, Richard) / 10. Complicated (Jagger, Richard) / 11. Miss Amanda Jones (Jagger, Richard) / 12. Something Happened To Me Yesterday (Jagger, Richard).

22

The Stones appear on ITV's variety show *Sunday Night At The London Palladium.* They mime to their latest record but refuse to mount the revolving carousel with all the other performers at the end of the show. This is regarded as unprecedented rudeness and the press erupts in predictable outrage. Mick tells the *New Musical Express:* "The only reason we did the show at the Palladium was because it was a good national plug. Anyone who thought we were changing our image to suit a family audience was mistaken."

The show's director said, "They're insulting me and everyone else."

24

The Stones recording at Olympic Studios.

25

The Stones record a session for BBC-TV's *Top Of The Pops* in London.

26

The Stones record a session for a future BBC Radio *Top Gear.*

The Stones appear on BBC TV *Top Of The Pops.*

27

'Between The Buttons' released in the USA where it reaches No. 2 in the album charts.

Mick and Marianne fly to Nice. Marianne is participating in the San Remo Pop Festival in Italy. There are

a week of rehearsals with the house orchestra prior to the event so Mick goes along to keep her company.

FEBRUARY

2

BBC TV's *Top Of The Pops* repeats their recent Stones recording.

4

Mick and Marianne, still on the Riviera, attend the International Record and Music publishing Market in Cannes where the Stones receive a special award as best selling British act.

5

The *News Of The World* claims that Mick Jagger has taken LSD at The Moody Blues' house in Roehampton. He is reported as saying, "I don't go much on it now the cats have taken it up. It'll just get a dirty name. I remember the first time I took it, it was on our tour with Bo Diddley and Little Richard." The reporter continued, 'Later at Blaises, Jagger showed a companion and two girls a small piece of hash and invited them to his flat for "a smoke".' The source of the paper's 'facts' was a year-old conversation with Brian Jones, whom the *News Of The World* reporter had mistaken for Jagger.

Jagger appears on ABC-TV's *Eamonn Andrews Show* and announces that he is suing the *News Of The World* for libel. The Stones also play on the show.

7

Jagger issues a libel suit against the *News Of The World.*

10

Mick, Keith, Marianne and Donovan attend a Beatles' recording session at Abbey Road to see The Beatles and a 40 piece orchestra record 'A Day In The Life'.

Hamilton and The Movement's 'I'm Not The Marrying Kind' (Wyman, Gosling) produced by Bill, released on CBS.

12

Police raid Redlands, Keith Richard's home in West Sussex after waiting

for George Harrison and Pattie Boyd to leave the weekend party. Mick and Marianne, as well as the other guests, are searched. Police seize sun-tan lotion, Earl Grey tea and other suspect substances for analysis. Marianne has just taken a bath and is wrapped in a fur rug when police arrive. Police also regard antique dealer Christopher Gibbs's attire as unorthodox until it is pointed out that it is the Pakistani national dress. It is widely believed that the *News Of The World* had kept Richard's house under surveillance and tipped the police off about the party in retaliation for Jagger's libel suit.

19

Though the police did not make the raid on Richard's house public, the *News Of The World* carries a carefully worded report, headlined, 'Drug Squad Raid Pop Stars' Party'.

23

For the world première of Roland Petit's ballet 'Paradise Lost' danced by Rudolf Nureyev and Margot Fonteyn, Mick and Marianne arrive at the Royal Opera House, Covent Garden eight minutes late. This causes a great scandal because Princess Margaret is present.

MARCH

Dates: Indoor Hall, Malmö, Sweden (25); Indoor Hall, Örebro, Sweden (27); Stadthalle, Bremen, Germany (29); Sporthalle, Cologne, Germany (30); Westfalenhalle, Dortmund, Germany (31).

Keith, Brian, Anita Pallenberg and a friend called Deborah Dixon leave London by car for Tangier to get away from the depressing atmosphere caused by the drugs bust at Redlands.

4

Mick flies to Tangier to be there when Keith and Brian arrive. Christopher Gibbs and Robert Fraser also fly out to Tangier to join the party.

6

Driving through the French Department of Tarn, on their way to

Morocco via France and Spain, Brian has a severe asthma attack and is hospitalised in Albi. The others continue without him. With Brian out of the way, Keith and Anita begin a long lasting affair.

8

Mick becomes a Friend of Covent Garden Opera House.

9

Marianne flies from Naples to join Mick in Tangier.

10

Brian flies from Nice to London where he enters the West London Hospital.

A press release announces that Brian has composed the soundtrack for Volker Schlondorff's *Mort Und Totschlag (A Degree of Murder)* which stars Anita Pallenberg. Brian recorded it at IBC Studios in London with Marianne Faithfull's producer Mike Leander. The film is chosen as Germany's entry for the 1967 Cannes Film Festival.

15

Brian flies to Morocco to rejoin his party who are now all in Marrakech.

16

Brion Gysin takes Brian to the great Djemaa el Fna public square to

record Moroccan trance music and smoke hashish with the Mejdoubi brothers who, in Gysin's words, "go into their long drawn out mint tea routine which can take a whole afternoon." While Brian is away from the hotel, Keith and Anita Pallenberg, accompanied by Mick and Marianne, fly back to London from Tangier, leaving him stranded in Morocco without even a note to say where they were.

18

A distraught Brian Jones flies back to London.

25

The Stones begin a European tour. The London *Evening News* reports: "Swedish customs officers have searched The Rolling Stones from head to toe for drugs. The pop group, arriving from Copenhagen, said they were delayed for nearly an hour as officers inspected sixteen pieces of luggage. 'They were looking for pot,' said Mick Jagger, 'and they went through every bit of clothes we had, even our underclothes'."

26

The audience riots at the Stones' Swedish concert and attack the stage. The police wade in with dogs and batons. Jagger asks, "Why do you have to hit girls on the head with batons?"

APRIL

Dates: Ernst-Merke-Halle, Hamburg, Germany (I); Stadthalle, Vienna, Austria (2); Palazzo dello Sport, Bologna, Italy (5); Palazzo dello Sport, Rome, Italy (6); Palazzo dello Sport, Milan, Italy (8); Palazzo dello Sport, Genoa, Italy (9); The Olympia, Paris, France (11); Sala Kongresowej, Palace Of Culture, Warsaw, Poland (13); Hallen Stadium, Zurich, Switzerland (14); Hautreust Hall, The Hague, Netherlands (15); Panathinaikos Football Stadium, Athens, Greece (17).

Above: In Green Park, London, January 11, 1967. Below: In the Mayfair Hotel on the same day.

2

A fan throws a smoke bomb and a riot breaks out at the Stones' concert in Vienna. 154 fans are arrested.

5

The Stones fly into Bologna.

6

Brigitte Bardot and Gina Lollobrigida are in the audience for the Stones' Rome concert.

8

The *Daily Express* reports: "Olympic gold medallist Lynn Davies clashed with The Rolling Stones yesterday over what happened in the dining room of an hotel in Germany where they were all staying. Said Davies: 'I felt sick and ashamed to be British as they poured out swear words at the breakfast table. They are tarnishing the name of their country in a foreign land...' Rolling Stones 22-year-old leader Mick Jagger in Rome replied: 'The accusations are disgusting and completely untrue. We deny that we were badly behaved. I cannot remember when we have behaved better. We hardly used the public rooms in this hotel. They were crammed with athletes behaving very badly'."

10

The Stones are searched by Customs officials when they arrive in Paris. Jagger says, "I feel as if I am being treated as a witch."

12

Customs officials at Le Bourget again search the Stones for drugs, this time on their way out of France. They take such a long time harassing them that the group misses their flight to Warsaw. Jagger loses his temper with an airport official who reacts by punching him.

13

At the Stones' first appearance behind the Iron Curtain, held at the Palais of Culture, Warsaw, police use batons and tear-gas to break up a crowd of 3,000 teenagers trying to storm the building. Hundreds of police, some wearing steel helmets, seal off the square in front of the skyscraper long before the group is due to arrive. When the Stones arrive about 1000 fans who were unable to get tickets for the concert break down the crush barriers and charge the iron gates of the building. The police draw batons and wade into the crowd then fire tear gas shells. They are met with a barrage of bottles and stones. About 30 people are arrested. Next, a crowd of about 2,000 tries to force its way into the building through an entrance at the other side of the square. Police attack with tear gas and batons. After breaking up the crowd the police bring up two water cannons in readiness for the second performance but there are no further incidents.

14

A fan breaks through a cordon of 300 policemen at the Stones' concert in Zurich and throws Jagger to the ground. The *Daily Mirror* reports: "The youth hoisted himself onto a twenty foot high stage, specially built to keep fans at bay, and rushed Jagger from behind. He grabbed Jagger by the lapels of his floral jacket and flung him to the floor. Then he began jumping on the singer. Detectives rushed to Jagger's rescue but the Stones' road manager, Tom Keylock, yelled at them to stand aside. He waded in with an uppercut at the youth's jaw, and broke his hand."

17

After the concert in Athens, Brian and Anita, still friends, fly to Cannes for the International Film Festival where *A Degree Of Murder* is the German entry. Keith sets off to join them, driving from Athens to Cannes by car. Mick and Charlie fly to London while Bill stays on in Greece for a week's holiday.

MAY

Chris Farlowe's cover of 'Yesterday's Papers', produced by Mick released on Immediate.

10

Mick and Keith, together with art dealer Robert Fraser, appear in court at Chichester, Sussex, and are released on bail of £100 each to be tried at West Sussex Quarter Sessions on 22 June. Manager Allen Klein is in court.

Brian Jones and his friend Stash de Rollo (Prince Stanislaus Klossowski) are arrested at Brian's flat in South Kensington and charged at Chelsea police station with unlawful possession of drugs. Brian is remanded on £250 bail to appear at the Magistrates Court the next day.

11

Brian appears at Marlborough Street Magistrates Court in Soho and his bail is extended.

Mick Jagger attends a Beatles recording session at Olympic Studios in Barnes. Notes on the tape box suggest that Mick may have joined in the chorus on 'Baby You're A Rich Man'.

16-19

The Stones record at Olympic Studios, Barnes.

21

Mick appears on BBC-TV's *Look Of The Week*, discussing with Professor John Cohen of Manchester University the relationship between performers and audiences.

JUNE

The 'Flowers' Stones compilation album released in the USA. It reaches No. 2 in the US charts.

FLOWERS

A - London PS 509 (USA).
Released: June 1967.
Producer: Andrew Loog Oldham.
Studios: Tracks 11 and 12: RCA, Hollywood. Track 6: Olympic, London.

Side 1: 1. Ruby Tuesday (Jagger, Richard) / 2. Have You Seen Your Mother, Baby, Standing In The Shadow? (Jagger, Richard) / 3. Let's Spend The Night Together (Jagger, Richard) / 4. Lady Jane (Jagger, Richard) / 5. Out Of Time (Jagger, Richard) / 6. My Girl (Robinson, White)

Side 2: 7. Back Street Girl (Jagger, Richard) / 8. Please Go Home (Jagger Richard) / 9. Mother's Little Helper (Jagger, Richard) / 10. Take It Or Leave It (Jagger, Richard) / 11. Ride On Baby (Jagger, Richard) / 12. Sittin' On A Fence (Jagger, Richard).

Notes: Tracks 6, 11 and 12 did not appear in the UK for several years. Track 11 was originally recorded by Chris Farlowe (on 'The Art Of Chris Farlowe' album) and track 12 was

originally recorded by Twice As Much. This compilation was never released in the UK.

3

Marianne Faithfull collapses on stage during a performance of Chekov's *Three Sisters* at the Royal Court Theatre, London.

8

Paul McCartney invites Brian to play on a track they are working on at Studio 2 at Abbey Road Studios. He arrives with his saxophone when they were expecting him to play guitar. He plays the amusing solo on 'You Know My Name (Look Up The Number)'.

25

Mick, Keith and Brian add their voices to the many dozens of others at The Beatles' live BBC-TV *Our World* telecast recording of 'All You Need Is Love'.

27

The London *Evening Standard* reports: "Chichester. Mick Jagger was found guilty at Chichester today of the illegal possession of two drugs found in his jacket at the house party given by a second member of The Rolling Stones pop group, Keith Richard. Jagger was remanded to Lewes jail overnight and may be sentenced tomorrow after a charge against Richard of allowing his Sussex house to be used for smoking hemp, has been heard.

The jury at West Sussex quarter sessions took six minutes to reach their verdict. They had retired after a ruling by the chairman, Judge Block, that Jagger had no defence to the charge. Det. Sgt. Cudmore agreed that during the police raid on the house at West Wittering Jagger had 'cooperated fully throughout and behaved in an entirely adult manner'."

29

The London *Evening Standard* reports: "Rolling Stones Mick Jagger and Keith Richard and Mayfair art gallery director Robert Fraser were jailed this afternoon at Chichester for drug offences at Richard's house party in Sussex four months ago.

The sentences imposed at West Sussex quarter sessions were Richard: one year and ordered to pay £500 towards costs; Jagger three months and £100 costs. Fraser: six months; £200 costs." Mick is taken to Brixton jail. Keith goes to Wormwood Scrubs.

Opposite: Brian at Top Of The Pops, 1967.

30

The London *Evening Standard* reports: "Rolling Stones Mick Jagger and Keith Richard jailed at Chichester yesterday for drug offences, were granted bail in the High Court this afternoon in the sum of £7,000 each". Robert Fraser remains in jail and serves four months for possession of heroin.

Several newspapers, including the *Evening Standard*, carry special advertisements placed by The Who: "The Who consider Mick Jagger and Keith Richard have been treated as scapegoats for the drug problem and as a protest against the savage sentences imposed upon them at Chichester yesterday, The Who are issuing today the first of a series of Jagger/Richard songs to keep their work before the public until they are again free to record themselves." The Who cover 'The Last Time' and 'Under My Thumb'.

Most of the audience at the underground UFO Club leave the premises to stage a demonstration outside the *News Of The World* newspaper which is widely believed to have set up the arrest of Mick and Keith. There are scuffles and many people are taken to the police station but only two are actually charged. Fans also gather at Piccadilly Circus, chanting 'Free The Stones!' At UFO the audience returns at about 2:00am and joins in the chorus of 'Revolution' by Tomorrow who were playing that night.

JULY
1

The Times leader, written by editor William Rees-Mogg, is headlined WHO BREAKS A BUTTERFLY ON A WHEEL?

"Mr Jagger has been sentenced to imprisonment for three months. He is appealing against conviction and sentence, and has been granted bail until the hearing of the appeal later in the year. In the meantime the sentence of imprisonment is bound to be widely discussed by the public. And the circumstances are sufficiently unusual to warrant such discussion in the public interest.

"Mr Jagger was charged with being in possession of four tablets containing amphetamine sulphate and methyl amphetamine hydrochloride; these tablets had been bought perfectly legally in Italy, and brought back to this country. They are not a highly dangerous drug or in proper dosage, a dangerous drug at all. They are of the Benzedrine type and the Italian manufacturers recommend them both as a stimulant and as a remedy for travel sickness.

"In Britain, it is an offence to possess these drugs without a doctor's prescription. Mr Jagger's doctor says that he knew and had authorised their use, but he did not

give a prescription for them as indeed they had already been purchased. His evidence was not challenged. This was, therefore, an offence of a technical character which before this case drew the point to public attention any honest man might have been liable to commit. If after his visit to the Pope, the Archbishop of Canterbury had bought proprietary air sickness pills on Rome Airport and imported the unused tablets into Britain on his return, he would have risked committing precisely the same offence. No one who has ever travelled and bought proprietary drugs abroad can be sure that he has not broken the law.

"Judge Block directed the jury that the approval of a doctor is not a defence in law to the charge of possessing drugs without a prescription, and the jury convicted. Mr Jagger was not charged with complicity in any other drug offence that occurred in the same house. They were separate cases, and no evidence was produced to suggest that he knew Mr Fraser had heroin tablets or that the vanishing Mr Snidermann had cannabis resin. It is indeed no offence to be in the same building or the same company as people possessing or even using drugs, nor could it reasonably be made an offence. The drugs which Mr Jagger had in his possession must therefore be treated on their own as a separate issue from the other drugs that other people may have had in their possession at the same time. It may be difficult for lay opinion to make this distinction clearly, but obviously justice cannot be done if one man is to be punished for a purely contingent association with someone else's offence.

"We have therefore, a conviction against Mr Jagger purely on the grounds that he possessed four Italian pep pills, quite legally bought, but not legally imported without a prescription. Four is not a large number. This is not the quantity which a pusher of drugs would have on him, nor even the quantity one would expect in an addict. In any case Mr Jagger's career is obviously one that does involve great personal strain and exhaustion; his doctor says that he approved the occasional use of these drugs, and it seems likely that similar drugs would have been prescribed if there was a need for them. Millions of similar drugs are prescribed in Britain every year, and for a variety of conditions. One has to ask, therefore, how it is that this technical offence, divorced as it must be from other people's offences, was thought to deserve the penalty of imprisonment. In the courts at large it is most uncommon for imprisonment to be imposed on first offenders where the drugs are not major drugs of addiction and there is no question of drug traffic. The normal penalty is probation, and the purpose of probation is to encourage the offender to develop his career and to avoid the drug risks in the future. It is surprising therefore that Judge Block should have decided to sentence Mr Jagger to imprisonment and particularly surprising as Mr Jagger's is about as mild a drug case as can ever have been brought before the courts.

"It would be wrong to speculate on the judge's reasons, which we do not know. It is, however, possible to consider the public reaction. There are many people who take a

primitive view of the matter, what one might call a pre-legal view of the matter. They consider that Mr Jagger has "got what was coming to him". They resent the anarchic quality of The Rolling Stones performances, dislike their songs, dislike their influence on teenagers and broadly suspect them of decadence, a word used by Miss Monica Furlong in the *Daily Mail*.

"As a sociological concern, this may be reasonable enough, and at an emotional level, it is very understandable, but it has nothing at all to do with the case. One has to ask a different question: Has Mr Jagger received the same treatment as he would have received if he had not been a famous figure, with all the criticism his celebrity has aroused? If a promising undergraduate had come back from a summer visit to Italy with four pep pills in his pocket, would it have been thought necessary to display him, handcuffed,

to the public? There are cases in which a single figure becomes the focus for public concern about some aspects of public morality. The Stephen Ward case, with its dubious evidence and questionable verdict, was one of them, and that verdict killed Stephen Ward. There are elements of the same emotions in the reactions to this case. If we are going to make any case a symbol of the conflict between the sound traditional values of Britain and the new hedonism, then we must be sure that the sound traditional values include those of tolerance and equity. It should be the particular quality of British justice to ensure that Mr Jagger is treated exactly the same as anyone else, no better and no worse. There must remain a suspicion in this case that Mr Jagger received a more severe sentence than would have been thought proper for any purely anonymous young man."

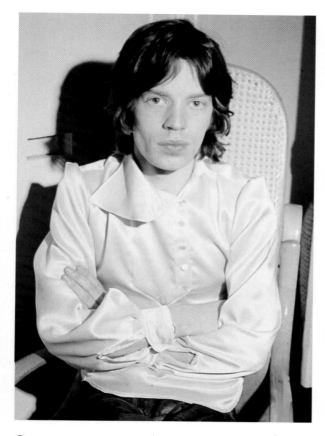

2

John Gorton writes in the *Sunday Express*: "Was Jagger convicted of taking one of the evil drugs like heroin or cocaine? Or LSD with which some of The Beatles confess that they have been experimenting? Not at all. Did he smoke marijuana which some experts say is evil but others, equally expert, say is not so evil? That wasn't alleged against him. He merely had four Benzedrine tablets, legally purchased abroad, which, with the knowledge and approval of his doctor, he took to keep him awake while he worked."

6

Brian Jones is hospitalised, suffering from strain.

7 - 20

The Stones record at Olympic Studios, Barnes.

12

Brian is well enough to join the others in the studio.

23

Brian and his new girlfriend Suki Potier fly to Marbella for a short holiday. Nicky Browne, the widow of Tara Browne, goes with them.

31

The Appeals Court lifts the sentences against Mick and Keith. They hold a press conference afterwards. Mick says: "I simply ask for my private life to be left alone. My responsibility is only for myself. I had prepared myself mentally, physically and business-wise for the possibility of going to jail. It felt lovely to be sure of freedom."

That evening Mick appears on ITV's *World In Action*. Filmed out-of-doors Mick arrives by helicopter for a discussion with William Rees-Mogg, the editor of *The Times*; Lord Stow Hill; Dr. John Robinson, the Bishop of Woolwich and Father Thomas Corbishley, a Jesuit priest. Mick says: "I am a rebel against society, but not an obvious one. Many people like me feel that things are wrong. Society has pushed me into this position of responsibility."

AUGUST

Anita Pallenberg attends the Venice Film Festival and her new boyfriend, Keith, goes along for the ride.

Early in the month, the Stones spend a week recording at Olympic Studios.

1

The Times reports "The Court quashed the conviction of Keith Richards for permitting, as an occupier, his house at West Wittering to be used for the purpose of smoking cannabis resin, contrary to section 5 (1) of the Dangerous Drugs Act, 1965, because the chairman of West Sussex Quarter Sessions, Judge Block, did not warn the jury that there was only tenuous evidence which could make them sure that a girl at the house, dressed only in a rug, smoked cannabis resin and that Mr Richards must have known it. Their Lordships allowed his appeal against conviction, on separate trial from Mr Michael Jagger. He had been sentenced to 12 months and ordered to pay £500 costs of the prosecution. Mick Jagger stood in the High Court yesterday, five days after his 23rd birthday and heard Lord Parker of Waddington, the Lord Chief Justice, substitute an order for conditional discharge for a sentence of three months' imprisonment imposed on him last month. Lord Parker warned him of the responsibilities he bore 'as an idol to a large number of people'."

5

Mick produces two tracks for Marianne's new album at Decca studios. Paul McCartney is in the studio to add encouragement when she sings his composition 'When I'm 64'.

12

Mick and Marianne go on holiday to Ireland.

18

'We Love You'/ 'Dandelion' released in UK and USA. It enters the charts at No. 13 reaching No. 9. In the USA, 'Dandelion' enters at No. 74 and climbs to No. 14 while 'We Love You' enters at No. 86 and gets to No. 50. It is intended as a 'thank you' to all of those who supported Mick and Keith through the trial. John Lennon and Paul McCartney sing back-up vocals on 'We Love You' and poet Allen Ginsberg is also in the studio lending support.

The *Daily Sketch* reviews 'We Love You': "The new Rolling Stones record 'We Love You' opens with an ironic comment on the group's trials and tribulations of the last few months. It's the sound of a prison warder's footsteps, accompanied by the clanking of chains and the banging of a prison cell door. It was recorded while Jagger and Richard were waiting for their appeal on drug charges to be heard. Mick Jagger describes the record as a 'thank you' to fans and supporters for their help during the trial and appeal period."

Meanwhile, the BBC have banned the promotional film made by the Stones for the single because it features Mick, Keith and Marianne acting scenes from *The Trials of Oscar Wilde*.

WE LOVE YOU Jagger, Richard / **DANDELION** Jagger, Richard

S - Decca F 12654 (UK) and London 905 (USA).
Released: August 1967.
Producer: Andrew Loog Oldham.
Studio: Olympic Sound.
Side A: August 1967 / Side B: November 1966.

Notes: Paul McCartney and John Lennon sing backup vocals on Side 'A'.

26

Mick and Marianne travel with The Beatles by train to see the Maharishi at his summer seminar held at a teachers' training college in Bangor, North Wales, but are not impressed. Mick: "Maybe he is the reincarnation of the Buddha for all I know. I never really got into it that much. He never seemed like he was to me. Maybe Christ would have used television. Maybe he would have, but he would have understood it before he started, don't you think? It's become an issue to laugh at, really."

SEPTEMBER

1
A three day recording session is planned. Keith interrupts his holiday in Rome with Anita Pallenberg to fly in. Brian interrupts a holiday in Marbella and flies in the same day.

3
Brian announces that he has applied for a pilot's licence.

5-7
The Stones recording at Olympic Studios. After the sessions, Brian returns to Marbella and Keith flies to Rome.

8
Keith is granted permission to build a nine foot brick wall around his house.

14
Mick flies into New York from Paris. Brian, Keith, Bill and Charlie fly in from London. Mick and Keith are questioned by Customs and Immigration officers about their drugs trial and have to attend further meetings at the immigration headquarters on Broadway.

The Americans are reassured when British authorities confirm that their convictions were successfully appealed.

16
The Stones begin long business meetings with Allen Klein at his Broadway office. After the meetings, Mick Jagger and Michael Cooper, designer of the sleeve for their forthcoming album, go to Mt. Vernon, New York to supervise the sleeve manufacture at Pictorial Productions Limited which is the only place, apart from a plant in Tokyo, where 3-D images are manufactured. The 3-D sleeve costs $50,000 to produce because the 3-D plastic images cost $1 apiece to make.

29
The Stones return to England from the USA. It is announced that Andrew Oldham will no longer be their manager, nor will he produce their records. Their new manager will be Allen Klein and they will produce their records themselves. This ends months of speculation in the press and music industry.

OCTOBER

1
Thieves steal Marianne Faithfull's jewellery and furs from Mick's house in Cheyne Walk.

3
Keith's guard dogs are shot at and wounded for worrying local livestock.

5
Keith flies to Rome to join Anita.

15
The *People* reports that "The Beatles and The Rolling Stones are planning to get together on a business venture. They are looking for new studios in London - probably to record unknown pop groups. And they may make films together. There is no question of the two pop groups merging."

It is also reported that Bill Wyman has applied for membership of the Royal Horticultural Society.

20
Brian flies to the Costa del Sol to get himself in shape for his upcoming appearance in court.

30
Brian Jones admits to possession of cannabis and allowing his flat to be used for smoking it but pleads not guilty to possession of cocaine and methedrine. He is found guilty and sentenced to nine months in prison. He is taken to Wormwood Scrubs. Fans demonstrate in the Kings Road and seven, including Mick Jagger's brother Chris, are arrested for obstruction.

31
Brian Jones released from the Scrubs on £750 bail, pending an appeal.

NOVEMBER

12
Rolling Stones PR Leslie Perrin releases a statement on their behalf, objecting to the contents of a speech made by Judge Leslie Block at a formal dinner given by the Horsham Ploughing and Agricultural Society in which he said, "We did our best, your fellow countrymen, I and my fellow magistrates, to cut these Stones down to size, but alas, it was not to be, because the Court of Criminal Appeal let them roll free... I can only suppose that the Court of Criminal Appeal was influenced by the words of Shakespeare when he wrote his own epitaph in these words, 'Blest be the man who spares these stones'." In view of Brian's upcoming appeal, Perrin questioned whether the Judge's words were helpful and suggested that an unbiased hearing might now be very hard to achieve.

19
'In Another Land' / 'The Lantern' is released in the USA.

IN ANOTHER LAND
Wyman / **THE LANTERN**
Jagger, Richard
S- London 907.
Released: December 1967.
Producer: The Rolling Stones.
Studio: Olympic Studios, London.

27
'Their Satanic Majesties Request' is released in the USA. It ships gold before release and quickly reaches No. 2, selling $2,500,000 worth of copies by Christmas.

'She's A Rainbow' / '2,000 Light Years From Home' is released in the USA. It enters the charts at No. 77 and reaches No. 25.

SHE'S A RAINBOW Jagger, Richard / **2000 LIGHT YEARS FROM HOME**
Jagger, Richard
S - London 906 (USA).
Released, November 1967.
Producer: The Rolling Stones.
Studio: Olympic Studios, London.
Notes: Taken from 'Their Satanic Majesties Request' album.

30
Mick, Brian and Charlie are interviewed for BBC Radio's *Top Gear*.

Left: Brian with One Plus One director Jean LucGoddard.
Above: Keith with Anita Pallenberg, Rome, September 1967.

DECEMBER

3
Mick, Brian and Charlie's interview broadcast on *Top Gear*.

12
Magistrates set Brian's sentence aside when three psychiatrists describe him as 'an extremely frightened young man', one of them even saying he had 'suicidal tendencies'. Brian is given three years on probation and a £1,000 fine instead. Lord Justice Parker tells him: "Remember, this is a degree of mercy which the court has shown. It is not a let-off. You are still under the control of the court. If you fail to cooperate with the probation officer, or you commit another offence of any sort, you will be brought back and punished afresh."

Brian's probation officer William Hornung says: "I will not treat him as a celebrity. To me, Brian Jones is the same as any other offender who has been placed on probation."

15
The *Daily Mirror* reports: "Rolling Stone Brian Jones collapsed yesterday. He was rushed to hospital after an ambulance answered a 999 call to his London flat. But an hour later Jones told doctors at St George's hospital: 'I'm going home'. Last night, Dr Flood said: "There is no cause for alarm. He is just tired and suffering from overstrain. He has also had some teeth out'."

18
'Their Satanic Majesties Request' is released in the UK. It enters the charts at No. 10 and climbs to No. 3. Brian says: "Yes, of course the album is a very personal thing. But The Beatles are just as introspective. You have to remember that our entire lives have been affected lately by socio-political influences. You have to expect these things to come out in our work."

21
BBC-TV's *Top Of The Pops* features tracks from the Stones' 'Satanic Majesties Request' album.

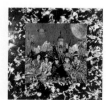

THEIR SATANIC MAJESTIES REQUEST
A - Decca TXS 103 (UK) and London NPS 2 (USA).
Released: December 1967 (UK) and November 1967 (USA).
Producers: The Rolling Stones.
Engineer: Glyn Johns.
Studio: Olympic Studios, London.

Side 1: 1. Sing This All Together (Jagger, Richard) / 2. Citadel (Jagger, Richard) / 3. In Another Land (Wyman) / 4. 2000 Man (Jagger, Richard) / 5. Sing This All Together (See What Happens) (Jagger, Richard).

Side 2: 6. She's A Rainbow (Jagger, Richard) / 7. The Lantern (Jagger, Richard) / 8. Gomper (Jagger, Richard) / 9. 2000 Light Years From Home (Jagger, Richard) / 10. On With The Show (Jagger, Richard).

Notes: The US single of tracks 6 and 9 was released before the album was released in the UK. The US album was released a month earlier also.

26
BBC-TV's *Top Of The Pops* repeats their film of the Stones recorded on January 25 in their year-end roundup.

1968

JANUARY
The Stones spend most days at a rehearsal hall in Surrey, just jamming and getting together again rather than consciously rehearsing the album tracks.

4
The *Daily Sketch* reports: "The University of California in Los Angeles is insisting that students taking a degree in music must study The Rolling Stones. The music professor feels they have made an important contribution to modern music."

20
Brian is rumoured to have been among the celebrities in the studio with Paul McCartney, contributing a few saxophone notes to the album 'McGough & McGear' he was producing. Known to be on the album are Jimi Hendrix, Zoot Money, Graham Nash, Dave Mason and Brian's friend, Prince Stash de Rollo.

FEBRUARY
The Stones spend February through to June recording at Olympic Sound, with holiday breaks. The sessions run from 7pm until dawn. After a few sessions, Jimmy Miller is brought in as producer: "Mick contacted me and said he likes the things I did with Traffic. He had been producing The Rolling Stones but he says he doesn't want to be on two sides of the control room window now."

5
Mick is interviewed on ABC-TV's *Eamonn Andrews Show* in London.

26
Brian is in Paris for his 26th birthday.

MARCH
15
Jimmy Miller takes over production duties on The Rolling Stones' new album.

16
Linda Keith, Brian Jones' girlfriend, collapses at her Belgravia flat in Chesham Place.

Brian and Mick are interviewed on BBC Radio's *Scene And Heard*.

17
Jimmy Miller's second session with the group.

18
Serafina Watts born to Charlie and Shirley.

Olympic Studios in Barnes, recording 'Beggars Banquet' before the film cameras for Jean Luc Goddard's movie One Plus One.

APRIL

Recording sessions at Olympic continue until April 18 when the group takes a break. During these sessions Brian Jones approaches Mick and asks: "What can I play?" "Yeah, what can you play Brian," is Mick's cynical response.

20

Mick and Marianne go to Ireland for a holiday.

28

The Stones film three promotional clips for their new single 'Jumpin' Jack Flash'.

MAY

Date: *New Musical Express Poll Winners Concert*, Empire Pool, Wembley, Middlesex (12).

Mick buys a house on Cheyne Walk, overlooking Chelsea Bridge, "I'm moving house next week. I've bought a house in Chelsea and I've also got a house in Hampshire, it's a huge great place."

11

It is announced that Mick Jagger will write the soundtrack for, and star in, *Performers* [sic] a movie directed by Nick Roeg and Donald Cammell. He will play opposite James Fox and Anita Pallenberg.

12

At the *NME* concert the Stones turn up unexpectedly and give their first public performance in Britain for nearly two years. Also on the bill are Lulu and Dusty Springfield. They play their new single, 'Jumpin' Jack Flash' and 'Satisfaction'. At the end of the concert, Mick throws a pair of white shoes into the audience. Mick: "It was just like old times. In fact, it was better than old times. One of the best receptions we have ever had. We were all delighted."

Southern TV broadcast the concert live. Mick gives an interview to Tony Blackburn for his TV show.

13

The Stones are back at Olympic recording their new album.

15

Mick and Brian are interviewed on BBC Radio's *Top Gear*. Brian is interviewed on BBC Radio's *Scene and Heard*.

18

The Stones segment of the *NME Poll Winners Concert* is shown on ITV's *Time For Blackburn* as well as Tony Blackburn's interview with Mick. BBC Radio repeats Brian's interview of May 15.

21

The police continue their campaign to break Brian Jones and arrest him once again, this time at his flat in the Kings Road. He appears at Marlborough Street Magistrates' Court charged with possessing cannabis and is released with bail set at £2,000.

23

BBC-TV's *Top Of The Pops* shows the Stones' promo film of 'Jumpin' Jack Flash'.

24

'Jumpin' Jack Flash' / 'Child Of The Moon' released in UK and USA. It enters the UK charts at No. 12 and goes to the top. In the States it enters at No. 63 and reaches No. 1. Mick tells *Rolling Stone*: "It's very basic, but we didn't say: 'Right, we'll go backwards.' All you are really saying is that it has a good beat - it's not weird and full of electric sounds. We could do it on stage. In fact we have done - for a film for *Top Of The Pops*. We did it live, with no backing track or anything. We didn't do it as a single. We are over half way through the new album and it was difficult, picking which track should be the single because they are all quite good for singles... We did some of the single on a cassette tape recorder, which is a pretty mad way of making a record. We were all

round at my house and we were recording everything. We got such weird sounds on drums and guitar with the cassette that we decided to use it. Charlie was just playing toy drums but we liked it and thought 'So why not use it'. We recorded again over the top of it."

JUMPIN' JACK FLASH
Jagger, Richard /
CHILD OF THE MOON
Jagger, Richard
S - Decca F 12782 (UK) and London 908 (USA).
Released: May 1968.
Producer: Jimmy Miller.
Studio: Olympic, London.

26

Charlie is interviewed on BBC-TV's *Line Up* in London.

31

It is announced that the Stones will take part in Jean-Luc Godard's next film.

JUNE
5

Jean-Luc Godard begins filming Rolling Stones recording sessions for his film, *One Plus One*. He works

fast and is through by the middle of the month. Jagger tells the *Los Angeles Free Press*: "It's not a movie really... just a lot of footage of the Stones playing in some improvised scenes, I was very turned on by Godard; he's very quiet and very good. I like his work very much. Very unobtrusive and pleasant. I think it will be ready in about two months. Movies are kind of interesting. I'm going to learn a lot, from movies, not just from acting but about making a movie."

Mick tells *Rolling Stone*: "We are very excited about this. We have been great admirers of Godard's work for a long time, and have a great respect for him."

6

BBC-TV's *Top Of The Pops* repeats the Stones' promo film of 'Jumpin' Jack Flash'.

Mick is interviewed by John Peel on UH Radio.

11

At 4:15am the fire brigade is called to put out a fire on the roof of Olympic Sound Studios which was set ablaze

by a faulty arc lamp on the Godard / Stones film set. Three fire engines arrive, interrupting the recording and filming session that is in progress. Mick: "The fire brigade was so thorough in extinguishing the blaze, our Hammond organ and all the electrical equipment was completely drenched. The sequence will have to be retaken."

Charlie Watts comments, "It was bloody frightening."

14

It is announced that the film Mick Jagger will work on is now called *Performance*.

26

The Stones make a recording for BBC-TV's *Top Of The Pops*.

27

BBC-TV's *Top Of The Pops* plays 'Jumpin' Jack Flash' with still photographs of the Stones and studio dancers.

Above: 'The Beggars Banquet' sessions. Below: Marianne looks on from the control room.

JULY

4

BBC-TV's *Top Of The Pops* shows the Stones' film recorded June 26.

7

Mick, Keith, Marianne, Anita and Jimmy Miller fly to Los Angeles. Mick and producer Jimmy Miller were so dissatisfied with the mix done in London on 'Beggars Banquet' that they called in Glyn Johns to re-do it in Los Angeles and flew in mid-July to supervise the work. Mixing took a week, working from midnight to four or five in the morning at Studio 3 in Hollywood.

Jagger is asked by the *L.A. Free Press* if the Stones were going to have any trouble getting into the States now that Brian has been busted again: "We're here aren't we, Charlie and I?... We don't know what will affect it really. It's so silly. I've had friends that have been busted ten times, who come to America to work and have no trouble getting in. It's the only country in the world where they question anyone's right to come in. My friends get through, but with us it's different. We're 'that other group from England', and they see what school (London School of Economics) I went to on the form and it's supposed to be left wing or something. People forget that John Kennedy went there.

"You have to fill out all these forms... 'I am not now, nor have I ever been' ... it's so silly. What's this got to do with me? The Stones have never advocated drugs. I don't agree with endorsing drugs. The Beatles with that ad for marijuana, really! Those people come on strong, six months later they change. Forget it. There is no announcing or denouncing drugs."

8

Charlie and Shirley Watts join the others in Los Angeles. Jagger comments, "Charlie came over for a holiday - he's doing the mixing just as an excuse to come here, that's all."

11

Brian Jones is committed for trial at Inner Court Sessions.

17

BBC Radio's *Scene and Heard* repeats their Brian interview of May 15th for the third time.

20

Chris Farlowe's cover of 'Paint It Black', produced by Mick released on Immediate.

In Hollywood, Mick goes to a Doors concert and hangs out with Jim Morrison afterwards. Brian is in Morocco with Suki Poitier where he records more Jajouka music.

26

'Beggars Banquet', the Stones new album, should have been released, but is held up because Decca will not agree to use the Stones' cover showing the graffiti on a lavatory wall.

'Street Fighting Man' / 'No Expectations' released in the USA. It enters the charts at No. 84 but only reaches No. 48.

STREET FIGHTING MAN
Jagger, Richard /
NO EXPECTATIONS
Jagger, Richard
*S - London 909 (USA).
Released: August 1968.
Producer: Jimmy Miller.
Studio: Olympic Studios, London.
Notes: Taken from the album 'Beggars Banquet'. (The album originally had an August release date scheduled but Decca refused to use the sleeve depicting 'toilet graffiti' that the Stones provided and the album was delayed by four months in stalemate.)*

29

Brian is in Tangier to record the Jajouka musicians. Brion Gysin and Hamri, then head of Musicians Union, take him to the Atlas mountains where he records the musicians in their home village.

AUGUST

3

Mick and Marianne go on holiday to Ireland.

24

Both Decca and London Records are still insisting that they will not release the Stones' new album with the toilet wall sleeve they designed in New York with Tom Wilkes of A&M Records.

SEPTEMBER

'Introspection', an album by The End released on Decca. Produced by Bill Wyman.

3

Mick records an interview for Associated Rediffusion-TV's *David Frost Show* in London.

4

The London *Evening Standard* reports, "The Rolling Stones' latest single disc is being banned by some American radio stations. The reason given by the station executives: 'It could incite further riots here.' Mick Jagger said today: 'I'm rather pleased to hear they have banned 'Street Fighting Man' as long as it's still available in the shops. The last time they banned one of our records in America it sold a million'."

5

The *Daily Mirror* reports: "A lavatory wall is standing between The Rolling Stones and the release of their new LP Beggar's Banquet. The wall has nothing to do with the disc's brilliant tracks, all written by Stones Mick Jagger and Keith Richard. It is on the album's sleeve - and is studded with up-to-the-minute graffiti. Record chiefs in London and the US are fighting shy of that wall. America's London label thinks the sleeve does give offence."

6

Mick's recorded interview appears on the *David Frost Show*.

12

Mick begins work on *Performance* which is being shot in London, mostly in Notting Hill.

The London première of Jack Cardiff's *Girl On A Motorcycle* starring Alain Delon and Marianne Faithfull causes a press sensation because Marianne appears completely nude. It is released in America with the title, *Naked Under Leather*.

14

Mick is interviewed on BBC Radio's *Scene and Heard*.

21

Mick is interviewed on BBC Radio's *The Voice of Pop*.

26

Brian Jones is fined £50 with £105 costs at the Inner London Sessions, after being found guilty of unauthorised possession of cannabis. Brian: "It's great not to be in jail. I was sure I was going to jail for at least a year. I never expected that I would be going home. It was such a wonderful relief... This summer has been one long worry to me. I knew I was innocent, but everything seems to happen to me." Mick, Keith and Brian's girlfriend Suki Poitier were in court. Mick Jagger says "We are pleased that Brian didn't have to go to jail. Money doesn't matter."

Above: Mick and Brian, hirsute, January 1968.

OCTOBER

3

The *Daily Mail* reports: "The Rolling Stones have lost their fight to keep a photograph of a lavatory wall on the sleeve of their new LP. Their dispute with Britain's Decca Records and American London Records has held up the LP 'Beggars Banquet' for more than three months. The Rolling Stones refused to change the sleeve. Record chiefs said they would not issue the record in it. Jagger said 'I don't find it at all offensive. Decca has put out a sleeve showing an atom bomb exploding. I find that more upsetting'."

4

Marianne announces that she is pregnant. Mick: "I'm happy about Marianne having our baby. It's real groovy. We'll probably have another three. But marriage? Can't see it happening. We just don't believe in it." Marianne says: "Why should we marry? We've got along fine together so far. The baby is not going to change the way we feel about each other."

12

Mick appears on TV's *David Frost Show.*

NOVEMBER

9

Mick and various record company executives work out a compromise sleeve for 'Beggars Banquet', showing an invitation card. Mick Jagger says that he has lost interest in the controversy surrounding the sleeve: "It is an unnecessary loss of time." The sleeve appears years later on the CD of the album.

The Stones all attend Tiny Tim's concert at the Royal Albert Hall.

11

Mick finishes shooting his part in *Performance.*

17

Mick is interviewed by John Peel on BBC Radio *Top Gear.*

19

Marianne is admitted to a London nursing home.

20

Marianne loses her baby at five and a half months. Mick Jagger tells the press: "Marianne has lost the baby following pregnancy complications. She is alright but we are both very upset."

21

Brian buys A.A.Milne's old house, Cotchford Farm, near Hartfield, Sussex, where the Christopher Robin books were written.

27

'Beggars Banquet' is finally released in the US where it rises to the No. 2 position in the album charts.

29

Jean Luc Godard's *One Plus One* (correctly written *1 + 1*) is premièred at the London Film Festival.

30

Mick is interviewed on the BBC-TV show *Release.*

DECEMBER

4

The Stones appear on Associated Rediffusion-TV's *David Frost Show.*

5

'Beggars Banquet' is finally released in the UK by Decca. It enters the album charts at No. 3, which is the highest it gets.

A banquet to launch the album is held at the Kensington Gore Hotel's Elizabethan Rooms in London where waitresses are dressed as serving wenches. The next day the *Daily Mail* reports: "The Rolling Stones, those apostles of present-day grooviness, came out with the oldest gag in show business yesterday - custard-pie throwing. It came at the end of a £1,000 'Beggars Banquet' named after their new LP. Suddenly they began pelting their guests - including Lord Harlech, who had been handed boxes and told 'Don't open until next Wednesday'."

Film of the reception is shown on ITN television news that evening.

BEGGARS BANQUET
A - Decca SKL 4955 (UK) and London PS 539 (USA).
Released: (UK) December 1968 (USA release): November (Originally scheduled for August but Decca refused to use the sleeve provided by the Stones).
Producer: Jimmy Miller.
Engineer: Glyn Johns.
Studio: Olympic Studios, London.

Side 1: 1. Sympathy For The Devil (Jagger, Richard) / 2. No Expectations (Jagger, Richard) / 3. Dear Doctor (Jagger, Richard) / 4. Parachute Woman (Jagger, Richard) / 5. Jig-Saw Puzzle (Jagger, Richard).

Side 2: 6. Street Fighting Man (Jagger, Richard) / 7. Prodigal Son (Rev. Robert Wilkins) / 8. Stray Cat Blues (Jagger, Richard) / 9. Factory Girl (Jagger, Richard) / 10. Salt Of The Earth (Jagger, Richard).

Notes: Nicky Hopkins and 'many friends' are credited with playing on this album.

8

The *Sunday Express* reports: "In a week's time two members of the group, Mick Jagger and Keith Richard, are off to Rio de Janeiro - to see a magician. 'We have become very interested in magic and we are very serious about this trip,' says Keith. 'We are hoping to see this magician who practises both white and black magic. He has a very long and difficult name which we cannot pronounce - we just call him Banana for short'." This is a classic Stones put-on, eagerly lapped up by the press.

12

Rock and Roll Circus, a TV special by The Rolling Stones is filmed at Intertel Studios, Wembley, featuring John Lennon and Yoko Ono, The Who, Eric Clapton, Taj Mahal, Jethro Tull, Mitch Mitchell, Marianne Faithfull and many others. The Stones are dissatisfied with their performance which is badly out of tune and scrap the entire project.

14

Mick is interviewed on BBC Radio's *Scene and Heard.*

18

Mick, Keith, Marianne and Anita fly to Rio de Janeiro, Brazil, to find their magicians.

Below, left: Brian with Diana Ross, January 1968. Below, right: At the party to launch 'Beggars Banquet'.

1969

JANUARY

4
The London *Evening News* reports "Rolling Stones guitarist Brian Jones now on holiday in Ceylon is 'furious' with several hotel managers there. Jones... complained that several hotel managers in Kandy had refused them accommodation, thinking he was an unkempt penniless beatnik. Jones, clad in a tight fitting pink suit with a psychedelic scarf pulled out a bundle of notes and said 'I am not a beatnik. I work for my living. I have money and I do not wish to be treated as a second class citizen'."

18
The *Daily Sketch* reports: "Rolling Stones Mick Jagger and Keith Richard have been barred from an exclusive hotel for wearing op art pants - and nothing else. They were asked to leave the Hotel Crillon in Lima, Peru, after refusing the manager's pleas to change clothes. Last night the two Stones... were staying in the equally exclusive Hotel Bolivar."

FEBRUARY

22
'Something Better' (Goffin, Mann) / 'Sister Morphine' (Jagger, Richard, Faithfull) by Marianne Faithfull, produced by Mick, is released on Decca. Marianne co-wrote the 'B'-side with Mick and Keith.

APRIL
Mick and Keith combine a holiday with working on new songs in Rome and Positano. Towards the end of the month the Stones hold recording sessions at Olympic Studios.

MAY

28
Mick and Marianne are busted at Mick's house on Cheyne Walk, Chelsea. Mick tells the press:

"The police, about six or seven of them, arrived at about a quarter to eight, just after Marianne and I had our tea. They were in the house for about an hour. We went in my car, not a police car."

It is announced that Mick will star in the film of Ned Kelly. ('To 36 year old Mrs Kelly a son: Ned.')

29
Mick and Marianne appear before magistrates at Marlborough Street Court and are remanded until June 23.

JUNE

7
Keith crashes his car near his home in Sussex. Anita, seven months pregnant, breaks her collar bone and is taken to hospital in Chichester.

9
The *Daily Sketch* headlines: BRIAN JONES QUITS THE STONES AS GROUP CLASH OVER SONGS.

"Rolling Stone Brian Jones last night quit the group after a clash with Mick Jagger and the three other Stones. Jones said at his Sussex home: 'I no longer see eye to eye with the others over the discs we are cutting.' An unknown guitarist is to replace him. He is Mick Taylor, 20 year old lead guitarist with the John Mayall group, who lives in Paddington, London. Mick Jagger said last night: 'I've been looking at Mick for a long time...'."

13
Mick Taylor officially joins The Rolling Stones. Mick Jagger later explained how he found him,

"I figured that John Mayall always had good guitar players, so I went and asked him, and he said, 'You can have mine. Take him.' He played with us and he seemed all right, nice. He's a good player too, actually, and he'll get much better. He's very level-headed. I don't think he'll have any trouble."

14
Mick Taylor: "I was invited to do a session with The Rolling Stones. It puzzled me. I had never met Mick Jagger in my life and here he was phoning me. I went down and played on some tracks and thought little more about it. Then they asked me if I wanted to be a Stone. I was amazed. I said I'd love to be a Stone, and that was that."

Mick Jagger: "He doesn't play anything like Brian. He's a blues player and wants to play rock'n'roll, so that's okay."

16
The Stones record a session for the Associated Rediffusion-TV's *David Frost Show*. It is shown in the States the next month.

24
The Stones rehearse at The Beatles' Apple Studios, in Savile Row. *Rolling Stone* magazine reported on July 12: 'Last week the Stones were rehearsing for the gig at Apple Studios with new guitarist Mick Taylor. They sounded a lot fuller than the Stones of old, with some nice solo swapping between Keith Richard and Mick Taylor. Possibly because they're now a group with two lead guitarists, they seem to be producing more complex rhythm frameworks within the context of a heavy blues / rock idiom.'

27
'That's The Way God Planned It' (Preston) / 'What About You' (Preston) by Billy Preston is released on Apple (UK) with Keith Richard featured on guitar.

JULY
Dates: Free Concert in Hyde Park, London (5).

3
Brian Jones dies. The next day the *Daily Mirror* reports: "Pop guitarist Brian Jones, who quit The Rolling Stones last month, was found dead early today. His body was discovered by friends who called at his £30,000 home at Hartfield Sussex.

It is believed to have been in the swimming pool, at the house which 25-year-old Jones moved into a few months ago."

Before they hear of Brian's death, the group record a session for BBC-TV's *Top Of The Pops*.

4
'Honky Tonk Woman' / 'You Can't Always Get What You Want' released. It enters the UK charts at No. 15 and spends five weeks at No. 1. In the US charts it enters at No. 79 and spends four weeks at No. 1.

Mick says that the free concert in Hyde Park will go on: "Brian would have wanted it to go on. We will now do the concert for him. I hope people will understand that it's because of our love for him that we are still doing it."

The Stones appear on BBC TV's *Top Of The Pops*.

HONKY TONK WOMAN
Jagger, Richard /
YOU CAN'T ALWAYS GET WHAT YOU WANT
Jagger, Richard
S - Decca F 12952 (UK) and London 910 (USA).
Released: July 1969.
Producer: Jimmy Miller.

Notes: On 'You Can't Always Get What You Want' vocals arranged by Jack Nitzsche. Al Kooper plays piano and organ.

Above: Mick and Marianne leave Marlborough Street Magistrates Court after being remanded on drugs charges, June 23, 1969. Below, left: Brian with Suki Poitier.

5

1:00pm. The Stones hold a free concert in Hyde Park. Rather than cancel the concert, they dedicate it to the memory of Brian Jones. Also on the bill are a number of groups associated with Blackhill Enterprises, the organisers of the event: The Third Ear Band, The Battered Ornaments, Screw and King Crimson.

Before the concert begins, Mick Jagger says, "All you want in an audience, for you, the performer, is all that feeling - that they want to have a good time, and if they want to have a good time, they make you have such a good time. Then you give it back and it goes round and round and round... I think this afternoon people will come to have a good time, be outside, dig the Stones, dig the other groups that are on, like the music, enjoy the sunshine. A concert's not to hear the music as it really is, that's for the studio to do, when you produce a record that's as near as you want it to sound, to get a totally integrated thing, but when you do a concert, they come to see what you're doing. No, they come for an excuse - as well as a groove - for them all to come together and all to join hands and all to embrace each other and have a common feeling."

In the Stones concert HQ in a nearby hotel, Mick tells the group, "We'll go on, and like they'll all be up, up, up. And I'll calm 'em right down and try and keep 'em as quiet as possible and then I'll say - and it'll take about two minutes - a speech."

Jagger tells an interviewer, "Oh Brian'll be at the concert, he'll be there! When we get there this afternoon, he's gonna be there. I don't believe in Western bereavement, like I can't suddenly drape a long black veil and walk the

hills but it still is very upsetting. I want to make it so that Brian's send-off from the world is filled with as much happiness as possible."

On stage Mick asks the audience, "Okay, now listen. Now will you just cool it just for a minute because I really would like to say something for Brian, and I'd really dig it if you would be with us, with what I'm gonna say... and Brian just going when we didn't expect him to." Mick reads from Shelley's *Adonais*. A film of the concert was released entitled *Stones In The Park*.

Newsreel film of the concert is shown on television news that evening.

6

Mick and Marianne fly to Australia to film *Ned Kelly*, the story of the legendary outlaw, born at Beveridge, 20 miles outside Melbourne in mid 1855. His father, John Kelly, came from Tipperary but had been transported to Australia for pig stealing. By the age of 17, Ned had been arrested and sentenced to three years hard labour for horse stealing, although he claimed that he was innocent. From this time on he was constantly in trouble with the police. The action which brought Ned, his brother Dan, and the other 'sympathisers' into a life of bush-ranging was the arrest of his mother on a trumped-up charge of having helped her sons in the attempted murder of police constable Fitzpatrick. In an attempt to raise money for her defence, Ned and the Kelly Gang, as it had become known, searched for gold in the hills and ran a sawmill. Then in October, 1878, the Stringybark Creek massacre of police by the Kelly Gang set the seal on their ultimate fate. Ned's famous armour, a metal can with an eye-slit, forged to protect him from gunfire, was his undoing. It restricted his

movements during the famous battle of Glenrowan and did nothing to protect the most vulnerable part of his body - his legs. Finally he was captured and was hanged on November 11, 1880, in Pentridge Gaol, Melbourne. His last words were: "Such is life."

BBC Radio's *Scene and Heard* transmits an interview with Mick.

7

Billy Preston's 'That's The Way God Planned It', featuring Keith Richard on guitar is released on Apple (USA).

8

Marianne is found in a coma from a drug overdose in her room at the Chevron Hotel, Sydney. She is taken to St. Vincent's Hospital and does not regain consciousness for five days. Actress Diane Craig is brought in to replace her in the film.

9

Bill and Diane Wyman are divorced.

10

Brian Jones is buried in Cheltenham after a funeral in the same church where he used to sing as a choirboy. He wrote his own epitaph which was read at his funeral service, "Please don't judge me too harshly". Bill, Keith and Charlie attend the funeral which is shown on national television news. Mick is in Australia.

BBC-TV's *Top Of The Pops* shows their July 3 recording of the Stones.

13

First day of filming *Ned Kelly* in Melbourne.

Above: Mick recites Shelley's *Adonais* in Hyde Park. Below: A Hell's Angel watches over the VIP area during the Stones' performance.

SEPTEMBER

2

'Through The Past Darkly (Big Hits Volume Two)' is released in the USA. It reaches number two in the charts and grosses over $1 million in the first two weeks.

Granada TV transmit their film 'The Stones In The Park'.

THROUGH THE PAST DARKLY (BIG HITS VOLUME 2) Compilation

A - London NPS 3 (USA).
Released: September 1969.

Side 1: 1. Honky Tonk Woman (Jagger, Richard) / 2. Paint It Black (Jagger, Richard) / 3. Street Fighting Man (Jagger, Richard) / 4. She's A Rainbow (Jagger, Richard) / 5. Jumpin' Jack Flash (Jagger, Richard) / 6. Dandelion (Jagger, Richard).

Side 2: 7. Ruby Tuesday (Jagger, Richard) / 8. Have You Seen Your Mother, Baby, Standing In The Shadow? (Jagger, Richard) / 9. Let's Spend The Night Together (Jagger, Richard) / 10. 2000 Light Years From Home (Jagger, Richard) / 11. Mother's Little Helper (Jagger, Richard).

Notes: This US compilation again differs from the UK one. The US sticks totally to a compilation of the 'A' or double -'A' sides of singles whereas the UK version included a track never before released in the UK.

10

It is announced that the Stones plan to tour the USA. The London *Evening Standard* reports Keith as saying, "The groupies are going to be even bigger than before on this tour."

15

Mick is interviewed on Australian radio from Sydney.

17

BBC-TV's *Top Of The Pops* repeats their July 3 recording of the Stones.

31

BBC-TV's *Top Of The Pops* repeats their July 3 recording of the Stones.

AUGUST

8

Mick is interviewed on BBC-TV's *Top Of The Pops*.

10

Keith Richard and Anita Pallenberg's son, Marlon, born at King's College Hospital.

18

Mick is accidentally shot in the hand on the *Ned Kelly* set but he is back at work a few days later.

22

'That's The Way God Planned It' by Billy Preston is released in the UK on Apple. It is produced by George Harrison and featuring Keith Richard on electric guitar.

When the *Los Angeles Free Press* asks Keith if he had been doing a lot of session work he replies: "Yeah. I did some things with Eric (Clapton), Billy Preston and Ginger (Baker), George (Harrison) on George's album, you know, 'Do What You Want'. I usually end up playing bass."

12

Mick finishes his part in the film *Ned Kelly* and flies to Bali for a rest.

'Through The Past Darkly (Big Hits Volume Two)' is released in the UK. It enters the charts at No. 14 and reaches No. 1.

THROUGH THE PAST DARKLY (BIG HITS VOLUME 2) Compilation

A - Decca SKL 5019.
Released: September 1969.
Producers: Compilation of the work of several producers: tracks 2, 4, 5, 6, 9, 10 and 11 by Andrew Loog Oldham. Tracks 1, 7 and 12 by Jimmy Miller. Tracks 3 and 8 by The Rolling Stones.

Side 1: 1. Jumpin' Jack Flash (Jagger, Richard) / 2. Mother's Little Helper (Jagger, Richard) / 3. 2,000 Light Years From Home (Jagger, Richard) / 4. Let's Spend The Night Together (Jagger, Richard) / 5. You Better Move On (Arthur, Alexander) / 6. We Love You (Jagger, Richard).

Side 2: 7. Street Fighting Man (Jagger, Richard) / 8. She's A Rainbow (Jagger, Richard) / 9. Ruby Tuesday (Jagger, Richard) / 10. Dandelion (Jagger, Richard) / 11. Sittin' On The Fence (Jagger, Richard) / 12. Honky Tonk Woman (Jagger, Richard).

Notes: This was the first British release of 'Sittin' On The Fence' which appeared in the USA on the 'Flowers' album in June 1967. Matrix number XDR 38704 it was recorded at RCA, Hollywood after 'Paint It Black' and before 'Have You Seen Your Mother, Baby, Standing In The Shadow?'

14

Chris Farlowe's album, 'The Last Goodbye' is released by Immediate and features the Jagger produced tracks from 'Farlowe In The Midnight

Hour' as well as a new track 'Looking For You' produced by Mick.

OCTOBER

The Stones mix their new album, 'Let It Bleed' in Los Angeles.

THE ROLLING STONES (Promotional album) Compilation

A- London RSD-I (USA) and Decca RSM-I (UK). Australian Decca. Released: October 1969 (US version first).

Side 1: 1. Route 66 (Troup) / 2. Walking The Dog (Dixon) / 3. Around And Around (Berry) / 4. Suzie Q (Hawkins, Lewis) / 5. Everybody Needs Somebody To Love (Burke, Wexler) / 6. Off The Hook (Jagger, Richard) / 7. I'm Free (Jagger, Richard) / 8. She Said Yeah (Jackson).

Side 2: 9. Under My Thumb (Jagger, Richard) / 10. Stupid Girl (Jagger, Richard) / 11. 2000 Man (Jagger, Richard) / 12. Sympathy For The Devil (Jagger, Richard) / 13. Prodigal Son (Rev. Wilkins) / 14. Love In Vain (Payne).

Notes: This album was released in the USA as a promotional compilation to accompany the two US Greatest Hits albums. It was designed for radio station use only giving DJs three albums to select cuts from and hopefully increasing Rolling Stones airplay. Decca pressed up about 200 copies for the UK most of which went to the press since there was no commercial radio in the UK at the time. Since then Australian Decca have released a version which was available in the UK but with a different track selection. The version of 'Love In Vain' seems to be a different mix to that which appeared the next month on 'Let It Bleed'.

16

Mick returns to London from Indonesia.

Above, right & left: Mick filming Ned Kelly in Melbourne. **Left:** Mick with one of the African drummers who joined the Stones during 'Sympathy For The Devil'.

17

The Rolling Stones fly to Los Angeles to prepare for their US tour. Mick, Keith and Mick Taylor stay with Steven Stills at his secluded mansion in Laurel Canyon where the Stones are able to conduct daily closed rehearsals in Stills' studio in the back of the house. Bill stays at the Beverly Wilshire. Charlie takes his family with him and rents a house in Oreole Drive, high in the Hollywood Hills overlooking Sunset Boulevard, which the group uses as their tour HQ.

The group are criticised in the press because of ticket prices of $7.50. The concert promoters, Concert Associates and Radio Station KRLA, had reserved the first 20 rows for their "friends" in the industry who were paying $12.50 for the privilege. Tickets sold out in eight hours. Wherever the Stones go, to see Taj Mahal at the Ash Grove and Delaney and Bonnie at the Brass Ring, the gossip columnists report their every move, right down to what they eat and in which restaurants they ate it.

At a press conference held at the Beverley Wilshire, Jagger gets into a good natured banter with gossip columnist Rona Barrett:

Barrett: Do you consider yourselves an anti-establishment group or are you just putting us on?
Mick: We're just sort of putting you on (laughter, applause).
Keith: We're taking you all for a ride.
Mick: Yeah, reckless.

Rona Barrett: Do you like making money?
Mick: We like making records. Fortunately that's made us a lot of money.

Rona Barrett: How did you enjoy eating at Yamamoto's last night? (laughter)
Mick: Wow! What - she was under the table actually. (laughter)...

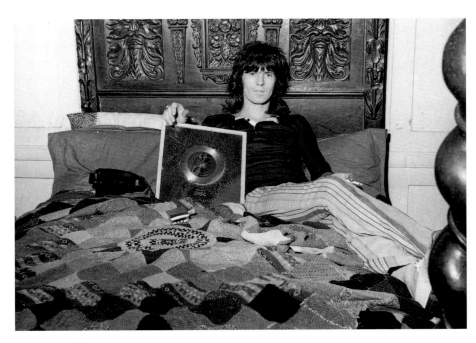

17

'Everything's All Right' (Preston, Troy) / 'I Want To Thank You' (Preston) by Billy Preston is released on Apple (UK) featuring Keith Richard on guitar

23

The Stones appear on CBS-TV's *Ed Sullivan Show*.

26

The Stones throw a party for Bill Wyman's 33rd birthday at Steve Still's house. Bill: "Someone had made a hash cake and Mick, Keith and Mick Taylor, who were staying there, looked on smilingly as they saw me innocently eating. I became stoned very quickly, felt awful and panicky, and spent a lot of time in the bathroom splashing my face..." The other Stones had often tried to turn on Bill who says in his autobiography, "My lack of interest in drugs has been a recurring problem in the Stones."

28

The Stones record new material at Elektra Records studio.

NOVEMBER

Dates: State University, Fort Collins, Colorado (7); The Forum, Los Angeles, California (8); Coliseum, Oakland, California (9); Sports Arena, San Diego, California (10); Coliseum, Phoenix, Arizona (11); Moody Coliseum, Dallas, Texas (13); University Coliseum, Auburn, Alabama (14); Assembly Hall, University of Illinois, Champagne, Illinois (15); International Amphitheater, Chicago, Illinois (16); The Forum, Los Angeles, California (20); Olympia Stadium, Detroit, Michigan (24); The Spectrum, Philadelphia, Pennsylvania (25); Civic Center, Baltimore, Maryland (26); Madison Square Garden, New York (27-28); Boston Garden, Boston, Massachusetts (29); International Raceway, West Palm Beach, Florida (30).

5

Keith Richard tells the *Los Angeles Free Press*, "Mick Taylor is the newest Stone. We call him the kid, but he's cool you know. I mean, I've been living with him for three weeks now and he's cool. If you can live with anyone for three weeks, he's cool. You know then."

9

The *Daily Express* reports: "The Rolling Stones on their first American tour for three years, relax on a hot Sunday afternoon in closely guarded ranch-style mansion near Hollywood. A dreamy eyed little blonde admirer in a maxi length knitted dress saunters by as the group pose for cameraman Terry O'Neill. 'Get your clothes off and get into the picture,' says head Stone, Mick Jagger, with all the enthusiasm of a man ordering a British Railways cup of tea. The young lady promptly obliges."

10

The *Daily Mirror* headlines: GUARDS TRAMPLED AS JAGGER FANS GO WILD.

"Thousands of frenzied pop fans gave The Rolling Stones an amazing welcome back to America yesterday. They swept aside barriers, trampled security guards and stormed the stage as the Stones launched their first US tour for three years with a pre-dawn rock concert. Scenes reminiscent of early Beatlemania erupted at the Los Angeles Forum. A line of security men guarding the stage, some with riot helmets and clubs, were brushed aside and trampled on by waves of teenagers."

13

Volker Schlondorff's film *Michael Kohlhass - Der Rebell* premières at the New Victoria Cinema, London. Both Keith Richard and Anita Pallenberg act in it.

Above & below: Keith at his Cheyne Walk home, August 1969.

24

The Rolling Stones hold a press conference at the Rainbow Grill, 30 Rockefeller Plaza, NYC, at 3:30pm.

"What are your impressions of the US?"
Jagger: "It's great. It changes."

"What are your views on the war in Vietnam?"
Jagger (letting out a long groan): "Just leave and get it over with as soon as you can."

"What about Ed Sullivan blocking some of your vocals out?"
Jagger: "It doesn't matter. It's all a joke..."

"How do you feel about a press conference like this?"
Jagger: "It's like being in the front row of a concert in Philadelphia."

"What do you think about the world-wide revolutionary movement of young people?"
Jagger (smiling): "How long have I? You can't ask a question like that at a thing like this."

"You sang you couldn't get 'no satisfaction'. Are you any more satisfied?"
Jagger: "How do you mean sexually or other? Sexually satisfied. Financially satisfied. Philosophically trying."

"Why don't you do a free concert in New York?"
Jagger: "New York is too cold. You can't do it outside. San Francisco is into that sort of thing."

"How did you like your Hyde Park concert this summer?"
Jagger: "It was very weird. We never played to that many people before."

"What do you think about Lennon returning the MBE?"
Jagger: "At last, he should have done it sooner."

"Would you have done it?"
Jagger: "We would never have gotten it in the first place."

"What do you think about the new sexual morality as reflected in all the sex newspapers? Is it catching up with you?"
Jagger: "No."

After twenty-five minutes of this banality, Jagger suddenly said: "Thank you gentlemen and God bless you all." The Stones leave in single file, as suddenly as they came in.

Mick poses for photographer Cecil Beaton for a *Vogue* magazine cover.

28

'Let It Bleed' is released in the USA where it reaches No. 2.

30

At the West Palm Beach Pop Festival, West Palm Beach, Florida, the Stones appear at 5:00am with Keith stripped to the waist despite the cold. Also on the bill is a classic Sixties line-up of Jefferson Airplane, Janis Joplin, Johnny Winter, Spirit, Iron Butterfly, Country Joe and The Fish, Vanilla Fudge and Grand Funk Railroad.

Mick Jagger, talking about the tour so far: "Compared to the way we sounded later along, we were terrible in San Francisco. Ragged. By the time we got to Detroit, I'd say, it was like a one hundred per cent improvement. The band got better. The sound system improved, and we got better accustomed to performing again. It's really a matter of confidence. It takes awhile to get that up.

"It's more of a band now [with Mick Taylor replacing Brian Jones]. It's definitely a different band. It's fucking incredibly hard now. I mean, we haven't got a lot of the things Brian could do. Like none of us play dulcimer and those things. I guess we could but we don't. I mean, I like to play autoharp, but I wouldn't do it on stage. At home, yes; you know? But not on stage. Those were things Brian did that we don't have now.

"But we're so hard now as a band... And, with Mick - Mick's really good - and it means Keith can sort of lay out and tune up in the middle of a tune. There's more time to think. And sometimes they'll get to tossing solos back and forth between the guitars, like on 'Sympathy For The Devil,' and it's just great! It's beautiful to hear, and it's something we've never gotten into just that way before.

"When we think back about the tour, well, it's all happened so quickly, you know? It's all like one big blur and it's hard to distinguish one place from another. Like in Chicago, it was just like last time: a lot of screamers, a lot of young girls, really young, like

12 or 14. And other places there were some who don't listen to the music at all; it's just a fantasy experience for them. Like in Boston, that crowd had almost an identical response to what they gave us last time. But on the Coast, and a lot of other places, there was a very large cross section of people, all kinds of people, and they listened. A lot of them did. That was new in some ways."

DECEMBER

Dates: Altamont Speedway, Livermore, California (6); London, Savile Theatre (14); Lyceum Ballroom, London (21).

The Rolling Stones spend the week before the Altamont concert in Muscle Shoals, Alabama, recording and negotiating an artist / label deal with Atlantic Records' chiefs Ahmet Ertegun and Jerry Wexler.

5

'Let It Bleed' released in the UK. It gets to No. 1.

The Stones fly to San Francisco.

LET IT BLEED

A - Decca SKL 5025 (UK) and London NPS 4 (USA).
Released: December 1969 (UK) and November 1969 (USA).
Producer: Jimmy Miller.
Engineer: Glyn Johns. Assisted by Bruce Botnick, Jerry Hansen and George Chiantz.
Studio: Olympic Studios, London.

Side 1: 1. Gimmie Shelter (Jagger, Richard) / 2. Love In Vain (Woody, Payne) / 3. Country Honk (Jagger, Richard) / 4. Live With Me (Jagger, Richard) / 5. Let It Bleed (Jagger, Richard).

Side 2: 6. Midnight Rambler (Jagger, Richard) / 7. You Got The Silver (Jagger, Richard) / 8. Monkey Man (Jagger, Richard) / 9. You Can't Always Get What You Want (Jagger, Richard).

Notes: Track 2 appeared in a different mix (as matrix XDR 45752) on a radio promotion album 'The Rolling Stones'. Mary Clayton sings vocals on track 1. Nicky Hopkins plays piano on tracks 1, 2, 7 and 8. Nicky Hopkins plays organ on track 7. Jimmy Miller plays percussion on tracks 1 and 8. Jimmy Miller plays drums on track 9. Ry Cooder plays mandolin on track 2. Nanette Newman sings vocals on tracks 3 and 9. Byron Bertine plays fiddle on track 3. Leon Russell plays piano on track 4. Bobby Keys plays tenor sax on track 4. Ian Stewart plays piano on track 5. Al Kooper plays piano on track 9. Al Kooper plays French horn on track 9. Al Kooper plays organ on track 9. Madeleine Bell sings vocals on track 9. Doris Troy sings vocals on track 9. Rocky Dijon plays percussion on track 9. The London Bach Choir sing on track 9. The record was issued with a full colour poster of the group included in the sleeve.

Above: Mick with Jimmy Savile. Below: Mick Taylor may have joined the Stones but he is not yet a stone.

6

The Stones play a free concert at the Altamont Speedway near Livermore in Northern California. They are advised by The Grateful Dead's manager Rock Scully to use Hell's Angels as security since the Angels will turn up and cause trouble anyway but they do not realise how different the American Angels are from the English variety that policed the free Hyde Park concert. Inflamed by drugs and alcohol, the Angels lay into the crowd, beating fans with billiard cues and driving their motorcycles straight at people, breaking one girl's ankle. One of their bikes is overturned in the crush, causing great dismay among the Angels, and not helped by Mick's sarcastic remark from stage, "Oh dear, someone's motorbike's fell over." A member of the Jefferson Airplane, also on the bill, is knocked unconscious on stage by an Angel, and dozens of people are injured. The climax of the violence comes when the Angels stab an 18-year-old black man, Meredith Hunter, to death with their billiard cues. Characteristically, the American underground press blame the Stones for the violence instead of looking at their own brand of "hip" culture.

Keith Richard says, "I thought the show would have been stopped, but hardly anybody seemed to want to take any notice. The violence in front of the stage was incredible. Looking back I don't think it was a good idea to have the Hell's Angels but The Grateful Dead, who've organised these shows before, thought they would be the best. I believe the alternative would have been The Black Panthers. I wouldn't like to say whether they would have been more vicious."

The Stones make a hurried departure from Altamont by helicopter but the incident will dog their career for years to come.

8

Keith and Charlie fly back to London. Mick Jagger flies to Switzerland to see Prince Rupert Lowenstein on business. Bill and Mick Taylor remain in the States for a few days

11

Marianne Faithfull, who has been living in Rome with Mario Schifano, an Italian film producer, is waiting at Heathrow Airport with her son Nicholas for Mick when he gets off the plane. His opening words are reported as, "Hello girl. Wop in your bed, eh?"

12

The Stones record their segment for BBC-TV's *Top Of The Pops Christmas Show* in London.

18

Mick is fined £200 plus 50 guineas (£52.10.0d) costs at Marlborough Street Magistrates' Court for being found guilty of possession of cannabis resin. Marianne is acquitted. At the hearing police say that when they stopped Jagger in Chelsea last May 28, he rushed to his house and shouted, "Marianne, Marianne, don't open the door. It's the police. They're after the weed." Jagger allegedly asked the police, "Why don't you leave us alone? I haven't got any drugs." The police, however, produce a search warrant and claim to have found a box of marijuana downstairs and another cache upstairs. At the hearing it is reported that when Jagger was asked what was in the box he replied: "I don't think I'd better answer that."

Jagger reveals in court that Detective Sgt. Robin Constable suggested to them: "We can do something about it... a man can be guilty and plead not guilty and in that way he can get off. How much is it worth to you?" Jagger says he remained silent, and the detective proposed the sum of £1000, saying: "Don't worry, you can have your money back if it doesn't work." In court, the officer heatedly denies the singer's charges, calling them malicious and untrue. Scotland Yard orders a senior detective to investigate Jagger's charges, and Mick says he'll give "every possible assistance" to the inquiry.

21

CBS-TV shows the *Ed Sullivan Show - The Swinging Soulful Sixties*, using repeats of the Stones on the show.

25

BBC-TV's *Top Of The Pops Christmas Show* features film of the Stones specially recorded on December 12th and also repeat film.

27

Clips of the Stones are featured in LWT's show *A Child of the Sixties*.

28

Film of the Stones is used in BBC-TV's show *Ten Years Of What*.

31

Film of the Stones is used in BBC-TV's *Pop Go The Sixties*.

Above left: Marianne.

1970

JANUARY

15

'LiveR Than You'll Ever Be', the first Stones bootleg, recorded at their November 9, 1969 concert in Oakland, is reported on the market in the States. Later, with one track less, it becomes the first UK Stones bootleg.

20

It is reported that the Stones have built a mobile recording studio, known as the Mighty Mobile. The Rolling Stones Mobile later became one of the most used mobile studios in the UK.

FEBRUARY

'The People Band' an album by The People Band is released on Transatlantic Records. Produced by Charlie Watts and featuring Charlie and eight other musicians. The album consists of seven extracts from a continuous performance by The People Band.

The Stones are working at Olympic Studios, mixing the tapes of the recent US tour for the live album released as 'Get Yer Ya-Yas Out!'.

7

Mick and Keith work at Trident Studios in Soho, London, re-mixing the live tapes of their second Madison Square Garden concert. The Maysles Brothers film them viewing the rushes of the concert at Altamont.

MARCH

Mick and Marianne are reported to be back together again. According to Mario Shifano who lived with Marianne for a short time, she is living with Jagger again. "I suppose they're inseparable. After all they were together for a long time."

Jagger himself refuses to talk about his private life, saying only, "We are still good friends and I hope that we shall remain so."

11

Jean-Luc Godard's *One Plus One* is released in the USA featuring long shots of the Stones recording 'Sympathy For The Devil'. To Godard's anger and distress, the film's producer Ian Quarrier changes the name of the film to the song title and destroys the film's intention - that we never see the final completed version of the song - by adding footage of a complete take of the song against Godard's wishes. In his review on April 27th of the national release, The *New York Times* critic

Roger Greenspun says: "An English language movie by Jean-Luc Godard opened theatrically yesterday at the Murray Hill. If you go on Monday, Wednesday, Friday or Sunday, you will see Godard's film, which is properly known as *1 + 1*. On other days, you will see a film popularly advertised as *Sympathy For The Devil*, which exactly resembles *1 + 1* except that in the latter part of the last reel a complete version of the song 'Sympathy For The Devil', which The Rolling Stones have been rehearsing and recording in cuts throughout the film, is played on the soundtrack. Several monochromatic stills of the film's last shot are added to fill out the song's time.

The changes and additions are the work of the producer, Ian Quarrier. Why anyone, given the choice, would prefer a producer's version of a movie to a director's escapes me. The movie to see at the Murray Hill is *1 + 1*. Not only does the use of the song impose a sense of emotional fulfilment (and, I think, the wrong sense of fulfilment) upon a conclusion that does not ask for it, but also the use of the song's title for the movie suggests a meaning that is less interesting in context than, say, the proposition 1 + 1 equals 2.

"For *1 + 1* is a heavily didactic, even instructional, film, like much recent Godard, and it builds upon repetition, or, if you will, addition. The Rolling Stones' repeated assays upon 'Sympathy For The Devil' in their recording studio, the rote repetitions of passages and slogans passed back and forth among black-power revolutionaries... all suggest a concern with ways of putting things together."

In June 1969, *Rolling Stone* magazine asked Godard what he wanted to do with The Rolling Stones in *1 + 1*: "I just wanted to show something in construction. To show that democracy was nowhere, not even constructive. Not destructive, of course, just saying: 'We are against war' but doing nothing for peace, not having the strength to follow the Black man who is going to be a revolutionary... That's why I was so angry with that ending. We should know only a little bit of it. We don't know what kind of song it is. It's just words, the beginning of words. It never goes to the end. Because The Rolling Stones are still at the very beginning."

24

Alameda County District Attorney Lowell Jensen arrests Alan David Passaro, a 21-year-old Hell's Angel, for the murder of Meredith Hunter at The Rolling Stones' disastrous free concert at Altamont. He is taken into custody at Soledad Prison, where he is already serving a term for grand theft and sale of grass. Jensen says Passaro was out on bail, awaiting trial on those charges on the day of the concert. *Rolling Stone* magazine

reports that Passaro has a long prison record dating back to 1963 in Antioch, when he was arrested for auto theft and sent to Juvenile Hall. He has been arrested six times in the past, four of them resulting in convictions. At the time of his arrest for murder, he was serving time for back-to-back convictions in June and July of 1969 in San Jose.

During the three-month investigation police interviewed over 1000 people. The key evidence, they said, was footage by crews of the Maysles Brothers, who filmed the entire concert for their documentary on the Stones tour. Several crews had the murder on film. The Alameda County Coroner's report on Hunter confirms that he was beaten as well as stabbed though the cause of death is listed as shock and haemorrhage due to multiple stab wounds. The viciousness of the knifing is best seen in the stab wounds themselves, which ranged from two and three-quarters to four and one-quarter inches in depth.

MAY

'Leon Russell' an album by Leon Russell is released on A&M. A large number of star session men contribute to the album though not all at the same time. Since there is no indication as to who played on which track it has to be assumed that Charlie Watts and Bill Wyman appear on one or more tracks. To avoid contractual problems the line-up simply has the album dedicated to them as follows: "This album is dedicated to: Chris Stainton / George Harrison / Ringo Starr / Charlie Watts / Bill Wyman / Eric Clapton / Klaus Voormann / B.J. Wilson / Alan Spenner / Jim Gordon / Greg Dempsey / Stevie Winwood / Jim Horn / Mr & Mrs Bramlett / Bobby Whiplash / Clydie King / Merry Clayton and Joe Cocker, for their inspirational music."

JUNE

24

The film *Ned Kelly* has its première at the London Pavilion. Jagger's comments on the film are: "That was a load of shit. I only made it because I had nothing else to do. I knew Tony Richardson was a reasonable director and I thought he'd make a reasonable film. The thing is, you never know until you do it whether a film will turn out to be a load of shit and if it does, all you can say is, 'Well, that was a load of shit' and try to make sure you don't do anything like it again."

The soundtrack is released in the UK on Liberty / United Artists Records as 'Mick Jagger Is Ned Kelly' and contains one Jagger track, 'Wild Colonial Boy' (Silverstein).

28

A guitar, clothes and other items are stolen from Mick's Bentley, parked near his home in Cheyne Walk.

JULY

It is reported in *Rolling Stone* magazine that Mick Jagger, having lost Marianne Faithfull to the 39-year-old Irish photographer Lord Patrick Rossmore, has got himself

a new girl friend: "19-year-old New York model Patti D'Arbanville, a busty, flashy-eyed blonde who moved into a flat next door to Mick in Cheyne Walk two weeks after meeting him in mid-June. Says Patti: 'Mick is so exciting but at the same time so peaceful to be with'.

The Stones record new songs at Olympic Studios and also use their mobile facility.

20

'Street Fighting Man' / 'Surprise, Surprise' released in the UK.

STREET FIGHTING MAN
Jagger, Richard /
SURPRISE, SURPRISE
Jagger, Richard
S - Decca F 13203 (UK).
Released: July 1970.
Producers: Side A: Jimmy Miller.
Side B: Andrew Loog Oldham.

Notes: Released in the UK two years after the USA due to timidity on the part of Decca.

Below: Mick and Marianne arriving Marlborough Street Magistrates Court where they appeared on drugs charges on January 26, 1970.

28

The film *Ned Kelly* is premièred in Glenrowan, near Melbourne, Australia.

29

The Stones release a statement saying, "Neither Allen Klein nor ABKCO Industries Inc, nor any other company have any authority to negotiate recording contracts on their behalf in the future." Klein's office counters by saying, "This development will not alter the rights of ABKCO Industries under existing agreements including the right to manufacture Rolling Stones records in the future."

31

The Stones contract with Decca Records expires with the group owing the company one final track. They deliver 'Cocksucker Blues' containing sexually explicit lyrics which ensure that Decca will not release it. (Though later German Decca include it in a boxed set which is quickly withdrawn.)

AUGUST
1

Performance, co-directed by Donald Cammell and Nick Roeg, starring Mick Jagger, James Fox, Anita Pallenberg, and Michele Breton is finally released by Warner Bros. Warner's put up the entire $1,100,000 production fee.

Nick Roeg: "Jagger's approach is so natural - he didn't care about actors' protocol - but about what was going to be on the screen. He's not a fool. He's not unaware that people are out to get him. People use him as a yardstick. People don't like him that have never seen him. He's not a guru but he represents behaviour. He was so far into the part. He's clever.

"He's an extraordinarily honest man. He's true to his own self. I've been in movies a helluva long time and I've never worked on one that was such a generous act by those three people - writer, director and artist - sympathy for what is truthful being allowed onto the screen. Jagger said in effect 'screw the contract. I'm not going to get up and sing a song, it has to come out of the film' so the two scenes where he sings are essentially part of the film. He's got to sing at that point, but it was terribly difficult to find that point."

Sandy Lieberson: "The whole idea of Mick Jagger being in it was

that it was going to be a movie in which he played a very important part. There's a certain element of Mick Jagger in the film. But he's not playing himself. Don't forget that the script was written with each of those people in mind so we had to extract the strongest aspects of their character and personality and use those as characters within the film."

Mick Jagger: "I think Turner is a projection of Donald's fantasy or idea of what I imagine how I am. The thing is that it's very easy for people to believe that's what I'm like. It was easy to do in a way because it's just another facet of me if I felt inclined to go that way. But now when I look at it there's so many things I could have done to make it stranger or to make it more real, to my mind, of how Turner would be and how he would live. I think it was a bit

too much like me in a few ways. But he's not quite hopeless enough a person. "I don't think there's many people like that individual. I found his intellectual posturing very ridiculous - that's what sort of fucked him up. Too much intellectual posturing in the bath when you're with two women is not a good thing - that's not to be taken too seriously! It made me skin go all funny! I know people like that. He's an amalgam of different people I've seen.

"I feel I did create something. It was enjoyable as far as that's concerned. That's what made it such hard work. It was shot just like a regular movie. You had to know what you were doing before you got on camera. We'd suddenly stop shooting one day because I'd say I wasn't going to say those lines. There were all kinds of situations like that and the regular technicians would go 'Blimey I've never seen anything like it!' and all that. Donald's whole thing is casting people for what they are and how they fit into the part, to make them work out and create the part, rather to work on things that were already in their own minds.

"There's two important things about the film to Donald. There's the sexual thing - not only physically sexual, but the interrelating of the sexes and the interchanging of roles. And the role

of violence and the role of women, vis à vis the role of violence of a man. How the two things can balance each other out. And the ritualistic significance of violence. That's one of the main themes if you can gain any conclusion out of it. Donald's really hung up on the ritual of violence not being the thing any more where certain people can go through certain moods - like a tournament or a small war - but now that that's not being used anymore that's very dangerous. He's deploring the lack of ritual in violence. The way of coping with the violence is to sort of act it out theatrically.

"I don't understand the connection between music and violence. Donald's always trying to explain it to me and I just blindly carry on. I just know that I get very aroused by music, but it doesn't arouse me violently. You can only really get into the feeling if you're with a group of people like that. The only time I've felt violent was in some street demonstration and you really get the feeling of being in with a crowd which wants to do something and you get really carried along whether they're right or wrong. Whether the policeman is doing his job or whether the cause that you're hitting the policeman for is really right, what's it fucking matter? The point

is that the act of violence is more powerful than the intellectual political act."

Sandy Lieberson: "The film was shot chronologically and very few scenes were shot out of sequence. Especially when we got into the house - we had no idea of what was going on from day to day. It sort of 'evolved'."

The random aspect of the film was intensified by deliberate randomness in the editing process. Roeg visited film-maker Antony Balch to find out the principles behind the random cuts in the film *Cut-Ups* he made with William Burroughs, and employed some completely random cuts in *Performance*. Other cuts were insisted on by Warner Brothers and the censor, who objected to full frontal nudity on Jagger's part.

15

The Stones announce that their new record label, Rolling Stones Records, will be headed by Marshall Chess in the USA and Trevor Churchill in the UK.

Above: Mick with Ike and Tina Turner. Below: Mick as Turner in Performance.

29

The Stones stop in Copenhagen, Denmark, for a press conference on their way to Helsinki for the first concert of their European tour.

It lasts all of 15 minutes: "Foolish questions," said Mick. "Let me get out of here."

The Scandinavian press asked:
Do you like Simon and Garfunkel?
Mick: "Oh, come on."

Who is the greatest person in show biz today?
Keith Richard: "Shirley Bassey."

Jagger, are you satisfied with your part in *Ned Kelly*?
Mick: "No, it's not worth seeing."

Your opinion on dope?
Mick: "Oh, come again another day!"

Just before the Helsinki concert Mick told a reporter, "We are not making any money out of this tour. It has only been arranged as a friendly gesture for our European fans. The contact with the audience makes us feel happy. There's nothing to replace it." The Stones were joined on stage by Jim Price (late of Delanie and Bonnie) on trombone and trumpet and Bobby Keys on saxophone. Stones road manager Ian Stewart, as usual, sits in on piano. Also on the tour is Chicago guitarist Buddy Guy's group, featuring Junior Wells on harmonica.

SEPTEMBER

Dates: Olympic Stadium, Helsinki, Finland (2); Malmö, Sweden (3); Royal Tennis Hall, Stockholm, Sweden (4); Tennis Stadium, Aarhus, Denmark (9); The Forum, Copenhagen, Denmark (12); Ernst Merck Halle, Hamburg, Germany (14); Deutschlandhalle, Berlin, Germany (16); Festhalle, Cologne, Germany (18); Killesberg, Stuttgart, Germany (20); The Olympia, Paris, France (22); Palais des Sports, Paris (23); Stadthalle, Vienna, Austria (27); Palazzo dello Sport, Rome (29).

6

The live album of the 1969 US tour 'Get Your Ya's Out!,' is released in the UK. It enters the charts at No. 28 and reaches No. 1.

In the USA, it enters the charts at No. 27 and reaches No. 5.

GET YER YA-YA'S OUT!
A - Decca SKL 5065 (UK) and London NPS 4 (USA).
Released: September 1970.
Producers: The Rolling Stones and Glyn Johns.
Studio: Recorded live at Madison Square Garden.
November 27 and 28, 1969.

Side 1: 1. Jumpin' Jack Flash (Jagger, Richard) / 2. Carol (Berry) / 3. Stray Cat Blues (Jagger, Richard) / 4. Love In Vain (Trad: Arr. Jagger, Richard) / 5. Midnight Rambler (Jagger, Richard).

Side 2: 6. Sympathy For The Devil (Jagger, Richard) / 7. Live With Me (Jagger, Richard) / 8. Little Queenie Berry / 9. Honky Tonk Woman (Jagger, Richard) / 10. Street Fighting Man (Jagger, Richard).

Note: Ian Stewart plays piano at both concerts.

13

The Stones give a press conference in Hamburg.

16

50 fans are arrested before the concert in Berlin in clashes with the police.

19

'Performance, starring James Fox - Mick Jagger', a solo Mick Jagger album released as Warner Brothers BS 2554 (USA) WS 2554 (UK). The one Jagger track is entitled 'Memo From Turner' (Jagger, Richard).

The Stones are interviewed on Radio Luxembourg.

22

At the Paris Olympia concert, several police are injured in the crush outside the hall. The apres-gig party is held at the Hotel George V.

28

The Stones fly into Rome. Mick punches a photographer "for asking stupid questions" at a press conference.

OCTOBER

Dates: Palazzo dello Sport, Milan, Italy (1); Palais des Sports, Lyon, France (3); Festhalle, Frankfurt, Germany (6); Grughalle, Essen, Germany (7); Rai Halle, Amsterdam, Netherlands (9); Olympiahalle, Munich, Germany (11).

1

Police tear gas fans in Milan as 2,000 riot trying to enter the already full hall. There are 63 arrests.

12

Mick Jagger flies into London with a new girlfriend, Bianca Perez Moreno de Macias.

30

Mick pays £200 costs as John Dunbar is granted a decree nisi from Marianne Faithfull citing Mick as co-respondent.

NOVEMBER
7

'Memo From Turner' is released as a Mick Jagger solo single on Decca F 13067. It reaches no higher than No. 32 in the UK charts.

24

Mick and Bianca leave for a two-week holiday in Nassau.

DECEMBER
5

Gimmie Shelter, the Maysles Brothers' documentary film of the ill-fated 1969 US tour premières at the Plaza Theater in New York City.

18

Keith Richard throws a Christmas party at Olympic Studios.

Above: Adopting Brian's role as the Stone's fashion plate, Bill experiments with an interesting Amero-Indian look.

1971

JANUARY
4
Performance is premièred at the Warner West End theatre in London as a benefit for the charity Release. Warner wished to simply bury the film because of the drug use shown in it but was contractually bound to screen it for Release which operated an emergency service for people arrested on drugs charges. Warner pulled the film after two weeks though it has subsequently been shown on television.

6
Rose Miller, Mick Taylor's girlfriend, gives birth to their daughter Chloe at Wimbledon Hospital, London.

19
Hell's Angel Alan Passaro is declared "not guilty" by the jury in the death of 18-year-old Meredith Hunter, stabbed to death at the Stones' Altamont concert. *Rolling Stone* magazine reports: "Passaro, 22, threw back his head and let out a whoop as the verdict was read. The eight-man, four-woman jury deliberated 12½ hours following 17 days of testimony. Passaro, who had been a member of the Angels for four months at the time of the concert, was arrested and charged with murder after being identified as a suspect from film footage shot by Albert and David Maysles at the concert. The film clip, from *Gimmie*

Shelter, the Maysles' documentary of the Stones' tour was also run many times during the course of the trial. During his testimony, Passaro said he had acted in what he believed to be self-defence... Passaro testified that he had 'stabbed at' Hunter, but said he wasn't sure if his six-inch knife blade had penetrated the Berkeley youth's body. The prosecution could round up only one witness from the multitudes near the stabbing who would testify against Passaro. Paul Cox, 18, nervously told the court that he had seen Passaro stab Hunter twice (the autopsy revealed that Hunter had been stabbed five times). Immediately after the trial, Passaro was returned to jail. He is currently serving a 2-to-10-year sentence for possession of marijuana."

FEBRUARY
6
The Stones confirm that they are about to become Britain's first rock'n'roll tax exiles.

Bill Wyman attends the UK première of the film of Joe Cocker's Mad Dogs and Englishmen tour.

MARCH
Dates: Newcastle City Hall (4); Free Trade Hall, Manchester (5); Coventry Theatre, Coventry (6); Green's Playhouse, Glasgow (8); Big Apple, Brighton (10); Liverpool Empire, Liverpool (12); University of Leeds (13); The Roundhouse, Camden Town, London (14); The Marquee, London (26).

2
BBC Radio broadcasts Michael Wale's documentary *A Story of Our Time - Brian Jones, The Rolling Stones.*

5
Mick loses £300 in a casino after the concert in Manchester.

13
Mick Jagger places an advertisement in the music press responding to an article in the March 5th *Daily Telegraph*: "Comment, I feel, on behalf of The Rolling Stones should be made on reports which estimate that The Rolling Stones' fortune from recordings alone is reckoned to be £83,000,000... The sum mentioned is ludicrous; in our opinion it most probably exceeds the collective recording earnings of The Beatles, Elvis Presley, ourselves and others."

20
The Rolling Stones place advertisements in the music press condemning Decca's release of 'Stone Age' a compilation album of old material. They say they were not consulted and "it is, in our opinion, below the standard we try to keep up, both in choice of content and cover design". It is signed by the whole group.

26
The Stones play before an invited audience at the Marquee Club in Soho to film two television shows, one for Britain, one for Europe. In an argument with Harold Pendleton, owner of the Marquee, Keith swings his guitar at Pendleton's head, but misses. Eventually the invited audience is thrown out by Mick Jagger because they are not showing sufficient enthusiasm for the band who, it must be said, tend to stop, start and repeat numbers with annoying regularity while the audience slopes off to the bar muttering that they'd seen better rehearsed bands in their local pubs most Saturday nights.

30
The Stones hold a farewell Britain party at Skindles Hotel in Maidenhead before departing for the Côte d'Azur. John Lennon and Yoko Ono, Eric Clapton and other stars attend. Film-maker Kenneth Anger: "The party was given in an inn decorated with huge flowering trees.

At about 2:00am the sound system went dead... Mick asked why this had happened and was told that a village ordinance forbade music after 2:00am. Mick promptly picked up the table and threw it through an enormous plate glass window that overlooked the Thames. The piece of glass must have cost $20,000. That was *his* gesture towards having the music turned off."

APRIL
1
Marshall Chess, son of Leonard Chess, founder of Chess Records, is announced as the head of Rolling Stones Records.

Bill and Astrid Lundström rent a house La Bastide Saint-Antoine near Grasse.

announcing a date am I?' Bianca, an exotic 21-year old South American graduate of the Sorbonne, full-lipped like Mick Jagger, is a former girlfriend of actor Michael Caine and one-time fiancée of record producer Eddie Barclay... 'The band is not retiring just because we're going away. We'll remain a functioning group, a touring group, and a happy group. We're not going to stay in the South of France for a whole year, we're going on the road. I couldn't live in France for a whole year'."

The Stones appear on BBC-TV's *Top Of The Pops*.

16

'Brown Sugar' / 'Let It Rock' released in the UK. It enters the charts at No. 18, reaching No. 1.

The US edition has 'Bitch' on the 'B' side and also makes No. 1.

BROWN SUGAR
Jagger, Richard /
BITCH Jagger, Richard /
LET IT ROCK Anderson
S - Rolling Stones RS 19100 (UK)
RLS 19100 (USA).
Released: April 1971 (UK)
May 1971 (USA).
Producer: 'Brown Sugar' and
'Bitch' by Jimmy Miller.
'Let It Rock' by Glyn Johns.
Studio: 'Brown Sugar' recorded at
Muscle Shoals, December, 1969.
'Let It Rock' recorded live in Leeds.

Notes: The extra track was on the UK version only.

23

'Sticky Fingers' album released in US and UK on Rolling Stones Records. The cover features an Andy Warhol design incorporating a real zip on a pair of jeans. Andy used Jed Johnson as the model for the jeans on the cover, and the underpants, which are revealed when the zip is lowered, were modelled by critic Glenn O'Brien.

STICKY FINGERS
A - Rolling Stones Records
COC 59100 (UK and USA).
Released: April 1971 (UK)
June 1971 (USA).
Producer: Jimmy Miller.
Engineers: Glyn and Andy Johns.
Assisted by: Chris Kimsey,
Jimmy Johnson.
Studios: Olympic Studios and
Rolling Stones Mobile.

Side 1: 1. Brown Sugar (Jagger, Richard) / 2. Sway (Jagger, Richard) / 3. Wild Horses (Jagger, Richard) / 4. Can't You Hear Me Knocking (Jagger, Richard) / 5. You Gotta Move (Fred McDowell).

Side 2: 6. Bitch (Jagger, Richard) / 7. I Got The Blues (Jagger, Richard) / 8. Sister Morphine (Jagger, Richard) / 9. Dead Flowers (Jagger, Richard) / 10. Moonlight Mile (Jagger, Richard).

Notes: Ian Stewart plays piano on tracks 1 and 9. Bobby Keys plays sax on tracks 1, 4, 6 and 7. Nicky Hopkins plays piano on track 2. Paul Buckmaster organised the strings on tracks 1 and 10. J. Dickinson plays piano on track 3. Billy Preston plays organ on tracks 4 and 7. Jimmy Miller plays percussion on tracks 4 and 6. Rocky Dijon plays congas on track 4. J. Price plays trumpet on tracks 6 and 7. J. Price plays piano on track 10. Ry Cooder plays guitar on track 8. Jack Nitzsche plays piano on track 8.

STONE AGE
Compilation
A - Decca SKL 5084.
Released: April 1971.
Producer: All tracks are by Andrew Loog Oldham. For some reason Jimmy Miller is given co-production credit.

Side 1: 1. Look What You've Done (Margonfield) / 2. It's All Over Now (B. Womack, S. Womack) / 3. Confessin' The Blues (Brown, McShann) / 4. One More Try (Jagger, Richard) / 5. As Tears Go By (Jagger, Richard, Oldham) / 6. The Spider And The Fly (Nanker, Phelge).

Side 2: 7. My Girl (Robinson, White) / 8. Paint It Black (Jagger, Richard) / 9. If You Need Me (Pickett, Bateman, Sanders) / 10. The Last Time (Jagger, Richard) / 11. Blue Turns To Grey (Jagger, Richard) / 12. Around And Around (Berry).

Studios: 1. RCA, Hollywood, 1965 / 2. Chess Chicago, June 10, 1964 / 3. Chess, Chicago, June 11, 1964 / 4. Chess Chicago / RCA, Hollywood, May, 1965 / 5. RCA Hollywood, January, 1966(?) / 6. Chess, Chicago / RCA, Hollywood, May, 1965 / 7. Olympic, London, 1967 / 8. RCA, Hollywood, 1966 / 9. Chess, Chicago, June 11, 1964 / 10. RCA, Hollywood, 1965 / 11. RCA Hollywood, 1966 / 12. Chess, Chicago, June 11, 1964.

Notes: Tracks and 11 appeared on US 'December's Children' album. Both tracks from same session as 'As Tears Go By'. Track 4 first appeared on the US 'Out Of Our Heads' album. Track 7 first appeared on the US 'Flowers' album.

6

Beginning of the new UK tax year. All the Stones are now resident in France and can only visit Britain for a maximum 90 days a year before becoming liable for tax. Mick has a house in Biot; Charlie has a farmhouse in the Cevennes; Mick Taylor lives in Grasse, centre of the French perfume industry; Keith rents Nellcot, a huge villa on the coast at Villefranche-sur-Mer which is used as the group's HQ for recording and business purposes. The Stones Mobile, a large trailer truck that has been painted khaki, "for camouflage", and containing £100,000 worth of 16-track equipment is brought to France to convert Keith's basement into a studio.

It is announced that Stargroves, Mick Jagger's country mansion,

left vacant by his move to France, is being outfitted as a total live-in recording studio complete with cooks, fireplaces, and round-the-clock facilities. It can be rented for £2,500 a week.

In Cannes the Stones arrive by yacht at Port Pierre to sign a distribution contract with Kinney National which owns the Atlantic, Warner-Reprise, and Elektra record labels. The Stones label will be run by their own international corporation based in Geneva, with branches in London and New York. Effectively, Marshall Chess and the Stones will direct activities. Jagger says, "By signing this contract, we are guaranteeing to produce six new albums over the next four years; this includes 'Sticky Fingers'. Additionally perhaps there may be some solo albums projecting

The Rolling Stones individually over this period."

At the party afterwards at the Canto Club House, attended by a contingent from the UK press flown over that day and accommodated in the swish Carlton Hotel, the Stones' guests include Steven Stills and the president and founder of Atlantic Records, Ahmet Ertegun. Bianca attracts swarms of photographers by wearing a sheer see-through top.

15

The *Daily Mirror* reports from St. Tropez that Mick is apparently living with Bianca: "At the Byblos Hotel, trendiest place in town, he admitted yesterday, 'It's quite true that I have been seeing this girl for some time. But I'm not the sort of bloke who would make a big fuss of

Above: Bianca Rose Perez Moreno de Macias.

MAY

2

For Bianca's birthday, Mick flies her to Paris for a dinner party in her honour and gives her a £4,000 diamond bracelet.

8

Mick flies from Nice to Paris to collect two wedding rings he has had specially designed.

11

Mick's parents and some of the wedding guests including Paul McCartney, Linda and children, Ringo and Maureen, fly to Nice in a chartered jet from Gatwick Airport.

12

Mick and Bianca are married in St. Tropez; first in a civil ceremony at the wedding chamber of the Town Hall then in a Roman Catholic ceremony. *Rolling Stone* reports: "At four in the afternoon, Mick and his bride to be, whose name on the wedding certificate is Bianca Rosa

Perez-Mora, 26, daughter of a Nicaraguan businessman, were still entrenched in the Byblos Hotel in the centre of St. Tropez. They'd heard that a hundred photographers were crammed into the wedding chamber of the local town hall, where the mayor was waiting to perform the civil ceremony. He wasn't going through with it unless that lot were cleared out. 'Impossible,' the mayor told anybody willing to listen. 'The hall is a public place, and as such everyone had a legal right to be there.' Picking up his tri-color sash, the mayor sashayed out, leaving the chief of police to calm down the atmosphere. So 50 minutes late, protesting that he doesn't want to be married in a 'fish bowl', surrounded by flying fists, agitated shrieks and popping flash bulbs, Mick arrived with his lady: Bianca Perez Moreno de Macias... After posing for photographers and facing the glare of television lights for several minutes, the couple went through a brief civil ceremony in the mayor's office. This was followed by a

Roman Catholic ceremony performed by the Rev. Lucien Baud at the 17th century chapel of St. Anne's." Jagger had been taking religious instruction from the Bishop of Fréjus and from Father Lucien Baud, who conducted the service. A selection of tunes from *Love Story* was played on a harmonium, reportedly requested by Bianca. Roger Vadim and Nathalie Delon were the witnesses.

The reception, which did not end until 4am, is held at the Café des Arts where Steve Stills, Bobby Keys, Nicky Hopkins and Michael Shrieve and David Brown of Santana lead the jam session. Mick joins Doris Troy and P.P. Arnold in the chorus for a 25-minute soul-standard session. Mick would have liked the Stones to play but Keith was out of it, flat on his back with his mouth open. Mrs Jagger told a reporter, "I hope my other son doesn't become a superstar." Les Perrin, the Stones' PR man describes it as "the most difficult day in my 21 years in the business."

The following week *Private Eye*, the satirical UK magazine, features a picture of the couple at the altar with the words "Are you taking the Mick?" attributed to the Rev. Lucian Baud.

13

Mick and Bianca leave Cannes by yacht.

16

Mick and Bianca change yachts at Micinaggio in Italy, and set sail for a nearby château which can be reached only by sea.

The Stones appear on the *Dave Lee Travis Show* which they pre-recorded before leaving Britain.

23

'Workers Playtime', an album by B.B. Blunder is released on United Artists. Mick Taylor plays bottleneck guitar on 'New Day'.

24

Granada TV broadcasts their film *Stones In The Park*.

26

At Beaulieu-sur-Mer, near his home, Keith crashes his Jaguar into a car driven by an Italian tourist. In the ensuing argument, the police are called and Keith is charged with assault. He continues to the Cannes Film Festival where the film *Gimmie Shelter* has been entered.

30

Mick and Bianca return to St. Tropez from their honeymoon.

The Stones appear on John Peel's BBC Radio show, *Sunday Concert*, with live recordings from their recent tour.

JUNE

Mick Taylor is featured on two albums released this month: 'Reg King' by Reg King released on United Artists and 'Back To The Roots' by John Mayall on Polydor.

3

Shirley Watts is sentenced *in absentia* to six months in jail and a £30 fine for assaulting Customs officers and using abusive language to Nice Airport officials.

12

'Wild Horses' / 'Sway' released in the USA where it reaches No. 18.

WILD HORSES Jagger,
Richard / SWAY Jagger,
Richard
S - Rolling Stones Records
RLS 101 (USA).
Released: June 1971.
Producer: Jimmy Miller.
Studio: Olympic Studios, London
and / or Rolling Stones Mobile.
Notes: Both tracks taken from the
'Sticky Fingers' album.

26

Decca release re-packed oldies: 'Street Fighting Man' / 'Surprise, Surprise' / 'Everybody Needs Someone To Love' as a maxi-single. It enters the charts at No. 27 and reaches No. 17.

JULY

An album and a single by Tucky Buzzard, produced by Bill Wyman are released on Capitol.

10

Using The Rolling Stones Mobile, the Stones begin work on a new album at Nellcot, Keith's villa at Cap Ferrat which is by now referred to as "Keith's coffee house". In France for the sessions are Nicky Hopkins,

Bobby Keys, Jim Price and Gram Parsons. Sessions continue until the end of the month.

26

Rolling Stone reports: "In a flash and unexpected move, attorneys representing The Rolling Stones have filed a whopping $7.5 million suit against Allen Klein ABKCO Industries, and ABKCO Klein Corporation, alleging that Klein, either through ABKCO Industries or other companies which Klein had established to handle the music publishing and subsidiary rights to the Stones' material, had made 'false or fraudulent' representations with intent to 'deceive and defraud' the group and various of its individual members... Klein is reported to be awaiting trial in New York on tax charges."

30

Arriving at London Heathrow, Mick and Bianca tell the press that Bianca is expecting a child. They were in London en route to Leixlip Castle in Ireland home of the Guinness family.

31

Keith and Anita attend the UK premier of the Maysles Brothers' film *Gimmie Shelter* at the Rialto Cinema, London.

AUGUST

5

Shirley Watts' six months jail term is reduced to fifteen days suspended on appeal at Aix-en-Provence.

20

'The London Howlin' Wolf Sessions', featuring Bill Wyman, Charlie Watts and Ian Stewart is released on Rolling Stones Records COC 49101 (UK) and Chess CH 60008.

28

'Sun, Moon and Herbs' by Dr. John, the Night Tripper, featuring Mick on vocals, is released on Atlantic.

31

Mick Jagger, Keith Richard, Bill Wyman, Charlie Watts, and Brian Jones' father file a High Court writ against ex-Stones' managers Andrew Oldham and Eric Easton, charging that they made a "secret" deal with Decca Records in 1963 to deprive the group of record royalties. The suit alleges that Oldham persuaded Brian Jones to accept six percent of the wholesale record price as the Stones' share while Decca was paying Oldham and Easton 14 percent. At the same time, Oldham had a 25 percent management contract with the Stones themselves. The four original Stones plus Lewis Jones are also suing Allen Klein for persuading them to sign over all the North American rights to their songs to a company called Nanker Phelge

Music, Inc. The Stones' claim is that they were led to believe they ran the company when in truth it was controlled by Klein.

OCTOBER
1

Keith has 11 guitars stolen from Nellcot. He says he will pay a "reasonable reward" for information leading to their return.

8

The album 'Brian Jones Presents The Pipes Of Pan In Joujouka' is released on Rolling Stones Records featuring the Master Musicians of Joujouka, recorded in the foothills of the Rif Mountains of Morocco by Brian Jones in 1968. Brion Gysin, who took Jones to see the musicians enact the Pipes of Pan ceremony, wrote the sleeve notes. The Maalimin of Joujouka, the Master Musicians of Morocco were recorded by Brian Jones on a Uher at 7 ½ ips. The final album was edited down at Olympic from many

hours of tape. Bou Jeloud means: 'The father of skins' and the ceremony, which lasts a whole week, is the surviving festival of the goat-God, Pan. The album was almost ready for release when Jones died in July 1969 but legal tangles prevented its release until the Stones started their own record company. It was the first album released on Rolling Stones records. The US pressings were shipped to the UK so there was no UK version.

20

It is reported that the Stones have recorded 20 new songs at Nellcot but none of them have been mixed since the Stones Mobile is a recording facility, not designed for sophisticated mixing.

21

A daughter, Jade, is born to Mr and Mrs Jagger at the Belvedere Nursing Home in Paris.

26

Mick makes an appearance on the TV documentary *Beaton On Bailey* about photographers Cecil Beaton and David Bailey.

NOVEMBER
7

Bill Wyman produces the album 'Loudwater House' by Tucky Buzzard.

23

The recording sessions at Nellcot end with the Stones having produced enough material for a double album.

30

Keith, Mick, Bianca, Jade fly to the States. Keith going first to Nashville to replace the guitars stolen at Nellcot.

Mick going straight to Los Angeles where he and Keith are to finish work on the new album.

DECEMBER
3

Keith's claim of self-defence in his fight with an Italian motorist is accepted by French magistrates and charges against him are dropped.

4

The Stones begin mixing the new album at Sunset Sound Studios, Los Angeles.

11

Mick and Bianca reported to be house hunting in California and planning to stay on the Coast until the Stones' US tour begins in the Spring.

20

The Stones are in the audience at a B.B. King concert in Las Vegas.

28

Mick makes an appearance at a gold disc award ceremony for The Who.

JANUARY

'Nick Hopkins, Ry Cooder, Mick Jagger, Bill Wyman, Charlie Watts: Jamming With Edward' released on Rolling Stones Records COC 39100, produced by Glyn Jones and recorded at Olympic Studios, London, in late 1969, during the 'Let It Bleed' sessions. The absence of Keith Richard was apparently due to animosity between him and Ry Cooder - since he didn't show up in the studio, the remaining musicians decided to jam. The results were released, several years later as a cut-price album for fans.

Mick, "Keith wasn't there, and we were sitting around and played continuously for about two hours. We got some good piano playing, and I sort of try to sing - I sang through the harmonica mike, just anything that came into my head. It's mostly instrumental. Nicky and Ry seemed to be keen on having it out, so why not?"

10

The Stones continue recording and mixing their new album, 'Exile On Main Street' in Los Angeles. *Rolling Stone* reports: "Mick Jagger took some time out from mixing and overdubbing work at Sunset Sounds in Hollywood to come to the phone and tell us what's been happening with the Stones' album, the tour, and the various scenes around L.A.

'We've just been screwing around,' he said, sounding relaxed. 'It's nice to be here, really, nice to be somewhere where you can get to some music. Charlie likes to see jazz bands - Kenny Burrell... Dexter Gordon... I saw The Who and... what you call her, that chick... Merry Clayton - she was good, she was fine.'

"In the studios, the Stones have completed maybe ten tracks, all quite short; no lengthy jams. We haven't really finished yet, we're about half-way through. Keith and I are writing the songs, and it was mostly recorded in the South of France. We might take it to London and put on an orchestra."

29

Mick, Keith and Ian Stewart join Chuck Berry on stage at a concert at the Hollywood Palladium but, uncharacteristically, Chuck is not satisfied with the sound and they only play three numbers together.

FEBRUARY

1

Mick and Bianca attend the wedding in San Francisco's China-town of John Phillips (ex Mamas and Papas) and Genevieve Waite.

12

The Rolling Stones box office records in Europe are broken by Jethro Tull.

15

The Stones continue work on 'Exile On Main Street' in Los Angeles.

18

The Stones are granted an injunction against KDAY Radio, Los Angeles which has been playing two new Stones tracks non-stop for 18 hours. The tapes were stolen from Marshall Chess' house.

MARCH

Keith is in such bad condition from drug addiction during the mixing of 'Exile On Main Street' that he has to be flown to Switzerland to take a cure.

APRIL

7

Mick takes Bianca and Jade to Bali for a three week holiday.

14

Release of 'Tumblin' Dice' / 'Sweet Black Angel', two tracks from the forthcoming album. It enters the UK charts at No. 13 reaching No. 5. In the US, it enters the charts at No. 26 and reaches No. 10.

TUMBLING DICE Jagger, Richard / SWEET BLACK ANGEL Jagger, Richard
S - Rolling Stones RS 19103 (UK)
RLS 19103 (USA)
Released: April 1972.
Producer: Jimmy Miller.
Studio: Keith Richard's house with the Rolling Stone Mobile Unit at Villefranche, South of France

Notes: Both tracks taken from the forthcoming album 'Exile on Main Street'.

17

Keith and Anita's daughter, Dandelion, is born in Geneva, Switzerland.

24

Mick returns from Indonesia to London.

29

Bill and Charlie attend the Wilson Pickett reception at WEA Records' London offices.

MAY

'Manassas' an album by Steven Stills and Manassas released on Atlantic. Bill Wyman plays bass on a number of tracks but the liner notes do not say which. Wyman does not play on 'The Love Gangster', the one number he co-wrote with Stills.

Right: Mick and Mick Taylor on stage at Newcastle City Hall, March 4, 1971.

10

Les Perrin, the Stones' publicist, issues the following statement: "The Rolling Stones and ABKCO Industries Incorporated and Allen Klein jointly announce the settlement of all outstanding differences to the satisfaction of all parties. Both Allen Klein and The Rolling Stones wish it to be made clear that ABKCO no longer act as business managers for The Rolling Stones."

12

In Los Angeles Mick has lunch at Sardi's with Rudolph Nureyev and in the evening joins John and Yoko who are recording at the Record Plant.

16

Bianca models hairstyles and wigs for Ricci Burns at the Oxfam Maytime Fair, Grosvenor House, London.

17

The Stones fly to Montreux, Switzerland, to rehearse for their upcoming tour.

23

The Rolling Stones go to the U.S. Embassy, Grosvenor Square, London, to collect their work permits for their upcoming American and Canadian tour - and all of them miss the plane except for Bill.

25

Mick, Keith, Charlie and Mick Taylor leave Heathrow for the USA.

26

'Exile On Main Street', first double album from The Rolling Stones is released. It enters the UK charts and goes to No. 1. In the States it enters the charts at No. 14 and gets to No. 1.

**EXILE ON MAIN STREET
(Double album)**
A - Rolling Stones Records COC 69100 (UK) and COC 2-2900 (USA).
Released: May 1972.
Producer: Jimmy Miller.
Engineers: Glyn and Andy Johns, Joe Zaganno and Jeremy Gee.
Studios: Rolling Stones Mobile Unit.
Recorded at Wellcote, Villefranche, France. Mixed at Sunset Sound, Hollywood.

Side 1: 1. Rocks Off (Jagger, Richard) / 2. Rip This Joint (Jagger, Richard) / 3. Shake Your Hips (James Moore a.k.a. Slim Harpo) / 4. Casino Boogie (Jagger, Richard) / 5. Tumbling Dice (Jagger, Richard).

Side 2: 6. Sweet Virginia (Jagger, Richard) / 7. Torn And Frayed (Jagger, Richard) / 8. Sweet Black

Angel (Jagger, Richard) / 9. Loving Cup (Jagger, Richard).

Side 3: 10. Happy / 11. Turd on the Run (Jagger, Richard) / 12. Ventilator Blues (Jagger, Richard) / 13. I Just Want To See His Face (Jagger, Richard) / 14. Let It Loose (Jagger, Richard).

Side 4: 15. All Down The Line (Jagger, Richard) / 16. Stop Breaking Down (Trad. arr. Jagger, Richard, Wyman, Taylor, Watts) / 17. Shine A Light (Jagger, Richard) / 18. Soul Survivor (Jagger, Richard).

Notes: Bill Plummer plays upright bass on tracks 1, 11 and 15. Ian Stewart plays piano on tracks 2, 6 and 16. Clydie King sings background vocals on tracks 5, 13, 14 and 17. Vanetta sings background vocals on tracks 5, 13, 14 and 17. Tammi Lynn sings background vocals on track 14. Shirley Goodman sings background vocals on track 14. Mac Rebbennack sings background vocals on track 14. Joe Green sings background vocals on tracks 14 and 17. Al Perkins plays steel guitar on track 7. J. Price plays organ on track 7. Jimmy Miller plays percussion on tracks 8, 9, 13 and 15. Jimmy Miller plays drums on tracks 10 and 17. Bobby Keys plays percussion on track 10. Kathy McDonald sings background vocals on track 15. Billy Preston plays organ on track 17. Jerry Kirkland sings background vocals on track 17. The musicians credits for all tracks include Bobby Keys, saxophone; J. Price, trumpet and trombone; Nicky Hopkins, piano.

JUNE

Dates: Pacific Coliseum, Vancouver (3); Coliseum, Seattle, Washington (4); Winterland, San Francisco, California (6); Winterland, San Francisco, California (8); Hollywood Palladium, Los Angeles, California (9); The Forum, Los Angeles, California (11); International Sports Arena, San Diego, California (13); Civic Arena, Tucson, Arizona (14);

University of New Mexico, Albuquerque, NM. (15); Coliseum, Denver, Colorado (16); Sports Center, St. Paul, Minnesota (18); International Amphitheater, Chicago, Illinois (19-20); Municipal Auditorium, Kansas City, Missouri (22); Fort Worth, Texas (24); Hoffeinz Pavilion, Houston, Texas (25), Auditorium, Mobile, Alabama (27); University of Alabama, Tuscaloosa, Alabama (28).

**HAPPY Jagger, Richard /
ALL DOWN THE LINE Jagger, Richard**
S - Rolling Stones Records RLS 19104 (USA).
Released: June 1972.
Producer: Jimmy Miller.
Studio: Keith Richard's house with Rolling Stones Mobile Unit, Villefranche, South of France.

Notes: Both tracks taken from the 'Exile on Main Street' album.

3

The Vancouver concert is a sell-out and 2,000 disappointed fans try to gatecrash. Thirty policemen are injured and charges are brought against eight people. Stevie Wonder opens for the Stones throughout the tour.

13

More riots with sixty fans arrested and fifteen injured at the concert in San Diego.

14

Police at Tucson, Arizona, use tear gas to disperse 300 fans trying to gatecrash.

22

Princess Lee Radziwill, and writers Truman Capote and Terry Southern join the Stones' entourage at Kansas City.

24

After the Fort Worth gig, the Stones leave without an encore to drive the 30 miles to Dallas where they are staying at the Hyatt House. The next

morning, Princess Lee Radziwill departs for New York after being told there was no room for her on the Stones' chartered McCullough Airlines jet.

25

Mrs Mary Whitehouse, the self-appointed anti-pornography campaigner, complains to the BBC about the alleged obscenity of two tracks from 'Exile On Main Street' - without actually hearing them. Lord Hill writes her an Open Letter suggesting 'she was zealous in discovering obscenity and perhaps heard what she wanted to hear'.

Between their two concerts in Houston, the group returns to the Ramada Inn where there is a party in Ahmet Ertegun's suite.

26

Mick, Keith and several others drive from Houston to New Orleans in 100 degree heat. In Houma, Louisiana, they are asked to leave the Stone Bar because two coloured men are in their party. They arrive late for a party hosted by Ahmet Ertegun in their honour at Camp's Jazz City, a recording studio in a shabby part of town. Blues shouter Roosevelt Sykes, guitarist Snooks Eaglin and the legendary Professor Longhair are on hand to play for them.

27

Charlie tells writer Richard Elman: "We each have our own lives. We tour so we can have the experience in common to make music together. The other groups they just stopped playing together, and you saw what happened..."

Bill accepts the key to the City of Mobile, Alabama, from the Mayor on behalf of the other Stones. After the concert, the Stones fly back to their hotel in New Orleans.

28

Keith stays over in Tuscaloosa to party with the Stevie Wonder Band

who are the support band on the tour. When he drives into Nashville the following afternoon, Keith tells Richard Elman he's had a good time "fucking and sucking".

JULY

Dates: Robert F. Kennedy Stadium, Washington, DC (4); The Scope, Norfolk, Virginia (5); Coliseum, Charlotte, North Carolina (6); Civic Arena, Knoxville, Tennessee (7); Keil Auditorium, St. Louis, Missouri (9); Rubber Bowl, Akron, Ohio (11); Convention Center, Indianapolis, Indiana (12); Cobo Hall, Detroit, Michigan (13-14); Maple Leaf Gardens, Toronto, Canada (15); The Forum, Montreal, Canada (17); Boston Garden, Boston, Massachusetts (18-19); The Spectrum, Philadelphia, Pennsylvania (20-21); Civic Arena, Pittsburgh, Pennsylvania (22); Madison Square Garden, New York City (24-26).

'Bootleg Him', an album by Alexis Korner, is released on RAK. Covering Korner's career from the beginning to the Seventies, it features Charlie Watts on 'I'm A Hoochie Coochie Man', the one track by the original line-up of *Blues Incorporated* as follows: Alexis Korner, electric guitar; Cyril Davis, vocal; Dave Stevens, piano; Dick Heckstall-Smith, tenor saxophone; Jack Bruce, string bass; Charlie Watts, drums.

4

The Stones play an Independence Day Concert at Robert F. Kennedy Stadium, Washington, with Robert Kennedy Jr. in the audience. Probably the oldest spectator was Mr Lee Hurley from Baltimore, aged 72. Hobbling into the stadium with a walking stick, he told a reporter: "I wanted to have a new experience."

Above: Mick on stage at Newcastle in 1971. Below: In 1972.

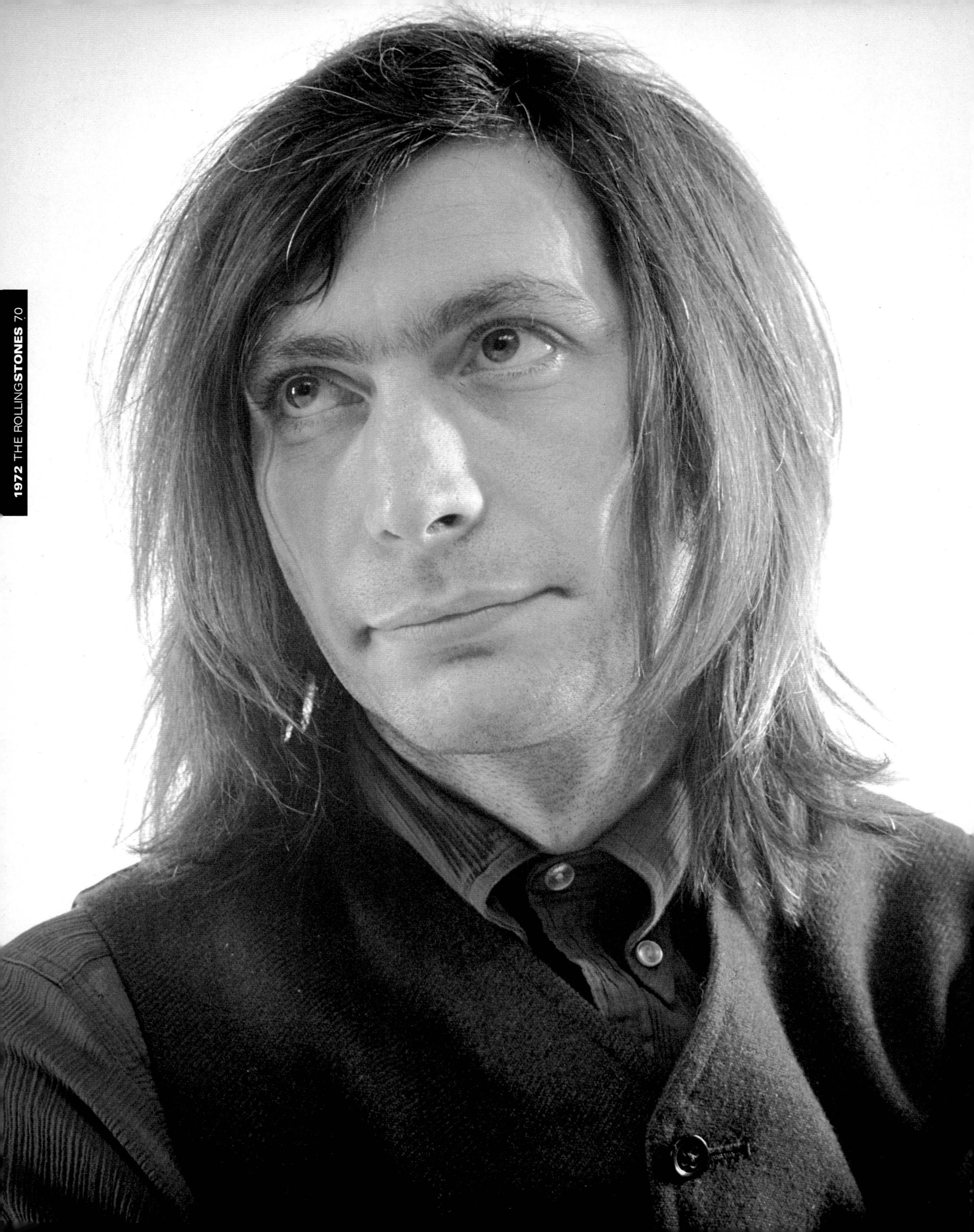

11

The Stones appear on BBC-TV's *The Old Grey Whistle Test*, in material filmed in the Côte d'Azur and in Montreux.

15

'Happy' / 'All Down The Line' is released in the USA. It enters the charts at No. 23 and rises to No. 14.

17

A bomb goes off under the Stones' equipment truck in Montreal. French separatist extremists are blamed. The concert at the Forum starts 45 minutes late while replacement gear is flown in from Los Angeles. Meanwhile fans riot outside the hall after 3,000 forged tickets are discovered to have been sold. During the concert Mick is hit by a bottle.

18

Fog causes the Stones to land at Warwick, Rhode Island, en route from Montreal to Boston. Mick, Marshall Chess and film-maker Robert Frank are charged with obstructing a police officer and Keith is charged with assault after a scuffle at the airport with a photographer and reporter. Boston's mayor, Mr Kevin White, goes to the jail and bails them out so they can

meet their commitment to play Boston's Garden Theater. The audience give him a standing ovation. The Stones go on two hours late.

24

At a party held for the Stones at the Four Seasons on Park Avenue, Mick Jagger leaves after seven minutes.

26

Atlantic Records boss, Ahmet Ertegun, holds a party for 500 on the top floor of the St. Regis Hotel, New York City, to celebrate Mick Jagger's 29th birthday and the end of the Stones' successful US tour. The Count Basie Orchestra and Muddy Waters entertain the guests which include Bob Dylan, Zsa Zsa Gabor, Woody Allen, George Plimpton, Truman Capote, and Andy Warhol. A huge birthday cake is wheeled in and out jumps Gerri Miller, the star of Andy Warhol's *Flesh* and *Trash* movies, wearing pasties on her nipples, a black garter belt on one thigh and nothing else. She does a suggestive dance which makes Mick applaud but causes Keith to look away in embarrassment. Among Mick's birthday presents are a snuff box for coke and a silver cross. Mick joins Stevie Wonder for a brief jam with Muddy Waters. The party breaks up at dawn.

AUGUST
9

Keith, Anita and their children take up residence in Montreux, Switzerland.

10

Mick and Bianca visit the Oval Cricket Ground for the Test Match against Australia.

26

Peter Rudge, the Stones' tour co-ordinator, announces that the US tour grossed over £1.5 million and that the group played to more than three-quarters-of-a-million people. The gross would have been higher but for the Stones' insistence on a top ticket price of $6.50.

28

Mick and Bianca arrive at the Earl of Gowrie's house in Ireland for a holiday.

SEPTEMBER
7

Charlie and Bill, the only Stones in France, are taken before a judge in Nice and formally arrested and charged. Suspects arrested in Marseilles had told police that they had seen members of The Rolling Stones taking drugs in Keith's house so all group members come under

suspicion, even the two Stones known for their non-drug lifestyles. The judge tells them that their names will be removed from the suspect lists until the trial comes to court. The next time Bill flies into Nice he is frog-marched away and questioned by police. His complaints and request for an apology fall on deaf ears.

22

Mick and Bianca, Charlie and Shirley, and Mick Taylor attend a party at WEA for Shirley Arnold, Personal Secretary to the Stones for nine years who is leaving to work with The Faces. She is succeeded by Anna Menzies.

OCTOBER

Mick is working at Olympic Studios, editing the tapes recorded on their US tour for a future live album.

10

Former co-manager Eric Easton announces in the High Court that he is suing Andrew Oldham (his ex-partner), Allen Klein, Decca Records, London Records and Nanker Phelge Music. Mick Jagger and everyone else named are counter-suing. The lawyers are overjoyed.

GIMMIE SHELTER
Compilation
A - Decca SKL 5101.
Released: October 1972.
Recorded: Side 1: previously issued material / Side 2: Live at the Royal Albert Hall, September 23, 1966.

Side 1: 1. Jumpin' Jack Flash (Jagger, Richard) / 2. Love In Vain (Trad. Arranged Jagger, Richard) / 3. Honky Tonk Woman (Jagger, Richard) / 4. Street Fighting Man (Jagger, Richard) / 5. Sympathy For The Devil (Jagger, Richard) /

6. Gimmie Shelter (Jagger, Richard) Side 2: 7. Under My Thumb (Jagger, Richard) / 8. Time Is On My Side (Meade, Norman) / 9. I've Been Loving You Too Long (Redding, Butler) / 10. Fortune Teller (Neville) / 11. Lady Jane (Jagger, Richard) / 12. (I Can't Get No) Satisfaction (Jagger, Richard).

Notes: The tracks on side two are taken from the US album 'Got Live If You Want It' (London PS 493) which was not released in the UK. The other tracks are re-issues of already released material.

NOVEMBER
2

The Stones drug case comes before the court in Nice and is adjourned for a month. Mick flies back to London.

6

Bill Wyman appears at Chelmsford Magistrates Court and is fined £20 and banned from driving for speeding in his Mercedes on the A12 near Chelmsford.

20

'You're So Vain' (Simon) / 'His Friends Are More Than Fond Of Robin' (Simon) by Carly Simon released on Elektra. Mick sings in the chorus on the 'A' side which was rumoured to be about him... or Cat Stevens or Warren Beatty.

22

Mick in New York to work with John Lennon on Yoko Ono's new album

23

The Rolling Stones arrive in Kingston, Jamaica to record at Byron Lee's Dynamic Sound studios. Lee has equipped the studio with £40,000 worth of equipment including a grand piano and a Hammond B3 organ which they specially request. The Stones stay at Hotel Terra Nova, once the family home of Chris Blackwell, owner of Island Records.

Above: Mick with Stevie Wonder in New York, 1972.

30
Mick, Keith and Mick Taylor fly to Los Angeles to work on the planning stages of their Far Eastern tour.

DECEMBER
2
The police in Nice issue warrants for Keith and Anita in connection with drug offences at Nellcot and on his yacht, The Mandrax.

The Stones fly from Jamaica to London.

3
Keith buys a villa at Point of View, Ocho Tios, Jamaica.

4
Mick, Bill, Charlie and Mick Taylor fly to Nice to discuss allegations of drug use at Keith's house, Nellcote and on board *The Mandrax*. Mick issues a statement saying, "Charlie Watts, Bill Wyman, Mick Taylor and myself deny categorically that we have been charged by the French police with the buying and use of heroin. It has never been suggested that we used or bought heroin. The four of us were not freed on 'provisional liberty' because we had never been arrested on any charge... at no time did we hold drug parties in our homes."

On behalf of the French police, Sergeant Maurey says, "We have been investigating the case in secret for the past thirteen months and three arrests have been made. No other members of the group

have been involved - they were given a thorough going-over in Nice recently and are clean." One of those arrested worked for Keith as a cook.

17
The Trials of Oz, which has songs by John Lennon and Mick Jagger opens on 2nd Avenue, New York, across from the Fillmore and closes shortly afterwards.

21
The Stones finish recording in Jamaica. Mick: "One of the benefits of recording away from home in an isolated place like Jamaica is that there are no distractions. We can work without interruptions and that is what we have been doing... Finding something to eat has been a problem. We usually get up too late for lunch and too early for dinner. When we return from the studio it's too early for breakfast."

26
Mick and Bianca fly to Kingston, Jamaica, en route to Nicaragua.

28
Mick and Bianca charter a private jet and fly to Managua, Nicaragua, to search for Bianca's mother, taking 2,000 anti-typhoid injections with them. They find Mrs Macias and some other relatives all safe.

23
An earthquake shatters Managua, Nicaragua - Bianca's birthplace, leaving 6,000 dead.

1973

JANUARY
Dates: Los Angeles Forum (18); International Sports Center, Honolulu (21-22).

4
After being reported missing, Mick and Bianca turn up safely in Managua.

It is announced that one of The Rolling Stones is banned from entering Australia by the Immigration Ministry - no name or reason is given.

8
Japanese authorities ban Mick Jagger from entering the country because of his 1966 drug conviction. This puts a big hole in the middle of a costly tour. Mick denies that the band are depressed because of it. "It's just a minor sort of frustration. The main thing that bugs us is that we got nothing to do for ten days, but that's about it. It's not a great financial loss."

9
Mr Albert Grassy, Australian Immigration Ministry, announces

that the ban on the entry of a member of The Rolling Stones group is lifted.

10
Mick announces that he wants the Stones to give a benefit concert to aid the earthquake victims in Managua.

14
In Los Angeles the Stones rehearse for their Australian tour. All Japanese concerts are now cancelled even though they all sold-out.

18
The Stones play a concert at the Los Angeles Forum as a benefit for the victims of the Nicaraguan earthquake. Santana and Cheech & Chong support. Before the concert, Bill Graham presents the Stones with a 11 by 14 ft tapestry of his Stones-at-Winterland poster. The concert grosses $516,810, the biggest house ever for a charity concert.

Rolling Stone magazine reports March 1: "LA station KMET-FM had a week-long telephone auction of Stones paraphernalia to further aid the Nicaraguans. Among the souvenirs: the studded velvet costume Mick wore at the LA benefit, starting price $1,000 and autographed: 'To the owner, much love, Mick Jagger'. Also on the block was The Rolling Stones tongue pillow that graced the stage during part of the last US tour, which Mick agreed to personally stain, somehow, to make it all the more valuable."

The readers of *Playboy* magazine name Mick Jagger as Best Male Vocalist of 1972. He receives his award after the Earthquake Benefit.

20
The Stones fly to Honolulu, Hawaii for two concerts where they take over the thirtieth floor of the Hawaii Hilton. At dinner at Nick's Fish Market, the Stones' party of 20 drinks 16 bottles of 1957 Château Margaux at $85 each.

22
Mick takes a cruise six miles out of Honolulu on an 82 foot restored 1929 schooner, the *Flying Cloud*.

23
The Stones return to Los Angeles.

Mick Taylor helps out on Nicky Hopkins' new album.

25
The Stones begin an eight-day stint in the studio, working on material laid down in Jamaica.

29
Radio KMET ends the bidding for Stones memorabilia during its week-long auction.

Above: Keith and Anita.

FEBRUARY

Dates: Hong Kong Football Stadium (5); Western Springs Stadium, Auckland, NZ (11); Milton Park Tennis Courts, Brisbane, Australia (13-14); Kooyong Tennis Courts, Melbourne, Australia (17-18); Memorial Park Drive, Adelaide, Australia (20-21); Western Australia Cricket Ground, Perth (24); Royal Randwick Racecourse, Sydney, Australia (26-27).

8
The Stones fly into Sydney.

9
The Stones hold a press conference in Sydney.

10
The Stones fly to Auckland, New Zealand.

13
Pillowcases and 16 cotton sheets used by the group while in Auckland are auctioned piece by piece and raise £550 for a local boys' recreation centre.

17
The Stones give a press conference at Montsaluat Castle, 20 miles outside Melbourne.

21
At the second concert in Adelaide, 5000 fans rioted resulting in 21 arrests.

28
The tour over, the Stones go on vacation: Mick goes first to Jamaica with Keith, continuing on to the States; Bill Wyman flies straight back to California; Charlie Watts goes to France; Mick Taylor visits Indonesia.

MARCH
6
Mick, Keith and Bill are back in the studio in Los Angeles mixing their next album.

APRIL
7
A six-week series, *The Rolling Stones Story* starts on BBC Radio One.

In Warwick, Rhode Island, Judge Orion Orton upholds charges against Mick and Keith over an incident with local photographers in July 1972. They will be tried the next time they are in the States.

16
Tucky Buzzard's album 'All Right On The Night', produced by Bill, is released on Purple Records.

29
'Sad Day' / 'You Can't Always Get What You Want' released as part of Decca and London's plan to milk the Stones' back catalogue for everything they can get. 'Sad Day' has not previously been available in the UK.

30
Mick and Bianca attend a party for Bette Midler in New York given by *After Dark* magazine.

MAY
2
A portrait of Mick Jagger by Cecil Beaton sells for £220 at Sotheby's.

9
The Rolling Stones benefit concert in January for the earthquake victims of Nicaragua raises $352,274 for the relief fund after expenses. Mick and Bianca with Bill Graham, who produced the concert, fly into Washington from New York to present the cheque to Senator Jacob Javits in a quick ceremony in his chambers. Javits then gives the cheque to Sy Rotter, executive director for the Pan American Development Foundation. Graham says no final decisions on ultimate disbursement of the money will be made without further consultations with him and Jagger. Audited figures showed that ticket sales at the concert reached $410,285. Graham sheltered the money under a tax- exempt non-profit corporation called Benefits, Inc., which was incorporated less than a week before the concert; the money earned $2744 in interest from short-term investments. Expenses came to $60,755, leaving the donated $352,274. *Rolling Stone* reports:

"The cheque presentation was attended by various consuls, delegates and children of Senators, there to ogle Jagger. At one point a consul referred to the benefactor as 'Mike Yaeger'. The whole thing was bombastic, there was no real emotion to it. Just these bodies there looking at this man giving them a lot of money. It was a glimpse of 'politicorama'... Jagger played the gentleman, thanking everyone for coming, then joining his summer-dressed wife and the suited Graham for lunch with Mrs. Javits."

10
Firemen put out a blaze at Stargroves, Mick's English country house.

Mick and Bianca see The J. Geils Band at the New York Academy of Music.

11
Bianca flies to London and attends the Liza Minnelli midnight concert at the London Palladium.

17
Mick and Bianca attend the first rock reception to be held at the Ritz Hotel to launch G&M Records - Chris Jagger is one of the label's first signings.

28
The Stones are mixing their new album, 'Goat's Head Soup' at Island Records Studios in London, though Keith is said to be missing some of the sessions.

JUNE
6
Mick and Bianca attend a birthday party for G&M Records' owner Billy Gaff given in his Fulham home. Fans swarm all over the building.

7
Paul McCartney gives a party after Wings play the Hammersmith Odeon. Present are Mick and Bianca, Keith and Anita, Charlie, as well as Eric Clapton, The Who, Elton John, Chris Jagger and various Small Faces.

10

Party at the Edmonton Sundown to celebrate a decade of The Rolling Stones.

14

The film *Jimi Hendrix* opens in London, including conversations between Jimi and Mick.

18

Mick, Bianca and Jade fly to Italy for a vacation.

Marsha Hunt files a paternity suit against Mick Jagger at Marylebone Magistrates Court, claiming he is the father of her two year old daughter, Karis.

19

At the request of Mick Jagger's attorney, Magistrates at Marylebone Court order Mick and Marsha Hunt to have blood tests and the hearing is adjourned.

25

Mick Taylor joins Mike Oldfield for a performance of 'Tubular Bells' at the Queen Elizabeth Hall, London. Mick Jagger is in the audience.

26

Keith and Anita are busted by the drug squad at their Chelsea home on Cheyne Walk, and charged with possession of marijuana and firearms. They are released next day on bail. "Stash" de Rollo, the Prince of Pop, is arrested with them.

27

Keith is remanded on £1,000 bail until August 1 but his passport is returned so that he can fulfil commitments abroad.

JULY

'The Tin Man Was A Dreamer', an album by Nicky Hopkins which features Mick Taylor, is released on CBS.

4

Mick and Bianca attend David Bowie's "retirement" party at the Café Royal following David's final concert with The Spiders From Mars at Hammersmith Odeon.

24

The Stones shoot a promotional film for their next single.

25

The *Daily Mirror* runs a spread of Bianca modelling Yves St Laurent clothes from his new collection.

26

A birthday party for Mick's 30th is held at the Stones office in London.

30

Mick Jagger seen watching the Test Match at the Oval.

31

Keith Richard's house in West Wittering, Sussex, is badly damaged by fire. He and Anita escape with

the children, and salvage a few antiques, books and pieces of equipment.

Keith and Anita are remanded on bail for their drugs bust at Marylebone Magistrates Court in their absence.

At the same court, Marsha Hunt's paternity suit against Mick is adjourned until the blood tests have been taken.

AUGUST
14

Keith and Anita remanded until September 12.

It is announced that the Stones have changed the name of the track 'Starfucker' to 'Star Star' in case delicate souls get offended.

18

The Stones fly to Rotterdam to rehearse for their upcoming European tour.

20

Rolling Stones Records release 'Angie' / 'Silver Train'. It enters the UK charts at No. 28 and climbs to No. 2. In the States it enters at No. 27 and gets to the top.

ANGIE Jagger, Richard / SILVER TRAIN Jagger, Richard
S - Rolling Stones RS 19105 (UK) RLS 19105 (USA).
Released: August 1973.
Producer: Jimmy Miller.
Studio: Dynamic Sound Studios, Kingston, Jamaica, November-December, 1972.

Notes: Both tracks taken from the forthcoming 'Goat's Head Soup' album.

31

'Goat's Head Soup' released. It enters the UK album charts at No. 7 and reaches No. 1. In the States it enters at No. 9 and also reaches No 1.

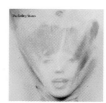

GOAT'S HEAD SOUP
A - Rolling Stones COC 59101 (UK and USA).
Released: August 1973.
Producer: Jimmy Miller.
Engineer: Andy Johns, assisted by Carlton Lee, Howard Kilgour and Doug Bennett.
Studio: Dynamic Sound Studios, Kingston, Jamaica, November 25, 1972 until Christmas 1972.

Side 1: 1. Dancing With Mr. D. (Jagger, Richard) / 2. 100 Years Ago (Jagger, Richard) / 3. Coming Down

Again (Jagger, Richard) / 4. Doo Doo Doo Doo Doo (Heartbreaker) (Jagger, Richard) / 5. Angie (Jagger, Richard)

Side 2: 6. Silver Train (Jagger, Richard) / 7. Hide Your Love (Jagger, Richard) / 8. Winter (Jagger, Richard) / 9. Can You Hear The Music (Jagger, Richard) / 10. Star Star (Jagger, Richard).

Notes: Nicky Hopkins plays piano on tracks 1, 3, 5, 8 and 9. Billy Preston plays clavinet on track 2. Billy Preston plays piano on track 4. Ian Stewart plays piano on track 6. Ian Stewart plays jangles on track 10. Horns: Bobby Keys on tenor and baritone sax. Jim Horn on flute and alto sax. Chuck Finley on trumpet. Horns on track 4 by Jim Price. Percussion by Pascal, Rebop and Jimmy Miller. String arrangements on tracks 5 and 8 by Nicky Harrison. Track 10 remixed for American pressings to disguise the word "pussy".

NOVEMBER

13
The Stones fly to Munich for recording sessions at the Musicland Studio where they are joined by Billy Preston and pianist Nicky Hopkins. Mick Taylor is described as having a "mysterious illness" and does not join them.

24
The Stones finish recording at Musicland.

DECEMBER

15
'Doo Doo Doo Doo Doo (Heartbreaker)' / 'Dancing With Mr. D' released in the USA. It enters the charts at No. 24 and reaches No. 10.

DOO DOO DOO DOO DOO (HEARTBREAKER) Jagger, Richard / DANCING WITH MR. D Jagger, Richard
S - Rolling Stones RS 19109 (USA). Released: December 1973.

Rock' maxi-single re-issued by Rolling Stones Records.

14
The Stones return to Munich for a further two weeks recording at Musicland Studios.

FEBRUARY

2
New Musical Express runs an interview with Marianne Faithfull in which she tells Andrew Taylor that she once went backstage, without Mick Jagger, to visit Otis Redding after a concert in the Sixties: "We went in and said 'That was a great version of "Satisfaction" Otis,' and he said 'Yeah, do you like that song? I just wrote it.' And we just went 'Huhh' and then we thought, well perhaps he did write it. I mean he's black. He knows. So then we went back and said 'Ere Mick, you didn't write "Satisfaction", Otis Redding wrote it.' And then we had this big argument about who wrote it.

Otis swore blue that he wrote it. But I don't think he did. I think Mick wrote it."

10
Cricket fan Mick Jagger is in Trinidad to attend the England v West Indies Test Match at Port of Spain.

15
The Bottom Line opens in New York. Dr. John "The Night Tripper" performs with Mick Jagger in the audience.

25
Mick Jagger is present at a David Bowie recording session in London.

Above left: Keith with sax player Bobby Keyes. Right, top & below: the 'It's Only Rock 'n' Roll' video where Charlie was submerged in foam.

1974

SEPTEMBER
Dates: Stadthalle, Vienna, Austria (1); Eisstadion, Mannheim, Germany (3); Sporthalle, Cologne, Germany (4); Empire Pool, Wembley (7-9 four shows); Bellevue, Manchester (11-12); City Hall, Newcastle-upon-Tyne (13); The Apollo, Glasgow (16-17); The Odeon, Birmingham (19); Innsbruck, Austria (23); Festhalle, Berne, Switzerland (25-26); Olympiahalle, Munich, Germany (28); Festhalle, Frankfurt (30).

5
The Stones fly to London from Cologne.

6
The Stones hire Blenheim Palace for a big party.

10
BBC bans 'Star Star' from 'Goat's Head Soup'.

12
Keith and Anita remanded for trial until October 24.

OCTOBER
Dates: Ernst Mercke Halle, Hamburg, Germany (2); Scandinavium, Gothenburg, Sweden (6); Brondby Halle n, Copenhagen, Denmark (7); Grughalle, Essen, Germany (9-11); The Ahoy, Rotterdam (13-14); Palais de Sport, Antwerp, Belgium (15); Forêt Nationale, Brussels, Belgium (17); Deutschlandhalle, Berlin, Germany (19).

2
The Stones appear on BBC TV *Old Grey Whistle Test* in a pre-recorded session.

15
Keith and Anita are given one-year suspended sentences and fined 5,000 francs each by a French court for throwing drugs parties at their villa in Villefranche-sur-mer in 1971. Keith is also banned from France for two years. Bobby Keys, the sax player with the Stones, also receives a suspended sentence.

18
Radio Luxembourg broadcasts the October 17 concert on their French language service.

24
Keith is fined £205 and given a conditional discharge at Marlborough Street Magistrates Court for four drug charges, including heroin, Mandrax and cannabis and three firearms offences. Anita is given a one-year conditional discharge for possession of Mandrax. Their lawyer claims that the drugs were left in the house by people using it while the couple were abroad.

25
At Billy Preston's concert at the London Rainbow Theatre, Mick and Mick Taylor join him on stage to the delight of the audience.

JANUARY

5
Bill Wyman is in the studio in Los Angeles cutting his first solo album. Guests include Dr. John, Mick Jagger, Mick Taylor, Leon Russell, Dallas Taylor, Joe Lala, Danny Kootch, Lowell George and various members of Billy Preston and Ike Turner's bands.

12
'Brown Sugar' / 'Bitch' / 'Let It

MARCH

1

The documentary film of the Stones' US tour, *Ladies and Gentlemen, The Rolling Stones* is previewed in New York.

3

Los Angeles. Mick Jagger and John Lennon attend the American Film Institute's tribute to James Cagney in which he receives a special Oscar.

25

Mick Jagger joins John Lennon and Harry Nilsson at the Record Plant in Los Angeles for a recording session for Nilsson's 'Pussycats' album.

27

Artist Guy Pellaert's *Rock Dreams* book is published. Mick invites Guy to the Stones' recording sessions in Munich to think of ideas for the Stones' next album sleeve. Pellaert designs the sleeve for 'It's Only Rock'n'Roll'.

APRIL

'London Underground' by Herbie Mann, featuring Mick Taylor on guitar, is released on Atlantic.

6

Mick holidays in the West Indies.

14

Ladies and Gentlemen, The Rolling Stones is premièred at the Ziegfield Theater in New York.

MAY

8

Bill Wyman is interviewed on BBC-TV's *Old Grey Whistle Test* which also plays 'White Lightnin'' a track from his forthcoming solo album 'Monkey Grip'.

10

Bill Wyman's solo album 'Monkey Grip' is released on Rolling Stones Records COC 59102 (UK and USA). The personnel on this album are mostly LA session men: Danny Kootch, electric guitar and 12-string; Joe Lala, percussion; Mac Rebennack, piano; Dallas Taylor drums; Leon Russell, piano; Lowell George, guitar; Hubie Heard, piano and organ; Jackie Clark, electric guitar; Abigale Haness, backup vocals; John McCuen, dobro, mandolin and banjo; Joey Murcia, electric guitar; Duane Smith, piano; George Terry, slide guitar; William Smith, piano; Byron Berline, country fiddle; and the Boneroo Horn section.

Bill is one of the guests at the launch of the new Swan Song label, owned by Led Zeppelin, at the Bel Air Hotel, Los Angeles.

18

Keith and Ron Wood are in the audience at The Who's concert at Charlton Athletic Ground.

20

The Stones mix their new album at Island Records studios in London.

28

Mick Jagger and Mick Taylor join in a recording session at Ron Wood's home where he is making a solo album. Also present are George Harrison, Eric Clapton and Keith Richard who is living there while visiting London from his home in Switzerland.

JUNE

15

'Monkey Grip Glue' (Wyman) / 'What A Blow' (Wyman) by Bill Wyman released by Rolling Stones Records, as RS 19112, both taken from his solo album.

28

Bill Wyman appears on stage with Muddy Waters at the Montreux Jazz Festival, Switzerland. He also jams with The Buddy Guy and Junior Wells All Stars.

JULY

9

The Stones appear on BBC-TV's *Old Grey Whistle Test* to promote their new single 'It's Only Rock'n'Roll (But I Like It)'.

13

Mick Jagger attends Eric Clapton's concert at Madison Square Garden.

Keith joins Ron Wood on stage at the Kilburn Gaumont.

14

Keith Richard joins Ron Wood on stage for the second night of Ron's solo concerts away from The Faces.

25

Mick Jagger has his hair cut short by Anthony at Ricci Burns.

26

There is a big party for Mick's birthday at interior designer David Mlinaric's house in Chelsea. 'It's Only Rock'n'Roll' / 'Through The Lonely Nights' released. It enters the UK charts at No. 27 and reaches No. 10. In the States it enters at No. 28 and reaches No. 18.

IT'S ONLY ROCK 'N' ROLL
Jagger, Richard /
THROUGH THE LONELY NIGHTS Jagger, Richard
S - Rolling Stones Records
RS 19114 (UK) RS 19301 (USA).
Released: July 1974.
Producer: Side A: The Glimmer Twins / Side B: The Glimmer Twins with Jimmy Miller.
Studio: Side A: Begun on a Revox in Ronnie Wood's studio and completed at Musicland Studios, Munchen, Germany, Winter 1973-74 / Side B: From the Goat's Head Soup' sessions, Dynamic Sound, Kingston, Jamaica, November 25, 1972 - Christmas 1972.

Notes: Side A originally featured Mick Jagger and Ronnie Wood on guitar, Willie Weeks on bass, Kenny

The LA Express, The Band and Jesse Colin Young play to an audience of 75,000 at the Wembley stadium. Ron Wood escorts Bianca to the after-concert party at Quaglino's restaurant in St James.

Mick is in Nassau, at a party to celebrate the opening of Stevie Wonder's American tour.

18

Mick Jagger rents a house in Andy Warhol's compound in Montauk, Long Island. He and Bianca have spent much of the summer staying next door in Andy's own house.

27

'I've Got My Own Album To Do', a Ron Wood solo album released on Warner Brothers K 56065 (UK). The

basic band on the album consists of Willie Weeks, bass; Andy Newmark, drums; Andy McLagan, keyboards; Keith Richard, guitars/ vocals and Ron Wood, guitars/vocals. The additional presence of Mick Jagger and Mick Taylor on some tracks makes this almost a Rolling Stones album. It was during the sessions for this album that the original backing track for 'It's Only Rock'n'Roll' was laid down.

29

Mick and Bianca see Eric Clapton at the Nassau Coliseum, N.Y.

Centre: Mick, Keith and Bill in 1975. Below: Bill with Astrid Lundstrom.

Jones on drums and David Bowie on backing vocals before the track was transferred to multi-track in the studio and the Stones proper got to work on it. Side B is rumoured to have Jimmy Page playing guitar somewhere in the mix.

AUGUST

'Billy Preston's Live European Tour' by Billy Preston, featuring Mick Taylor on lead guitar, is released on A&M and 'Reggae' by Herbie Mann, also featuring Mick on guitar, is released on Atlantic.

17

The film *Ladies and Gentlemen, The Rolling Stones* premiers in Los Angeles with proceeds going to the LA Free Clinic.

18

Mick is in Los Angeles to supervise the mastering of the new album.

24

The Stones video three numbers for the US-TV's *Don Kirshner Show*.

SEPTEMBER

14

Crosby, Stills, Nash & Young, Joni Mitchell with Tom Scott and

Rolling Stones Records. It enters the charts at No. 21 and gets to No. 15.

AIN'T TOO PROUD TO BEG Whitfield, Holland / **DANCE LITTLE SISTER** Jagger, Richard
S - Rolling Stones Records RS 19302 (USA).
Released: October 1974.

Notes: Both tracks taken from the album 'It's Only Rock 'n' Roll'.

26

Keith Richard applies for planning permission to rebuild Redlands, his Sussex home, which was largely destroyed by fire in 1973.

Mick and Bianca are guests at a party at the Four Seasons on Park Avenue, New York, in honour of Charlotte Rampling after the premier of *The Night Porter* in which she stars. Mrs Levine, wife of the film's producer, tries to throw them out for being "scruffy".

30

Bianca reported to be in Jamaica.

NOVEMBER

'White Lightnin'' (Wyman), a Bill Wyman solo single, released on Rolling Stones Records RS 19115 (UK and USA), as is 'I Can Feel The Fire', a solo single by Ron Wood on Warner Brothers K 16463.

14

Keith Richard goes to Switzerland to get himself a new set of teeth. He says, "I'm changing my image. I've arranged a whole series of dental appointments in Switzerland... I only ever get ill when I give up drugs."

17

Mick and Bianca at a party at the Hippopotamus Club, New York.

22

Mick and Bianca are guests at a party for Elton John held at the Grand Ballroom of the Pierre Hotel in New York.

26

Mick and Bianca are in Managua, Nicaragua, to monitor the distribution of the charity money they helped to raise.

DECEMBER
4

Mick Jagger and Mick Taylor are in the audience at Eric Clapton's concert at the Hammersmith Odeon and attend the party afterwards. Mick Jagger: "When we went to Eric Clapton's concert at Hammersmith, Mick said he wanted to do something else. He'd played with us for five years and he felt he wanted to play some different kind of music. So I said, 'OK, that's fine' and that was that."

OCTOBER
1

BBC-TV's *Old Grey Whistle Test* previews the upcoming Stones' album with 'Ain't Too Proud To Beg', and an interview with Keith Richard.

A Leni Reifenstahl photo spread on the Jaggers is published in the *Sunday Times*.

Robert Greenfield's *STP - Stones Touring Party* book on the 1972 American tour is published.

17

Mick spends a week in Paris where he sees Nathalie Delon.

18

Rolling Stones Records release 'It's Only Rock'n'Roll'. A graffiti campaign announces the new album all over London. It enters the UK charts at No. 14 and reaches No. 4. In the States it enters at No. 34 and reaches the top of the album charts.

IT'S ONLY ROCK 'N' ROLL
A - Rolling Stones Records COC 59103 (UK), COC 79101 (USA).
Released: October 1974.
Producer: The Glimmer Twins.
Engineers: Andy Johns and Keith Harwood.
Overdub Engineer: George Chkiantz.
Assisted by Tapani Tapanamen, Rod Thear and Howard Kilgour.

Studio: Musicland, Munchen, Germany. Track 3 begun at Ron Wood's home studio in London.
Recorded: Winter 1973-4.

Side 1: 1. If You Can't Rock Me (Jagger, Richard) / 2. Ain't Too Proud To Beg (Whitfield, Holland) / 3. It's Only Rock 'n' Roll (Jagger, Richard) / 4. Till The Next Goodbye (Jagger, Richard) / 5. Time Waits For No One (Jagger, Richard).

Side 2: 6. Luxury (Jagger, Richard) / 7. Dance Little Sister (Jagger, Richard) / 8. If You Really Want To Be My Friend (Jagger, Richard) / 9. Short and Curlies (Jagger, Richard) / 10. Finger-print File (Jagger, Richard).

Notes: Track 3 was started at Ron Wood's home studio during the recording of his 'I've Got My Own Album To Do' album. It featured Willie Weeks on bass and Kenny Jones on drums. It was then considerably changed during the making of this album but apparently retained the original backing tracks under all the layers of overdubs. Billy Preston plays piano, clavinet on tracks 1, 2 and 10. Nicky Hopkins plays piano on tracks 4, 5, 6, 8 and 10. Ian Stewart plays piano on tracks 3, 7 and 9. Charlie Jolly plays tabla on track 10. Ed Leach plays cowbell on track 2. Ray Cooper plays percussion on all tracks. Blue Magic sing backing vocals on track 8. Kenny Jones plays drums on track 3 (original track). Willie Weeks plays bass on track 3 (original track).

25

'Ain't Too Proud To Beg' / 'Dance Little Sister' released in the USA on

7
The Stones are in Munich to record, with Glyn Johns as engineer and overseer for the first time since 'Sticky Fingers'.

12
Mick Taylor officially leaves The Rolling Stones.

13
The Stones finish recording in Munich.

14
New Musical Express reports "Mick Taylor has left The Rolling Stones, the band he joined in 1968 as replacement for Brian Jones, and has joined a new outfit currently being formed by Jack Bruce. The Stones, at present recording as a four-piece in Munich, will engage a new guitarist in time for a major new concert tour of America in May."

Mick Taylor issues a statement: "The last 5½ years with the Stones have been very exciting, and proved to be a most inspiring period. And as far as my attitude to the other four members is concerned, it is one of respect for them, both as musicians and as people. I have nothing but admiration for the group, but I feel now is the time to move on and do something new."

Mick Jagger issues a statement: "After 5½ years, Mick wishes a change of scene and wants the opportunity to try out new ventures, new endeavours. While we are all most sorry that he is going, we wish him great success and much happiness."

21
Rumours circulate that Mick Taylor had left the group because he was dissatisfied with the financial arrangements. He tells *Sounds*, "There was no personal animosity in the split, nothing personal at all. There was no row, no quibbling or squabbling. I'm very disturbed by the stories going around that it was all to do with credits and royalties, things like that. It had nothing whatever to

do with those things. I'm very upset by the rumours because I really like all the guys in the Stones. I've really loved working with them these past five years, we've had some great times."

1975

JANUARY
'7-Tease' an album by Donovan is released on Epic. Produced by Andrew Loog Oldham, Bill Wyman plays bass on the track 'Rock and Roll Souljer' (Donovan) which is also released as a single.

22
The Stones fly to Rotterdam to record, taking Alexis Korner with them. Keith had recently played on the title track of Korner's album 'Get Off Of My Cloud'.

FEBRUARY
9
The Stones complete their recording sessions. Keith returns to London, Mick flies to New York.

15
Keith, again staying with Ron Wood, rehearses with guitarist Wayne Perkins in Ron's home studio. Sessions for Ron's next solo album continue until the end of the month.

MARCH
Mick Jagger and Charlie Watts begin working on the stage design and lighting for the upcoming Americas tour. Mick: "I've been working mostly in posters and things. Artwork. Been heavily into design and stage design... It should be nice, you know?"

Mick and Stones tour co-ordinator Peter Rudge fly to New York to plan their forthcoming US tour.

8
Mick and Rudge, who also manages The Who's US affairs, see John Entwistle's Ox at the New York Academy of Music.

11
Mick shows up at the Los Angeles Record Plant to jam with Ron Wood and various members of Wings.

15
It is reported that Mick Jagger has settled Marsha Hunt's paternity suit out of court.

22
The Stones return to Musicland Studios in Munich for more recording sessions.

30
Ron Wood flies to Munich to join the Stones at Musicland.

APRIL
4
The Stones finish their recording sessions and return to London. Mick flies straight on to New York with the others following on in a few days. The group will rehearse for their US tour at Andy Warhol's secluded estate on the coast near Montauk, Long Island.

14
It is announced that Ron Wood of The Small Faces is hired as lead guitarist for the 58 concert, three month summer tour but he will not be joining the Stones permanently as he is committed to staying with The Small Faces. Ron, meanwhile, is in Amsterdam, still recording tracks for his solo album.

Mick, when asked about Ron Wood's selection, said, "He had to please me and Keith both. I can sort of tell a good guitar player but probably Keith can tell better than me. Remember, Keith used to be the lead guitarist for The Rolling Stones. Woody seems a natural in the respect that both he and Keith are brilliant rhythm guitarists. It allows a certain cross-trading of riffs not previously possible. They can both

play solos; maybe Keith's going to have to do more solos.

"I wanted someone that was easy to get on with, you know, and that was a good player and was used to playing on stage. It's quite a lot to ask someone to come and do a big American tour with a band like the Stones. Not that I think the Stones are any big deal, but it tends to be a bit of a paralysing experience for people - you know what I mean? Woody can sing - a little. He can sing. He's starting to get it together; the first singing he did was his album. Woody's personality would seem to fit the bill also... Onstage he's got a lot of style. And it's got to be fun on the road. That's what it's all about, isn't it?"

MAY
1
The Stones call a press conference at the Fifth Avenue hotel at 9th Street in Greenwich Village, but waiting pressmen soon become aware of music in the street outside as the Stones, using a portable generator, play 'Brown Sugar' on the back of a flat bed truck. They drive slowly past the hotel, throwing leaflets to the press detailing the venues for their upcoming US tour and astonishing passers-by. Traffic is halted and fans block the street. The Stones jump down from the truck and into waiting limousines and are gone. The group got the idea from Charlie Watts who told them that New Orleans jazzmen used to advertise upcoming concerts by driving around town playing on the back of a truck.

The Stones return to Montauk to begin rehearsals with Ron Wood for the tour.

18
Mick cuts his hand on a glass door at a restaurant in Montauk, needing 20 stitches. He says "It's a bit messy but I won't need a cast or anything."

21
The Stones new lotus-shaped stage made by Robin Wagner to designs by Mick and Charlie is unveiled at an aircraft hangar at Stewart Airport, Newburgh, N.Y. The five petals project out into the audience. In an advanced version for concerts in New York City, Chicago and Los Angeles, the petals are raised and lowered hydraulically.

I DON'T KNOW WHY
Wonder, Riser, Hunter, Hardaway / **TRY A LITTLE HARDER** Jagger, Richard
S - Decca F 13584 (UK)
ABKCO 4701 (USA).
Released: May 1975.

Notes: First 1000 credit Jagger, Richard as the composers of Side A. The tracks were received by Decca as part of the ABKCO agreement which gave them the tapes on 'Metamorphosis'. Both tracks appear on 'Metamorphosis'. The Decca matrix numbers cannot be used for dating purposes since they were assigned only when ABKCO received the tapes.

30

The Stones fly from New York to New Orleans from Newark, N.J. airport.

31

At the Louisiana State University Assembly Center, Baton Rouge, the Stones hold their final rehearsal before their American tour. Staying at the Royal Orleans Hotel, New Orleans, Keith says: "If everything's working well, the general idea is that you should be able to hear what you want to on stage. Charlie wants to hear me; Mick needs to hear me, drums and himself, and the bass wants to hear the drums. The amps are so directional, I basically just hear myself. I don't care what I hear as long as I hear something. Over the years, you know, we've virtually lost control over our sound - now it's some guy at a mixing board who we may never have met and has maybe never heard us play. Is there any way to beat that system? Sure, to beat that guy."

JUNE

Dates: Louisiana State University Assembly Center, Baton Rouge, Louisiana (1); Convention Center, San Antonio, Texas (3-4); Arrowhead Stadium, Kansas City, Missouri (6); Milwaukee County Stadium, Milwaukee, Wisconsin (8); Civic Center, St. Paul, Minnesota (9); Boston Garden, Boston,

Massachusetts (11-12); Municipal Stadium, Cleveland, Ohio (14); Municipal Auditorium, Buffalo, New York (15); Maple Leaf Gardens, Toronto, Canada (17-18); Madison Square Garden, New York (22-27).

METAMORPHOSIS
A - ABKCO ANA 1 (USA).
Released: June 1975.
Producers: Andrew Loog Oldham and Jimmy Miller (individual tracks are not credited).

Side 1: 1. Out Of Time (Jagger, Richard) / 2. Don't Lie To Me (Berry) / 3. Each And Every Day Of The Year (Jagger, Richard) / 4. Heart Of Stone (Jagger, Richard) / 5. I'd Much Rather Be With The Boys (Oldham, Richard) / 6. Try A Little Harder (Jagger, Richard).

Side 2: 7. I Don't Know Why (Wonder, Riser, Hunter, Hardaway) / 8. If You Let Me (Jagger, Richard) / 9. Jiving Sister Fanny (Jagger, Richard) / 10. Downtown Suzie (Wyman) / 11. Family (Jagger, Richard) / 12. Memo From Turner (Jagger, Richard) / 13. I'm Going Down (Jagger, Richard).

See Decca version entry for details (except for tracks 3 and 8).

2

The Stones fly into San Antonio, Texas in the Starship, a Boeing 707,

specially fitted out for wealthy rock groups on tour. They check into the Hilton Palacio Del Rio. The head of the local police Vice Squad threatens to bust the Stones if they unveil the huge inflatable penis which is part of the stage set. Rather than disrupt the tour, the Stones agree not to corrupt the morals of the locals. Nonetheless, police barge backstage during the show but back down when threatened with legal action.

4

Mick plays rhythm guitar on Leslie West's album, 'The Great Fatsby', released today.

5

The Stones visit the Alamo for a photo session.

6

Allen Klein's ABKCO label releases 'Metamorphosis', a compilation of early tracks, in the States. It enters the charts at No. 19 and gets to No. 8. The UK version, on Decca, contains 16 tracks, two more than the US version. It enters the UK chart at No. 27.

Charlie: "It's just a lot of junk really."

Bill: "We wanted to have it done historically, so that it would have at least had a value to collectors."

Charlie: "We spent months going over material."
Bill: "And we provided an album which he [Klein] turned down. I selected about 18 titles, laid it all out historically, with details."

Charlie: "We gave him our album and he said no."

METAMORPHOSIS
Compilation
A - Decca SKL 5212 (UK).
Released: June 1975.
Producers: Andrew Loog Oldham and Jimmy Miller (individual tracks are not credited).
Recorded: These tracks are mostly demo tapes done to enable other artists to record the songs. The remainder are out-takes from albums thought at the time not to be worth releasing. Decca received the tapes as part of the ABKCO settlement between Allen Klein and The Rolling Stones.

Side 1: 1. Out Of Time (Jagger, Richard) / 2. Don't Lie To Me (Richard) / 3. Some Things Just Stick In Your Mind (Jagger, Richard) / 4. Each And Every Day Of The Year (Jagger, Richard) / 5. Heart Of Stone (Jagger, Richard) / 6. I'd Much

Rather Be With The Boys (Oldham, Richard) / 7. (Walkin' Thru The) Sleepy City (Jagger, Richard) / 8. We're Wastin' Time (Jagger, Richard) / 9. Try A Little Harder (Jagger, Richard).

Side 2: 10. I Don't Know Why (Wonder, Riser, Hunter, Hardaway) / 11. If You Let Me (Jagger, Richard) / 12. Jiving Sister Fanny (Jagger, Richard) / 13. Downtown Suzie (Wyman) / 14. Family (Jagger, Richard) / 15. Memo From Turner (Jagger, Richard) / 16. I'm Going Down (Jagger, Richard, Taylor).

Notes: Track 1: This is the same backing track that Jagger used in his production of Chris Farlowe's hit version. This could be seen as an early arrangement of the number on the 'Aftermath' album - Probably made at RCA, Hollywood in early 1966. Track 3: Probably a demo for the version released by Vashti on Decca F 12157. (May 1965). Track 4: Probably a demo for the version

released by Thee on Decca F 12163 (May 1965). Track 5: This is an out-take from the 'Out Of Our Heads' album. Track 6: Probably a demo for the version released by The Toggery Five on Parlophone R 5249. (February 1965). Track 7: Probably a demo for the version released by The Mighty Avengers on Decca F 12198 (February 1965.) Track 8: Probably a demo for the version released by Jimmy Tarbuck on Immediate IM 018. Track 13: Recorded between 'Their Satanic Majesties Request' and 'Beggars Banquet'. Track 14: Beggars Banquet' outtake. Track 15: Probably the original demo for the number. If so, it features Stevie Winwood and Jim Capaldi. Late 1970. The US version of this album does not include tracks 3 and 8.

Opposite: On stage in American tour, 1975.

7

The Stones leave the Sheraton-Royal Hotel, Kansas City, and fly to Milwaukee.

10

In Jamaica, Anita Pallenberg is fined £200 for drugs offences and deported. The *Daily Express* reports that her first hearing was adjourned because she adopted "an unusual posture" in court.

13

Rolling Stones Records release a compilation album, 'Made In The Shade' to coincide with the tour. It enters the US charts at No. 25 and reaches No. 6. In the UK it enters at No. 17 and gets to No. 10.

MADE IN THE SHADE
Compilation
A - Rolling Stones Records COC 59104 (UK) COC 79101 (USA). Released: June 1975.

Side 1: 1. Brown Sugar (Jagger, Richard)/2. Tumblin' Dice (Jagger, Richard)/3. Happy (Jagger, Richard)/4. Dance Little Sister (Jagger, Richard)/5. Wild Horses (Jagger, Richard).

Side 2: 6. Angie (Jagger, Richard)/7. Bitch (Jagger, Richard)/8. It's Only Rock 'n Roll (Jagger, Richard)/9. Doo Doo Doo Doo Doo (Heartbreaker) (Jagger, Richard)/10. Rip This Joint (Jagger, Richard).

Notes: All tracks previously issued.

22

Eric Clapton joins the Stones on stage for the encore, 'Sympathy For The Devil'. Atlantic Records press officer, Earl McGrath hosts a party for the group afterwards at his home.

26

Some members of the Stones jam with Eric Clapton at Electric Lady Studio on 8th Street, New York.

27

Carlos Santana joins the group on stage for an encore at their sixth and final Madison Square Garden concert. Press reports suggest that the Stones grossed $1.25 million from the Madison Square Garden concerts. After the concert the Stones give a party for the Steel Bands Association to thank them for opening the New York shows.

JULY

Dates: Capital Center, Washington, D.C. (1-2); Memorial Stadium, Memphis, Tennessee (4); The Cotton Bowl, Dallas, Texas (6); Los Angeles Forum, California (9-13); Cow Palace, San Francisco, California (15-16); The Coliseum, Seattle, Washington (18); Hughes Stadium, Denver, Colorado (19); Chicago Stadium, Illinois (23-24); Indiana University Assembly Center, Bloomington, Indiana (26); Cobo Hall, Detroit, Michigan (27-28); The Omni, Atlanta, Georgia (30); The Auditorium, Greensboro, North Carolina (31).

'Now Look', Ron Wood's second solo album, released on Warner Brothers K 56145. The basic band on this album consists of Ronnie Wood, vocals and guitar; Bobby Womack, guitar; Ian McLagan, piano; Willie Weeks, bass; Andy Newmark, drums; and Jean Roussell, electric piano. In addition to this Keith Richard and Mick Taylor contribute guitar on certain tracks. A single by Ron, 'If You Don't Want My Love' is also on Warner Brothers K 16618.

4

The Memphis Vice Squad tell the Stones that they will arrest them if they perform 'Starfucker'. Mick tells them, in no uncertain terms, that he will sing what he likes and does so. Memphis cops in full riot regalia approach the stage. Stones' attorney, Bill Carter, tells them, "If you bust the Stones, these kids'll burn down this stadium and your city along with it. And the Stones will litigate you forever. These aren't some broke hippies. They will sue." Considering that a local radio station had been broadcasting the song all along without being charged with public obscenity, the cops back down.

5

The Arkansas Highway Patrol arrest Keith in Fordyce and charge him with carrying an offensive weapon and also hold Ron Wood who is driving with him. They are released on $162 bail. The incident happens when they rejoin the road after stopping at a roadside coffee shop. A crowd had gathered which attracted the police. Keith says, "I bent down to change the wave-band on the radio and the car swerved slightly. A police patrol vehicle then pulled out from a lay-by and stopped us. I was then questioned about having a 'concealed weapon', a penknife complete with tin-opener and a device for removing stones from horses hooves." What is not mentioned in the news stories is that Stones aide Fred Sessler is also in the car (described as a "hitch-hiker") and is arrested for possession of cocaine. He is released on $5,000 bail.

7

The Stones fly into Los Angeles for Ringo Starr's birthday party.

9

Diana Ross gives a party for the Stones after their star-studded opening night at the Los Angeles Forum.

11

After the concert, Ron Wood and Bill Wyman see Bob Marley and The Wailers play The Roxy.

19

Elton John joins the Stones on stage at their concert in Denver.

AUGUST

Dates: Gator Bowl, Jacksonville, Florida (2); Freedom Hall, Louisville, Kentucky (4); Coliseum, Hampton Roads, Virginia (6); Rich Stadium, Buffalo, N.Y. (8).

4

Louisville police announce they intend to bust the Stones the moment their private jet sets down on Kentucky soil. Stones lawyer, Bill Carter, who had previously worked for the Secret Service with Jack Kennedy, devises a plan where the Starship taxies to the deplaning ramp and parks where it blocks any police cars arriving at the ramp. The plane then taxies to safety as the Stones make a get-away in a bus hidden in a side ramp. The bus takes the group to the Coliseum, followed by police cars. A total of 40 narcotics officers gather outside the dressing rooms, ready for their big bust but a combination of bodyguards and lawyers prevent them from entering without a warrant. Attorney Carter calls the District Attorney complaining of police harassment and demands that he come to the scene immediately. The DA arrives, poses for pictures with the group and tells the cops to get the hell out of there.

Opposite: Ron Wood joins Mick at the mic on his debut Stones tour, 1975. Above: Mick with Billy Preston who joined the Stones for their 1975 US tour. Below: Ron, Billy Preston, Mick and Keith.

8

During the final concert of the tour 600 fans are injured and 170 arrested. The tour took the group to 27 cities where they played 47 concerts and grossed just under $13 million.

SEPTEMBER
3

A party given by Peter Sellers in Hollywood develops into an all-star jam with Ron Wood on guitar, Bill Wyman on bass, Bobby Keys on saxophone, Keith Moon on organ, David Bowie playing alto saxophone and Joe Cocker providing vocals.

13

Mick and Bianca vacation with the Guinness family at Leixlip Castle in Ireland. Mick announces that the Stones will tour Europe before Christmas.

15

Bill Wyman begins work on a solo album at the Record Plant in Los Angeles. On hand are Van Morrison, Sly Stone, Joe Walsh, Joe Vitale, Steve Stills and Leon Russell.

21

Mick in the audience at Circasia, a charity show in Dublin featuring Eric Clapton, Sean Connery, John Huston and Shirley MacLaine.

'Get Off Of My Cloud' an album by Alexis Korner is released by CBS Records featuring Keith Richard on guitar and lead vocal on the title track.

OCTOBER
4

Mick in the audience at a Johnny Cash concert in Dublin.

19

The Stones, with Ron Wood, fly into Montreux, Switzerland, to begin work on their new album at Mountain Recording Studios.

NOVEMBER
30

The Stones and Ron Wood complete their sessions at Mountain.

DECEMBER
3

The Stones continue work on their new album with Ron Wood at Musicland Studios in Munich.

Krissie Wood, Ron's wife, is arrested in London for possession of cannabis and cocaine when the drugs squad raid their home in Richmond. Also arrested was Audrey Burgon, giving the tabloids wonderful scope for their imagination since the two women were found sleeping together.

6

In Tallahassie, Florida, fanatical Christian teenagers burn Rolling Stones and Elton John records, after a local preacher, Charles Boykin, found them 'sinful'. His researches had shown that of 1,000 unmarried mothers, 984 had had sex while rock music was playing.

10

Krissie Wood and Audrey Burgon cleared of possessing cannabis but the jury fail to reach a verdict on the charge of possessing 15 milligrams of cocaine. A retrial date will be set later.

16

The Stones and Ron Wood complete their sessions at Musicland.

18

Rod Stewart leaves The Faces, effectively disbanding the group. His spokesman, Tony Toon says, "Rod feels he can no longer work in a situation where the group's lead guitarist, Ron Wood, seems to be permanently on loan to The Rolling Stones." This is seen by many people as leaving the way clear for Ron to join the Stones.

In 1974 Mick approached Ron Wood about joining the Stones. Ron: "I was sitting in the back seat of a car with Mick and Marshall Chess and Mick said to me, 'I don't want to split up The Faces - I really dig them - but if you ever want to move on, would you come with us?' I said, 'There's nothing I'd like more, but I am committed in every way to The Faces, so if you could find someone else, that would be better. If you get *real* desperate though, ring me up'.

"A year later, Mick tracked me down in LA and said, 'Woody, I'm desperate.' I said, 'Does that mean you want me? Things are a little rough with The Faces and I was planning on dropping by Munich to see how you're getting on.' After 'Black And Blue' and that first tour, I was willing to play with both bands - which I did for a while in 1975 - but then Rod threw in his cards and that made my choice easier. I thought, 'These are my marching orders to work with the Stones full time'."

19

In Paris, on his way to New York, Mick Jagger comments on Rod Stewart's decision to leave. "I don't think Ron even knows of this yet. All I can say at the moment is that no agreement has yet been signed between us. There's nothing finalised at all."

23

Mick, Bianca and Jade fly to Rio de Janeiro from New York for Christmas.

1976

JANUARY
BY INVITATION ONLY
Compilation
C - Atlantic Records K 60112 (USA).
Released: 1976.
Titles of Stones tracks: 1. Angie (Jagger, Richard) / 2. It's Only Rock 'n' Roll (Jagger, Richard)
Recorded: November-December 1972. Spring 1974.
Origin of Stones tracks: 1. Taken from single / 'Goat's Head Soup' album / 2. Taken from single / 'It's Only Rock 'n' Roll' album.

9

David Bowie rents Keith's house in Jamaica to rehearse for his forthcoming 'Station To Station' American tour.

10

Ron Wood and The Rolling Stones meet in New York for business discussions.

Left: Charlie on stage, 1975.

13

Mick goes to Andy Warhol's Factory in New York for Mick to co-sign the limited edition prints Andy made of him. Before Mick arrives Andy complains, "It's going to be just like the Sixties - waiting all night for a rock star." Mick arrives one and a half hours' late. "I had to get a haircut," he explains. There are 250 portfolios of ten prints each, offered at $7,500 a set. Individual prints go for $875.

Mick commissions Andy to paint his portrait. This means he will get four different coloured versions of the same image which is how Andy works.

15

At Bonham's Auction House in Chelsea, Mick Taylor sells his gold disc for 'It's Only Rock'n'Roll' for £75.

18

The Stones are in the studios of Atlantic Records in New York, mixing their next album.

FEBRUARY

'Big Bayou', a Ron Wood solo single by Ron Wood released on Warner Brothers.

7

The Stones are photographed on Sanibel Island, off the Florida coast, by fashion photographer Hiro for the sleeve of the new album, 'Black And Blue'. Afterwards Ron Wood flies on to the Bahamas to work on Eric Clapton's new album.

26

'Stone Alone', Bill Wyman's second solo album, is released on Rolling Stones Records COC 79103 (USA) COC 59105 (UK). Again, the personnel on the album are mostly L.A. session men but they also include Van Morrison, Joe Walsh, Ron Wood, Al Kooper and Bonnie Pointer.

27

Mick in hospital in New York suffering from severe influenza.

28

It is officially confirmed that Ron Wood is The Rolling Stones permanent new guitarist, replacing Mick Taylor and Brian Jones before him.

MARCH
12

The Stones announce details of their European tour.

26

Anita Pallenberg gives birth prematurely to her second son by Keith in Geneva, Switzerland. They name him Tara, after their friend Tara Browne who died in a car accident, but he is a sickly child and only survives for ten weeks.

31

Radio KHJ Los Angeles premiers the Stones' new album, 'Black And Blue' at 6:15pm. The Stones immediately bring an injunction to stop the broadcast to prevent bootleggers getting it on the market before the record is officially released.

APRIL

Dates: Festhalle, Frankfurt, Germany (28-29); Munsterlandhalle, Munster, Germany (30).

'A Quarter To Three', a Bill Wyman solo single, released on Rolling Stones Records RS 191 I9 (UK and USA).

1

Harry Goldsmith receives enough postal applications for tickets for The Rolling Stones' Earls Court concerts to fill the hall 67 times (over one million). The Stones add three extra shows.

6

Krissie Wood and Audrey Burgon are cleared of possessing cocaine. Krissie is charged £12,000 costs. She is three months pregnant and says, "All I want to do now is go home and wait for my baby."

10

The Stones begin rehearsals for their tour at Mougins, in the Côte d'Azur. Keith will join them later, but Billy Preston is present.

20

The new Stones album, 'Black And Blue' is released. It enters the UK charts at No. 30 and reaches No. 2. In the States it enters at No. 26 and goes to the top.

BLACK AND BLUE
A - *Rolling Stones Records COC 59106 (UK) COC 79104 (USA). Released: April 1976. Producer: The Glimmer Twins. Engineers: Keith Harwood, Glyn Johns, Phil McDonald and Lew Hahn. Studios: Tracks 1, 2, 3, 4, 5, 7 and 8: Musicland, Munchen, Germany. Track 6: Rolling Stones Mobile in Rotterdam, Netherlands. Work also done at the Casino, Montreux, Switzerland with Mobile. Recorded: December 12, 1974 - April 2, 1975: track 1: March 30, 1975 / track 2: March 25, 1975 / track 3: December 15, 1974 / track 4: March 31, 1975 / track 5: April 2, 1975 / track 6: January 23 1975 / track 7: December 12, 1974 / track 8: March 29, 1975.*

Side 1: 1. Hot Stuff (Jagger, Richard) / 2. Hand Of Fate (Jagger, Richard) / 3. Cherry Oh Baby (E. Donaldson) / 4. Memory Motel (Jagger, Richard).

Side 2: 5. Hey, Negrita (Jagger, Richard) / 6. Melody (Jagger, Richard) / 7. Fool To Cry (Jagger, Richard) / 8. Crazy Mama (Jagger, Richard).

Notes: Harvey Mandel plays electric guitar on tracks 1 and 4. Wayne Perkins plays electric guitar on tracks 2 and 7. Wayne Perkins plays acoustic guitar on track 4. Ronnie Wood plays electric guitar on tracks 3, 5 and 8. Billy Preston plays piano on tracks 1, 2, 5, 6 and 8. Billy Preston plays organ on tracks 5 and 6. Billy Preston sings backup vocals on tracks 1, 4, 5, 6 and 8.

Billy Preston plays string synthesizer on track 4. Ollie E. Brown plays percussion on tracks 1, 2, 5 and 8. Nicky Hopkins plays piano on track 7. Nicky Hopkins plays organ on track 9.

'Fool To Cry' / 'Crazy Mama' is released in the UK. It enters at No. 26 and reaches number four. In the US the 'B'-side is changed to 'Hot Stuff'. It enters the charts at No. 20 and reaches No. 9.

FOOL TO CRY
Jagger, Richard /
CRAZY MAMA
Jagger, Richard
S - *Rolling Stones Records RS 19121 (UK) ST DSKO 31990 PR (USA). Released: April 1976. Producer: The Glimmer Twins. Studio: Musicland, Munchen, Germany. Recorded: Side A: December 12, 1973 / Side B: March 29, 1975.*

Notes: Taken from the album 'Black and Blue'.

FOOL TO CRY
Jagger, Richard /
HOT STUFF
Jagger, Richard
S - *Rolling Stones Records RS 19304 (USA). Released: April 1976. Producer: The Glimmer Twins. Studio: Musicland, Munchen, Germany. Recorded: Side A: December 12 1973 / Side B: March 30, 1975. Notes: Taken from the album ' Black and Blue'.*

25

The Stones complete rehearsals and go their separate ways before the tour begins three days later in Frankfurt.

MAY
Dates: Osteenhalle, Kiel, Germany (2); Deutschlandhalle, Berlin, Germany

(3); Stadthalle, Bremen, Germany (4); Forêt Nationale, Brussels, Belgium (6-7); The Apollo, Glasgow (10-11); Granby Hall, Leicester (15); New Bingley Hall, Stafford (17-18); Earls Court, London (21-27); Football Stadium, The Hague, Netherlands (29-30).

1

British tabloid interest is still focused on the Stones. The *Daily Mirror* asks Keith if he and Anita plan to get married. He says, "I have been asked so often by the press and by both our families when are we going to get married that I thought we might as well. There are so many papers we have to produce, especially when we travel with the children, that it might just simplify things to have the same name on our passports."

2

The authorities in Hamburg refuse to allow the Stones to play the Congresscentrum, so the concert is switched at the last minute to Kiel.

In an interview in the *Sunday Mirror*, Ron Wood says he is planning to quit Britain. He feels persecuted by the police, particularly after they kicked his door down. "I love Britain, but I haven't lived there since last year mainly because I wouldn't feel safe in my own bed." Keith commented: "I think it was me and Anita the police were after. Before they came into Woody's home, they broke into a little cottage at the end of his garden where I sometimes stay when I'm in Britain. I was out of the country at the time but it looks as though they were hoping to pin something on Woody and me in one go."

Below, left: Ron with Billy Preston.

8

The Stones fly back to London. Mick is in the audience at David Bowie's concert at the Empire Pool, Wembley.

19

Keith writes off his Bentley at 5am when it hits the central barrier of the M1 near Newport Pagnell, Buckinghamshire. Anita, Marlon and Keith emerge unhurt but the police arrest Keith after a "substance" is found in the car.

21

The Stones open at Earls Court and are dissatisfied with the sound and the staging of the concert, which is panned by the critics. Jagger says, "This is the worst toilet I've played in, and I've seen toilets. There just aren't any places to play in London. It really is a problem that we have nowhere else." Princess Margaret goes backstage after the concert and the Stones hold a party afterwards at the Cockney Pride pub in Piccadilly.

JUNE

Dates: Westfalenhalle, Dortmund, Germany (1); Sporthalle, Cologne, Germany (2); The Abattoirs, Paris, France (4-6); Palais des Sports, Lyon, France (9); Barcelona, Spain (11); Parc de Sports de l'Ouest, Nice, France (13); Hallenstadion, Zurich, Switzerland (15); Olympiahalle, Munich, Germany (16-17); Neckarstadion, Stuttgart, Germany (19); Zagreb, Yugoslavia (21-22); Stadthalle, Vienna, Austria (23).

4

Tara, Keith and Anita's ten week old son, dies of a 'flu virus in the hospital in Geneva where he was born. He had been ill since birth. Keith keeps the news secret in order not to disrupt the tour.

9

The "substances" found in Keith's Bentley when he wrote it off on the M1 are identified by the police as cocaine. A rumour somehow reaches the newspapers that the Stones are unwittingly being used as drug couriers though a group less prone to being stopped and searched would seem more suitable for the job. "Drug Smuggling Shock For The Stones" and "Cocaine Hidden In Pop Star's Bentley" headlined the *Daily Mirror*. The coke

was hidden in a silver horn on a bracelet and inside the shell on a string of worry beads, Keith claimed it was "a mystery to me" how they got there. The police were looking for the owners. *The Daily Mirror* said, "Police and Customs men know drug gangs sometimes use pop groups' amplifiers and instruments to smuggle cannabis..."

17

Feminists in Los Angeles protest against the billboard on Sunset Strip advertising 'Black And Blue' which features a bruised girl, tied up.

18

News of the death of Keith and Anita's son Tara appears in the popular press.

28

At 5am, just as Eric Clapton was winding up a recording session at Electric Lady Studios on 8th Street, New York, in walk Mick, Keith, Charlie and Ron Wood. The jam session lasts until noon.

30

Having enjoyed themselves so much at Eric Clapton's studio jam, Mick, Keith, Ron and Charlie return for another seven-hour session, arriving a bit earlier this time and bringing Billy Preston and Ollie Brown with them.

JULY
26

Mick has a birthday party in the house he rents from Andy Warhol, in Montauk, Long Island. Andy and Paul Morrissey bought an oceanfront property there in 1971 consisting of one main lodge house, three smaller ones and a house for the caretakers.

AUGUST

Date: Knebworth House (21).

2

Ron Wood announces that he and Krissie are moving to Los Angeles and that she will have her child there. When they returned from a holiday in France, Krissie was stopped and searched for drugs.

Keith appears in court in Newport Pagnell on three driving offences and possession of cocaine and cannabis. He is remanded until September 6 and released on bail.

19
The Stones hold a sound check at Knebworth and disturb a Girl Guide campfire being held elsewhere in Knebworth Park. The stoutly built Guide Leader complains to the owners. "How can we hold our camp sing-song tonight with that dreadful racket going on?" she demands. When it is pointed out to her that the dreadful racket is, in fact, The Rolling Stones and that her Guides might prefer to listen, she is unimpressed. "I want it stopped," she insists. Eventually she marches up to the stage, elbows her way past security men and grabs Mick Jagger by the arm. "Young man," she shouts, "This noise must stop. My girls can't hear themselves sing." "Fuck off lady," replies Mick, but the Stones stop rehearsing anyway.

21
The Stones headline Knebworth where the support acts include Lynyrd Skynyrd, 10cc, Hot Tuna and Todd Rundgren's Utopia. The stage for the Stones' appearance at Knebworth is built in the shape of a gaping mouth and features a 100 yard long catwalk for Mick to run about on. The audience is over 100,000 and the group don't start their set until 11:30pm, thirty minutes after the concert was due to finish. They don't finish until 1:40am. Among the audience are Jack Nicholson and Paul and Linda McCartney. A police spokesman said, "The fans were as good as gold They were a damn sight better than football

crowds." Asked if this was the final Rolling Stones' concert, Mick said, "If all these people still want to see us who knows what will happen?"

SEPTEMBER
'Apache Woman', a Bill Wyman solo single is released on Rolling Stones Records RS 19303 (USA) RS 19120 (UK).

6
Keith appears in court at Newport Pagnell and is remanded on bail until October 6th.

20
Mick and Ron Wood listen to 150 hours of live concert tape in the studio in Los Angeles, selecting material for a live album.

OCTOBER
2
Mick and Ron in Atlantic Studios, New York, mixing the numbers selected for the live album. While there, they see Joe Cocker on the set of the TV show, *Saturday Night Live*.

6
Keith arrives in court at Newport Pagnell two and a half hours late, giving the excuse that his trousers were not returned from the cleaners on time. Mrs Mary Durbridge, Chairman of the Magistrates is not convinced. She says, "It strikes me as extraordinary that any gentleman of his stature can only afford one pair of trousers" and makes him forfeit his £100 bail. His bail is

renewed at £5,000 when he elects to appear before a jury.

22
Mike Maitland, President of MCA Records, and Mick Jagger meet in Los Angeles to discuss The Rolling Stones new record contract.

25
In an interview with *Woman's Own*, Mick says: "I got married for something to do. I thought it was a good idea... I've never been madly, deeply in love. I wouldn't know what

that feels like. I'm not an emotional person."

30
Krissie Wood has a baby boy, Jesse James, in Hollywood.

DECEMBER
18
Bianca and Andy Warhol finish packing Mick and Bianca's belongings at their suite in the Pierre Hotel and move them to the house that Mick has bought on 72nd Street. "It must be costing them a fortune,

this little house," comments Warhol. Bianca flies out to Montauk in a private plane.

24
Mick and Bianca eat Christmas dinner at Fred Hughes's flat on Lexington Avenue, New York. Carroll Baker, Paloma Picasso, Andy Warhol et al are also guests.

Below: Keith, Anita and their son Marlon.

1977

JANUARY
10 - 11
Keith appears in court at Aylesbury in connection with the drugs found in his car after he crashed it. He claims that he didn't know the drugs were there.

12
Despite an eloquent speech by his expensive council, Sir Peter Rawlinson, Keith is found guilty of possessing cocaine. However, he is cleared of the LSD charge. He is fined £750 plus costs of £250. Keith later commented, "In my court appearance at Aylesbury Assizes, the jury was incredibly young. I had been expecting a whole panel of housewives. But most of them were young and one chick was crying."

22
The *News of the World* somehow obtains stills from Robert Frank's movie *Cocksucker Blues* and Mick Jagger, Keith Richard, Charlie Watts and Bill Wyman take out an injunction to stop them from publishing them.

23
Robert Frank complains that Stones lawyers have asked him to return his own personal copy of *Cocksucker Blues*. He said, "I have refused. I regard the copy I have as my property and do not intend to return it."

Mick Jagger and Andy Warhol bump into each other shopping in Paris.

25
Mick and Bianca hold a Christmas party at their house on 72nd Street, New York. John Lennon and Yoko Ono, Halston and Loulou de la Falaise, Paloma Picasso, Andy Warhol and entourage are guests.

27
Bill Wyman sees Lynyrd Skynyd at the Rainbow Theatre, London and attends the party afterwards.

FEBRUARY
5
The Stones fly to Paris, then on to New York and eventually Los Angeles on a business trip to complete their new recording contract and to check out recording studios in which to finish mixing their live album.

In New York, Mick and Bernie Taupin, Elton John's lyricist, attend a concert by Queen at Madison Square Garden.

16
The Stones announce their new recording contract with EMI who will distribute everything on The Rolling Stones Records label throughout the world with the exception of North America. EMI are to get six albums and some publishing rights on the Jagger-Richards song catalogue. "In this Jubilee year, I think it only fitting that we sign with a British company," said Jagger, though the group almost signed with Polydor, only backing out when Polydor leaked news of the signing at Cannes.

17
Mick flies into Los Angeles on business. He spends the night with Bianca in Malibu before flying out the next day.

18
Keith fined £25 for driving without tax when he crashed his Bentley and arrested for drugs on May 19, 1976.

24
Keith and Anita arrive in Toronto, Canada. Anita is dressed in a very flamboyant outfit and attracts considerable attention by the fact that she is accompanied by 28 pieces of luggage. She is arrested when cannabis and heroin are found in one of the cases. She is released on a promise-to-appear notice.

27
After giving Keith a couple of days to score, Royal Canadian Mounted Police raid his rooms at the Harbour Castle Hotel and arrest both Keith and Anita for possession of heroin for re-sale. It takes the Mounties two hours before they can locate Keith's suite because, as usual, he has registered under another name and has booked a number of suites in the hotel as "floaters". Keith is released on $1,000 bail and Anita released with no bail being paid. If Keith is found guilty, he could go to jail for life.

MARCH
2
There is a party for Alan Dunn, the Stones' senior roadie, at the Harbour Castle Hotel, which all the Stones attend.

3
Anita's court appearance in Toronto for importing heroin and cannabis is postponed until March 14th. The Stones, especially Mick, are reported to be very despondent, fearing that Keith will go down for a long time, ruining the band and making their new live album their last.

4
The Stones play the El Mocambo Club in Toronto before an invited audience of 300 winners of a radio competition: "Why I Would Like To Go To A Party With The Rolling Stones." The concert is recorded for the live album. Mick says, "I wish we could make money doing gigs like this."

In the audience is Margaret Trudeau, wife of the Prime Minister who throws a party for them after the concert in the suite at the Harbour Castle Hotel that she has taken in order to be near them. She says, "It's quite a buzz, I've always been a Rolling Stones fan." Charlie Watts comments, "I wouldn't want my wife associating with us."

Though it is denied that Keith's drug bust has anything to do with it, Robert Stigwood announces the withdrawal of his $7,000,000 offer for the North American rights to the Stones catalogue. It is also rumoured that the EMI deal is in jeopardy if Keith goes to jail.

5
The Stones second gig at the El Mocambo Club is recorded for a live album. Girls climb on stage and feel Jagger's crotch. The next day he said, "It was fun on stage last night but all these girls were grabbing my balls. Once they started they didn't stop. It was great up to a point, then it got very difficult to sing." Afterwards the Stones and Margaret Trudeau go on to a private party together.

6
Talking about Margaret Trudeau, Mick says: "She just dropped by. Someone said she wanted to come to the gig, so we took her. I had never met her before but I guess she likes to go out to clubs and go rocking and rolling like everyone else - a young girl, you know."

7
Keith appears in court and is told that the second substance they seized in their raid has been analysed and is cocaine: a fifth of an ounce of it. Keith is attacked and grabbed by the hair outside the court. Things look very serious for Keith and the group holds a band meeting to plan for the future.

The Canadian dollar falls against the US dollar, said to be because of the alleged affair between Margaret Trudeau and Mick Jagger.

8
Keith appears in court at a private hearing. The date is still not set for his trial.

Canadian Customs refuse to allow Mick Jagger to take a flight to New York. Members of Mick's staff have to go to the airport in the early hours to exert pressure.

9
The remaining Stones, with the exception of Keith and Anita, fly to New York City. Margaret Trudeau also flies to New York to stay with her friend Princess Yasmin Khan on Central Park West. She is mobbed by the press when she and the Princess go to see Mikhail Baryshnikov dance at the City Center on West 55th Street.

Above left: 1975 American tour with Billy Preston.

10

Mick Jagger releases a statement to the press which says, "Margaret Trudeau is a very attractive and nice person but we are not having an affair. I never met her before and haven't seen her since I got to New York. In fact I haven't seen her since Sunday. What can I say? I'm in New York to be with my wife and daughter."

In the *Toronto Sun*, Margaret Trudeau says, "I'm very fond of him. I'd like to think he is a friend. But after all, I'm a married lady."

In the *New York Daily News*, gossip columnist Suzi suggests that it is Ron Wood, not Mick Jagger, that Margaret Trudeau is after.

11

Finally Pierre Trudeau, the Canadian Prime Minister, tells the *Toronto Sun:* "I think that if she goes to rock concerts she has to expect to be noticed and written about. I have no complaints about that, but I believe that my wife's private life is her affair and mine." He says that her engagements have been cancelled for an indefinite period and that she "wants to take the pressure off and become a private person for a while."

12

Margaret Trudeau flies to Ottowa from New York City. Peter Rudge, in charge of the Stones touring party, says, "I don't want her round us one minute longer. I'll be glad when she is as far away from us as possible." Mick and Bianca attend a cast party at Halston's apartment after his fashion show. Mick leaves early. An exhibition of Andy Warhol's signed silk-screens of Mick Jagger opens at the Pigeonhole Gallery on the Kings Road, Chelsea. The works are £3,700 each.

13

Photographer Annie Leibowitz keeps Keith up all night taking photographs for *Rolling Stone* magazine. He finally collapses with a needle in his arm and the next day he nods out in court from exhaustion, creating a wonderful impression.

14

Anita appears in court in Toronto on her initial charge of importing drugs and is fined $400. She says, "The judge was kind to me." The court retains her passport and begins deportation proceedings against her. Meanwhile, in another court, Keith is further remanded on bail until June 27.

18

In New York Mick and Bianca, Bill and Astrid Wyman, Ron and Krissie Wood hit the town. They watch Iggy Pop's concert at the Palladium from backstage where they can get a good view of David Bowie playing piano, then continue to The Eagles concert at Madison Square Garden.

26

The drugs squad raid Keith's house in Cheyne Walk, Chelsea, but find nothing. Keith hasn't been there for three months.

APRIL

1

Keith and Anita are permitted to fly to New York from Toronto to receive treatment for his drug addiction and attend important business matters.

The Rolling Stones re-sign with Atlantic Records for North America in a deal said to be worth $21 million over six albums. It is announced that Earl McGrath will replace Marshall Chess as head of Rolling Stones Records.

5

Mick is a dinner guest at Fred Hughes' apartment. Other guests include Andy Warhol, Diana Vreeland, Earl McGrath and Caroline Kennedy.

6

The Andy Warhol print of Mick Jagger is shown on the Barbara Walters TV show when Walters interviews the Empress of Iran about her art collection. The Empress says, "I like to keep modern."

10

Mick and Jade attend an Easter party given by Marsia Trinder and Lenny Holzer on Central Park West. They all play "hunt the Easter egg".

26

Mick drops in on Peter Frampton

who is recording at Electric Lady studios in the Village.

MAY

2

Halston holds a birthday party at Studio 54 for Bianca. Mick gives her a white horse as a present.

15

Ron Wood sees Muddy Waters at the Roxy in Los Angeles.

25

The Stones regroup in New York to begin editing live tapes for their next album.

JUNE

12

Back in Britain, Charlie plays a charity concert with a group of jazz musicians at the Swindon Arts Centre. He tells the press, "I have always liked this type of music. I listen to a lot of jazz and blues records, especially Charlie Parker when I'm at home. If we'd had about four gigs together then the sound would have been a lot better."

20

Mick and Keith begin mixing the 'Love You Live' at Atlantic Studios in New York.

27

Keith fails to turn up at a court hearing in Toronto called to fix the date of his trial because he is still undergoing treatment for drug addiction at the Stevens Clinic at Sutton Place in New York. Judge Gordon Tinker demands evidence of progress in his cure and says "I intend to treat Mr. Richard like everyone else." The hearing is postponed until July 19.

28

Mick and Jerry Hall attend a dinner party given by Peter Beard at the "21" in New York. Andy Warhol was there and wrote, "I thought things were fishy with Mick and Jerry, then the plot started to thicken. Mick was so out of it that I could tell the waiters were scared he'd pass out. His head was so far back he was singing to himself. The top part of his body was like jelly and the bottom half was tapping 3,000 taps a minute. He was putting his sunglasses on and off... I found out later from Fred [Hughes] that he's really passionately in love with Jerry, and it looks like there's trouble for Bianca."

Above: Mick with Angie Bowie at David Bowie's post-Ziggy 'retirement' party, the Cafe Royal, London, July 4, 1973. Below: Mick with Bianca Jagger.

JULY
2
Mick attempts to halt the publication of *The Man Who Killed Mick Jagger* by David Littlejohn, Associate Dean of the University of California, saying that it might encourage a crazy person to try it.

18
Mick visits the Pathé Marconi studios in Paris, looking for studios in which to record the Stones' next album.

Ron Wood's home in Richmond, The Wick, is sold for £300,000.

19
Keith's hearing in Toronto is postponed until December 2 after he again fails to turn up in court.

24
At the Montreux International Jazz Festival, in Switzerland, Bill Wyman plays on stage with the Clarence Brown Band.

AUGUST
25
The *Daily Mirror* reports that Mick and Bianca are on the Greek island of Hydra, trying to save their marriage, but are seen sitting at separate tables in local discos. A friend, photographer Nick Karantilion, tells the *Mirror*: "They both seemed very unhappy. Mick was in a very distressed mood. After spending an evening with them I am convinced they are busting up."

SEPTEMBER
12
Mick gives a press conference to promote 'Love You Live' at the Savoy Hotel in London.

13
'Love You Live' is launched with a promotional party at the Marquee Club in London. All the Stones except Keith attend.

14
Buddy Holly's old backing group, The Crickets, play the Kilburn Gaumont, London, as part of Paul McCartney's annual Buddy Holly Week. Mick and Ron Wood are in the audience.

A number of newspapers run interviews with Mick Jagger as part of the publicity for the new album. He tells the *Daily Express* that Keith "has been having treatment in a New York hospital and has now finished it. At present he is living in the country outside New York. We all know Keith could get nothing or life imprisonment. If he got life, I would carry on with the band but I don't know what I'd do. I'd be very upset. I'm sure Keith could write in prison, he'd have nothing else to do. I think the law's out to get us. Once you get any notoriety it seems to happen." He tells the London *Evening Standard*, "Rock'n'roll music is for adolescents. It's adolescent music. It's a dead end. I think the whole history of rock'n'roll has proved that. There is nothing wrong with it, but it's just for kids. My whole life isn't rock'n'roll. It's an absurd idea that it should be. But it's no more than anybody's whole life might revolve around working in Woolworth's. Keith Richard is the original punk rocker. You can't really out-punk Keith. It's a useless gesture."

16
'Love You Live' released. It enters the UK charts at No. 18 and reaches No. 3. In the States it enters at No. 18 and gets to No. 5. Andy Warhol designed the sleeve.

**LOVE YOU LIVE
(Double Album)**
A - Rolling Stones Records
COC 89101 (UK), COC 2-9001 (USA).
Released: September 1977.
Producer: The Glimmer Twins.
Engineers: Keith Harwood, Eddie Kramer, Ron Nevison, Dave Jordan, Jimmy Douglas.
Studios: Live recordings, Paris, 1976-7. Side 3 recorded at the El Mocambo Club, Toronto, Canada, 1977, March 4 and 5, 1977.

Side 1: 1. (Introduction) Excerpt from 'Fanfare For The Common Man' by Aaron Copeland / 2. Honky Tonk Woman (Jagger, Richard) / 3. If You Can't Rock Me (Jagger, Richard) / 4. Get Off Of My Cloud (Jagger, Richard) / 5. Happy (Jagger, Richard) / 6. Hot Stuff (Jagger, Richard) / 7. Star Star (Jagger, Richard).

Side 2: 8. Tumbling Dice (Jagger, Richard) / 9. Fingerprint File (Jagger, Richard) / 10. You Gotta Move (McDowell, Davis) / 11. You Can't Always Get What You Want (Jagger, Richard).

Side 3: 12. Manish Boy (London, McDaniel, Morganfield) / 13. Crackin' Up (McDaniel) / 14. Little Red Rooster (Dixon) / 15. Around And Around (Berry).

Side 4: 16. It's Only Rock 'n' Roll (Jagger, Richard) / 17. Brown Sugar (Jagger, Richard) / 18. Jumpin' Jack Flash (Jagger, Richard) / 19. Sympathy For The Devil (Jagger, Richard).

Notes: Also on the album are Billy Preston, playing keyboards and singing backup vocals. Ian Stewart on piano and Ollie Brown playing percussion.

20
BBC TV *Old Grey Whistle Test* screens an hour long live Stones concert filmed in Paris in 1976.

23
The documentary film *Ladies and Gentlemen, The Rolling Stones* has its European premier at the Rainbow Theatre in London.

27
'Love You Live' is launched in New York by the Stones with a party at the Trax Club.

29
Andy Warhol photographs The Rolling Stones at the Factory.

OCTOBER
6
Keith and Ron Wood fly to Paris from Washington DC on Concorde to join the rest of the Stones who are already there preparing to record a new album. Keith takes a cab to the apartment he owns in Paris but can't remember the exact address and has to telephone the Stones' office in New York to get it.

10
The Stones begin recording sessions at the Pathé Marconi studios in Paris.

19
It is reported in the French press that Mick is going out with Brian Ferry's girlfriend Jerry Hall, the Texan model.

28
Mick is in the audience at the Lyceum Ballroom, London, to see the Stiff Records Package Show featuring Elvis Costello, Ian Dury, Nick Lowe and Wreckless Eric.

NOVEMBER
17
In London, Bianca buys a Cecil Beaton print of Mick Jagger, taken during the filming of *Performance*, at a Sotheby's auction.

26
The Stones take a break from recording sessions so that Keith can attend a court session in Toronto. Mick flies to Tangier, Morocco with Jerry Hall.

Above: Mick with Andy Warhol at the 'Love You Live' launch party at Trax in New York, September 27, 1977. Left: all the band at the same party.

DECEMBER

2
Keith appears in court in Toronto and is remanded to a hearing in a higher court in February 1978. In court he says that he has made repeated efforts to get off drugs, but that every time the band goes on tour he begins to take them again.

5
The Stones get back to work at Pathé Marconi studios.

11
Bianca flies to New York from London on Concorde. Rumours of divorce fill the popular press.

21
The Stones take a Christmas break from recording. Mick and Jerry Hall spend Christmas in London. Keith and Anita fly back to New York.

27
Mick and Jerry Hall fly to Barbados for a winter vacation.

1978

JANUARY

6
Mick and Jerry Hall fly to New York, then on to London. Bianca is reported to be clubbing with Bjorn Borg in New York.

25
Mick is involved in a fight with a photographer outside the Elysée Matignon Club in Paris. Mick throws the first punch but the photographer knocks him to the ground.

26
Ron Wood signs with CBS Records for solo work. The contract is finalised at the MIDEM Festival in Cannes.

27
Charlie Watts is back in Swindon, playing behind Bob Hall and George Green. The Rolling Stones Mobile is on hand to record the gig which is released in a limited edition in August as 'Jamming The Boogie'.

FEBRUARY

3
Bianca issues a statement to the press through her agent: "There is

no disagreement between us and we are tired of the harassment and falsely attributed statements."

6
Keith's lawyers get the date of his court appearance in Toronto moved to March 6.

15
William Seward, the officer who arrested Keith in Toronto, is killed in an automobile accident.

16
Ron's wife Krissie is hospitalised after a car crash in London.

MARCH

1
Mick offers to pay a reward for the return of the jewellery he gave Jerry Hall for Christmas. She lost a bracelet and ear-rings on the Paris Metro.

3
The Stones finish recording their new album at Pathé Marconi Studios. Mick and Keith stay on in Paris to mix the tapes then fly to New York to do the final mix at Atlantic Studios. Charlie returns to London, Ron Wood flies to Los Angeles and Bill and Astrid fly to Barbados for a holiday.

6
A date is finally fixed for Keith's trial. He will appear in the High Court on October 23.

9
Krissie Wood files for divorce against Ron, citing a model Jo Howard as co-respondent.

APRIL

3
Mick and Jerry Hall, Margaret Trudeau and Tom Sullivan attend the Academy Awards party given by Polaroid at Studio 54 and hosted by Truman Capote and Andy Warhol.

8
Andy Warhol and Bob Colacello take Mick and Jerry to dinner at La Grenouille in New York. Afterwards Mick takes them back to the Pierre Hotel where he now lives after breaking up with Bianca. They pick up the new Stones record from Earl McGrath's house and take it to

Studio 54 to play it, arriving very late. Shortly after this Mick and Jerry move to the Carlyle Hotel where Jerry is registered as "Miss Philips".

19
Ian Stewart joins Alexis Korner on stage for the latter's 50th Birthday concert in London.

27
Mick and Keith fly to Jamaica to see the One Love Peace Concert. They have signed Jamaican reggae singer Peter Tosh to Rolling Stones Records.

MAY

TIME WAITS FOR NO ONE: ANTHOLOGY 1971-1977
Compilation

C - Rolling Stones Records COC 59107 (UK).
Released: May 1978.
Producers: Tracks: 1, 7, 8, 9 and 10 by The Glimmer Twins. Tracks 2, 3, 4, 5 and 6 by Jimmy Miller.
Recorded: Track 2: 1971. Track 3: 1972. Tracks 4, 5 and 6: 1973. Track 1: 1974. Tracks 8, 9 and 10: 1976. Track 7: 1977.

Side 1: 1. Time Waits For No One (Jagger, Richard) / 2. Bitch (Jagger, Richard) / 3. All Down The Line (Jagger, Richard) / 4. Dancing With Mr. D (Jagger, Richard) / 5. Angie (Jagger, Richard).

Side 2: 6. Star Star (Jagger, Richard) / 7. If You Can't Rock Me / Get Off Of My Cloud (Jagger, Richard) / 8. Hand Of Fate (Jagger, Richard) / 9. Crazy Mama (Jagger, Richard) / 10. Fool To Cry (Jagger, Richard).

Notes: This is the second compilation on Rolling Stones Records to feature 'Angie' and 'Bitch', which were both on 'Made In The Shade'.

Below: Keith attracts headline without the words 'drugs' or 'charges' sensation.

5

Mick is in the audience when Muddy Waters plays the Roxy in Los Angeles.

14

Bianca files for divorce against Mick in London.

The Stones rehearse at Todd Rundgren's Bearsville compound near Woodstock, New York. The arrangements are not up to scratch but they have little choice but to continue there. Keith is badly strung out on heroin and much of the band effort is devoted to helping him kick his habit.

19

'Miss You' / 'Far Away Eyes' released on Rolling Stones Records. It enters the US charts and peaks at No. 2. It enters at No. 23 in the USA and gets to the top.

MISS YOU Jagger, Richard / GIRL WITH THE FARAWAY EYES Jagger, Richard
S - EMI 2802 (UK) Rolling Stones Records RS 19306 (USA).
Released: May 1978 (12" version released June 1978 as 12EM12808 and released in USA as ST-DSKO 35247-PR).
Producer: The Glimmer Twins.
Studio: EMI Paris and the Rolling Stones Mobile Unit.
Notes: Both tracks taken from the forthcoming 'Some Girls' album.

JUNE

Dates: Civic Center, Lakeland, Florida (10); Fox Theater, Atlanta, Georgia (12); Capitol Theater, Passaic, New Jersey; (14); Warner Theater, Washington, D.C. (15); John F. Kennedy Stadium, Philadelphia, Pennsylvania (17); The Palladium, New York City (19); The Coliseum, Hampton Roads, Virginia (21); Convention Center, Myrtle Beach, South Carolina (22); Midsouth Coliseum, Memphis, Tennessee (28); Rupp Arena, Lexington, Kentucky (29).

9

'Some Girls' is released on Rolling Stones Records. It enters the UK album charts at No. 11 and reaches No. 2. In the States it enters at No. 18 and goes to the top. Keith comments: "The reason that 'Some

Girls' was a hit was because I'd kicked junk. We hadn't been in the studio for some time and everybody, including most of the Stones, were thinking, 'Oh well, Keith has finally ridden himself into the dirt.' We got together for that. We threw ourselves together working in a great studio in Paris. It was just another one of those things that it was impossible to put your finger on. But it worked."

SOME GIRLS
A - Rolling Stones Records CUN 39108 (UK and USA)
Released: June 1978
Producer: The Glimmer Twins.
Engineers: Chris Kimsey except track 8: Dave Jordan. Assistant engineers: Barry Sage, Ben King.
Studios: EMI Studios, Paris, and on the Rolling Stones Mobile Unit.

Side 1: 1. Miss You (Jagger, Richard) / 2. When The Whip Comes Down (Jagger, Richard) / 3. Imagination (Whitfield, Strong) / 4. Some Girls (Jagger, Richard) / 5. Lies (Jagger, Richard).

Side 2: 6. Far Away Eyes (Jagger, Richard) / 7. Respectable (Jagger, Richard) / 8. Before They Make Me Run (Jagger, Richard) / 9. Beast Of Burden (Jagger, Richard) / 10. Shattered (Jagger, Richard).

Notes: Ian 'Mac' McLagan plays piano on track 1. Ian 'Mac' McLagan plays Hammond organ on track 3. Mel Collins plays sax on track 1. Sugar Blue plays harmonica on tracks 1 and 4. Some details of the original sleeve had to be changed for legal reasons. After the initial release there was an interim sleeve before the final one.

17

Mick has 'flu and performs in Philadelphia against specific orders from his doctor not to go on. After the concert he flies to New York

and sees Bob Marley play Madison Square Garden.

28

Keith is asked why their new album is called 'Some Girls'. He replies: "Because we couldn't remember their fucking names."

29

At the Lexington, Kentucky, concert one fan is shot and seventeen arrested in a confrontation with the police.

JULY

Dates: Municipal Stadium, Cleveland, Ohio (1); Rich Stadium, Buffalo, New York (4); Orchard Park, New York (5); Masonic Temple, Detroit, Michigan (6); Soldiers Field, Chicago, Illinois (8); The Coliseum, St. Paul, Minnesota (10); Keil Auditorium, St. Louis, Missouri (11); Louisiana Super Dome, New Orleans, Louisiana (13); Folsom Field, Boulder, Colorado (16); Will Rogers Memorial Center, Fort Worth, Texas (18); Sam Houston, Coliseum, Houston, Texas (19); Community Center, Tucson, Arizona (21); Anaheim Stadium, Los Angeles, California (23-24); Oakland Coliseum, Oakland, California (26).

Raquel Welch and Lucille Ball threaten legal action against the Stones, Atlantic Records and EMI, claiming that the images of themselves which appear through cut-outs on the sleeve of "Some Girls" are unflattering and humiliating. The sleeves are withdrawn and the offending images blacked out. These are then replaced with a temporary sleeve bearing the message "Please accept our apologies. We are being reconstructed."

Meanwhile some Black radio stations refuse to play tracks from the album because they find the lyrics to the title track racist.

5

At the upstate New York gig, fans riot when the Stones refuse to play an encore.

8

Mick attends a Lefty Dizz concert at the Kingston Mines in Chicago.

9

Mick, Keith, Ron and Charlie all join Muddy Waters on stage at his gig at the Quiet Knight in Chicago.

10

While leaving the stage after the concert in St. Paul, Bill falls nine feet and is knocked unconscious. He spends the night in the local hospital. X-rays show he has broken a knuckle in his left hand as well as cut his head and torn a shoulder muscle. He is ordered to rest for a month but discharges himself the next morning and plays the remaining nine shows with his fingers taped up.

17

The Stones fly into Dallas and check into the Fairmont Hotel. Tickets for the show are being sold for as much as $300 to desperate fans.

18

Jagger tells the audience in Fort Worth, Texas, "If the band's slightly lacking in energy, it's because we spent all last night fucking. We do our best." After the show, there is an all-night party in honour of Ian Stewart's birthday. Chet Flippo reported, "Someone had rounded up a bunch of incredibly glossy, high-tech, sex-drenched, friendly Dallas female Stones fans. 'We are the encore,' one of them told me. She said she was there because 'The Stones are the only ones that still make me quiver and shake'."

19

The Stones fly to Houston in their private Convair 580 turbo-prop. They fly back to the Fairmont Hotel in Dallas after the show.

21

In her home town, Linda Ronstadt joins the Stones on stage to duet with Mick on 'Tumblin' Dice'.

22

The Stones fly into Los Angeles and check into the Westwood Marquis. That night Mick, Jerry Hall, Mick's daughter Jade and Diana Ross attend Bob Marley's concert at the Starlite Amphitheater in Burbank.

24

The Stones are joined on stage by Nicky Hopkins and Bobby Keys at their second night in L.A.

25

Mick's share of the concert money from the Los Angeles concerts is frozen by a Los Angeles judge until Marsha Hunt's suit to increase Mick's weekly child support for their daughter Karis from £8.50 to £300 is settled. Marsha Hunt is represented by the Hollywood lawyer Marvin Mitchelson, a specialist in divorce and child support cases.

26

Mick and Jerry Hall stay with tour promoter Bill Graham for a few days in his house at Corte Madera, Marin County outside San Francisco. Brian Jones' 14 year old son Julian joins them there.

AUGUST
1

The Stones are in Los Angeles for a month to mix the live tapes recorded during the tour at the RCA Studios and record new material.

7

Les Perrin, publicist for the Stones from the early years, dies in London at the age of 57.

28

'Beast of Burden' / 'When The Whip Comes Down' released in the USA. It enters the charts at No. 27 and gets to No. 7.

BEAST OF BURDEN Jagger, Richard / WHEN THE WHIP COMES DOWN Jagger, Richard
S - Rolling Stones Records RS 19309 (USA).
Released: August 1978.
Producer: The Glimmer Twins.
Studios: EMI Paris and the Rolling Stones Mobile unit.

Notes: both tracks taken from the album 'Some Girls'.

SEPTEMBER

The Stones begin recording at Wally Heider's Studio in Hollywood. It is thought that they are stockpiling material in case Keith is jailed.

Keith and Ron are reported to have recorded with Alice Cooper, who is in the studio in Los Angeles working on his new album, 'From The Inside'.

At 5:00am, Mick and Jerry Hall are disturbed by noises coming from a closet in their rented Los Angeles mansion. Mick investigates and sees a "bare, dark leg" sticking out. He slams the door and runs downstairs with Jerry to call the police. The man runs past them, making what Jerry describes as "a very crazy sound" and appears to be naked except for his shoes and socks. They identify the man as James Harrington, a 26 year old black belt karate expert who was Jagger's bodyguard on their last tour. $10,000 in jewellery and $3,000 cash is stolen. Harrington is arrested five days later in Queens, New York, and brought to trial.

Keith rents a house in Laurel Canyon and wakes up to find the bedroom filled with smoke. There had been a big party and someone had not-quite turned off a gas fire. The leaking gas was eventually ignited by a stick of incense burning in the room.

Keith: "I'm in the bedroom with the flavour of the month, my girlfriend of the hour. I wake up and the room's full of smoke... I open the door to the bedroom and I'm looking at a fireball rushing down the corridor towards the oxygen... and me!" Keith throws his girlfriend out of the window and follows her as fire engulfs the room. "There's the two of us stark naked. Half the house is already destroyed, the roof is falling in on us but we've managed to get through - with a few burns here and there - to the swimming pool... Stark fucking bollock naked with this blonde, bless her heart, good girl, solid gold, saying to me, 'Do something'. And I said, 'What d'you want me to do? Piss on it?'" Just as he hears the unwelcome sound of police sirens, "Suddenly this car stops and it's Anita's cousin! And I never know how she recognised me because she could only see my cock! And she goes, 'Get in!' and she just scooped us up and whisked me off so nobody could find me for a couple of days."

The house burns to the ground except, miraculously, part of the wardrobe containing Keith's passport, jewellery, a gun and 500 rounds of ammo plus his favourite tapes, all of which are retrieved by an assistant from the smoking ruin the next day.

13

Bill and Charlie attend the funeral in London of Keith Moon, drummer with The Who, who died on September 7.

15

'Respectable' / 'When The Whip Comes Down' released in the UK. It enters the charts at No. 26 but only reaches number No. 22.

RESPECTABLE
Jagger, Richard / WHEN THE WHIP COMES DOWN
Jagger, Richard
S- EMI 2861 (UK).
Released: September 1978.
Producer: The Glimmer Twins.
Studios: EMI Paris and the Rolling Stones Mobile unit.

Notes: Both tracks taken from the 'Some Girls' album.

29

Peter Tosh's single '(You Gotta Walk) Don't Look Back' is released on Rolling Stones Records with Mick singing backup vocals.

OCTOBER
3

The controversy over the lyrics to 'Some Girls' continues. It is reported in the press that Mick wrote the song after spending a night with two black girls. The lyrics read, "Black girls want to get fucked all night, but I just don't have that much jam..."

7

The Reverend Jesse Jackson campaigns against 'Some Girls' saying "It is an insult to our race and degrading to our women." He demands that the album be

withdrawn. Mick maintains that the whole thing is a parody citing that the other lyrics parody other received stereotypes about women.

20

Mick flies to London.

Keith spends his last two days before appearing in court resting quietly at his country property, Frog Hollow in South Salem, Westchester County outside New York.

22

Jo Howard gives birth to a daughter, Leah, by Ron Wood in Los Angeles.

Keith and his girlfriend Lilly fly into Toronto in a private Lear jet and check into the Four Seasons Hotel.

23

Keith appears in court in Toronto before Judge Lloyd Graburn. He arrives with two of the most famous members of the Canadian entertainment community: producer Lorne Michaels and Dan Akroyd from the TV show *Saturday Night Live*. The Canadian authorities are clearly embarrassed by the international spotlight focused on the case and are doing their best to

get rid of the problem. The Justice Department muzzled the Royal Canadian Mounted Police by forbidding them from making use of Richard's lengthy previous record and after successful behind the scenes plea bargaining, the Crown Prosecutor was told that Keith would be charged only with possession of heroin; the charges of trafficking and possession of a large amount of cocaine would be dropped. Keith pleads guilty to possession of heroin. It is generally thought among the old time court reporters that an expensive, complicated fix was on, one which possibly emanated from the highest levels of government.

A doctor testifies that Keith and Anita were in "a desperate condition from opium abuse" when they arrived in Canada. Prince Rupert Loewenstein, Keith's financial adviser, provided documents showing that Keith's casual spending had gone from $170,000 in 1975, to $300,000 in 1976 and $350,000 in 1977, almost all of it going on drugs. The Turning Point Clinic, where he had kicked his habit using the black box method gave a lengthy testimonial saying how well he was doing.

In his speech in Keith's defence, his lawyer, Austin Cooper, says, "He should not be dealt with as a special person, but I ask your honour to understand him as a creative tortured person, as a major contributor to art form. He turned to heroin to prop up a sagging existence. I ask you to understand the whole man. He has fought a tremendous personal battle to rid himself of this terrible problem." Sylvia Plath, Vincent Van Gogh, Aldous Huxley, Judy Garland and F.Scott Fitzgerald are all cited as creative individuals under great strain. Keith tells the judge, "If you want to get off it, you will, and this time I really wanted it to work. I've got to stay on the treatment if I want to stay off it for good." He promises to donate $1,000,000 to a drug rehabilitation clinic.

Judge Graburn says he will give his verdict at 10am the next day. "This is a matter of great importance to Keith Richards and Canada," he tells the court.

24

Judge Graburn tells the court that Keith was arrested with a very large quantity of heroin and says, "The Crown seeks a jail term, but I will not incarcerate him for addiction and wealth... No jail or fine is appropriate." Citing the successful drug cure he orders that Keith be free to create his music and complete his treatment for addiction. He gives Keith one year probation, no fine and no jail term. He is to continue his treatment at the Turning Point Clinic and to report to his probation officer within 24 hours and at dates over the next year. He is ordered to give a benefit performance for the Canadian

Institute for the Blind within the next six months.

Later, in a television interview, Keith theorised that the judge had made his decision because of "the Blind Angel". Keith said, "This little chick from Toronto was totally blind but there was nothing that would stop this girl from turning up at gigs. So I'd fix her up, 'give the girl a ride', because I just had visions of her being run over. God knows what could happen to a blind chick on the road. This chick went to the judge's house in Toronto, personally, and she told him this simple story. And from there, he figured out the way to get Canada and himself and myself out of the whole mess."

Keith flies back to New York that night and sees himself on television.

25

Keith sees Rockpile, Nick Lowe and Dave Edmunds' band, play the Bottom Line, a small Greenwich Village club. The audience cheer him and send him drinks. Keith jams on 'Let It Rock' and 'Down Down Down'. As he leaves the club, a number of New York police shake his hand and congratulate him.

26

Mick flies out of London to Jamaica before Bianca's represent-atives can serve divorce papers on him. A spokesman says, "I think Mick Jagger left as soon as he heard they were after him. He has a feeling about these sort of things."

28

The Stones issue a press release: "It never occurred to us that our parody of certain stereotypical attitudes would be taken seriously by anyone who has heard the entire lyrics of the song in question. No insult was intended and if any was taken, we sincerely apologise."

Ahmet Ertegun, chairman of Atlantic Records says, "Mick Jagger is certainly not a racist. He is con-sciously anti-racist. He owes his whole being to black people and black music." Ertegun urges the Stones to re-edit the track but they refuse. Jagger's private views are reported as "If you can't take a joke, it's too fucking bad."

29

Keith flies to Jamaica from New York. Mick flies to New York from Jamaica.

In Canada, the right wing press campaign against the leniency of Keith's sentence. *The Toronto Sun* says, "Imagine the laughter among Rolling Stones fans throughout the world... Their hero got busted and got off." This was countered by the *Toronto Globe* which praised the verdict as "a model of enlightened sentencing, one which should pave the way for a more equitable and civilised treatment of convicted drug addicts in Canadian courts."

NOVEMBER

**SHATTERED Jagger,
Richards / EVERYTHING
IS TURNING TO GOLD**
Jagger, Richards
*S - Rolling Stones Records RS 19310.
Released: November 1978.
Producer: The Glimmer Twins.
Side 1: From the album 'Some Girls' /
Side 2: Later appeared on 'Sucking
In The Seventies'.*

22
In Toronto, Crown Prosecutor
John Scollin wins an extension until
May 3, 1979, to appeal against Judge
Lloyd Graburn's sentence.

29
'Shattered' / 'Everything Is Turning
To Gold' is released in the USA on
Rolling Stones Records. It enters
the US charts at No. 27, but does
not climb.

DECEMBER
3
Mick and Jerry Hall fly to
Washington D.C. for the first annual
Kennedy Center Awards Gala.

Keith's first solo single 'Run Rudolph
Run' (Richard) / 'The Harder They
Come' (Richard) is released in the
States as Rolling Stones Records
RSR 102.

10
Ian Stewart, Charlie Watts and
Alexis Korner all play in a Big Band
assembled to celebrate the fiftieth
anniversary of boogie woogie at
Dingwall's Dance Hall in Camden
Town, London.

15
The Japanese authorities
announce that they have withdrawn
their ban on The Rolling Stones.

18
Keith throws a party in New York
to celebrate his 35th birthday and his
freedom, then returns to London to
spend Christmas with his family.

25
Mick is in Hong Kong for Christmas.

1979

JANUARY
18
The Stones fly to Nassau in the
Bahamas where they are to record
their new album at Compass Point
Studios.

23
Mick is ordered to pay $1,500

a week to Marsha Hunt in child
support for their daughter Karis by
a Los Angeles court.

24
Mick is granted an eviction order
against the caretakers of his former
home, Stargroves. Although they
had worked for Jagger for ten
years, Mr and Mrs White had not
been informed that the house was
sold until the estate agents told
them. Mick waived the order for
28 days to give them time to find
somewhere else to live. They did
not dispute the fact that they should
move, just felt they should have
been informed. Mick's lawyers did
not ask for costs and the Judge
replied, "I am glad to hear that, in
all the circumstances."

FEBRUARY
8
Alan Dunn, a Stones roadie since
1963, and his girlfriend Ramona
Herman, go missing on a boating trip
off the Bahamas. The Stones hire a
plane and fly out to sea to search for
him. Fortunately Alan and Ramona
are picked up safely by the crew of
the yacht *Drummer*.

16
'Run Rudolph Run' / 'The Harder
They Come', Keith's solo single, is
released in the UK, a little late for
the Christmas market.

MARCH
20
Keith announces that he will

give two concerts for the Canadian
National Institute for the Blind in
Toronto in April. This means that the
Justice Minister, who has now been
granted leave to appeal against
Keith's sentence, can serve him the
notice of appeal when he sets foot in
Canada.

24
Keith and Ron show up at
Fiorucci's, New York, where Andy
Warhol is signing copies of *Interview*.
Warhol reports, "It was the first time
I was seeing them in the daylight
and they looked so old and beat-up.
Their girlfriends looked young and
fresh."

APRIL
Dates: The New Barbarians:

Oshawa Civic Stadium, Oshawa,
Canada (21); Ann Arbor, Michigan
(24); Denver, Colorado (25); St. Louis,
Missouri (26); Cobo Hall, Detroit,
Michigan (28); Sports Arena,
Milwaukee, Wisconsin (29); The
Amphitheater, Chicago, Illinois (30).

5
Bianca's legal team, led by Marvin
Mitchelson who also represented
Marsha Hunt against him, is finally
able to serve divorce papers on
Mick in New York. The demand is
for half of his estimated £10 million
fortune, even though Mick made her
sign a marriage agreement stating
that their property be kept separate.

Above: Mick and Keith in 1978.

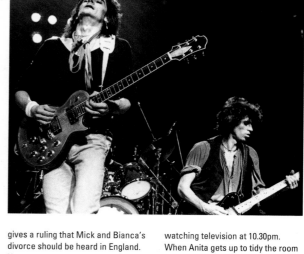

6

Judge Graburn upholds his own sentence, rejecting the Crown's claim that Keith had turned Canada's court system into a "laughing stock".

As soon as he arrives on Canadian territory Keith is served with a notice of appeal of his sentence and appears in court to discuss his progress with Judge Graburn.

21

Keith forms a pick-up group, The New Barbarians, consisting of himself and Ron Wood, plus Bobby Keys, Stanley Clarke, Joseph Modelliste and Ian McLagan. The band was given its name by Neil Young. Both The New Barbarians and the Stones proper play at the court-ordered benefit for the blind in Oshawa, thirty miles from Toronto. Despite the venue seating only 4,500 people, the entire Rolling Stones touring apparatus arrives in Toronto from Dallas, complete with lighting rigs, accountants, bodyguards and technicians, taking over a large section of the Four Seasons Hotel. The expense is enormous. The Stones are putting on a very special show.

MAY

Dates: The New Barbarians: Pittsburgh, Pennsylvania (2); Cincinnati, Ohio (3); Capital Center, Largo, Washington (5); Madison Square Garden, New York (7); Richfield Coliseum, Cleveland, Ohio (8); Birmingham, Alabama (10); The Summit, Houston, Texas (12); The Tarrant County, Dallas, Texas (13); Tucson, Arizona (16); Phoenix, Arizona (17); The Coliseum, Oakland, California (20); The Forum, Los Angeles, California (21); Rocket 88: The Venue, London (12).

4

Mick attends a private hearing at the High Court in London to discuss his divorce. The meeting lasts three hours and is thought to concern whether his divorce should be heard in the USA or the UK. British property laws would be in his favour but Bianca would prefer the hearing to be in the USA.

9

The haggling over Mick and Bianca's divorce settlement begins. She claims £6,500,000, being half of the money she says he has earned since their marriage in 1971. Mick says he has only £2 million left. His lawyers issue a statement saying that although the last time Mick and Bianca had sex was in October 1977, their marriage "was over in every true sense in 1973".

11

'Gimme Some Neck', a solo album by Ron Wood, is released as CBS 83337 (UK). Mick, Keith and Charlie all appear on the record.

12

Charlie Watts follows Keith's lead and forms his own group, Rocket 88, featuring himself, Ian Stewart, Alexis Korner and Dick Morrissey.

13

Mick and Bill Wyman are at the party following the screening of The Who's films *Quadrophenia* and *The Kids Are All Right* at the Cannes Film Festival. Mick is vacationing at Bill Wyman's house in St. Paul in the South of France for a few weeks. Bianca is in Los Angeles.

14

At a hearing in Los Angeles, Judge Harry Shafer is told by Bianca's lawyers that Mick has cut her allowance from £8,000 to £1,000 a month. Shafer orders Mick to maintain Bianca in the "sumptuous style" to which she has become accustomed. He says Mick must not attempt to "starve her into submission."

20

Mick and Charlie are guests at Eric Clapton's wedding reception at Clapton's house at Ewhurst in Surrey. Eric married Pattie Boyd in Arizona on March 27. Among the other guests are Paul McCartney, George Harrison and Ringo Starr who perform together on stage for the first time since The Beatles played collectively for the final time on the Apple rooftop on January 30, 1969.

JUNE

2

In court in Los Angeles, Judge Shafer orders Mick to pay Bianca £1,500 a week until a final divorce settlement is reached.

18

The Stones meet up in Paris to begin work on a new album at Pathé Marconi Studios. They record throughout the month. They have block-booked the studio so that they can come and go as they please, sometimes recording for 18 hours at a stretch then taking a day off.

27

The appeal against Keith's sentence opens in Toronto. Keith's lawyers tell the five Appeal Judges that Keith is no longer an addict, but that a jail sentence would very likely cause a relapse. They file an affidavit in which Keith says, "I have grimly determined to change my life and abstain from any drug use. I can truthfully say that the prospect of ever using drugs again in the future is totally alien to my thinking. My experience has also had an important effect not only on my happiness, but on my happiness at home in which my young son is brought up."

The Crown Prosecutor John Scollin still argues that Keith belongs in jail and that Canadian justice will be called into disrepute if he is not put there. The court reserves its judgement.

30

Worried by the civil war in Nicaragua, Bianca flies to Managua to try and rescue her family and relatives.

JULY

6

Mick breaks off recording and returns to London for seven days of private hearings on his divorce proceedings. The hearings cost him £20,000.

9

Bianca arrives in London to raise money for medical aid for the victims of the Nicaraguan civil war. She tells the press that her family are safe but, "I can do nothing to help them financially at present because I have no money. Although Mick was told by a judge in the United States to pay me money, he hasn't done so. After the divorce hearing, I intend to fly back to Nicaragua to work for the Red Cross, although it will be a very stiff task to raise my fare."

16

In the High Court, Justice Eastham gives a ruling that Mick and Bianca's divorce should be heard in England. However, he does not prevent her from petitioning in the USA as that would be "discourteous" to the American judiciary. In the event, the proceedings are heard in London.

20

There is a shooting accident in Frog Hollow, Keith and Anita's country house in South Salem, Westchester County. 17-year old Scott Cantrell, from Norwalk, Connecticut, is in bed with Anita, watching television at 10.30pm. When Anita gets up to tidy the room he shoots himself in the head with a .38 Smith and Wesson revolver. The police are called and Cantrell is taken to Northern Westchester Hospital but dies just after midnight. Anita is arrested and questioned for 12 hours by local police.

Mick and Jerry dine with Andy Warhol and his entourage at Castel's in Paris. Mick and Jerry tell Andy about the shooting, referring to Cantrell as "Anita's boyfriend".

Lady Studios. Ron flies to Los Angeles. Bill and Charlie remain in Paris. Charlie goes on to play several Rocket 88 gigs in Germany and the Netherlands.

NOVEMBER

2
Bianca is granted a decree nisi and given custody of Jade.

10
It is reported that Charlie Watts, Ian Stewart and Jeff Bradford, who played guitar with the Stones in an early line-up, have been recording a blues album with Brian Knight.

19
A Westchester County Grand Jury clears Anita Pallenberg of any involvement in the death of Scott Cantrell but she pleads guilty on two charges of illegal possession of a weapon. Cantrell's father says, "I think they were lovers and she had supplied him with drugs. A 37 year old woman should have known better than to associate with a 17 year old boy in her bedroom. I feel she is fully responsible for the death of my son, no matter how they wrap it up." Keith telephoned Anita from Paris, angry about the loss of the gun. The incident put a final end to their long common-law marriage. Anita later said, "That boy of seventeen who shot himself in my house really ended it for us. And although we occasionally saw each other for the sake of the children, it was the end of our personal relationship."

21
Anita is released on bail of $500 and her passport held. She is charged with possession of stolen property as the gun (one of Keith's) was stolen in Fort Lauderdale, Florida. She tells the police that Cantrell had been playing with the gun all evening and talking about Russian Roulette.

23
Jeffrey Sessler, who called the police to Anita's house after the shooting, says that he was in a downstairs room with Anita and Keith's son Marlon when it happened. He tells reporters, "The two were watching a programme to commemorate the tenth anniversary of man setting foot on the moon. She felt very sorry for him. He didn't seem to have a friend in the world. He told us his mother committed suicide on Christmas Day and that no-one loved or cared for him. Anita invited him to come and live at the place about a month ago. She wanted to let him work for the family as an odd job man, but quite honestly I don't think he could adapt to the warmth and love he was being shown here. Although Anita cared for him it was not a sex-type relationship."

26
The sensational tabloid, the *New York Post*, begins digging the dirt on Anita. They report that detectives were shocked at how filthy the house in South Salem was when they arrived after the shooting. The sheets were grey with dirt and one detective is reported as saying, "There was a powerful unpleasant smell in the room as if there was a dead cat somewhere."

28
The Stones are still working on 'Emotional Rescue' in Paris, forcing Keith and Ron to postpone the proposed New Barbarians gig at Knebworth until August 11.

AUGUST
Dates: The New Barbarians: Knebworth (11).

'Seven Days', a Ron Wood solo single is released on CBS 7785.

Late in the month, the Stones take a break from recording. Ron and Keith remain in Paris, Bill flies to the States, Mick and Charlie go to London.

16
The latest revelation from the *New York Post* has Anita and Scott Cantrell connected with a local witches' coven. They quote a 15-year-old neighbour, Steve Levoie, as saying that Anita had invited him "to pot and sex orgies. She's a sick person, she should be put away. The house was filthy, really dirty, and Anita was dirty herself. She even asked my sister if she wanted some coke... She had a lot of young boys who would come to the house all the time. She would ask for sex and talk of sex quite often. She never asked me, but who would want a dirty old woman like that."

17
The *Post* continues its series on Anita, reporting that nuns at a local convent told police that they heard "strange chants, gun shots and loud music", and local boys report finding dogs and cats "sacrificed" near the house. Considering how secluded the Richards estate is, it is hard to imagine how so many neighbours saw so much.

SEPTEMBER

2
Bill Wyman joins Ringo Starr, Dave Mason, Kiki Dee and Todd Rundgren on stage in Las Vegas for the *Jerry Lewis Muscular Dystrophy Telethon* live TV broadcast.

12
The Stones regroup in Paris to continue recording.

17
In Toronto the five Appeal Judges reject the Crown Prosecutor's appeal to jail Keith Richard saying they recognise that Keith's cure has been a success and that he is no longer a drug addict.

OCTOBER

19
The Stones finish recording their new album at Pathé Marconi Studios. The album has the tentative title of 'Saturday, Where The Boys Meet' which is later changed to 'Emotional Rescue'.

20
WNEW-FM in New York broadcasts a 24-hour *Rolling Stones Special*.

21
Mick flies to London to attend Jade's eighth birthday party.

NBC-TV pays CBS-TV $250,000 to use a short clip of the Stones playing on the *Ed Sullivan Show* in 1964 for a history of television specials.

22
All of the Stones attend Leah Wood's first birthday party in Paris.

26
Mick and Keith fly to New York from Paris to spend a month mixing the Stones' new album at Electric

DECEMBER

Dates: Rocket 88: The Venue, London (18).

15
The Rolling Stones office denies a rumour that Bill Wyman is leaving the group.

18
Keith meets fashion model Patti Hansen at his birthday party held at the Roxy Roller Disco in New York.

30
Charlie Watts, Alexis Korner and Jack Bruce play Dingwalls Dance Hall in London.

31
At Lewisboro Town Court, New York, Anita is indicted on one charge of illegal possession of a weapon. The charge of possession of a second gun is dropped. She will appear in court in March 1980.

Ron Wood and David Bowie see Sam and Dave at Trax in New York City.

Also in New York, Mick and Jerry Hall attend Woody Allen's New Year's Eve Party at Harkness House on 75th Street. Andy Warhol reported, "Mick came in with Jerry and Bianca ran over and was charming. I don't know how she did it but she got it over with, she broke the ice, they talked for about half an hour. She wanted to get Jerry nervous which she did. Mick shaved off his beard so he looks really good."

1980

FEBRUARY
22
Ron and his girlfriend Jo Howard are arrested for possession of 200 grams of cocaine on St. Marteen in the Dutch Antilles.

25
Mick and Bianca are both dinner guests at Ahmet Ertegun's New York apartment along with Andy Warhol and his entourage. Jerry Hall is out of town.

26
Ron and Jo are released and charges dropped when it is revealed that the cocaine was planted on them by zealous police.

MARCH
1
Mick has dinner with William Burroughs at Burroughs' "Bunker", an old gymnasium on the Bowery. Andy Warhol joins them.

3
Anita is fined $1,000 and given a one year conditional discharge by Judge George Hunter Roberts for possession of the stolen .38 that Scott Cantrell used to kill himself.

13-14
Bill Wyman in Pye Records London studios mixes the live tapes by Buddy Guy and Junior Wells recorded at the 1974 Montreux Jazz Festival in Switzerland.

18
Mick attends a party at Diane Von Furstenberg's in New York. Other guests include Bryan Ferry, Richard Gere and Andy Warhol.

APRIL
Late in the month, the Stones get together in New York to film the promotional video clips for their new album, 'Emotional Rescue'. Bill and Charlie return to Europe, Ron flies to Los Angeles. Mick and Keith stay on in New York to remix some of the tracks.

27
Mick at a birthday party for Averil Meyer at Hector's on 82nd Street and 3rd Avenue. Also on his table was Diane Vreeland from *Vogue*.

JUNE
18
Mick and Jerry Hall attend an "all-in-red" party at the Pré Catalan in Paris given by South American millionaire Nelson Seabra. Bianca arrives with Andy Warhol.

20
'Emotional Rescue' / 'Down In

The Hole' released. It enters the UK charts at No. 13 and reaches No. 8. In the States it enters at No. 22 and gets to No. 3.

EMOTIONAL RESCUE
Jagger, Richards /
DOWN IN THE HOLE
Jagger, Richards
S - Rolling Stones Records RSR 105 (UK), Atlantic RS 20001 (USA). Released: June 1980. Produced: The Glimmer Twins. Associate producer and engineer: Chris Kimsey.

Notes: Taken from the album 'Emotional Rescue'.

23
The Stones' new album, 'Emotional Rescue' is released. It enters the UK charts at No. 23 and spends a month at No.1. In the States it enters at No.5 and spends seven weeks at the top.

The Stones hold a launch party for the album at the Duke of York's Barracks in Chelsea. They all attend except Keith who remains in New York.

EMOTIONAL RESCUE
A - Rolling Stones Records CUN 39111 (UK), Atlantic COC 16015 (USA). Released: June 1980. Produced by The Glimmer Twins. Associate Producer: Chris Kimsey. Engineer: Chris Kimsey. Assistant engineers: Sean Fullen, Brad Samuelsohn, 'Snake' Reynolds and Jon Smith. Arranged by Jack Nitzsche. Recorded at Pathe-Marconi Studios, Paris, France, Compass Point Studio, Nassau, Bahamas and The Rolling Stones Mobile.

Side 1: 1. Dance (Jagger, Richards, Wood) / 2. Summer Romance (Jagger, Richards) / 3. Send It To Me (Jagger, Richards) / 4. Let Me Go (Jagger, Richards) / 5. Indian Girl (Jagger, Richards).

Side 2: 6. Where The Boys Go (Jagger, Richards) / 7. Down The Hole (Jagger, Richards) / 8. Emotional Rescue (Jagger, Richards) / 9. She's So Cold (Jagger, Richards) / 10. All About You (Jagger, Richards).

Notes: Ian Stewart, piano. Bobby Keys, saxophone. Nicky Hopkins, piano. Sugar Blue, harmonica. Michael Shrieve, percussion. Max Romeo sang back-up vocal on track 1.

**Above: Keith with David Bowie.
Bottom: Mick with Jerry Hall.**

JULY
26
Mick spends his birthday in Tangier with Jerry Hall.

SEPTEMBER
16 - 21
Robert Frank screens 'Cocksucker Blues' at the Whitney Museum of American Art in New York. In his agreement with the Stones, the film can be shown only four times a year for "educational and artistic" purposes and Frank has to be present for each screening.

Mick and Keith are in London, editing tracks left over from 'Emotional Rescue' for possible future use.

18
Mick buys Château Fourchette, a mid-18th century château built for the mistress of the owner of the Château d'Amboise on the Loire at Poce-sur-Cisse near Amboise. Restoration is not completed until the summer of 1986.

19
'She's So Cold' / 'Send It To Me' released. It enters the British charts at No. 29 but only rises to No. 27. In the States it enters at No. 25 and gets to No. 21.

SHE'S SO COLD Jagger, Richards / SEND IT TO ME Jagger, Richards
S - Rolling Stones Records RSR 106 (UK) Atlantic RS 21001 (USA). Released: September 1980. Producer: The Glimmer Twins.

Notes: Taken from the album 'Emotional Rescue'.

OCTOBER
1
Art Collins takes over from Earl McGrath as president of Rolling Stones records. He was previously vice-president.

3
Bill Wyman begins work on a soundtrack for Ernest Day's film thriller *Green Ice* at his villa in the Côte d'Azur.

11
The Stones assemble at the Pathé Marconi studios in Paris to edit tracks they have in the can and record material for a new album. The sessions continue until the beginning of November.

Mick and Jerry Hall rent an apartment on the Ile de la Cité in the middle of the Seine.

NOVEMBER
1
The Stones continue work at the Pathé Marconi studios in Paris for much of the month. When recording is finished, Bill returns to his villa to continue work on the soundtrack for *Green Ice*, Ron flies to New York and Charlie returns to Britain. Mick and Keith remain in Paris to mix the tapes.

2
Mick and Bianca attend the High Court in London for the judgement on their divorce settlement. The amount is kept secret but it is thought that Bianca receives £1,000,000 plus costs. The question of custody of 9-year old Jade will be decided at a separate hearing.

3
Mick back in Paris to continue recording.

10
The Warhol crowd are in Paris and Mick meets with Fred Hughes from Andy Warhol's *Interview* magazine in the afternoon.

DECEMBER
8
After hearing that John Lennon has been murdered, Bill Wyman telephones WNEW-FM from his home in France to talk about John live on the air.

22
Mick and Jerry entertain Andy Warhol and entourage to dinner at Jerry's new apartment at 135 Central Park West. Jerry gives Andy a complete set of china from the Concorde as a present. He is overjoyed.

24
Mick and Jerry give a Christmas lunch for Andy Warhol, Earl McGrath, Ahmet Ertegun and Jerry's family.

27
Mick flies from New York to Peru to begin work on Werner Herzog's movie *Fitzcarraldo*.

JANUARY
Keith Richards' neighbours in New York attempt to get him evicted because of the high volume of the music he plays all night.

Bill Wyman's soundtrack for *Green Ice* is launched at the MIDEM festival in Cannes. The film, which stars Ryan O'Neal and Omar Sharif, was panned by the critics.

27
A live album, 'Rocket 88' is released on Atlantic Records, K 50776 featuring Charlie Watts and Ian Stewart. Produced by Ian Stewart from a live recording made at the Rotation Club in Hanover, Germany in November 1979.

Keith Richards attends Jerry Lee Lewis's concert at the Ritz in New York.

FEBRUARY
The filming of *Fitzcarraldo* is stopped when Jason Robards gets sick and Amazonian Indians attack the film set in a small jungle town called Iquito. The crew returns to Munich. When the shooting is rescheduled for May, Mick drops out of the project claiming prior commitments. He and Jerry return to New York. Mick: "I went down there and I was in the jungle in South America for about three months and we had Jason Robards as the star at that point and I was playing his brother or something, although the part I played wasn't in the final version. Then Robards got sick and I finished my contract and by the time they started shooting again in the autumn I was on the road so I couldn't do it."

8
At the Lone Star Café on Fifth Avenue, Keith Richards joins Etta James on stage to play 'Miss You'.

MARCH
Mick, Jerry, Keith and Patti take a short holiday in Barbados.

4
The anthology 'Sucking In The Seventies' is released in the USA on Rolling Stones Records. Despite a number of American stores refusing to sell it because of its title, it enters the US charts at No. 29 and reaches No. 17.

Above: Mick escorting Jerry Hall. Below: Rolling Stones Records boss Earl McGrath with Charlie and Mick in 1980.

APRIL
Mick and Jerry spend Easter in Mustique.

Back in New York, Mick and Keith finish off the Stones' new album at Atlantic Records studios. Ron Wood is in Los Angeles working on a solo project.

13
The anthology 'Sucking In The Seventies' is released in the UK on Rolling Stones Records.

```
THE ROLLING STONES
SUCKING IN THE SEVENTIES
THE ROLLING STONES
SUCKING IN THE SEVENTIES
THE ROLLING STONES
SUCKING IN THE SEVENTIES
THE ROLLING STONES
SUCKING IN THE SEVENTIES
```

SUCKING IN THE SEVENTIES Compilation
A - Rolling Stones Records EMI CUNS 39112 (UK), Atlantic COC 16028 (USA).
Released April 1981 (UK), March 1981 (USA).
Producer: The Glimmer Twins.

Side 1: 1. Shattered (Jagger, Richards) / 2. Everything Is Turning To Gold (Jagger, Richards, Wood) / 3. Hot Stuff (Jagger, Richards) /
4. Time Waits For No One (Jagger, Richards) / 5. Fool To Cry (Jagger, Richards).

Side 2: 6. Manish Boy (London, McDaniel, Morganfield) / 7. When The Whip Comes Down (Live version) (Jagger, Richards) / 8. If I Was A Dancer (Dance Pt. 2) (Jagger, Richards) / 9. Crazy Mama (Jagger, Richards) / 10. Beast Of Burden (Jagger, Richards).

JUNE
Bill Wyman's film soundtrack 'Green Ice' is released on Polydor POLS 1031. Polydor also release a single taken from the soundtrack: 'Tenderness' (Wyman)/'Noche De Amour' (Wyman) as Polydor POSP 291.

Bill sues the Daily Star for claiming that he is quitting the group. "The Rolling Stones are the biggest project in my life and always will be," Bill tells the press.

Charlie Watts and Ian Stewart are featured on Brian Knight's album, 'A Dark Horse' released on PVK Records. Brian Knight's Blues By Six used to share the bill with the Stones at the Haringay Jazz Club back in 1963 and they remained friends.

In New York, Mick, Keith and Patti, Charlie and Shirley with Bobby Keys

all see Jimmy Cliff play the Ritz. Also this month, Keith and Patti go backstage at the Ritz to visit Chuck Berry after his set there but Chuck does not recognise Keith and he gets a punch in the eye.

JULY
Keith's neighbours finally succeed in getting him evicted from his apartment.

Bill's solo single, '(Si, Si,) Je Suis Un Rock Star' (Wyman) /'Rio De Janeiro' (Wyman) is released on A&M AMS 8144. It enters the UK charts at No. 26 and rises to No. 11. It is also a hit in a number of European countries and he does a lot of solo press on it.

2
The Stones shoot a promo video directed by Michael Lindsay-Hogg for 'Waiting On A Friend' at the St. Marks Bar and Grill in Greenwich Village. After the filming, the group play a few numbers for the startled patrons of the bar but leave before too large a crowd gathers. Further filming is done later at the Taft Hotel.

Mick and Jerry throw a party at Mr. Chow's in New York. Andy Warhol is one of the guests.

20
Stones logistics chiefs Alan Dunn and Ian Stewart fly to Long View recording studio, in Brookfield, Massachusetts on an overnight visit to inspect the rehearsal facilities there. They are favourably impressed.

24
Mick flies to Bombay, India, from New York.

27
Keith, Patti and Alan Dunn fly to Worcester to inspect Long View Farm. Keith spends three days hanging out.

AUGUST
Mick returns to New York, stopping over in Paris en route.

12
Keith flies to Rome from New York to get his American visa fixed.

15
Ian Stewart flies to Worcester, Massachusetts, as an advance guard for the Stones.

16
WMMR-FM in Philadelphia somehow gets hold of a copy of the Stones new album, 'Tattoo You' and becomes the first radio station in the world to play it.

17
'Start Me Up'/'No Use In Crying' released on Rolling Stones Records. It enters the UK charts at No. 30 and climbs to No. 4.

START ME UP
Jagger, Richards /
NO USE IN CRYING
Jagger, Richards, Wood
S - Rolling Stones Records RSR 108 (UK), Atlantic 21003 (USA).
Released: August 1981.
Producer: The Glimmer Twins.

Notes: Taken from the 'Tattoo You' album.

18
The Stones begin to assemble for six weeks' rehearsals at Long View Farm. Mick, Charlie and Mick's daughter Jade, fly into Worcester from New York. Bill Wyman and Astrid fly in from Bill's villa in the South of France, Ron arrives from Los Angeles the next day.

26
Mick announces details of the Stones' forthcoming American tour at a press conference held at the JFK Stadium in Philadelphia where the tour will open.

31
'Tattoo You' is released on Rolling Stones Records. It sells a million copies in the USA in its first week of release and goes to No. 1 in both the UK and USA.

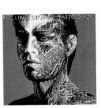

TATTOO YOU
A - Rolling Stones Records EMI CUNS 39114 (UK), Atlantic COC 166052 (USA).
Released: August 1981.
Producer: The Glimmer Twins.
Associate producer and engineer: Chris Kimsey. Remixed by Bob Clearmountain. Mastered by Greg Calbi at Sterling Sound.

Side 1: 1. Start Me Up (Jagger, Richards) / 2. Hang Fire (Jagger, Richards) / 3. Slave (Jagger, Richards) / 4. Little T&A (Jagger, Richards) / 5. Black Limousine (Jagger, Richards, Wood) / 6. Neighbours (Jagger, Richards).

Side 2: 7. Worried About You (Jagger, Richards) / 8. Tops (Jagger, Richards) / 9. Heaven (Jagger, Richards) / 10. No Use In Crying (Jagger, Richards, Wood) / 11. Waiting On A Friend (Jagger, Richards).

Above left: The Stones press conference, July 1980 at Danceteria, NYC.

SEPTEMBER
Dates: Sir Morgan's Cove, Worcester, Massachusetts (14); JFK Stadium, Philadelphia, Pennsylvania (25-26); Rich Stadium, Buffalo, New York (27).

1
The Stones announce that they have done a deal with Jovan perfume to sponsor their upcoming US tour. It is the first time that this type of funding has ever been applied to a rock tour.

2
Ron Wood's fourth solo album '1234' is released on CBS 85227 (UK) and CBS 37473 (USA).

Produced by Ron Wood and Andy Johns, the line-up features Charlie Watts, Bobby Keys, Nicky Hopkins, Jim Keltner, Ian McLagan, Alan Myers, Carmine Appice and Bobby Womack.

14
The secret warm-up gig at the 350 seater Sir Morgan's Cove club in Worcester almost turns into a riot when a radio station broadcasts details of the gig in retaliation for a rival station, WAAF, being given the job of distributing the 300 forgery-proof tickets. Some 4,000 fans besiege the club and 11 are arrested, mostly for underage drinking, but police restore order by opening the club doors to let fans gathered outside hear the music.

21
Despite requests from every major TV channel, wire service and newspaper in the country, Mick only grants one interview during rehearsals and that is to two girls, aged 12 and 13, from the North Brookfield Junior High School for their school newspaper.

24
The Stones leave Brookfield, Massachusetts and fly to Philadelphia in a private F28 Fokker jet. They check into the Barclay Hotel facing Rittenhouse Square.

25
Over 90,000 people attend the opening concert of the tour in Philadelphia. The band uses the biggest of its three stages, the others being for medium and smaller shows. Each stage has a hydraulic lift which can wave one of the band out over the audience and Mick has one all of his own. The drums are on a revolving platform for venues with behind the stage seating. The Stones hire a Boeing 707 for the duration of the tour to travel from city to city.

OCTOBER
Dates: The Metro, Rockford, Illinois (1); Folsom Field, Boulder, Colorado (3-4); San Diego Stadium, California (7); Los Angeles Coliseum, California (9, 11); The Kingdom Stadium, Seattle, Washington (14-15); Candlestick Park, San

Francisco, California (17-18); Tangerine Bowl, Orlando, Florida (24-25); The Fox Theater, Atlanta, Georgia (26); The Astrodome, Houston, Texas (28-29); The Cotton Bowl, Dallas, Texas (31).

15
A 16-year-old fan, Pamela Lynn Melville falls 50 feet to her death from a ramp leading into the Kingdom Stadium on to the parking lot below after repeatedly being warned by ushers not to lean over. At the same concert a woman is arrested after threatening Mick's life.

17
The 146,000 crowd at Candlestick Park is the biggest ever gathered in San Francisco.

20
Mick appears on public service television with Dianne Feinstein, Mayor of San Francisco, on a "Save The Cable Cars" appeal. Afterwards he has dinner with Jackie Onassis.

21
Mick holds a party for Jade's tenth birthday at the Roller Disco in New York.

24
The Stones celebrate Bill's 45th birthday at a private party held on a rented boat, floating around Disney World in Orlando, Florida.

28
A 16-year old boy shoots and kills a 22-year fan outside the Astrodome in Houston.

31
Mick, Keith, Bill and Ron appear on CFOX-FM radio in Dallas to talk about the tour.

NOVEMBER
Dates: The Cotton Bowl, Dallas, Texas (1); Freedom Hall, Louisville, Kentucky (3); Byrne Arena, Meadowlands, New Jersey (5-7); Civic Center, Hartford, Connecticut (9-10); Madison Square Garden, New York City (12-13); Richfield Coliseum, Cleveland, Ohio (16-17); Checkerdrome, St. Louis, Missouri (19); Unidome, Cedar Falls, Iowa (20); Civic Center, St. Paul, Minnesota (21); Rosemont Horizon, Chicago, Illinois (23-25); Carrierdrome, Syracuse (27-28); Silverdome, Pontiac, Michigan (30).

3
Directly after the show in Louisville, the Stones fly back to New York City where there have been four million postal applications for their New York area concerts.

4
Mick appears live by telephone on BBC Radio Rock On.

5
Mick appears on BBC-TV in a taped interview with Rona Barrett, the syndicated gossip columnist.

Tina Turner opens for the Stones at all three Meadowlands concerts. She duets with Mick on 'Honky Tonk Woman' during the second show.

9
12 fans are injured and 56 arrested when fans trying to gatecrash clash with security in Hartford, Connecticut.

12
Screamin' Jay Hawkins opens for the Stones at their Madison Square Garden concerts.

Bill Wyman gives a 90 minute guitar lesson to tennis star John McEnroe in his hotel suite. Among the stars in the audience at the Madison

Square Garden concerts are Paul McCartney, Bob Dylan, Jack Nicholson, Angelica Huston, Robert Redford, Tina Turner, Carly Simon, Ali McGraw, Shelley Duval and Peter O'Toole.

20
'Waiting On A Friend'/' Little T&A' released in the States on Rolling Stones Records and promoted with a video shot in Greenwich Village.

WAITING ON A FRIEND
Jagger, Richards / LITTLE T&A Jagger, Richards
S - Rolling Stones Records RSR 109 (UK), Atlantic RS 21004 (USA). Released: November 1981. Producer: The Glimmer Twins.

Notes: Taken from the 'Tattoo You' album.

22
Mick, Keith and Ron jam with Muddy Waters, Buddy Guy and Junior Wells on stage at the Checkerboard Lounge, Chicago.

Above: Tina Turner joins the Stones on stage at Meadowlands, 1981.

back to London and Bill flies to Nice to spend Christmas at his villa in the south of France.

26
Ron, Jo and family fly to London.

1982

JANUARY
11
'Hang Fire' / 'Neighbors' is released in the USA on Rolling Stones Records.

HANG FIRE Jagger, Richards / NEIGHBORS Jagger, Richards
S - Rolling Stones Records - Atlantic 21300.
Released January 1982.
Producer: The Glimmer Twins.

Notes: Taken from the album 'Tattoo You'.

FEBRUARY
3
Mick and Keith fly to Los Angeles to work on the film of the tour with director Hal Ashby.

18
In New York Ron Wood is at Bobby Womack's concert at the Ritz and joins him on stage for a jam. They are joined by Steve Marriott and Wilson Pickett.

MARCH
Mick and Keith begin editing the live tapes from the tour for a live album at the Power Station studio in New York.

5
A new solo single by Bill is released: 'A New Fashion' (Wyman) / 'Girls' (Wyman). Ripple AMS 8209.

18
Keith and Ron drop by the Hit

Factory in New York where Jimmy Cliff is making a new album and jam with him.

25
Mick and Charlie are guests at a dinner given for Fred Hughes by Lord Jermyn at the Odeon, New York.

26
Bill releases a solo album: 'Bill Wyman' on A&M Records, AMLH 68540. It reaches No. 25 in the UK album charts.

APRIL
The Stones, minus Bill who is doing promotion for his solo album, are in New York making the final selections and mixes of their forthcoming live album 'Still Life'.

17
In New York Ron joins Toots and The Maytals on stage at the Ritz and plays six numbers with them.

28
Mick holds a press conference at Le Beat Route in London to announce the itinerary of the European leg of the Stones' World Tour. Also on the bill are The J. Geils Band and various local bands. As usual, Ian Stewart will be the pianist. Bobby Keys and Gene Barge will constitute the horn section and Chuck Leavell will play keyboards. The tour will be managed by Bill Graham.

MAY
Dates: Capitol Theatre, Aberdeen, Scotland (26); Apollo Theatre, Glasgow, Scotland (27); Green's Playhouse, Edinburgh, Scotland (28); The 100 Club, Oxford Street, London (31).

26
The Stones' tour opens in Aberdeen. Advance copies of their new album, 'Still Life' are available for sale at the venue.

27
Mick is interviewed for BBC Radio's *Round Table* in Glasgow.

DECEMBER
Dates: Silverdome, Pontiac, Michigan (1); Superdrome, New Orleans, Louisiana (5); Capital Center, Washington, D.C. (7-9); Rupp Arena, Lexington, Kentucky (11); Sun Devil Stadium, Phoenix, Arizona (13); Kemper Arena, Kansas City, Missouri (14-15); Hampton Coliseum, Hampton Roads, Virginia (18-19).

1
Radio KBFH records the show in Pontiac for later transmission. Iggy Pop and Santana are support on both shows.

4
The Stones hold a party on a riverboat on the Mississippi.

7
Radio KBFH records the Washington, D.C. show for future transmission.

14
Mick Taylor joins the Stones on stage in Kansas City.

18
The Hampton Roads concert is broadcast live on television across America.

After the show there is a joint birthday party backstage for Keith and Bobby Keys. Marlon and Dandelion, accompanied by Keith's mother, Doris, flew in for the concert and party.

19
The Stones fly back to New York directly after the second Hampton Roads show, the final date of the tour. More than 2,000,000 attended the shows and the tour grossed over $50,000,000. Merchandising brought in over $10,000,000, Jovan gave them $4,000,000 for sponsorship rights and they sold about $1,500,000 worth of records. The tour was also filmed by Hal Ashby which promised future income. It was their longest and most financially rewarding tour ever.

Ron and Jo stay in their Greenwich Village apartment for Christmas. Mick spends a few days in his Central Park West apartment before flying to France to spend Christmas in his château. Charlie and Keith fly

28

BBC's *Round Table* with Mick's interview is broadcast.

31

The Stones play a surprise gig at the 100 Club, in Oxford Street, London which holds only 400 people.

JUNE

Dates: Feijenoord Stadiom, Rotterdam, Netherlands (2,4-5); Niedersachsen Stadium, Hanover, Germany (6-7); Waldbuehne, Berlin, Germany (8); Olympic Stadium, Munich, Germany (10-11); Hippodrome d'Auteuil, Paris (13-14); Stade de Gerland, Lyon, France (16); Nya Ullevi Stadium, Gothenburg, Sweden (19-20); Newcastle United Football Ground, Newcastle-upon-Tyne, Northumberland (23); Wembley Stadium, Wembley, Middlesex (25-26); Bristol City Football Ground, Bristol, Avon (27); Festhalle, Frankfurt, Germany (29-30).

1

'Still Life' is released on Rolling Stones Records. It enters the UK charts and reaches No. 2. A single: 'Going To A-Go-Go' / ' Beast Of Burden' is also released. It enters the UK charts at No. 23 and gets to No. 19. In the States it reaches No. 20.

STILL LIFE AMERICAN CONCERT 1981
A - Rolling Stones Records EMI CUN 39115 (UK), Atlantic COC 39113 (USA). Released: June 1982. Producer: The Glimmer Twins. Recorded: Bob Clearmountain and David Hewitt using the Record Plant Remote. Mixed: Bob Clearmountain at Power Station Studios. Mastered by Vlado Meller at CBS, New York.

Side 1: 1. Intro: Take The A Train (performed by Duke Ellington and his Orchestra (studio recording) (B. Strayhorn) / 2. Under My Thumb (Jagger, Richards) / 3. Let's Spend The Night Together (Jagger, Richards) / 4. Shattered (Jagger, Richards) / 5. Twenty Flight Rock (N. Fairchild) / 6. Going To A Go Go (Robinson, Tarplin, Moore, Rogers).

Side 2: 7. Let Me Go (Jagger, Richards) / 8. Time Is On My Side (N. Meade) / 9. Just My Imagination (Running Away With Me)(Whitfield, Strong) / 10. Start Me Up (Jagger, Richards) / 11. (I Can't Get No) Satisfaction (Jagger, Richards) / 12. Outro: Star Spangled Banner (Trad: This version arranged and performed by Jimi Hendrix).

Notes: Ian Stewart plays piano. Ian McLagan plays keyboards. Ernie Watts plays saxophone.

GOING TO A GO GO
Robinson, Moore, Tarplin, Rogers / BEAST OF BURDEN Jagger, Richards
S - Rolling Stones Records RSR 110 (UK) Atlantic RS 21301 (USA). Released: June 1982. Producer: The Glimmer Twins.

Notes: Both tracks recorded live during the 1981 US tour. Side 1 from the 'Still Life' album.

3

In the Hague, Mick goes to see George Thorogood at a club and joins him on stage.

8

Fans start two fires at the Hippodrome d'Auteuil racetrack in Paris, where the Stones are due to perform, in protest at the Fr.75,00 admission charge for the concerts.

10

In New York, Patti Hansen, Anita Pallenberg and Andrew Oldham are all in the audience for Marianne Faithfull's concert at the Ritz.

11

Even though it is pouring with rain, 50,000 show up to see the Stones in Munich.

18

The Stones are given a thorough body search when they land at Gothenberg airport in Sweden.

23

When the Stones play Newcastle, it rains throughout the entire eight-hour show. Bill Graham cannot understand why the British have never built large indoor stadia for sports and music events like the Americans.

24

Bill receives the Silver Clef Award for Outstanding Achievement on behalf of the Stones at the *British Music Industry's award ceremony* in London.

Keith is interviewed live on BBC-TV's *Newsnight*.

25

In an interview published by the London *Evening Standard*, Keith says: "I don't like to regret heroin because I learned a lot from it. It was a large part of my life. It is something I went through and dealt with. I'd regret it if I hadn't dealt with it, or if I had OD'd. I would definitely regret it then. A lot of my friends, who should by rights be around, aren't because of it. I don't think it makes a damned bit of difference to anyone going to get into it being told 'don't'. In fact it sometimes reinforces the desire to take it. Having been on it, I know. If there is anything I do regret, it's its accessibility to very young kids."

Bill's solo single 'Visions' (Wyman) / 'Nuclear Reactions' (Wyman) is released by Ripple Records as AMS 8227.

27

Mick holds a press conference for seven European television companies and tells them how important the 75,000 a night sell-out concerts in London were: "These shows mean a lot to us and they'd better be good as well. We'll get our share of attention unless she has another baby or something." [referring to Princess Diana.]

At the concert in Bristol the Stones exceed the permitted noise level by 20 decibels and in November are fined £200 by the local authority.

JULY

Dates: Festhalle, Frankfurt, Germany (1); Prater Stadium, Vienna, Austria (3); Mungersdorfer Stadium, Cologne, Germany (4-5); Vicente Calderon Stadium, Madrid, Spain (8-9); Comunal Stadium, Turin, Italy (11-12); St. Jakob Stadium, Basle, Switzerland (15); San Paolo Stadium, Naples, Italy (17); Parc des Sports de l'Ouest, Nice, France (20); Slane Castle, near Dublin, Eire (24); Roundhay Park, Leeds, Yorkshire (25).

7

A proposed concert on this date at the Espanol Football Stadium, Barcelona, is cancelled by the Spanish football authorities on June 15 for "security" reasons after 20,000 tickets have already been sold. Another concert in Madrid on July 29, is cancelled for the same reason.

9

The Stones fly to Nice directly after their concert in Madrid.

13

The Stones fly back to Nice from Turin. Mick has dinner with Roman Polanski at his house in Ramatuelle just outside St. Tropez.

15

The Stones fly straight back to Nice after the concert in Switzerland.

17

The Stones fly to Naples for that night's sell-out concert to 83,000 people. Michelangelo Antonioni visits them backstage.

25

In Leeds, a thief steals a tour map presented by the Stones to tour manager Bill Graham which shows all the tour venues and is covered with messages to him from the band members.

26

Mick holds a fairly quiet birthday party at Langan's Brasserie in Mayfair, London.

30

Mick flies to Paris on business. Keith flies to his house in Jamaica to rest after the tour.

AUGUST

8

Bill Graham offers a £1000 reward for the recovery of the tour map stolen from him backstage at the Leeds concert.

31

It is announced that the premier of Hal Ashby's film of the Stones' tour will occur as part of the fiftieth anniversary celebrations of the Venice Film Festival, shown on a wide screen in St. Marks Square. The following day the Venice authorities lose no time in prohibiting the screening, fearing damage to the ancient structures surrounding it.

SEPTEMBER

Les Blank's *Burden of Dreams*, a documentary of the making of Werner Herzog's film *Fitzcarraldo* in the Amazonian jungle is released in the States, starring, among others, Mick Jagger who was not in the final film.

The 12 hour special radio documentary *Rolling Stones Past and Present* is transmitted by 275 stations across Canada and the USA on various dates during the month. It is produced by David Pritchard and Alan Lysaght and includes interviews with all of the Stones as well as Alexis Korner and many others involved in their career.

Mick's literary agent signs a deal with Weidenfeld and Nicholson for his autobiography. It will be ghost-written and the advance is rumoured to be in the region of £1,000,000. Eventually Mick has to return the money because he can't remember enough interesting material from his past and early draft copies of the manuscript are deemed by the publishers to be 'boring'.

Rumours persist in the popular press that Jerry is now going out with millionaire racehorse owner Robert Sangster who is apparently even richer than Jagger. They first met at Ascot and were seen together at the Keenland Yearling horse sales in Kentucky.

1

Redlands, what is left of Keith's Tudor mansion in Sussex, is yet again engulfed in fire. The thatched roof is destroyed but no-one is hurt. 65 firemen fight the blaze.

'Time Is On My Side' / 'Twenty Flight Rock' is released in the States. In the UK, there is also a 12" version which adds 'Under My Thumb'.

TIME IS ON MY SIDE
Berns, Ragavoy /
TWENTY FLIGHT ROCK
Fairchild, Cochran
S - Rolling Stones Records RSR 111 (UK), Atlantic RS 7-99978 (USA).
Released: September 1982.
Producer: The Glimmer Twins.

Notes: Both tracks recorded live during the 1981 US tour. Side 1 from the 'Still Life' album.

25

Mick and Jade arrive at JFK Stadium in Philadelphia by helicopter to see The Who and The Clash.

OCTOBER
4

Mick, accompanied by Cornelia Guest, one of the Warhol entourage, goes to a party held at Regine's in New York. Afterwards they go on to Xenon where Mick meets up with Valerie Perrine, providing more fuel for the gossip columnists.

NOVEMBER
7

Mick, Keith and Ron begin work on a new album at the Pathé Marconi studios in Paris, beginning with a run-through of left-over unreleased material from previous sessions.

11

Bill and Charlie fly from London to Paris to join the other Stones at EMI's Pathé Marconi studios.

12

The *Sun* reports: "Tearaway Rolling Stone Keith Richards is to get married at last. His bride-to-be is his beautiful model girlfriend Patti Hansen. They are planning a huge white wedding in New York within a month... 'Yes, it's true,' a spokesman for the 38-year old Stones' guitarist said yesterday. 'Keith was trying to keep it secret, but if the *Sun* knows

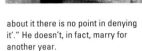

about it there is no point in denying it'." He doesn't, in fact, marry for another year.

Jerry flies from New York to Paris to join Mick. They begin arguing at the airport when Mick picks her up.

13

Victoria Vicuna, the Venezuelan model flies to Paris to join Mick.

17

Gossip columnist Nigel Dempster writes in the *Daily Mail*: "Mick started at Jerry as soon as he met her at the airport. She really can't take his abuse any longer and has split. She does not want to see him again."

DECEMBER
17

The Stones stop work on their new album and return home for their Christmas break. Mick remains in Paris.

20

Mick and Jerry fly to Mustique, where Mick is having a house built. Jerry rejoined Mick in Paris earlier in the month and they have apparently patched up their relationship.

1983

JANUARY

Charlie buys a 17th century Grade II listed building near Barnstaple in North Devon. It has three reception rooms, six bedrooms and enough stabling for Charlie and Shirley's ten horses. There are 20 acres of meadows surrounding it.

9

Mick and Jerry fly to Los Angeles.

14

Mick shoots scenes for the Showtime Cable TV *Faerie Tale Theater* series, playing the Chinese Emperor in *The Nightingale* by Hans Christian Andersen.

18

Mick, Keith, Ron and Charlie attend a private screening of Hal Ashby's film of the Stones' tour, *Let's Spend The Night Together*, in New York.

30

Keith, Ron and Jo fly to Paris to continue work on the next album.

FEBRUARY
11

LET'S SPEND THE NIGHT TOGETHER Jagger, Richards / **START ME UP** Jagger, Richards
S - Rolling Stones Records RSR 112 (promotional release only)
Released: February 1983.
Producer: The Glimmer Twins.
Notes: Side 1: recorded live at Hampton Coliseum, Hampton Roads, Virginia, December 18, 1981 / Side 2: recorded live at the Rosemont Horizon, Chicago, Illinois, November 25, 1981. Issued to promote the film 'Let's Spend The Night Together'. Taken from 'Still Life' album.

Hal Ashby's *Let's Spend The Night Together* is premièred at Loew's Theater in New York.

25

After auditioning a number of writers, *Sunday Times* literary editor John Ryles is hired as "technical writer" for Mick's autobiography for a fee of £50,000.

MARCH
24

Hal Ashby's film of the Stones' tour, *Let's Spend The Night Together*, goes on release at Classic cinemas across Britain.

Above left: Ron and Jo Wood and family. Above right: Mick with Prince Rupert Lowenstein, the Stones' financial advisor.

Records are all contenders for a new distribution deal for Rolling Stones Records. The winner gets all the back catalogue on the group's own label as well as new product - but not, of course, the classic recordings made for Decca during the Sixties. Prince Rupert Lowenstein, the Stones' business manager, shuttles back and forth across the Atlantic working on the deal.

2
Mick gives a birthday party for Jerry Hall at Mr Chow's in New York. The tabloid, the *Daily Star* runs an interview with Mick in which he says, "When you get to my age you really have to work at staying young. You've got to be fit because rock requires a tremendous amount of energy and I find that if your body is alive, your mind becomes alive. That's vital in a business that is as fast as this. Once I led the typical life of a dissipated rock star, full of drugs, booze and chaos. But these days my health is my most treasured possession. When I'm on tour I never touch hard liquor and I try to get as much sleep as I possibly can. I like to get as much as ten hours a night. I don't go to clubs or discos except to pick up girls."

4
Keith appears on stage with Jerry Lee Lewis in Los Angeles and the resulting jam is recorded for a forthcoming *Salute* TV show.

AUGUST
Bill and Astrid separate after 14 years together. She says she resents sharing him with "thousands of other women".

10
Keith is one of the guests at his son Marlon's 14th birthday party held at his old house in Long Island where Anita Pallenberg and Marlon still live.

20
A son, Tyrone, is born to Jo Howard and Ron Wood at Mount Sinai Hospital in New York City.

25
The Stones sign the biggest

record deal ever seen in the record business. CBS records signs a deal in Paris (for tax reasons) giving them $6,000,000 per album for a total of four albums plus a promotion budget in the region of $1,000,000 per album- potentially $28,000,000 in all. They will continue to use their own tongue logo on their records.

Above left: Mick with Jimmy (left) and Stevie Ray Vaughan (right) at NBC Studios, New York, for Saturday Night Live. Above right & below: Keith with son Marlon and, below left, with Marlon and father Ben Richards.

APRIL
Bill and Astrid, after living in France for 11 years, take a three month trip around the world, stopping in Los Angeles, Maui, Hawaii, Fiji, Australia, Bali and spend a month in Japan before moving back to Gedding Hall in Suffolk, England. Not long after returning to Britain, they buy a house on Mulberry Walk, Chelsea.

10
Mick and Jerry vacation in Mustique so that Mick can oversee the construction work on his new house and begin work on his autobiography.

28-29
At the 25th anniversary celebrations for the Marquee, Bill and Charlie join Alexis Korner on stage to play blues.

MAY
4
Keith flies to San Francisco to join Patti Hansen who is filming *Hard To Hold*.

Mick and Ron begin mixing and editing the new album at the Hit Factory in New York. Keith returns later in the month to join them.

JUNE
In an unprecedented move, Keith leaves New York for his home in Jamaica, leaving Mick to continue working alone on the new album, overdubbing the Sugarhill Records rhythm section and horns on to the tracks. Rumour has it that a rift has developed between them.

JULY
EMI, MCA, CBS and Atlantic

Studio: Compass Point, Nassau and EMI Studios, Paris.

Side 1: 1. Undercover of the Night (Jagger, Richards) / 2. She Was Hot (Jagger, Richards) / 3. Tie You Up (The Pain Of Love) (Jagger, Richards) / 4. Wanna Hold You (Jagger, Richards) / 5. Feel On Baby (Jagger, Richards).

Side 2: 6. Too Much Blood (Jagger, Richards) / 7. Pretty Beat Up (Jagger, Richards, Wood) / 8. Too Tough (Jagger, Richards) / 9. All The Way Down (Jagger, Richards) / 10. It Must Be Hell (Jagger, Richards).

Notes: Percussion by Moustapha Cisse, Brahms Coundoul, Ian Stewart, Martin Ditcham and Sly Dunbar. David Sanborn plays saxophone. Horns by CHOPS. Chuck Leavell plays keyboards on tracks 2 and 7. Ian Stewart plays piano on tracks 2 and 7. Jim Barber plays guitar on track 6.

SEPTEMBER
Dates: ARMS line-up: Royal Albert Hall, London (20-21).

20
An all-star line-up assembled by Glyn Johns, Bill and Charlie, including Jeff Beck, Jimmy Page, Eric Clapton, Joe Cocker, Ray Cooper, Stevie Winwood, Paul Rodgers, Kenney Jones, Andy Fairweather-Low and Ronnie Lane, play a charity concert at the Royal Albert Hall for ARMS (Action for Research into Multiple Sclerosis). Ronnie Lane, who suffers from the disease, has to be helped on to the stage to play.

21
The same line-up play a second Albert Hall gig, this time for The Prince's Trust with Prince Charles and Princess Di present.

24
Mick and Keith record promo videos for the 'Undercover' album in New York.

25
The recording of Keith jamming with Jerry Lee Lewis is broadcast on the *Salute* TV show.

OCTOBER
17
The Stones assemble in Paris to film the promo video for 'Undercover Of The Night'.

18
Julien Temple, director of the controversial Sex Pistols movie, *The Great Rock'n'Roll Swindle*, shoots footage for the 'Undercover Of The Night' single at the Bain Douches Club in Paris.

24
Mick and Jerry, Keith and Patti fly with Julien Temple to Mexico City to film sequences for the promotional video for 'Undercover Of The Night'.

28
A recording of an interview with Mick appears on the first edition of the ground-breaking Channel 4 TV rock show *The Tube* in Newcastle-upon-Tyne.

30
In Mexico, Mick and Keith finish work on the video for 'Undercover Of The Night'. Keith and Patti go on holiday to Cabo San Lucas, Mexico where he rents a large house on the main street of Cabo Bello, once the playground of Sinatra, Crosby and John Wayne. Mick and Jerry fly to Europe.

31
'Undercover Of The Night' / 'All The Way Down' is released by Rolling Stones Records. It enters the UK charts and reaches No. 8. In the US it enters at No.15 and reaches No. 9. In both countries censorship problems with the promo-video harm sales.

UNDERCOVER OF THE NIGHT Jagger, Richards / ALL THE WAY DOWN Jagger, Richards
S - Rolling Stones Records RSR 113 (UK), RS 7-99813 (USA). Released: November 1983. Notes: Taken from the album 'Undercover'.

NOVEMBER
Dates: ARMS line-up: Reunion Arena, Dallas, Texas (28-29).

7
The album 'Undercover' is released by Rolling Stones Records. It enters the UK charts at No. 18 and gets to the top position. In the States it enters at No. 13 and reaches No. 4.

UNDERCOVER
A - Rolling Stones Records EMI CUN 165 4361 (UK), Atlantic 90120-1 (USA). Released: November, 1983. Producer: The Glimmer Twins and Chris Kimsey. Mixed: Chris Kimsey at the Hit Factory, New York. Mastered : George Marino at Sterling Sound.

9
Bill Graham calls a press conference at Madison Square Garden to announce that the musicians who played the two Albert Hall concerts would do a benefit mini-tour of the US for ARMS, the multiple sclerosis charity. Bill, Charlie and Ian Stewart are on the bill.

10
Julien Temple's promo-video for 'Undercover Of The Night' is banned by BBC-TV's *Top Of The Pops* because in their opinion it is too violent. In the video, Mick is relaxing at the Mexico City Holiday Inn, when three terrorists, led by Keith, burst into his suite and shoot him in the head. Says Jagger, "A lot of 'Undercover Of The Night' was inspired by the things I read about all the people who've disappeared in Argentina."

11
The Independent Broadcasting Authority bans the video for 'Undercover Of The Night' and Mick goes on Channel 4 TV's music show, *The Tube* to defend it. "It follows the song. The song is about repression, it's about violence. We're not trying to dress it up and sell the record with advertising clichés. There's no gratuitous violence in it at all. We're not trying to glamorise violence. We're trying to make something interesting that has a point." The programme screened the video, minus the brief moment where Jagger is shot.

18
Instead of the 'Undercover Of The Night' video, Channel 4 TV's *The Tube* screens old Stones videos. Meanwhile the Stones are editing a sanitised version of the video suitable for BBC-TV's *Top Of The Pops*.

28-29
Charlie, Bill and Ian Stewart play one of the ARMS benefit concerts at the Reunion Arena, Dallas.

DECEMBER
Dates: ARMS line-up benefit concerts: Cow Palace, San Francisco (1-3), and The Forum, Los Angeles (5-6); Madison Square Garden, New York City (8-9).

16
Mick flies to La Paz, the nearest town to Cabo San Lucas, at the southernmost tip of Baja California, Mexico to join Keith and Patti. Keith's parents, together for the first time in 20 years, and Keith's children, all assemble in Cabo San Lucas.

The sleeve of 'Undercover' gets it banned in Singapore.

17
Mick and Keith hold a jam session at Keith's bachelor party and play their way through all the old rock'n'roll favourites.

18
Keith marries Patti Hansen in a secret ceremony held on his 40th birthday at the Finisterra Hotel, Cabo San Lucas. The location is about as remote as they can get and the only other Stone present is Mick. Julien Temple films the wedding.

21
Mick and Jerry give a Christmas party at their new house on West 81st Street, New York.

23
Mick tapes an appearance in the video promo for Bette Midler's new record, the Jagger / Richards composition, 'Beast Of Burden'.

Above left: Keith with Patti Hansen and David Bowie at the Ritz Club in New York, 1983. Above right: Keith with Tina Turner. Below: Charlie at a 1983 charity concert in Los Angeles.

1984

JANUARY
Mick gives £32,000 in sponsorship money to the British Olympic Gymnastic Team for the forthcoming Games in Los Angeles.

1
Alexis Korner dies at the Westminster Hospital. He was 55.

18-25
The Stones are back in Mexico again with Julien Temple to shoot the promo-video for their next single, 'She Was Hot', featuring the dancer Anita Morris from the Broadway musical *Nine*. First she enters Mick and Keith's bedrooms, then appears with the whole band, causing their trouser buttons to pop off. MTV, which happily showed the violent 'Undercover Of The Night' video, bans it saying, "We have had some raunchy videos before, but this was too much." A sanitised version is made for MTV.

23
'She Was Hot' / 'I Think I'm Going Mad' released on Rolling Stones Records. It enters the US charts at No. 83 and gets to No. 44 and in the UK it only reaches No. 40.

SHE WAS HOT Jagger, Richards / **I THINK I'M GOING MAD** Jagger, Richards
EMI S - Rolling Stones Records RSR 114 (UK), Atlantic 7-99788 (USA). Released: January 1984.

Notes: Side 1 from the album 'Undercover'.

FEBRUARY
3
The first part of an interview with Mick is broadcast on NBC-TV's *Friday Night Videos* in the States.

10
The second part of Mick's interview is broadcast on *Friday Night Videos*. They also show the sanitised version of the 'She Was Hot' video.

21
Bill presents a posthumous award to the wife of Alexis Korner at the *Daily Mirror* British Rock Awards held at the Lyceum, London. Bill goes with Julien Temple and they sit watching girls from various London clubs who have been brought in to dance. Bill: "I saw two stunning girls leaving the dance floor and my heart just jumped. She took my breath away." He asked Julien to go over and invite them for a drink. The girls were Nicola and Mandy Smith, aged 15 and 13. "I was totally besotted with Mandy from the moment I saw her..." So begins the Lolitaesque Bill Wyman-Mandy Smith saga, so loved by the popular press.

25
Keith flies to Paris on Concorde to look at possible studios for the next album.

MARCH
2
Jerry Hall gives birth to Elizabeth Scarlett. Mick is present at the birth in Lennox Hill Hospital, New York.

5
Death threats are received against Mick and his family so he is surrounded by bodyguards when he leaves the hospital with Jerry and her baby.

8
Bill arrives at the home of Patsy Smith, mother of Mandy, armed with flowers and chocolates and asks if he can take Mandy to dinner. She has no objections. Despite visits to Tramp and other night-clubs their affair was to be a well kept secret for two and a half years because she did not look under age.

17
Keith celebrates Patti's birthday with her parents in New York.

28
Keith and Patti see a screening of Patti's film *Hard To Hold* but are not happy with the way the film turned out.

30
Mick, Jerry and their two girls travel to Nassau in the Bahamas where Mick is to record a solo album at Compass Point Studios.

APRIL
4
Bill appears on the *News Nightwatch* TV show in New York by satellite to categorically deny making a series of derogatory remarks about the other Stones in an interview with the British tabloid *The Sun*.

10
Keith and Patti fly to Jamaica for a ten week holiday at Point of View.

Above left: Ron, Jo and daughter, 1983. Above right: Alexis Korner, who died January 1st, 1984.

16

Mick flies to New York in order to testify against Allen Klein in the Stones' lawsuit against their former manager. The *Daily Express* reports: "The two men have been personal enemies for years and have not spoken since Klein accused Jagger of insulting his daughter by pulling a face at her. Their amazing row ten years ago was over a contract giving Klein the rights to pre-1970 Rolling Stones material. The confrontation was described yesterday by Jagger at a Manhattan court, where he is fighting to have the contract nullified. Jagger said: 'I wanted to be reasonable and cool but the moment he walked in I blew my top and screamed at him "Where is my $800,000?"' Jagger explained that the rights Klein held were mainly to uncompleted recordings of practice sessions and how, throughout the Seventies, he feared Klein would damage the Stones' reputation by releasing the material. Mick says: 'The group are upset as this stuff is rubbish. I do not want him in my life. It's like dealing with the Russians'."

23

An arrangement is made whereby the Stones will drop their suit against Klein if he pays them their half-yearly royalties on time.

MAY
6 - 10

Mick works on a song with The Jacksons called 'State Of Shock' at A&R studios in New York.

10

Mick's publishers are upset at how dull Mick's autobiography is turning out to be. Futura, who bought the mass market paperback rights say, "No sex. No rock'n'roll. It's just boring stuff about his ordinary parents, and his ordinary upbringing. I was surprised at the poor quality."

12

Mick flies to Mustique to join his family for a brief holiday before returning to Compass Point Studio in the Bahamas. Among the all-star line-up on his album are Pete Townshend, Jeff Beck, Mike Shrieve, Herbie Hancock, Nile Rodgers, Bill Laswell, Jan Hammer and Sly and Robbie.

JUNE
1

Ron Wood has a walk-on part during the New York filming of Adrian Lyne's soft core movie *9½ Weeks*.

5

Charlie and Ian Stewart take part in a benefit concert in Nottingham with many other musicians, in memory of Alexis Korner in aid of cancer research.

11

The Jacksons' 'State Of Shock' with Mick and Michael Jackson on vocals is released on Epic Records. It enters the US charts at No. 30 and goes to No. 3. In the UK it enters at No. 20 and goes to No. 14.

14

The Stones are the first band to be awarded the Madison Square Garden Platinum Ticket for their 1981 concerts there. They also become the group included in the Madison Square Garden Hall of Fame.

24

Elizabeth Scarlett Jagger is christened at St. Mary Abbot's Church in Kensington, London. Shirley Watts is a godmother. In addition to Mick and Jerry, guests include Mick's other children Jade and Karis, Mick's parents, brother Chris and Charlie Watts.

26

The Stones, minus Ron, assemble for a business meeting at their London office.

29

The compilation album 'Rewind' is released in Europe on Rolling Stones Records. It enters the UK album charts at No. 28 and reaches No. 12.

The single 'Brown Sugar' / 'Bitch' is released in the UK on Rolling Stones Records.

REWIND (1971-1984)
Compilation

A - Rolling Stones Records
EMI CUN 1 EJ260 106 1 (UK),
Atlantic 90176-1 (USA).
Released: June 1984.
Producer: The Glimmer Twins.

Side 1: 1. Miss You (Jagger, Richards) / 2. Brown Sugar (Jagger, Richards) / 3. Undercover Of The Night (Jagger, Richards) / 4. Start Me Up (Jagger, Richards) / 5. Tumbling Dice (Jagger, Richards) / 6. Hang Fire (Jagger, Richards).

Side 2: 7. Emotional Rescue (Jagger, Richards) / 8. Best Of Burden (Jagger, Richards) / 9. Fool To Cry (Jagger, Richards) / 10. Waiting On A Friend (Jagger, Richards) / 11. Angie (Jagger, Richards).

BROWN SUGAR Jagger, Richards / BITCH Jagger, Richards

S - Rolling Stones Records
SUGAR 1 (UK).
Released: June 1984.

Notes: Re-issue of the first single on Rolling Stones Records released to promote the compilation album 'Rewind 1971-1984'.

JULY
2

The compilation album 'Rewind' is released in the States on Rolling Stones Records with some different tracks to the UK version.

The single 'Miss You' / 'Too Tough' is released in the States on Rolling Stones Records.

MISS YOU Jagger, Richards / TOO TOUGH Jagger, Richards

S - Rolling Stones Records
7-99724 (USA).
Released: July 1984.
Producer: The Glimmer Twins.

Notes: Taken from the compilation album, 'Rewind'.

23

Mick issues a denial that he is trying to build a solo career and the Stones are going to split: "Rumours like this come up regularly and have done since the Sixties. The truth is we're very much together as a band. In fact, we all met up three weeks ago in London to discuss future Stones projects. They include recording a new album in December and the possibility of touring next year. I am doing a solo album, but that was part of a record deal we signed a year ago. But the deal with CBS also involves making at least five albums together, so we'll be around for some time. Besides, the Stones have all done solo projects before. Bill Wyman has recorded three albums."

SEPTEMBER

Bill begins work on his 'Willy And The Poor Boys' project, provisionally called 'Up In Arms' the proceeds of which were to go to Ronnie Lane and his ARMS charity. Bill produced the album which featured Jimmy Page, Paul Rodgers, Charlie Watts, Andy Fairweather-Low, Kenney Jones, Chris Rea, Ringo Starr and Dire Straits' drummer Terry Williams. Bill also made a half hour video to promote it.

The Stones are all ready to record their first album for CBS but have to postpone it because Mick is still working on his solo album, mixing the tracks at the Power Station Studios in New York City. Members of Duran Duran drop by the Power Station to visit.

We also want to make a new generation aware of some of the music that inspired all of us when we were growing up. The music has its origin in the 1940s and 1950s. It's a combination of blues, swing, boogie and early rock styles. As a side benefit, this project will provide exposure for a number of excellent musicians who are not as well known as they should be."

18

At New York Hospital, Keith is present when Patti gives birth to Theodora Dupree. Keith: "I was half asleep when we got to the hospital. The next thing I knew they were putting me into gown and cap and I was standing in the delivery room. The only help I could give was to hang on tightly to Patti's hand and try not to trip up the doctors. Even for a hardened old cynic like me, it was a fantastic thing to see a baby being born. I have to admit I was close to tears. I'm a soft hearted guy when it comes to kids and things like that. I just love it."

OCTOBER

Mick is offered a fee of £1,000,000 to join the cast of the American soap *Dallas* but turns it down.

13

Mick and Jerry give a dinner party at their house in New York: among the guests are Jack Nicholson, Andy Warhol, Art Garfunkel, Whoopi Goldberg and Mike Nichols.

26

Ron is interviewed live on WNEW-FM radio from the Hard Rock Café in New York City.

NOVEMBER

Mick, Keith, Charlie and Bill hold business meetings in Amsterdam to plan future projects for the band. Afterwards they return to their various homes. Mick flies to New York.

Later in the month, Mick, Jerry and Julien Temple fly to Rio de Janeiro to begin work on a promo video for Mick's solo album.

8

Mick and Jerry attend a party at Diane Von Furstenberg's apartment in New York. Among the other guests were Bianca and Andy Warhol.

14

Vestron releases a collection of Rolling Stones promo-videos called Video Rewind including all three Julien Temple videos: 'Too Much Blood', 'She Was Hot' and the uncensored version of 'Undercover Of The Night'. It enters the video charts at No. 2 and goes to the top the week after.

28

Ron and Jo fly to Dallas, Texas, where Ron has an exhibition of his paintings at the Foster Goldstrum

Gallery. Called *Portraits Of Friends* the thirty or so works include portraits of Jimi Hendrix, Sid Vicious and the other Stones. The show runs until January 1985.

29

Bill Wyman attends West End première of Paul McCartney's *Give My Regards To Broad Street* at the Empire, Leicester Square and the party at the Hippodrome.

DECEMBER
9

Charlie and Ian Stewart play a benefit concert in Edinburgh in aid of the famine in Ethiopia.

25

Keith and Patti, and Mick and Jerry spend Christmas at their homes in New York, Ron and Jo fly back from New York to spend Christmas in England.

1985

JANUARY

Mick and Keith get together in Paris and work out ideas for the next Stones album at EMI Pathé Marconi studios. They are soon joined by the rest of the group and but for a number of small breaks the group spend the next six months recording in Paris.

3

Ron and Jo get married at St. Mary's Church in Denham, Buckinghamshire. Keith is best man and wedding guests include Charlie

and Bill as well as Rod Stewart, Eric Clapton and Peter Frampton. Mick can't make it, he is supervising the installation of a desalination pump at Stargroves.

11

Ron and Jo go to the party given by the *Daily Mirror* at the old Derry and Toms Roof Garden in Kensington to celebrate columnist John Blake moving to the *Daily Mirror* from *The Sun*.

FEBRUARY
4

Mick's solo single 'Just Another Night' (Jagger) / 'Turn The Girl Loose' (Jagger) is released as CBS Records A 4722. It is taken from Mick's forthcoming solo album 'She's The Boss'. It enters the UK charts at No. 30 but only reaches No. 27. In the States it enters at No. 28 and gets to No. 10.

5

In an interview with the *Daily Mirror* Mick says, "The other Stones might think it's possible that if the album did really well it might be the end of the Stones, but I know it won't be. But it was still strange, working without the others. It is rather like having a wife and a mistress. The Stones thing is like a long marriage. I know them very well, I know their strengths and weaknesses. I almost have telepathy with them after all these years."

MARCH

Charlie's 16-year old daughter Seraphina and another sixth form girl are reported to have been expelled from Millfield, the expensive co-ed progressive boarding school in Somerset. It is alleged that "an incident involving cannabis" was the cause.

1

Keith flies to New York from Paris to await the arrival of his and Patti's baby.

4

Mick's first solo album, 'She's The Boss' released as CBS Records 86310. Musicians featured include Jeff Beck, Pete Townshend, Herbie Hancock, Michael Shrieve, Bernard Edwards, Nile Rodgers, Robbie Shakespeare, Sly Dunbar, Colin Hodgekinson, Chuck Leavell, Ray Cooper and G.E.Smith.

It enters the British charts at No. 16 and climbs to No. 6. In the States it enters at No. 22 and gets to No. 8. Mick is said to be disappointed by the results even though it eventually sells over 2,000,000 copies in the USA alone.

11-12

Bill, Charlie and Ron record a video of six songs as part of the *Willie and the Poor Boys* charity project at Fulham Town Hall, London.

Bill says: "We had three goals in mind when we put together the *Willie and The Poor Boys* project. We want to raise money for ARMS, of course, and keep the public aware that money is always needed for multiple sclerosis research.

APRIL
1

Julien Temple and Mick begin work on the video to promote his next solo single, 'Lucky In Love'.

8

Mick appears on BBC TV's *Old Grey Whistle Test* in London.

11

After a slow start, the Stones reassemble in Paris to resume work on the new album at Pathé Marconi Studios. Steve Lillywhite is co-producing with The Glimmer Twins. The release date was originally set for June, this is now revised to September and the album does not in fact appear until March 1986.

19

Mick releases another solo single: 'Lucky In Love' on CBS A 6213. It enters the US charts at No. 65 and climbs to No. 38.

Above: Mick in Central Park, New York, with daughters Jade (left) and Karis. Below: Mick in the video for 'Lucky In Love'.

MAY

The Stones are approached by Bob Geldof to appear at the Live Aid charity concert and after a meeting in the Paris recording studio, the band decide not to take part. Later in the month Mick announces his participation in the event.

24

Bill releases the 'Willy And The Poor Boys' album on his own Ripple label as Bill 1. Musicians include Charlie Watts, Jimmy Page, Andy Fairweather-Low, Chris Rea, Ray Cooper, Micky Gee, Paul Rodgers, Kenny Jones, Henry Spinetti, Steve Gregory, Geraint Watkins and Bill Wyman, who also produced it.

A single 'Baby Please Don't Go' / 'Let's Talk It Over' from the 'Willy And The Poor Boys' album is also released.

JUNE

The Stones finish recording at Pathé Marconi in the middle of the month. They have laid down 30 tracks.

29

Mick and David Bowie had originally planned to perform a duet for Live Aid with one in the UK and the other in the USA but the technical problems were too difficult to overcome. Instead they go to a London recording studio and cut 'Dancing In The Street' in just 12 hours. After the session they film a video for it in London's East End to be screened during the Live Aid concert.

JULY
4

Mick and Jerry attend an Independence Day celebration on Malcolm Forbes' yacht which sails round the tip of Manhattan once all the millionaires are on board.

Above left: Backstage at Live Aid, clockwise - Keith, Darryl Hall, John Oates, Ron, Bob Dylan, Madonna, Mick and Tina Turner. Centre: Mick with Tina Turner. Bottom: Mick and David Bowie in their 'Dancing In The Street' video for Live Aid.

13

The Live Aid concerts, in aid of Ethiopian famine victims, are staged simultaneously (allowing for time differences) at Wembley Stadium, London and JFK Stadium, Philadelphia. The show is broadcast live by satellite to 1.6 billion people all over the world including the then USSR. In Philadelphia, backed by Hall and Oates and their band, Mick performs his first ever solo show before Tina Turner joins him for 'State Of Shock' and 'It's Only Rock'n'Roll'. The final act from Philadelphia is a very loose Bob Dylan backed by even looser Stones, Keith and Ron. Clearly unrehearsed, Dylan's set is an embarrassing shambles and the two wayward Stones share the blame. One of the main features of the event is the video of Mick and David Bowie dancing to 'Dancing In The Street'.

15

Mick is in Los Angeles to shoot a video for his next single, 'Hard Woman'.

16 - 17

Mick, Keith and Ron begin mixing the tapes for the new album at RPM Studios in New York City. While they are there, Jimmy Page drops by and overdubs guitar on to a couple of tracks.

26

A party is held for Mick's 42nd birthday in the Mike Todd Room of the Palladium Club in New York City.

AUGUST
4

Keith and Patti visit with Marlon, Keith's father and Anita Pallenberg at Anita's Long Island house.

9

The Stones assemble for a photo session with Annie Liebowitz

in New York. She does studio shots for the cover of the next album 'Dirty Work' and also takes them to Battery Park at the tip of Manhattan for outdoor shots.

16

Guitarist Les Paul visits Keith and Ron as they continue work on the new album.

17

The Stones take a three week break from mixing the album.

18

Charlie falls in the cellar of his house in Devon and breaks his leg in three places. His doctor orders him to rest it for three months.

23

Mick and David Bowie's version of 'Dancing In The Street' released worldwide as EMI America EA 204. In the UK it enters the charts at No. 1. In the States, where it is advertised by 20,000 posters and the promo-video is shown in 5,000 cinemas, it enters at No. 25 and gets to No. 7.

28

At Lennox Hill hospital in New York City, Jerry Hall gives birth to James Leroy Augustine Jagger.

SEPTEMBER

Mick, Keith and Ron resume work, mixing the new album.

30

On BBC-TV's *Terry Wogan Show* Jerry Hall says that Mick makes their new baby sleep by jumping up and down singing 'Jumpin' Jack Flash'.

OCTOBER
11

Mick attends a dinner for the Crown Prince of Belgium at Tuileries in New York.

12

Bono from U2, drummers Steve Jordan and Keith LeBlanc, record a track for the anti-apartheid charity album 'Sun City' at Right Track Studio in New York. Keith and Ron play back-up guitars.

15

Keith, Mick and Ron take a break from the mixing board and go on holiday. Keith, Patti, her mother and their daughter fly to Barbados. Ron stays home and has a recording studio installed in the basement of his house in New York. Mick stays in town for a week.

21

Mick and his brother Chris fly to India to go pony-trekking.

NOVEMBER
Dates: The Charlie Watts Big Band dates: Ronnie Scott's, London (18-25).

8

Mick and Jerry are in London for the christening of their son, James Leroy, at St. Mary Abbot's Church in Kensington. Anjelica Huston is godmother, Mick's financial adviser, Prince Rupert Lowenstein, and Mick's personal assistant Alan Dunn are the godfathers.

18

Charlie's 29 piece big band opens at Ronnie Scott's. Among the musicians are Jack Bruce on cello, Pete King on alto, Stan Tracey on piano and Jimmy Deuchar on trumpet. Mick, Keith and Ian Stewart all attend the opening night. Bill drops by later in the week.

25 - 27

Mick, Keith and Ron continue mixing which is now being done at Right Track Studios.

30

Tina Turner plays the Charlotte Coliseum in Charlotte, North Carolina and Mick joins her on stage for 'Honky Tonk Woman'.

DECEMBER
12

Ian Stewart, roadie and pianist with the Stones from the very beginning, has been suffering from acute respiratory problems for several

days and is visiting a specialist in a West London clinic when he dies of a massive heart attack. He was 47. Stewart was the only person in their entourage who had remained unaffected by the wealth and fame. He still herded them on stage by yelling, "Come on, my little shower of shit. You're *on!*"

20

Ian Stewart's funeral is held at Randall's Park Crematorium, Leatherhead, Surrey. All of the Stones attend, flying in from various parts of the world. Ian's ex-wife and 14-year son, Giles are there as well as Bill Wyman's ex-wife Diane and many of his musician friends, Eric Clapton, Jeff Beck, Glyn Johns, Kenney Jones and many others. The band are visibly affected, Mick with tears in his eyes. Keith says to Ron at the funeral: "Who's gonna tell us off *now* when we misbehave?"

23

Keith and Ron fly to New York to join Patti and Jo for Christmas. Mick flies back to Mustique where Jerry and the children are waiting for him. Bill and Charlie retire to their country houses.

Above: Ian Stewart who died December 12, 1985. **Below:** Mick with Pete Townshend and Roger Daltrey of The Who at JFK Stadium, September 25, 1982.

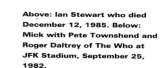

1986

JANUARY

2

Jamaican singer Patrick Alley sues Mick for plagiarism over the song 'Just Another Night' which he says bears a close resemblance to a song on his album 'A Touch Of Patrick Alley'.

23

Keith presents Chuck Berry with the first Rock'n'Roll Hall of Fame award. Keith tells the audience, "I lifted every lick he ever played."

FEBRUARY

Date: Rocket '88: 100 Club, London (7).

7

The Stones assemble in New York to work on the promo-video for 'Harlem Shuffle', their next single. It is shot at the Kool Kat Club in New York with the group singing among animated cut-out characters who look rather like them. Even before shooting ends, one of their accountants is trying to sell the set to minimise expenses.

23

Billed as Rocket '88, the name of Ian Stewart and Charlie Watts' blues band, the Stones play a memorial gig to Ian Stewart at the 100 Club on Oxford Street, London, temporarily burying the rumours that the break between Mick and Keith was irreconcilable and that the Stones would never play again. The death of their close friend brings everyone back to reality, and Mick and Keith leave with their arms around each other. They are joined on stage by Pete Townshend, Eric Clapton, Jeff Beck, Jack Bruce and Simon Kirk.

25

At 3am, the Stones receive a Grammy Lifetime Achievement award from Eric Clapton at the Roof Garden Club in Kensington in London. The presentation is broadcast live by satellite to Los Angeles where the Grammy Awards are being held. They use the occasion to reveal their new promo-video, 'Harlem Shuffle'.

MARCH

Dates: The Charlie Watts Orchestra: Fulham Town Hall, London (23).

3

'Harlem Shuffle' / 'Had It With You' is released on Rolling Stones Records, the first to be distributed by CBS instead of Atlantic. It enters the UK charts at No. 30 and rises to No. 7. In the States it enters at No. 47 and reaches No. 5.

HARLEM SHUFFLE
Relf, Nelson / HAD IT WITH YOU Jagger, Richards, Wood
S - Rolling Stones Records
CBS A 6864 (UK),
Columbia 38-05802 (USA).
Released: March 1986.

Notes: Taken from the album 'Dirty Work'.

23

The Charlie Watts Orchestra at Fulham Town Hall, London, are recorded by The Mobile Studio for a future live album.

24

The Stones new album 'Dirty Work' is released a day early because copies of the album were stolen from a truck in New York and quickly reached radio stations in the US and Europe who immediately began playing it. It enters the British charts at No. 12 and gets to No. 3. In America it enters at No. 21 and reaches No. 4.

DIRTY WORK
*A - Rolling Stones Records
CBS 86321 (UK),
Columbia OC 40250 (USA).
Released: March 1986.
Producer: The Glimmer Twins
and Steve Lillywhite.
Engineer: Dave Jordan.
Mastered: Bob Ludwig at
Masterdisk.
Studio: Recorded at Pathé Marconi
Studios, Paris.
Mixed: R.P.M and Right Track
Studios, New York City.*

*Side 1: 1. One Hit (To The Body)
(Jagger, Richards, Wood) / 2. Fight
(Jagger, Richards, Wood) /
3. Harlem Shuffle (Relf, Nelson) /
4. Hold Back (Jagger, Richards) /
5. Too Rude (Roberts).*

*Side 2: 6. Winning Ugly (Jagger,
Richards) / 7. Back To Zero (Jagger,
Richards, Leavell) / 8. Dirty Work
(Jagger, Richards, Wood) / 9. Had It
With You (Jagger, Richards, Wood) /
10. Sleep Tonight (Jagger, Richards).*

*Notes: Additional musicians include:
Bobby Womack, Don Covay, Chuck
Leavell, Jimmy Page, Patti Scialfa,
Jimmy Cliff, Tom Waits, Kirsty
MacColl, Ivan Neville, Anton Fig,
Steve Jordan, Charley Drayton,
Philippe Saisse, Dan Collette, John
Regan, Alan Rogan, Ian Stewart,
Janis Pendarvis, Dolette McDonald.*

Left: Stills from the 'One Hit To The Body' video.

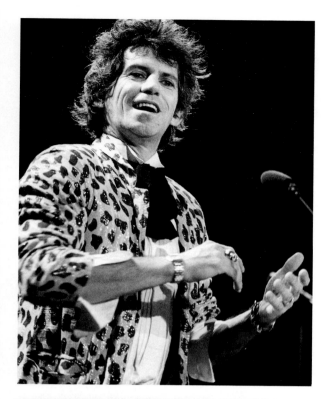

where he joins Chuck Berry on stage at a blues festival in Grant Park before 70,000 people.

7
Keith and Chuck go to Billy Mulligan's to see Dr. John's set then continue on to jam with Junior Wells at the Checkerboard Lounge.

8
Keith flies to Los Angeles where he joins Etta James on stage at the Vine Street Bar for a version of 'Miss You'.

11
Keith flies in to New York and records a video for NBC-TV's *Friday Night Videos* in which he is joined by Marcus Miller on bass and NBC's Paul Shaffer on guitar for a series of Rolling Stones classics.

20
In London Mick appears at a charity concert for the Prince's Trust to raise money to help young unemployed people. Also on the bill are Eric Clapton, Paul McCartney, Phil Collins, Elton John and Tina Turner. Afterwards Mick and David Bowie chat with the Prince.

JULY
5
The Faces are reunited as the climax to Rod Stewart's concert at Wembley Stadium. Ron Wood joins Rod Stewart on stage before an audience of 60,000, and Bill plays bass, deputising for Ronnie Lane who is crippled by multiple sclerosis.

6
Andy Warhol arrives in London on Concorde. Mick and Jerry are guests at Tina Chow's party for him held at Mr. Chow's.

7
Ron flies to Detroit to join Keith where they and Steve Lillywhite co-produce Aretha Franklin singing 'Jumpin' Jack Flash' at Tamla Motown's United Sound Studios. Keith and Ron provide the guitar backing for the track which will appear on her album 'Aretha'.

9
Aretha, Ron, Keith, Steve Lillywhite and Whoopi Goldberg all take part in a promo-video for Aretha's 'Jumpin' Jack Flash' shot at the Motown studios. Whoopi Goldberg will use the track as the title theme for a film of the same name.

12
Keith flies to St. Louis and he and Chuck Berry discuss the idea of a film based on Chuck's life at Chuck's house in Wentzville outside St. Louis, Missouri.

15 - 17
Ron joins Bob Dylan on stage three nights in a row at Madison Square Garden, New York City, to play on ten of Dylan's songs.

APRIL
Dates: The Charlie Watts Orchestra dates: Ronnie Scott's, London (19-26)

4
Mick flies to London from Mustique to work on the theme tune for Abrahams, Zucker and Zucker's Walt Disney production *Ruthless People* and to promote 'Dirty Work'.

15
The Jagger / Richards feud intensifies as *USA Today*, the US national newspaper, reports that Keith has received a cable from Mick telling him that he would not be touring to promote the Stones' 'Dirty Work' because he will be working on a solo album.

MAY
1
The Stones shoot a promo-video for their new single, 'One Hit To The Body' at Elstree Film Studios. It is directed by Russell Mulcahy. Mick and Keith are on good enough terms to stage a scuffle to parody the press stories about their feud though later in the month Keith is reported as saying, "If Mick tours without the band, I'll slit his throat."

19
'One Hit To The Body' / 'Fight' released.

ONE HIT (TO THE BODY) Jagger, Richards, Wood / FIGHT Jagger, Richards, Wood
S - Rolling Stones Records CBS A 7160 (UK), Columbia 38-05906 (USA). Released: May 1986.

Notes: Taken from the album 'Dirty Work'.

JUNE
2
Ron is in New Orleans to appear in a TV-Special on Fats Domino. He spends two days rehearsing with drummer Steve Jordan and Paul Shaffer from the NBC-TV *David Letterman Show*.

6
Keith arrives in New York on the QE2 and flies straight to Chicago

17
In the course of a long telephone conversation on her sixteenth birthday Bill and Mandy finally decide to break up.

21
'Ruthless People' / 'I'm Raining' Mick's solo single, the theme from the film *Ruthless People* is released on Epic in the States only as CBS 34-06211. It enters the US charts at No. 83 but only reaches No. 51.

23
Bill drives to Paris with a

girlfriend, en route to his house in Vence.

26
Mick holds a party for his birthday at his London home. Eric Clapton, Sting, Nick Rhodes and Tina Turner help him celebrate.

Centre: Keith on stage as Chuck Berry's rhythm partner in the movie Hail Hail Rock n'Roll. Below: Ron on stage with Rod Stewart during The Faces reunion at Wembley Stadium, July 5, 1986.

28

At the Lennox Hill Hospital in New York, Patti Richards gives birth to Alexandra Nichole.

30

Ron and Jo sell their house in New York and move back to their home in Wimbledon.

AUGUST
3

Bill's affair with Mandy Smith is "exposed" by the *News Of The World*. Mandy is quoted as saying, "My mother approved of my relationship with Bill. It was an unusual one." Mandy was in Marbella when she and Bill "broke up" by telephone on her sixteenth birthday. One evening at dinner in Marbella with some friends, including her new boyfriend Keith, Mandy innocently discussed the break-up. What she didn't know was that one of the party was a reporter who sold her story to the gutter press. She was not a party to it, nor did she benefit from it, despite inferences in the other tabloids.

She is mobbed by tabloid reporters in Marbella, and Bill cannot leave his villa in Vence because of the reporters parked outside. Bill writes, "I decided it was my responsibility to get her out of Spain to avoid the madness, so I arranged a quiet departure - and was immediately accused of surrounding her with the 'Stones Mafia'... It was a nightmare. I didn't think I'd done her any harm, whatever her age. Quite the reverse."

The press has a bean-feast. Bill's lawyer suggests that he stays in France until things cool down since there is a possibility of criminal charges.

9

Mick, Jerry and children fly to Paris, en route to their Loire Valley château for two weeks holiday.

29

Aretha Franklin's 'Jumpin' Jack Flash' is released on Arista. It enters the US charts at No. 61 and climbs to No. 21.

SEPTEMBER
14

Charlie flies to New York to discuss the possibility of releasing his Charlie Watts Orchestra album in the States and doing a short tour of the East Coast.

15

Mick pursues his solo career and flies to Los Angeles to discuss plans for his next album with Dave Stewart of Eurythmics.

16

A photographer intrudes upon Mick and Dave Stewart at dinner in Los Angeles. Mick punches him in the face.

28

Bill returns to London from Vence and contacts the police who tell him that the Director of Public Prosecutions is not interested in the case. "We've interviewed the mother and daughter. They don't want to press any charges. There is nothing we can do. Thank you very much. If we need you we'll be in touch."

OCTOBER
8 - 15

Keith flies to St. Louis for a week of rehearsals at Chuck Berry's house in preparation for Chuck's 60th birthday show. Also in the band are Bobby Keys on sax, Steve Jordan on drums, Johnny Johnson on piano, Chuck Leavell on keyboards and Joey Stampinato on bass.

16

Chuck Berry gives two concerts at the Fox Theater in St. Louis to celebrate his 60th birthday. Anita Pallenberg and Marlon are in the audience. The shows are filmed by Taylor Hackford for a movie to be called *Hail! Hail! Rock'n'Roll* for which Keith is the musical director.

NOVEMBER

Dates: Charlie Watts Orchestra dates: Music Hall, West Hartford, Connecticut (29).

Allen Klein's ABKCO Records release all of the Stones American London albums (everything up to 'Let It Bleed') on CD.

15

Mick begins work with Dave Stewart on his new solo album at the Wisseloord Studio in Hilversum, Netherlands. Among those helping out are Jeff Beck, Simon Phillips and Doug Wimbish.

23

Eric Clapton plays the Ritz, New York City and is joined on stage by Keith for 'Cocaine' and 'Layla'.

27

Charlie and his 33 man orchestra fly to New York. They will play eight dates on the East Coast to promote their new album.

Keith flies to Jamaica from New York.

DECEMBER

Dates: Charlie Watts Orchestra dates: Philadelphia, Pennsylvania (1); Ritz, New York (2-4); Boston, Massachusetts (5); Toronto, Canada (6).

1

'Live At The Fulham Town Hall', an album of jazz standards by Benny Goodman, Lester Young and Charlie Parker among others, performed by the Charlie Watts Orchestra is released as Columbia 450253-2 in the USA and UK. It was recorded live at Fulham on March 23, 1986. The orchestra was arranged and conducted by Alan Cohen and comprised Charlie Watts, John Stevens and Bill Eyden: percussion; Stan Tracy: piano; Jim Lawless and Bill Lesage: vibes; Ron Mathewson and Dave Green: bass; Jack Bruce: cello; Colin Smith, John Huckeridge, Steve Sidwell, Harry Beckett, Ted Emmett, Jimmy Deuchar and Dave Defries: trumpets; Paul Rutherford, Annie Whitehead, Chris Pyne and John Picard: trombones; Don Weller, Evan Parker, Alan Skidmore, Bobby Wellins, Danny Moss and Courtney Pine: tenor saxophones; Peter King, Ray Warleigh and Willie Garnett: alto saxophones; Gail Thompson: baritone saxophone; Olaf Vass: clarinet and flute.

2

Keith flies to New York from Jamaica.

3

Keith attends the final show of the Charlie Watts Orchestra at the Ritz.

13

Mick completes his work on his solo album at the Wisseloord Studio in Hilversum, Netherlands. He has laid down ten tracks.

18

Keith is back in Jamaica with Patti and the children for his 43rd birthday. Shortly afterwards he flies to New York for Christmas.

21

Mick, Jerry and family fly to Mustique, where David Bowie joins them for Christmas.

24

Mick and David Bowie sing at a carol service held at Mustique's Anglican church.

1987

JANUARY
6

Mick and Jerry fly from Mustique to Barbados where Mick continues work on his solo album at Blue Wave Studios.

21

Jerry drives to Grantley Adams Airport in Barbados to collect a package of clothes and make-up forwarded from Mustique. An employee of Mustique Airways says that another package has been delivered at their desk for her but that it is not addressed to her and they suggest that she open it to make sure it is in fact hers. She does so and is immediately jumped on by police and Customs officials who charge her with importing 20lbs of marijuana. She is locked in a cell overnight and Mick, who is recording, is not told of her arrest for six hours. Mick immediately pays $6,000 bail money. Jerry vehemently denies that the package is hers. She has to surrender her passport and report to Holetown police station twice a week until her case comes to trial on February 13. Jerry's New York lawyer, Peter Partcher flies in to advise and Mick hires top Barbadian lawyer Elliott Mottley to fight the case.

Opposite: Ron at home with his family. Above & centre: Keith with Patti Hansen and new arrivals.

FEBRUARY

Keith begins recording solo tracks at Studio 900 in New York.

Ron Wood continues work on his solo album in the studio at his home in Wimbledon.

13

Jerry appears in court in Barbados, pleads innocence and the trial is adjourned for three days.

16

Jerry is back in court again in Barbados. It soon becomes obvious that police and Customs officers are guilty of a crude attempt to fix Jerry up. Customs supervisor Casper Walcott admits perjury and now tells the court that he had been asked by detectives to be on the look out for a package containing marijuana and changes the evidence he previously gave the court in a number of important details. Despite overwhelming evidence of Jerry's innocence, the magistrate, Frank King, seems strangely reluctant to end the case and adjourns the trial for a further two days to consider the "complicated legal arguments" before pronouncing his verdict. Jerry bursts into tears.

20

Jerry appears in court again in Barbados to hear the verdict. The magistrate takes eight minutes before pronouncing her 'Not Guilty'. As soon as the case is over Mick and Jerry fly to New York where she tells the press that she has lost £130,000 in lost modelling jobs by being forced to stay in Barbados for this ridiculous affair and is very forceful in her opinions about Barbados in general. The unfortunate losers in the situation are Blue Wave Studios in Barbados because Mick transfers all further work on his solo album to the Right Track Studio in New York.

APRIL
1

Jerry, Bianca, Mandy Smith and Bill Wyman all attend the International AIDS day concert at Wembley Arena in London - separately.

8

Fire interrupts Keith's final night of recording his solo album at Studio 900, on 19th Street, New York, one of many studios he is using to lay down tracks. Keith, Ian Neville and drummers Steve Jordan and Charley Drayton salvage their equipment and jam in the street, waiting for the fire dept.

12

Keith flies to Jamaica for a two month holiday, taking his mother Doris and his daughter Angela (née Dandelion) with him.

13

Bill holds a press conference at the Champagne Exchange in London to announce AIMS, his latest charity project. He bought the Stones mobile when they decided they no longer needed it and plans to take it around Britain, giving unknown bands the opportunity to make decent recordings of their work. Bill will produce but take no percentage for his services. Together with sponsorship from Pernod he is able to give free recording facilities to fifty bands out of 1,200 who apply.

MAY
26

Ron and Jo fly to Italy where Ron spends nine days as an interviewer for the Italian TV station RAI. His guests include David Bowie, Peter Gabriel, Genesis and Prince.

27

Keith flies to Los Angeles from Jamaica for discussions with Virgin Records about signing with them for solo work and distributing the soundtrack to *Hail! Hail! Rock'n'Roll*.

JUNE

Date: The Charlie Watts Orchestra: Playboy Jazz Festival, Hollywood Bowl, Los Angeles (13-14); Avery Fisher Hall, Lincoln Center, New York City (23).

Above: Charlie at the head of his Big Band at the New York Ritz, December 1986. Centre: Ron and Jo Wood at the opening of Ron's Art Exhibition. Below: Ron and Bo Diddley.

14

Keith finishes work on the soundtrack album from the film *Hail! Hail! Rock'n'Roll* at Electric Lady studios in New York City.

23

Keith and Patti with Mick Taylor see Charlie's big band play Lincoln Center.

JULY

Date: The Charlie Watts Orchestra: Pistoia Blues Festival, Pistoia, Italy (4).

13

Keith and Richard Branson meet at the Westbury Hotel in New York to conclude discussions about Keith joining the Virgin label for solo work.

15

Bill organises a fund-raising banquet at the London Hilton in aid of his AIMS charity. All the Stones attend with the exception of Keith who is negotiating his contract with Virgin in New York.

17

Keith signs a deal for solo work with Virgin Records in New York.

20-21

Mick in New York City filming a promo-video for his next single, 'Let's Work'. The director is Zbigniew Rybczynski.

27-28

Mick in London films a promo-video for his solo track 'Say You Will' directed by Mary Lambert.

AUGUST
15

Keith and The X-Pensive Winos begin recording at Le Studio in Montreal, Canada.

29

Keith and Patti drive back to New York from Montreal.

31

Mick releases his solo single 'Let's Work' (Jagger, Stewart) / 'Catch As Catch Can' (Jagger) on CBS 65 1028-7. Produced by Mick Jagger and Dave Stewart. It enters the US charts at No. 75, climbing to No. 39. In the UK it enters at No. 35, but gets no higher.

Mick and Jerry are among the guests at Dave Stewart's marriage to Siobhan Fahey of Bananarama.

SEPTEMBER
7

Mick and Dave Stewart, from Eurythmics, work on new material at Dave's London home. Stewart co-wrote 'Let's Work' with Jagger.

9

Mick tapes a video of 'Let's Work' for BBC-TV's *Top Of The Pops*.

14

Mick's second solo album, 'Primitive Cool', is released on CBS 460 123-2. It is produced by Mick and Dave Stewart and the musicians involved include Jeff Beck and G.E.Smith on guitars, drummer Simon Phillips, David Sanborne on saxophone and Paddy Moloney on whistle and uileann pipes. It enters the UK charts at No. 23 and gets to No. 18. In the States it enters at No. 81 but only reaches No. 41.

25

Bill and Ringo Starr are both present at the opening of the La Brasserie night-club in Atlanta, Georgia, in which they have both invested. Bill and Ringo later jam with Jerry Lee Lewis.

OCTOBER
3

Chuck Berry's film, *Hail! Hail! Rock'n'Roll* for which Keith produced the music, is premiered at the New York Film Festival at Lincoln Center. Keith and Chuck are in the audience.

7

Keith and Patti attend the West Coast premier of *Hail! Hail! Rock'n'Roll* which is held at the AMC Century in Hollywood.

20

Mick records a promo-video of his next single, 'Throwaway' live on stage at the Country Club, Los Angeles, directed by Mary Lambert and before an audience of radio competition ticket winners. Backing him are Jeff Beck on guitar, Phil Ashley on keyboards, Doug Wimbish on bass and Zappa drummer Terry Bozio.

Beck was supposed to accompany Jagger on a tour to promote the album starting this month, but the tour was cancelled after Beck and Jagger argued. Jagger's spokesman said, "He had been rehearsing for the tour for a month. Jeff is well known for being difficult to work with and tempers finally snapped. But the tour has been postponed because Jeff is a brilliant guitarist and will be very hard to replace. It now looks like the tour will go ahead in the New Year."

In November, *The Sun* gave Beck's version of the row: "I quit the tour because Mick only offered me peanuts to play with him. It was laughable, an insult. I wanted to teach him a lesson because I believe if you want the best you have to pay for it. The kind of money he offered is what you pay an ordinary session musician. Mick's problem is that he's a meanie. He is no better than a glorified accountant. He counts every single penny. For someone with his money, I can't believe how tight he is. I'd still love to go on tour with the old geezer. He's just got to make me a proper offer. To show there's no hard feelings I went to Los Angeles with him to film the video for his next single 'Throwaway'."

29

'Decades', an exhibition of signed, limited edition lithographs by Ron Wood opens at the Katherine Hamnett Gallery. The last three decades are represented by portraits of well-known musicians.

31

Ron flies to Miami, Florida, where his night club and restaurant Woody's On The Beach has its unofficial opening.

NOVEMBER

Dates: Ron Wood and Bo Diddley's 'Gunslingers' tour: Newport Music Hall, Columbus, Ohio (4); The Riviera, Chicago, Illinois (5); Harpos, Detroit, Michigan (6); The Agora, Cleveland, Ohio (7); The Holliday House, Pittsburgh, Pennsylvania (8); The Copa, Toronto, Canada 10; The Grange, Poughkeepsie, New York (11); The Channel, Boston, Massachusetts (12); The Living Room, Providence, Rhode Island (13); Sundance, Long Island, New York (14) The Stone Balloon, Newark, Delaware (21) The Bayou, Washington, DC (24) ; The Ritz, New York City (25)(late date). Monroeville, Alabama [date unknown]; Raleigh, South Carolina [date unknown] For dates in Memphis, Tennessee and Dallas, Texas, [dates unknown] Bo Diddley is replaced by Charlie Sexton.

9

Mick's solo single 'Throw Away' (Jagger) / 'Peace Of The Wicked' (Jagger) is released as CBS THROW 1.

25

At the last date of their 'Gunslingers' tour, at the Ritz, New York, Ron and Bo Diddley are joined on stage by ex-Temptations David Ruffin and Eddie Kendricks. The set is recorded by the Westwood One Mobile studio and Ron goes immediately to Los Angeles to assist in the mixing which is done by Martin Adam at Secret Sound Studios.

DECEMBER
Dates: Ron Wood and Bo Diddley's 'Gunslingers' tour: Woody's On The Beach, Miami, Florida (19-20).

19

Woody's On The Beach in Miami, Florida, has its official open day. Ron and Bo Diddley are on stage to entertain the guests.

Above: Keith and Patti attend the opening of Bus Stop in New Jersey, July 26, 1988. Below left: Mick with Dave Stewart. Below right: Mick with Jerry Hall at the Royal Albert Hall, London June 6, 1988.

1988

JANUARY
7 - 8

Ron is still in Miami. Mick Taylor joins him on stage at Woody's On The Beach for two nights in a row.

20

The Beatles are inducted into the Rock'n'Roll Hall of Fame and Mick introduces George Harrison and Ringo Starr to the audience at the Waldorf Astoria in New York. Mick joins George and Bruce Springsteen on stage for 'I Saw Her Standing There', plays with Bob Dylan and Bruce Springsteen on 'Like A Rolling Stone' and performs 'Satisfaction' backed by Jeff Beck.

FEBRUARY

Mick begins rehearsals for a Japanese tour at the SIR studios in New York. His line-up includes Doug Wimbish on bass, Simon Philips on drums, Joe Satriani and Jimmy Ripp on guitars, Phil Ashley and Richard Cottle on keyboards. The tour is being promoted by Suntory Dry Beer.

Ron Wood and Martin Adam mix the live tapes of Ron Wood and Bo Diddley recorded at the Ritz, New York, at Secret Sound, Los Angeles. The tapes are released as the CD 'Live At The Ritz'.

20

Through his AIMS charity, Bill organises a benefit for the Great Ormond Street Hospital for Sick Children Wishing Well Appeal at the Royal Albert Hall, London. The top five young AIMS bands are featured, along with Elvis Costello, Chrissie Hynde, Chris Rea, and Bill's all-star band featuring himself, Ron Wood, Phil Collins, Terence Trent d'Arby, Eddy Grant, Ray Cooper, Kenney Jones and Ian Dury. Bill writes in his autobiography, "Harvey Goldsmith presented the concert and we raised over £30,000, which we gave to the Great Ormond Street Children's Hospital. Harvey sent the cheque... and Harvey got the letter of thanks."

MARCH

Dates: Mick Jagger solo tour: Osaka Castle Hall, Osaka, Japan (15-19); Karakuen Dome, Tokyo, Japan (22-23); Nagoya International Exhibition, Japan (25).

Ron Wood and Bo Diddley 'Gunslingers' tour: Two week tour of Japan (2-15); Los Angeles Palace, California (18); Magic Mountain Amusement Park, Los Angeles (26).

12

Ron and Mick meet in Mick's hotel room in Osaka. Ron is playing there, Mick is rehearsing.

23

Tina Turner joins Mick on stage at the Kerakuen Dome to sing 'Brown Sugar' and 'It's Only Rock'n'Roll'.

27

Mick joins Tina Turner on stage at the Osaka Castle Hall to sing 'Honky Tonk Woman'.

Ron visits an exhibition of his paintings in Sherman Oaks, Los Angeles, California.

APRIL
6

Despite legal action by Bill, Phillips Auction Rooms in London sell a three-track acetate of the Stones recorded in October 1962 at Curley Clayton's Studio in London for £6,000. They perform Muddy Waters' 'Soon Forgotten', Jimmy Reed's 'Close Together' and Bo Diddley's 'You Can't Judge A Book'. Tony Chapman is the drummer and the original session was arranged by Bill Wyman.

18

Proceedings open in Federal Court, White Plains, New York in a copyright infringement case in which Jamaican reggae musician Patrick Alley claims that Mick Jagger's song 'Just Another Night' plagiarised his song 'Just Another Night' which first appeared on his album 'Just A Touch of Patrick Alley' in 1982. He is suing both Mick and Columbia Records for $7,000,000 in estimated profits from Mick's 1985 'She's The Boss' album claiming that Mick copied both words and music. Mick is in court to defend his case.

20

Sly Dunbar, who played drums on 'She's The Boss' plays his drums in court to show how the beat on the two recordings is different. Patrick Alley says that Sly played on his record as well, and Sly admits that he might have, or it might have been someone copying him. Sly does so many sessions he can't remember which records he is on.

22

Mick sings a number of songs in court and plays demo tapes of 'Just Another Night', showing its development through various stages of completion.

26

Mick is pronounced innocent of any copyright infringement. He tells reporters, "My reputation is really cleared. If you're well known, people stand up and take shots at you. But the trial was a bit of a waste of time for everyone." All three American television News networks lead with the story of Mick's innocence

MAY
13

Mick puts his foot down and stops Jade from appearing as a young prostitute in a film.

18

The Rolling Stones hold a business meeting at the Savoy Hotel in London to discuss their future plans and projects. They decide to work together again in 1989, make a new album and consider the possibility of another tour.

27

The *Daily Telegraph* reports that Jade Jagger has been expelled from St. Mary's, her exclusive boarding school in Calne, Wiltshire, after sneaking out to meet her boyfriend Josh Astor after hours. "What shall I do?" she is reported to have said. "My dad will kill me."

JUNE

Dates: Ron and Bo Diddley's 'Gunslinger' tour: Hammersmith Odeon, London (28).

10

Bill folds his AIMS charity after Pernod stops its sponsorship and no other companies come forward. He tells *The Sun*: "All the firms are really mean. I just wanted to give some youngsters a break."

JULY

Dates: Ron and Bo Diddley's 'Gunslinger' tour: dates in Italy, Germany and Spain ending on the 29th.

22

Publishers Weekly announces "Viking Penguin and Viking / NAL in the US, have secured world English language rights to the autobiography of Rolling Stone Bill Wyman..." The book will be ghosted by former *Melody Maker* editor Ray Coleman and in fact will only cover the Sixties period, something that was unclear at the time of signing. When Mick had been unable to recall events in sufficient detail for *his* memoirs, he'd asked Bill - the band's unofficial archivist - for help, but Bill had turned him down.

26

Jerry Hall plays the lead as Cherie in *Bus Stop* at Montclair State College Theater in Montclair, New Jersey. The role was originally made famous by Marilyn Monroe. Afterwards they celebrate her first night and Mick's birthday with a party at Ten Park, in New York City.

Above left: Mick with George Harrison, and, right, with Bruce Springsteen at the Rock n'Roll Hall of Fame bash in New York. Centre: Springsteen, Bob Dylan and Mick join forces on 'Like A Rolling Stone'.

Australia (17); Boondall Entertainment Centre, Brisbane, Australia (22-23); Entertainment Centre, Sydney, Australia (26-27, 29).

9

Mick and his backing group arrive in Sydney, allowing themselves plenty of time to recover from the severe jet lag caused by the flight.

14

Mick holds a press conference in Sydney and says he will stop touring when he is fifty: "You can't be nineteen forever. I'll just want to sit back in a chair." Mick is 45.

17

Mick launches his Australian tour with a surprise gig held at the Kardomah Café in Sydney which only seats 400.

22

Keith is in Paris for press interviews to promote his forthcoming single and album.

23

Keith's solo single 'Take It So Hard' (Richards, Jordan) / 'I Could Have Stood You Up' (Richards, Jordan) is released on Virgin Records as VS 1125.

29

Ron has a party at the Hamilton Gallery in Mayfair to launch a book of his paintings, 'The Works'. Anita Pallenberg, Marlon and Mick's brother Chris are among the guests.

OCTOBER
Dates: Mick Jagger solo tour:

Entertainment Centre, Sydney, Australia (1-2); International Tennis Centre, Melbourne, Australia (6-7); Burswood Superdome, Perth, Australia (10-11); International Tennis Centre, Melbourne, Australia (14-15, 17); Entertainment Centre, Sydney, Australia (21); Stadion Utama Senayan, Jakarta, Indonesia (30).

4

Keith's first solo album, 'Talk Is Cheap' is released as Virgin CDV 2554.

Produced by Keith Richards and Steve Jordan, the musicians involved include Keith on lead and background vocals, guitars, percussion, Steve Jordan on drums, percussion, background vocals, Bootsy Collins on bass, Bernie Worrell on organ, Waddy Wachtel on guitar, Charlie Drayton on drums, Ivan Neville on keyboards, Maceo Parker on alto saxophone, Sarah Dash, Patti Scialfa and Sam Butler on background vocals, Joey Spanpinato on bass, Johnny Johnson on piano, Chuck Leavell on organ, Bobby Keys on tenor saxophone, Stanley "Buckwheat" Dural on accordion, and Michael Doucet on violin. It enters the US charts at No. 75 and gets to No. 24.

5 - 6

Keith rehearses his solo touring band, The X-Pensive Winos, at the American Sound Studios in New York City, ready for their upcoming tour.

Below: Ron with his own book of art work.

AUGUST
19

Mick flies to London from New York to work with Ron on new songs.

22

Mick flies to New York from London. At Heathrow Airport, he tells the press that the Stones will make a new album next year and do a tour.

23

Mick and Keith meet in New York to discuss future projects and writing the material for the proposed new album.

Ron, Jo and family fly to Antigua for a vacation.

24

Mick flies to San Francisco to begin rehearsals with his backing group for his forthcoming solo Australian tour which is sponsored by Reebok.

SEPTEMBER
Dates: Mick Jagger solo tour: The Kardomah Café, Sydney,

6

Mick and Keith's problems are put in perspective by Keith in an interview in *Rolling Stone* magazine. He says, "In the Seventies, when I was on dope and I would do nothing but put the songs together and turn up and not deal with any of the business of the Stones, Mick took all of that work on his shoulders and did it all and covered my ass. And I've always admired him very much for that. I mean, he did exactly what a friend should do. When I cleaned up, and 'Emotional Rescue' time came around - 'Hey, I'm back, I'm clean, I'm ready; I'm back to help and take some of the weight off your shoulders' - immediately I got a sense of resentment. Whereas I felt that he would be happy to unburden himself of some of that shit, he felt that I was homing in and trying to take control. And that's when I first sensed the feeling of discontent, shall we say. It wasn't intended like that from my point of view, but that's when I first got a feeling that he got so used to running the show that there was no way he was going to give it up."

16

Keith plays the *Smile Jamaica* benefit concert held in London in aid of Jamaican hurricane victims. His own house at Point Of View, Ocho Tios, was damaged by the hurricane. Keith is in London to promote his new album.

28

Keith gives a press conference at the Hard Rock Café in New York to announce his solo X-Pensive Winos tour.

NOVEMBER

Dates: Mick Jagger solo tour: Western Springs Stadium, Auckland, New Zealand (5).

Keith Richards' X-Pensive Winos tour: Fox Theater, Atlanta, Georgia (24); New Daisy Club, Auditorium, Memphis, Tennessee (25); Constitution Hall, Washington, D.C. (27); Beacon Theater, New York (29).

3

Keith attends the tenth anniversary party of *Beggars Banquet*, the official Rolling Stones fanzine, held at the US Blues Club in New York.

4

Keith and Patti take the kids to the circus.

9

Jerry Lee Lewis joins Ron on stage at Woody's On The Beach in Miami. David Bowie is in the audience but does not sit in.

10

Keith and Patti fly to Antigua for a week's holiday prior to Keith's X-Pensive Winos tour.

16

Ron receives an undisclosed amount of damages for libel from *The Sun* newspaper in the High Court in London after the paper alleged that he spent the night with a girl he picked up at a London nightclub. "Usually I just laugh at things that are written about me," he said when he issued the writ in May, 1987, "but this time things have gone too far. I have never even met this girl, let alone gone to bed with her." He also receives a public apology from the paper.

24

The X-Pensive Winos play their first gig at the Fox Theater in Atlanta. Keith's line-up consists of Waddy Wachtel on guitar, Bobby Keys on saxophone, Steve Jordan on drums, Charley Drayton on bass, Ivan Neville on keyboards and Sarah Dash singing back-up vocals.

29

After the audience leaves the Beacon Theater, Keith holds a party

in the lobby. Among the guests are Carole King, Brooke Shields, Steve Van Zant and Matt Dillon.

30

Keith does a record signing session at Tower Records on Broadway.

DECEMBER

Dates: Keith Richards' X-Pensive Winos tour: Tower Theater, Philadelphia, Pennsylvania (1-2); Orpheum Theater, Boston, Massachusetts (3-4); Music Hall, Cleveland, Ohio (7); Fox Theater, Detroit, Michigan (8); Aragon Ballroom, Chicago, Illinois (10); Henry J. Kaiser Convention Center, Oakland, California (13); Universal Auditorium, Los Angeles, California (14); The Palladium, Hollywood, California (15); Brendan Byrne Arena, New Jersey (17).

4

Mick, Jerry and their family leave London to spend Christmas in Mustique.

14

There is a backstage party after Keith's Los Angeles gig. Among the guests are Dan Aykroyd and Bill Murray.

17

Keith's tour end party is held in the bar at the Brendan Byrne Arena. Patti Hansen, Anita Pallenberg and their three children are among the guests. Keith is presented with a gold album for 'Talk Is Cheap'.

Above: Keith and Patti Hansen and, below, with their daughters Theodora and Alexandra in New York.

1989

JANUARY
10
Ron and Jo attend Rod Stewart's 44th birthday party at Langan's restaurant, London.

13
Mick and Keith get together in Barbados to write. Before leaving New York, Keith tells Patti, "I'll be back in either two weeks or 48 hours because I'll know in 48 hours whether this thing is going to work or if we're just going to start cattin' and doggin'." He stayed on. Bill Wyman writes: "Perhaps the earlier tension between them provided an impetus, for they worked with amazing speed."

16
Ron has an opening for his paintings at the Hamilton Gallery in Mayfair, London. The show runs for two weeks.

17
Mick and Keith fly to New York from Barbados. Ron flies to New York to join them and Mick Taylor, who lives in New York, in order to accept the Rock'n'Roll Hall of Fame award.

18
The Rolling Stones are inducted into the Rock'n'Roll Hall of Fame in a ceremony held at the Waldorf Astoria in New York City. The band were originally expected to perform but Bill objected, saying that the award was "too little, too late". Bill wrote, "Charlie and I didn't attend. It seemed ridiculous to me that we were being honoured by the Establishment of show business so late in our careers and I'd have felt hypocritical at a formal dinner as a Stone, dressed in a tuxedo and bow tie, an image we had vigorously opposed throughout our career."

The award is accepted by Mick, Keith, Ron and Mick Taylor. Pete Townshend gives a speech in which he says, "The Stones feel to me as if they still have a future. Guys, whatever you do, don't try to grow old gracefully. It wouldn't suit you."

Mick, accepting the award says, "It's slightly ironic that tonight you see us on our best behaviour, but we're being rewarded for 25 years of bad behaviour. And then, there's a bit of music on the side... but we're not quite ready to hang up the number yet." Mick, Keith and Pete Townshend pay tribute to Brian Jones and Ian Stewart.

Later Mick joins Stevie Wonder for a run through of 'Uptight' and 'Satisfaction', then Keith, Ron and Mick Taylor backed him and Tina Turner singing 'Honky Tonk Woman'. After a few more numbers, the four Stones concluded with 'Start Me Up'.

19
Charlie joins Mick, Keith and Ron in New York for a business meeting.

21
Ron, along with Bo Diddley, Percy Sledge, Duck Dunn, Eddie Floyd, Willie Dixon, Chuck Jackson, Dr. John, Carla Thomas, Steve Cropper, Albert Collins, Billy Preston and Koko Taylor all celebrate Republican President-elect George Bush's victory on stage at the Convention Center in Washington D.C. George Bush shows up to meet the musicians and be presented with a signed poster and a guitar, then Republican National Committee Chairman Lee Atwater who organised the bash, strapped on a red guitar and played 'Hi Heel Sneakers'. Out of the 8,500 attendees, there were more black people on stage than in the audience.

29
Mick and Keith return to Barbados for a week's recording.

FEBRUARY
6
Mick flies to London from Barbados.

8
Keith flies from Barbados to New York.

9
Keith makes a promo-video for his new single 'Make No Mistake' / 'Struggle'. It is shot at the North River Bar in New York and features X-Pensive Winos: Charley Drayton, Steve Jordan and Sarah Dash, as well as members of The Memphis Horns.

10
Mick flies from London to Barbados.

13
Keith returns to Barbados to continue working on new songs at the Blue Wave studios with Mick.

Ron and Bill attend the BPI Awards held at the Royal Albert Hall where they presented the Best British Newcomer Award.

18
Bill takes part in the Kampuchea Appeal concert held at the Ringwood Recreation Centre, Southampton.

In Barbados serious business discussions take place between Mick, Keith, Prince Rupert Lowenstein, Stones' US business manager Joseph Rascoff, their US music-business attorney John Branca and promoters Bill Graham and Michael Cohl, the head of CPI, who fly in from the States for the meeting.

20
Charlie flies in to Barbados to record rough demos of the new songs with Mick and Keith.

MARCH
9
Ron and Bill fly out to join the other Stones for rehearsals in Eddy Grant's studio in Barbados.

15
The biggest rock'n'roll contract in history is signed in Barbados between The Rolling Stones and Michael Cohl, of Concert Productions International. Toronto promoter Cohl guarantees the Stones between $65 and $70,000,000 for approximately 55 shows in the US and Canada. He will promote the tour, the associated merchandising and a pay-as-you-view TV special through his company Brockum.

21
The Stones break for ten days. They all fly to their various homes except Bill who holidays in Antigua with girlfriend Melissa from New York.

29
The Stones reassemble at George Martin's AIR studios in Montserrat to begin recording their next album.

31
The *Daily Express* breaks the story that Bill has asked Mandy to marry him. She says, "Bill asked me to marry him on Easter Sunday and I accepted immediately. It was really romantic. I'm delighted and so is he." Bill proposed over the telephone from Barbados.

APRIL
1
Bill holds a press conference in Antigua to announce that he and Mandy Smith will be getting married despite the fact that she is 19 and he is 52. He holds the conference in Antigua to keep the publicity away from the other Stones who are trying to get on with recording. While he is away, Ron takes over on bass and the Stones lay down four new tracks.

2
Bill flies to Montserrat to continue work on the next album.

3
It seems Bill and Mandy are having problems finding a church in which to get married. Bill tells the *Daily Express*, "Mandy is a Catholic and I am Church of England and she desperately wants the ceremony in June in a Catholic church: a white wedding with all the trimmings. But everywhere she has gone they have said 'No' because I am divorced. Surely there is a Catholic church somewhere in Britain who will make Mandy's dream come true."

Above: The Stones, including Mick Taylor, are inducted into the Rock n' Roll Hall of Fame and jam with Pete Townshend (centre) and Tina Turner (below).

29

The Stones finish recording at AIR Studios. The band recorded the basic tracks in only five weeks, recording everything live in the studio.

MAY

The Stones, working with producer Chris Kimsey, begin mixing their new album at Olympic Studios in Barnes.

2

Mick arrives in an outsize limo to watch a match at the Oval cricket ground.

9

An advance opening party is held at Bill's new restaurant, Sticky Fingers, in Kensington. Among Bill's guests are Mandy, Ron and Jo, Chris Jagger, James Hunt, Ringo's wife actress Barbara Bach and actress Emma Samms. Bill has filled the walls of the restaurant with Rolling Stones memorabilia, including Brian Jones' Gretsch guitar.

15

The Stones hold business meetings in Amsterdam. The evening ends in a brawl when Mick wakes Charlie at 5:00am by calling his room and yelling "Is that my drummer boy? Why don't you get your arse down here?" Charlie comes to Keith's room, approaches Mick, yells, "Don't ever call me your drummer again - you're my fucking singer!" and knocks Mick out with a single punch to the head. Keith told *The Sun*, "We were having a group meeting in Amsterdam and I figured Mick and I would go out for a drink. We had a great time and at five in

the morning Mick came back to my room. Mick was drunk and Mick drunk is a sight to behold. Charlie was fast asleep and Mick shouted those words at him. Charlie shaved, put on a suit and tie, came down, grabbed him and went BOOM! Charlie dished him in a walloping right hook. He landed in a plateful of smoked salmon and slid along the table towards the window. I just pulled his leg and saved him from going out into the canal below."

17

Bill's restaurant, Sticky Fingers, opens in Kensington.

18

Bill gets himself in the papers again by sticking his finger down the front of model Denise Lewis's dress at the opening of an exhibition of prints by photographer David Bailey.

28

Bill Wyman's XI play Eric Clapton's XI in a charity cricket match at the Stocks Country Club, Aldbury, Hertfordshire. They raise £25,000 for actress Emma Samm's Starlight Foundation for Terminally Ill Children. Among the all-star teams were Ron Wood, Gary Brooker, David Essex, Mike Rutherford and Andy Fairweather-Low. Eric Clapton misses his flight from New York and doesn't show.

Above: Bill and Mandy Smith marry at Bury St. Edmunds, June 2, 1989 and, below, attend a celebrity cricket match together on May 28.

31

Keith is given a statuette of Elvis Presley by Eric Clapton and proclaimed a "living legend" at the first annual International Rock Awards ceremony held in the Armory, New York. The X-Pensive Winos are joined on stage by Eric Clapton, Jeff Healy, Dave Edmunds, Clarence Clemons and Tina Turner. The show is broadcast live by ABC-TV to 50 countries. As soon as it is over, Keith flies back to London to continue work on the new album.

JUNE
2

Bill and Mandy get married at Bury St. Edmunds Registry Office, with Bill's son Steven and Mandy's sister Nicole as the only witnesses. That evening they appear on the *Terry Wogan Show:* "It was all over in 15 minutes," Bill says. "If I'd have known it was that easy, I'd have done it years ago."

5

Bill and Mandy receive a blessing at the Church of St. John the Evangelist in Hyde Park Crescent, London. The Anglican ceremony is witnessed by 170 guests and afterwards there is a reception for 400 at the Grosvenor House Hotel. All the Stones and their wives attend, as does Eric Clapton, Elton John, and many other musicians. Mick's wedding present is a £20,000 Picasso etching. As he presented it, Charlie joked, "You should have kept the original and given Bill a copy - he'd never know the difference."

10

Bill and Mandy continue their honeymoon at Bill's house in Vence in the South of France.

11

Ron and Jo leave London for a short holiday in Ireland.

16-17

BBC-TV's *Arena* team film the Stones recording at the 16th century Palace of Ben Abbou in Tangier, Morocco for a *Rhythms Of The World* programme. Mick, Keith and Ron record a backing track for the song 'Continental Drift' on the new album, using the music of the Master Musicians of Joujouka. Mick says, "It feels that there's a sort of twinning between the two bands here." In 1968 Brian Jones recorded the Joujouka musicians for an album which was not released until after his death. In 1968 he wrote, "They're not singing to an audience of mortals but rather an incantation to those on another plane." Once a year, the Joujouka musicians re-enact the rites of Pan, something they apparently have been doing for more than two thousand years.

There was an odd coincidence involving the Joujouka musicians as Mick explained, "When I was writing this song I said 'Oh this would be great if we could have someone like Joujouka on it. And a week later, I got a letter from them saying, 'Can we come and play on a show that you're doing'. The Stones had had no contact with them in 20 years. Director Nigel Finch also films Mick talking to the American writer Paul Bowles who has lived in Tangier since the Thirties and was one of the first Westerners to go to the mountains and hear the musicians of Joujouka.

20

Ron's Miami club and restaurant, Woody's On The Beach closes after pressure from neighbours about the noise.

Back in London from Tangier, Mick and Keith resume mixing the new album. Mick says, "The album is called 'Steel Wheels'. It was very quick for a Rolling Stones LP, which makes it more interesting for several reasons. It was written - apart from one song I did last year and one Keith did last year - all the songs were written in this rather compressed time frame. It presents us in the state we were then, rather than over the last five years. We had got into a terrible habit of meandering and being disorganised. I sat down with Keith and he said, 'We're never going to do an album.' Well maybe we won't but there isn't any harm in trying. If we get four good things, or six or even nothing but let's see what we can do. But the only way it's going to work is if we come in, write the songs, do the arrangements, have it all ready and go into the studio. It does sound very professional for The Rolling Stones and to be honest I never thought it would work... but it did. We wrote it in Barbados - Jerry won't go back there, but not me. I quite like Barbados though it has its downside, too many tourists, but we were quite far away from all of it in Eddie Grant's studio."

24

Keith watches Wimbledon tennis stars Vitas Gerulaitus, Pat Cash and Mats Vilander play Stones numbers at the Hard Rock Café in London.

Above left: Bill outside his Kensington restaurant Sticky Fingers and, right, with his celebrity cricket XI. Below: Keith with Eric Clapton.

JULY

At the beginning of the month the Stones begin rehearsals in the small town of Washington, Connecticut, not far from Waterbury in an attractive area of steep hills and lakes. They occupy an entire hotel and three additional houses. Wykham Rise, a former girls' boarding school has been rented for rehearsals and their entire compound is protected by steel gates and security guards. Mick has his own house a few miles up the road in New Preston at the bottom of Mount Bushnell where he undertakes a rigorous training régime. Mick says, "It will be more difficult than the last tour but I did play last year so I know what my body can do. It's pretty good.

I'm very lucky. I may be fitter than I was 20 years ago but I'm older. The real boring thing is that 20 years ago I only did a 45 minute set, when I could have done two hours. Now I would rather do 45 minutes I have to play for two hours. I don't have any problems with it. It's just the length of the tour. After 25 shows I can make it then it gets tougher. It depends how much I move, it's 5-10 miles on stage. The others don't keep fit at all. Charlie has to keep very fit because it's the second most physical job. Bill, well we could make lots of jokes about Mandy and we will."

Above & centre: The band in 1989. Below left: Mick trains with dancer Adrienne Eggleston.

1

Mick wins £5,000 on the Irish Derby by predicting the first three horses past the post.

9

Mick flies into New York on Concorde. The other Stones are already in town.

11

The Stones hold a press conference at Grand Central Station in New York to announce their 'Steel Wheels' tour. After keeping 500 reporters and milling fans waiting in 100 degree heat for an hour, the band arrived on track 42 in a 1920's caboose, featured in Francis Ford Coppola's film *The Cotton Club*, pulled by a chartered commuter train. They played 'Mixed Emotions' off the new album through a tinny ghetto blaster and gave details of the tour.

Reporter: "Some rock critics have charged that the only reason you're doing it is for the money."

Mick: "What about love and fame and fortune? Have you forgotten about all those things?"

Keith: "The glory, darlin', the glory."

16

Bill collapses, complaining of heart pains during rehearsals in Washington, Connecticut. The Stones' doctor diagnoses food poisoning.

19

The residents of Washington, Connecticut, form a "Roll The Stones Out Of Town" pressure group, complaining of harassment from Stones' security.

26

The Stones have a barbecue at the Mayflower Inn in the small town of Washington to celebrate Mick's 46th birthday.

AUGUST

Dates: Toad's Place, New Haven, Connecticut (12); Veterans' Stadium, Philadelphia, Pennsylvania (31).

3

The Stones tape a video for "Mixed Emotions".

12

At Toad's Place, a 700 capacity club in New Haven, Connecticut, it is just another Saturday Night Dance. Young people pay $3.01 admission to attend a "Rock Party With The Cruiser", expecting to dance to a local act, Sons Of Bob. Even Sons Of Bob don't realise they are opening for the Stones until they see the equipment coming in. With no announcement Keith rips into 'Start Me Up' and the beginning of a solid 50 minute Stones set that gives the audience good value for their money.

13

The Stones decamp from Washington, Connecticut and check into the Garden City Hotel to continue their rehearsals at the Nassau Coliseum, in Long Island, where they can test out their stage and lighting. They play before a select audience of a 100 or so people each night at the Coliseum.

Mandy, whom Bill has hardly seen since he married her, is reported as unable to join him because she is suffering from a serious allergy.

17

'Mixed Emotions' / 'Fancyman Blues' is released by Rolling Stones Records. It enters the UK charts at No. 41 and gets to No. 33. In the States it enters at No. 47 and climbs to No. 5.

MIXED EMOTIONS Jagger, Richards / FANCYMAN BLUES Jagger, Richards
S - Rolling Stones Records CBS 655 193-7 (UK), CBS 38-69008 (USA). Released: August 1989.

Notes: Taken from the album 'Steel Wheels'

24

Thirteen love letters from Bill to "Babs" written in 1964 along with a gold bracelet inscribed "To Barbara, in gratitude, Bill Wyman 1967" are sold at Christie's rock auction in London for £1,430.

26

The Stones fly into Philadelphia and check into the Four Seasons Hotel for three days of rehearsals.

28

Hells' Angels reportedly threaten to kill Mick on stage as a 20th anniversary commemoration of Altamont. The threat is taken seriously and police stage a 24 hour guard over him.

29

'Steel Wheels' released in the US on Rolling Stones Records. It enters the charts at No. 44 and reaches the top.

31

The Stones begins the biggest rock' n'roll tour of all time. Over 2,000,000 people applied for tickets for the two Philadelphia concerts and some rich fans are so desperate they are paying forty times the ticket price to scalpers. 55,000 people see each show. There are minor skirmishes outside the auditorium when drunken fans clash with police, resulting in 52 injuries and 28 arrests. Mid-way through 'Shattered' the 550,000 watts sound system goes dead. It takes the stage crew three minutes to locate the problem and fix it. The Stones drop 'Shattered' from their set.

SEPTEMBER

Dates: Veteran's Stadium, Philadelphia, Pennsylvania (1); Exhibition Stadium, Toronto, Canada (3-4); Three Rivers Stadium, Pittsburgh, Pennsylvania (6); Alpine Valley Stadium, East Troy, Wisconsin (8-9, 11); Riverfront Stadium, Cincinnati, Ohio (14); Carter-Finley Stadium, Raleigh, North Carolina (16); Busch Stadium, St. Louis, Missouri (17); Cardinal Stadium, Louisville, Kentucky (19); Carrier Dome, Syracuse, New York (21-22); R.F.K. Stadium, Washington, D.C. (24-25); Municipal Stadium, Cleveland, Ohio (27); Sullivan Stadium, Boston, Massachusetts (29).

3
The Stones play their first concert in Canada in twelve years to an audience of 60,000.

6
The Stones play 'Mixed Emotions' live on MTV for the Video Awards ceremony via a satellite link to the Three Rivers Stadium in Pittsburgh.

10
Ron goes on stage at Buddy Guy's concert at Legends in Chicago to greet the audience but does not play.

11
'Steel Wheels' is released in the UK on Rolling Stones Records. It enters the British album charts at No.12 and gets to No. 2.

STEEL WHEELS
A - Rolling Stones Records CBS 465 752 1 (UK), Columbia OC 45333 (USA). Released: September 1989 (UK), August 1989 (USA). Producer: The Glimmer Twins and Chris Kimsey. Engineer: Christopher Marc Potter. Mastered: Ted Jensen at Sterling Sound. Studio: Recorded at AIR Studios, Montserrat.

Side 1: Sad, Sad, Sad (Jagger, Richards) / 2. Mixed Emotions (Jagger, Richards) / 3. Terrifying (Jagger, Richards) / 4. Hold On To Your Hat (Jagger, Richards) / 5. Hearts For Sale (Jagger, Richards) / 6. Blinded By Love (Jagger, Richards).

Side 2: 7. Rock And A Hard Place (Jagger, Richards) / 8. Can't Be Seen (Jagger, Richards) / 9. Almost Hear You Sigh (Jagger, Richards, Jordan) / 10. Continental Drift (Jagger, Richards) / 11. Break The Spell (Jagger, Richards) /

12. Slipping Away (Jagger, Richards).

Notes: Chuck Leavell plays piano and organ on tracks 1, 2 and 12. Chuck Leavell plays organ on t racks 3, 6 and 8. Chuck Leavell plays keyboards on tracks 7 and 9. Kick Horns (Simon Clarke, Roddy Corimer, Tim Sanders, Paul Spong) play brass on tracks 1, 2, 7 and 12. Bernard Fowler sings background vocals on tracks 1, 2, 5-10 and 12. Luis Jardin plays percussion on tracks 2, 6, 8 and 9. Sara Dash sings background vocals on tracks

2, 7, 9, 10 and 12. Lisa Fisher sings background vocals on tracks 2, 3, 7, 9, 10 and 12. Matt Clifford plays keyboards on tracks 3, 5-12. Roddy Corimer plays trumpet on track 3. Phil Beer plays fiddle and mandolin on track 6. Chris Jagger is literary editor on tracks 6 and 9. The Master Musicians of Jajouka play on track 10.

13
Mick and Charlie see Elton John play Riverbend Stadium, Cincinnati, Ohio.

16
The United Station Program Network transmits *The Rolling Stones Story*, a three-hour radio special, throughout the States.

OCTOBER
Dates: Sullivan Stadium, Boston, Massachusetts (1-2); Legion Field, Birmingham, Alabama (5); Cyclone Field, Ames, Iowa (7); Arrowhead Stadium, Kansas City, Missouri (8); Shea Stadium, New York City (10-11); Los Angeles Coliseum, California (18-19, 21-22); Shea Stadium, New York City (25-26, 28-29).

9
Charlie and Shirley celebrate their 25th wedding anniversary with a party at the English Speaking Union in New York. All the other Stones attend as guests.

11
Bill, Ron and Charlie fly to Los Angeles directly after their final Shea Stadium concert

14
Ron and Eric Clapton go to the Santa Anita racetrack. Ron wins, Eric doesn't.

16
Bill presents an exhibition of the late Michael Cooper's photographs from the *Blinds and Shutters* book at the Earl McGrath Gallery in Los Angeles. Among the guests were John Mayall, Eric Clapton and Ron and Jo Wood.

17
Ron hosts a show of his paintings and drawings at the Madison Gallery. Among the guests are Alice Cooper, Eric Clapton and John McEnroe.

24
Bill celebrates his birthday with a party at the Red Zone Club in New York.

Centre: Bill with John Mayall, Eric Clapton and Al Cooper at the opening of the exhibition of photographs by the late Michael Cooper. Left: Charlie and Shirley Watts.

1990

NOVEMBER

Dates: B.C.Place, Vancouver, Canada (1-2); Alameda Stadium, Oakland, California (4-5); Astrodome, Houston, Texas (8); Texas Stadium, Dallas, Texas (10-11); Superdome, New Orleans, Louisiana (13); Orange Bowl, Miami, Florida (15-16); Tampa Stadium, Tampa, Florida (18); Grant Field, Atlanta, Georgia (21); The Gator Bowl, Jacksonville, Tennessee (25); Death Valley Stadium, Clemson, Utah (26); Metrodome, Minneapolis, Minnesota (29-30).

4

The Stones' Oakland concert is delayed because Mick is viewing the devastation in Watsonville which was the hardest hit by the October earthquake. He flies in by helicopter and spends an hour talking with residents and viewing the damage. The Stones donate $500,000 to help rebuild the town.

14

Mick and Bill see Buddy Guy play at Club Mu in Miami.

20

'Rock And A Hard Place' / 'Cook Cook Blues' released in the UK.

ROCK AND A HARD PLACE
Jagger, Richards /
COOK COOK BLUES
Jagger, Richards
*S - Rolling Stones Records
CBS 655 422-7 (UK),
CBS 38-73057 (USA).
Released: November 1989.
Producer: The Glimmer Twins
and Chris Kimsey.*

*Notes: Taken from the album
'Steel Wheels'.*

26

A concert in Death Valley Stadium in Clemson, South Carolina, is added to the Stones' tour after Hurricane Hugo strikes and $500,000 is donated to hurricane victims.

DECEMBER

Dates: Skydome, Toronto, Canada (3-4); Hoosier Dome, Indianapolis, Indiana (6-7); Pontiac Silverdome, Detroit, Michigan (9-10); Olympic Stadium, Montreal, Canada (14); Convention Center, Atlantic City, New Jersey (16-17, 19-20).

20

The final concert of the US leg of the tour is transmitted live over radio and cable TV simulcast. Eric Clapton gets up and jams and Axl Rose and Izzy Stradlin of Guns n' Roses do their Junior Glimmer Twins imitation on 'Salt Of The Earth'.

27

BBC-TV's *Arena* shows a special devoted to the history of The Rolling Stones.

JANUARY

ALMOST HEAR YOU SIGH
Jagger, Richards, Jordan /
BREAK THE SPELL
Jagger, Richards
*S - Rolling Stones Records
CBS 38-73093 (USA).
Released January 1990.
Producer: The Glimmer Twins
and Chris Kimsey.*

*Notes: Taken from the album
'Steel Wheels'.*

25

Mick and Jade attend the opening night of *Bus Stop* at the Palace Theatre, Watford, where Jerry Hall is playing the lead role of Cherie.

Axl Rose and Izzy Stradlin of Guns N'Roses joins the Stones on stage in New Jersey.

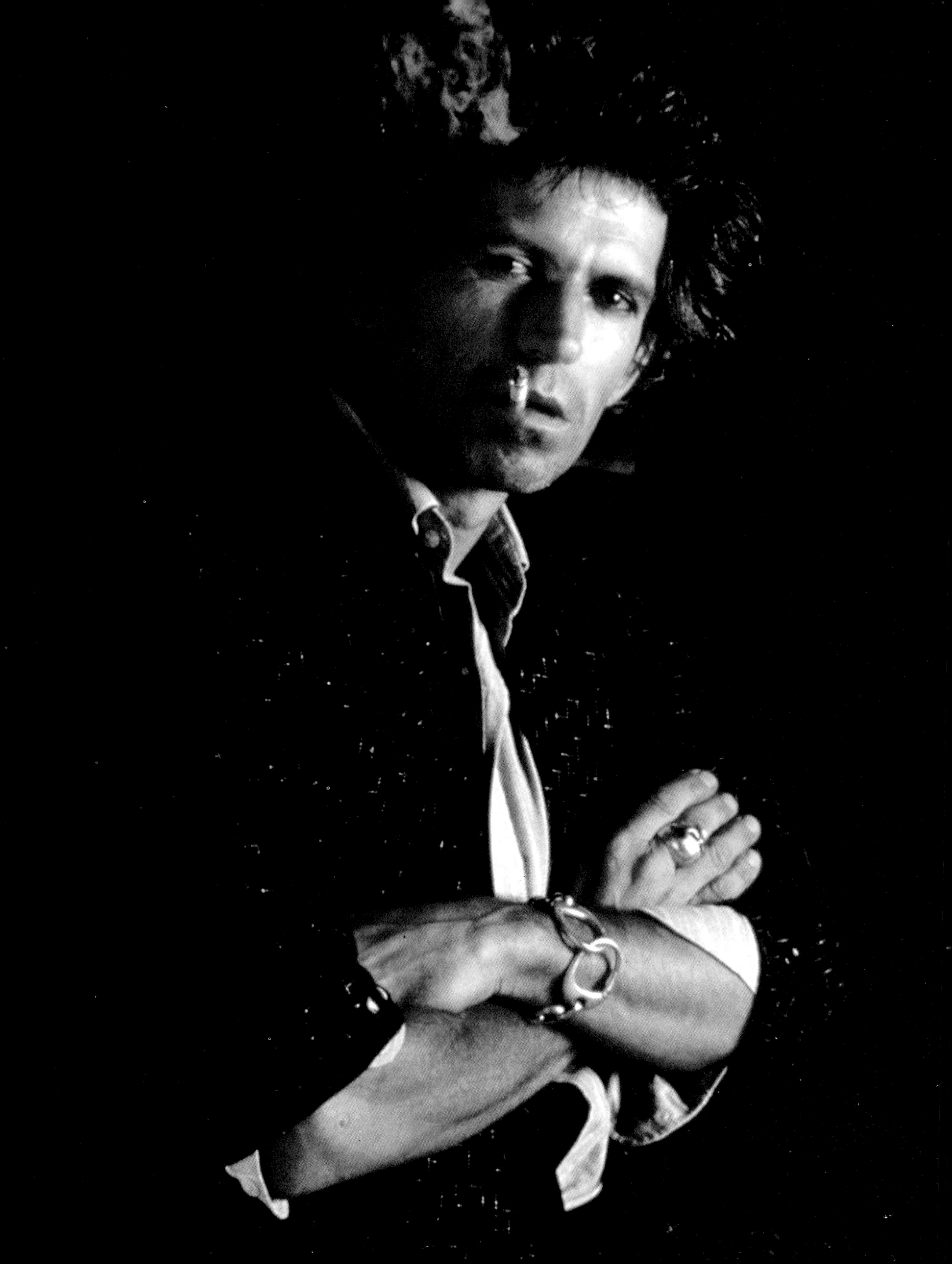

FEBRUARY

Dates: Korakuen Dome, Tokyo, Japan (14, 16-17, 19-21, 23-24, 26-27).

5
Keith and Ron Wood fly into Narita Airport, Tokyo, Japan, from London and check into the Okura Hotel.

6
Mick and Charlie fly into Narita Airport, from New York and check into the Okura Hotel. Bill is delayed in England because his father is very ill.

9
The Stones hold a press conference at Korakuen Hall, next door to the Korakuen Dome where they appear flanked by an honour guard of Samurai warriors. Bill misses the conference.

The Stones begin rehearsals at the Mza studio, Tokyo.

11
Bill flies into Tokyo.

Mick, Keith, Charlie and Ron attend the Buster Douglas - Mike Tyson fight at the Dome. Tyson wins the heavyweight crown.

12
The Stones hold their first full rehearsal with a full line-up.

14
Set designer and architect Mark Fisher meets with Mick and Charlie to finalise the design for the Urban Jungle set to be used during the Stones' European tour.

Opening night at the Korakuen Dome. Keith tells the sell out audience of 50,000 "I feel better than Mike Tyson."

15
Bill Wyman gives interviews at the Isetan department store to promote the book of Michael Cooper's photographs: *Blinds and Shutters*, which he helped to create. An hour later, at 8pm, Ron Wood hosts a reception for his paintings and drawings on a different floor of the same store which takes the form of a press conference, with Ron surrounded by translators.

16
After the concert, the Stones film some video sequences for a Fox-TV programme to be broadcast in April, 1990. They mime to the soundtrack of the Atlantic City pay-as-you-view concert, but had to shoot the 3-D footage in Japan.

17
Sony hosts an après-gig party for the Stones at the Okura where they receive gold CDs for *Steel Wheels*.

After the party, Ron, Bernard Fowler and Lisa Fisher spend the night drinking Lizard Juice in the Red Shoes bar in Roppongi.

21
Patti Hansen's mother, who is with Keith and Patti on the tour, suffers a heart attack and is rushed to hospital. Keith goes with her, takes a break to play the gig, then returns to the hospital. They keep her there for two weeks before she is allowed to fly back to New York.

22
Mick, Keith and Ron all take their children to the Korakuen Amusement Park next door to the Dome.

26
Just before he goes on stage, Bill Wyman is informed that his father has died.

27
The Stones attend the end-of-tour party. *Bus Stop* with Jerry Hall, transfers to the Lyric Theatre in the West End of London.

28
Bill flies to London to attend his father's funeral. Over the next few days, the Stones leave Japan. Mick flies to England (and Paul McCartney moves into his suite at the Okura, ready to play the Korakuen Dome), Ron flies to Eire, Charlie to England and Keith stays in Tokyo for a few days where he spends one night visiting with Paul McCartney before flying to Antigua.

MARCH

17
Keith in New York for Patti's birthday and to visit his mother-in-law in hospital.

18
Keith celebrates the birthday of his daughter Theodora.

19
Keith is interviewed by Flo and Eddie for a *Save The Rainforests* five station radiothon from New York. Afterwards he dines at Il Cantanori.

22
The Stones European tour is announced at a chaotic press conference held at the Tabernacle Club in London during which Mick trips over his microphone lead and is cut short by the ringing of his own telephone.

Keith flies back to Antigua from New York.

APRIL

30
The Stones begin two weeks of rehearsals for the forthcoming European leg of the world tour at the Château du Dangu, near Paris, using the dining room as their studio.

MAY

Dates: Feyenoord Stadium, Rotterdam, The Netherlands (18-19, 21); Niedersachsen Stadium, Hanover, Germany (23-24); Wald Stadium, Frankfurt, Germany (26-27); Mungersdorfer Stadium, Cologne, Germany (30-31).

12
The Stones check into the Rotterdam Hilton.

20
Charlie visits the Van Gogh Museum in Amsterdam.

22
The Stones check into the Intercontinental Hotel, Hannover.

30
The Stones Atlantic City concert, recorded December 19, 1989, is shown on Fox-TV in the States.

JUNE

Dates: Olympic Stadium, Munich, Germany (2-3); Olympic Stadium, Berlin (6); Alvalade Stadium, Lisbon, Portugal (10); Olympic Stadium, Barcelona, Spain (13-14); Vicente Calderon, Madrid, Spain (16-17); Stade Velodrome, Marseille, France (20); Parc des Princes, Paris, France (22-23, 25); St. Jacob Stadium, Basel, Switzerland (27).

1
Charlie and Ron hold a joint birthday celebration in the bar of the Vier Jahreszeiten Hotel in Munich. (Charlie's birthday is actually on the 2nd).

3
Immediately after the concert, Keith, Bill, Ron and Charlie take the train to Berlin where they stay at the Bristol Kempinski Hotel.

6
The Stones on ABC-TV's *Rock Awards* show. Their acceptance speeches and Keith's presentation of the "Living Legend" award to Eric Clapton were videotaped in Cologne and their "live" performance was taped in Munich.

15
Keith and Charlie record tracks at a Madrid studio. Keith plays a jazz solo on the Charles Mingus number "Please God, Don't Let 'Em Drop The Atom Bomb On Me" for a possible tribute album to the late bass player and composer.

16
Before the concert in Madrid, Mick meets the mayor Felipe Gonzalez. There is an after concert party at the Moon Club.

ALMOST HEAR YOU SIGH Jagger, Richards, Jordan / **WISH I'D NEVER MET YOU** Jagger, Richards / **MIXED EMOTIONS** Jagger, Richards
S - Rolling Stones Records
CBS 656 065-7 (UK).
Released: June 1990.
Producer: The Glimmer Twins and Chris Kimsey.

Notes: Taken from the album 'Steel Wheels'.

27
The Stones play a brilliant set in Basle, but it pours with rain throughout.

28
The Stones take a week off. Mick, Bill and Charlie go to France, Keith flies to London to stay in a rented house in Wimbledon. Ron flies to his new home in Ireland, taking Bobby Keys with him.

JULY

Dates: Wembley Stadium, London (4, 6-7); Hampden Park, Glasgow, Scotland (9); Cardiff Arms Park, Wales (16); St. James's Park, Newcastle (18); Maine Road, Manchester (20-21); Flamenio Stadium, Rome, Italy (25-26); Delle Alpi, Communal Stadium, Turin, Italy (28-29); Praterstadion, Vienna, Austria (31).

except Charlie get together for a quiet drink with President Václav Havel and his wife Olga in a local pub.

18

The Stones visit Hradcany castle and have dinner with the President and his wife before the concert. Keith: "That was an amazing gig." A ticket also acted as a one-day passport for fans coming from Poland, Hungary, and Russia. A lot of the reason you've got major shifts in superpower situations in the past few years has to do with the past twenty years of music. You'll never get rid of nationalism and so-called patriotism, but the important thing is to spread the idea that there's really this one planet - that's what we've really got to worry about." The Strahov Stadium holds 107,000 people and is full, despite the pouring rain.

The Stones donated their fee to a charity for disabled children.

19

The Stones fly into London and check into the Mayfair Hotel, except Mick who stays at the Halcyon.

21

Footage for a documentary is filmed in Keith's room at the Mayfair.

25

Final concert at Wembley Stadium. More than 2,000,000 people had seen them perform live, grossing more than $200,000,000.

The Stones hold an end of tour party at the Roof Garden in Kensington. Marianne Faithfull is among the guests.

27

Mick and Matt Cliford see Bernard Fowler play with his band Tackhead in Reading, not far from Mick's country house.

SEPTEMBER

Charlie and Shirley Watts go to Poland for a short holiday.

12

BBC Radio 1 broadcasts the Stones' August 24 Wembley Stadium concert.

19

Keith flies from New York to Jamaica.

22

Stones' assistant Miranda Guinness and Stones' stage designer Keith Payne are married in Basingstoke. Charlie and Shirley Watts attend the ceremony, Bill attends the reception afterwards in Miranda's parents' house. Seraphina Watts and Jade Jagger also attend.

3

The Stones check into the Mayfair Hotel for their London gigs, except Mick who stays at the Halcyon. Bill spends a couple of nights at his house in Chelsea and Keith, Patti and children rent a house in Wimbledon for some of the time.

5

Bill holds a party at his Sticky Fingers restaurant. Bobby Keys and The Uptown Horns all make a showing but no other Stones.

6

Keith holds a party in his hotel room. Woody and his brothers Art and Ted are among the guests.

9

Tuning up backstage in Glasgow. Keith pricks the middle finger of his left hand on a guitar string protruding from the machine head. After playing a two and half hour set, his finger becomes swollen and he has difficulty playing.

10

Keith's finger becomes stiff and infected and he runs a high fever. After examination in hospital he is ordered to take five days off to recover, causing two shows at Wembley Stadium and one at Cardiff Arms Park to be rescheduled. This is the first time ever that the Stones have missed a gig caused by personal illness. He stays in Wimbledon to recuperate.

14

The Stones, except Keith, hold a party at the Serpentine Gallery in Hyde Park. Among the guests were Elton John, Jeff Beck, Duran Duran, Bianca and Jade Jagger.

16

The Stones return to London immediately after their Cardiff gig.

17

Bill visits his wife Mandy in the Spring Hill Convalescence Home in Buckinghamshire where she has been recovering from Addison's Disease for the last two months.

26

Mick's birthday is celebrated with a party at the Excelsior Hotel, Rome.

TERRIFYING
Jagger, Richards /
ROCK AND A HARD PLACE
Jagger, Richards
S - Rolling Stones Records
CBS 656 122-7 (UK).
Released: July 1990.

Notes: Taken from the album 'Steel Wheels'.

AUGUST

Dates: Eriksberg Stadium, Gothenberg, Sweden (3-4); Vallehoven, Oslo, Norway (6-7); Idraetsparken, Copenhagen, Denmark (9); Weisensee, East Berlin, Germany (13-14); Parkstadion, Gelsenkirchen, Germany (16); Strahov Stadium, Prague, Czechoslovakia (19); Wembley Stadium, London (24-25).

15

SKY-TV, Europe, shows 90 minutes of the Stones' Barcelona concert.

17

The Stones arrive in Prague, Czechoslovakia, and check into the Palace Hotel. Then all

OCTOBER
24
Bill's autobiography, *Stone Alone* is published by Viking Penguin in London. The book is launched with a combination birthday party-book party at Bill's own Sticky Fingers restaurant. Bill blows out 54 candles on a cake shaped like the book.

NOVEMBER
1
Jo Wood's father dies of a heart attack at Ron and Jo's home in Wimbledon in the middle of a conversation.

12
Returning from his funeral in Devon, Ron and Jo and their children Leah and Tyrone are involved in a car crash on the M4 near Swindon, Wiltshire, at 7:15 on a rainy night. Jo was driving their BMW when it skidded on oil and spun 180 degrees. The car behind hit them head on. Jo received back injuries, Leah and Tyrone received head injuries requiring stitches. Ron hurt his left shoulder, but as he got out of the car a third vehicle hit the oil and struck the second car, trapping Ron between the second car and his own, breaking both his legs. Ron's car phone was used to call an ambulance and the family were taken to the Princess Margaret Hospital in Swindon where Ron was kept for several days before being transferred to the Cromwell Hospital in London, across the hallway from Mandy Smith who had been there for three months recovering from Addison's Disease which had reduced her weight to a mere 70lbs.

13
Bill attends the National Youth

Theatre Ball at the Grosvenor House Hotel, London. Prince Edward is the guest of honour.

21
Mick and Jerry are married in Bali, Indonesia, by a holy man called Ida Banjar. Alan Dunn is best man. The marriage is of questionable validity since they are not Hindus nor did they present the required paperwork. They had been sight-seeing in India, Nepal and Bhutan for six weeks before arriving in Indonesia.

22
Bill announces that his seventeen month marriage to Mandy Smith is over.

27
Ron, Jo and Jerry Hall attend a fashion show for designer Bruce Oldfield at a restaurant on Sloane Street.

DECEMBER
2
Keith flies to London from Jamaica to mix the live tracks for the album, *Flashpoint* at Metropolis Studios with Mick.

7
Mick's parents, Joe and Eva, celebrate their golden anniversary in what becomes a joint celebration with Mick and Jerry held at the Nayland Rock Hotel, Margate, Kent. Mick presents his parents with a gold chalice.

Keith flies to New York from London.

10
Ron has his plaster casts removed from his legs.

19
Keith held a celebration of his birthday and wedding anniversary at his and Patti's house outside New York.

20
Ron, Jo and family fly to Ireland.

25
Mick, Jerry and family in Mustique.

1991

JANUARY
4
Charlie, Shirley and Seraphina dine at Le Caprice in Mayfair.

Bill sighted at Tramp with Fergie, Duchess of York.

6
Ron, Jo and family fly to London from Ireland. Keith flies to London from New York.

12
Ron and Jo go to Kenya on safari.

7-26
The Stones are in the Hit Factory (CBS Studios) London to record a new single, 'Highwire' and 'Sex Drive'. Mick and Keith finish mixing *Flashpoint*, the live album of the Steel Wheels / Urban Jungle tour.

16
The Stones record 'Highwire' on the day that allied aircraft first bomb Baghdad.

24
Keith flies to New York.

29-30
Keith produces and plays on two tracks for Johnnie Johnson's solo album *Johnnie B. Bad.* at the Sorcerer Sound Studios, New York.

FEBRUARY
Keith and Patti spend the month on vacation in Antigua.

2
Ron joins the Irish band, The Wilfs, to play the Rock-a-Baby charity concert at the Hackney Empire, London, to help the maternity ward of the Homerton Hospital in East London. Paul Young and Dave Gilmour also play.

14
Mick flies to Atlanta, Georgia, to prepare for filming his part as the 21st century bounty hunter, Vacendak, in the Sci-Fi thriller *Freejack.*

16
Ron joins Bob Dylan on stage at the Hammersmith Odeon, London, for three numbers including "Like A Rolling Stone".

17
Ron and George Harrison walk on stage during Bob Dylan's show at the Hammersmith Odeon, London, to present him with a bunch of yellow roses. When he ignores them they stuff the flowers down his shirt front.

18
Mick begins filming his part in *Freejack.*

26-27
Charlie Watts records his solo album 'From One Charlie' at the Lansdowne Studios, London.

Ron attends Eric Clapton's concert at the Royal Albert Hall.

28
Bill also attends one of Eric Clapton's Albert Hall shows.

Ron and Charlie fly to New York to film the video for "Highwire" and check into the Plaza.

MARCH
Keith spends the month in New York working on material for his next solo album.

1
The Stones, except Bill, are in New York to shoot the promo-video for 'Highwire', their new single with director Julien Temple. The shoot takes place at Pier 3, now used for parking trains but once a WWII military pier. At 3am there is a break for a quick birthday party for Stones aide Alan Dunn. Shooting was completed at 6am.

Bill attends Eric Clapton's concert at the Royal Albert Hall, London, with Phil Collins.

2
A proper birthday party for Alan Dunn is held at the Plaza Hotel's Edwardian Room.

3
Charlie returns to London.

4
"Highwire" / "Sex Drive" released in USA.

5
Ron and Jo fly to London.

6
Charlie adds the string section to his album 'From One Charlie' at Lansdowne Studios. Recording the album has taken three days.

7-14
Ron and Jo holiday in Ireland.

21
"Highwire" released in the UK where it causes controversy because some critics claim its lyrics are critical of the Gulf War. In an act of censorship that the Stones are familiar with in Britain, the first verse is edited out by BBC-TV's *Top of the Pops.* Mick: "It's not about the war, it's about how it started."

HIGHWIRE
Jagger, Richards /
2000 LIGHT YEARS FROM HOME Jagger, Richards
S - Rolling Stones Records
Sony Music 656 756 (UK),
Columbia 38-73742 (USA).
Released: March 1991 (UK),
February 1991 (USA).
Producer: Chris Kimsey and The Glimmer Twins.

Notes: Side 1 taken from the album 'Flashpoint'

Above: Bill at the launch of his autobiography Stone Alone. Below: With Mandy.

FLASHPOINT

A - Rolling Stones Records
Sony Music 468 135 2 [CD].
Released: April 1991.
Producer: Chris Kimsey and
The Glimmer Twins.
Recorded live by Bob Clearmountain
and David Hewett on Remote
Recording Services and by Cedric
Beatty and Harry Braun on Dierk's
Recording Mobile.
Mixed: Christopher Marc Potter
except tracks 14 and 15, which
were mixed by Chris Kimsey and
Mark Stent.
Mastered: Bob Ludwig at
Masterdisk.

Side 1: 1. (Intro) Continental Drift
(Jagger, Richards) / 2. Start Me Up
(Jagger, Richards) / 3. Sad Sad Sad
(Jagger, Richards) / 4. Miss You
(Jagger, Richards) / 5. Ruby
Tuesday (Jagger, Richards) / 6. You
Can't Always Get What You Want
(Jagger, Richards) / 7. Factory Girl
(Jagger, Richards) / 8. Little Red
Rooster (W. Dixon).

Side 2: 9. Paint It Black (Jagger,
Richards) / 10. Sympathy For The
Devil (Jagger, Richards) / 11. Brown
Sugar (Jagger, Richards) /
12. Jumping Jack Flash (Jagger,
Richards) / 13. (I Can't Get No)
Satisfaction (Jagger, Richards) /
14. Highwire (Jagger, Richards) /
15. Sex Drive (Jagger, Richards).

Notes: Bobby Keys plays saxophone.
Chuck Leavell plays keyboards.
Matt Clifford plays keyboards and
the French horn. Bernard Fowler
sings background vocals. Lisa Fisher
sings background vocals. Cindy

Mizelle sings background vocals.
The Uptown Horns (Arno Hecht,
Paul Litteral, Bob Funk and Crispen
Cioe) play on all tracks. The Kick
Horns (Simon Clarke, Roddy Corimer,
Tim Sanders, Paul Spong) play on
track 5 on the CD version (missing
from vinyl release). Eric Clapton
plays guitar on track 8. Tessa Niles
sings background vocals on
track 15. Katie Kissoon sings
background vocals on track 15.
The CD release contains two extra
tracks: Rock And A Hard Place
(Jagger, Richards) and Can't Be
Seen (Jagger, Richards).
Tracks 2 and 13 were recorded at
Death Valley Stadium, Clemson,
November 26, 1989. Tracks 2 and 8
were recorded at the Convention
Center, Atlantic City, New Jersey,
December 19, 1989. Tracks 4 and 6
were recorded at the Gator Bowl,
Jacksonville, Florida, November 25,
1989. Track 10 was recorded at
the Korakuen Stadium, Tokyo,
February 26, 1990. Track 5 was
recorded at the Korakuen Stadium,
Tokyo, February 27, 1990. Track 7
was recorded at Wembley Stadium,
London July 6, 1990. Track 9 was
recorded at the Estadio Olimpico,
Barcelona, Spain, June 13, 1990.
Track 11 was recorded at the Stadio
delle Alpi, Torino, Italy, July 28, 1990.
The two studio tracks, 14 and 15
were recorded at the Hit Factory,
London, January 7-16, 1991.

10 - 19
Keith is in San Francisco working
on 'Crawling King Snake' a track for
John Lee Hooker's new album at
Russian Hill Studio.

16
Mick and Elton John are in the
audience for Bob Dylan's concert at
the Fox Theater, Atlanta, Georgia.

19
Keith flies from San Francisco to
Los Angeles to meet up with Patti.

26
Mick attends Noël Coward's
play Fallen Angels at the Marietta
Theater in the Square, Atlanta,
Georgia, while filming Freejack.

APRIL
Dates: The Charlie Watts Quintet:
Ronnie Scott's, London (3).

Keith flies to San Francisco
to produce a track for John Lee
Hooker's next album, 'Mr. Lucky'.
Keith also plays on it. Keith,
"John came on and did a couple
of songs at the Stones' last gig
in America in Atlantic City. I'd
heard a couple of his latest records,
including the one he'd put out in
'89, and I said, 'Nice job, John'.
Then at the beginning of this year
he calls up and says, 'I'd really like
you to do a track on this album.'
He asked me what song I wanted
to do. I said, 'I wanna do a song
about a subject you're really
interested in, John. Let's do
'Crawlin' Kingsnake'."

While in San Francisco, Keith
and Tom Waits get together to write
some songs.

2
'Flashpoint', the live album of the
Stones' recent world tour, released
in the USA.

3
Charlie plays his latest jazz
album at a press launch held at
Ronnie Scott's, London.

5
Charlie appears on the Jonathan
Ross TV show in London to promote
his new record / book.

8
'Flashpoint', the live album of the
Stones' recent world tour released
in the UK.

Charlie plays his latest jazz album
at a press launch held at Ronnie
Scott's, London. The album 'From
One Charlie' is released as

UFO 2 CD, and includes mostly
material by Pete King, the alto
saxophone player and Charlie's band
leader. Also on the album are Gerard
Presencer, trumpet; Brian Lemon,
piano; David Green, acoustic bass;
and a string section.

In 1964, Charlie published a small
book, Ode To A High Flying Bird, that
he had written in 1961, based on the
life of saxophonist Charlie Parker.
Almost 30 years later Charlie was
persuaded to allow a second edition
to be published and decided to
create some music to go with it.
He asked Peter King to compose
music to capture the flavour of the
Charlie Parker Quintet - which had
Red Rodney on trumpet - without
actually copying it. This he did.
When they recorded, they added
two original Parker numbers, Charlie
says: "This is a holiday into something
I love. And what I would hope for is
that people would a) like the book
and b) go out and buy a Charlie
Parker record. I think that's a good
thing to hope for."

MAY

1
In Atlanta, Georgia, Mick completes work on *Freejack* and flies back to New York. Mick: "Now here I am in an action film and it's great, a bit like *Bladerunner*, and I get to have lots of fire-fights, shooting high-tech machine guns which is what boys like."

2
Bill and Ron collect trophies for the Stones for their Outstanding Contribution To British Music at the Ivor Novello Awards at the Grosvenor House Hotel in London.

4
Mick and daughter Karis see the Broadway play, *I Hate Hamlet*, at the Walter Kerr Theater.

9
Mick flies to London from New York.

14
Mick flies to France to attend the Cannes Film Festival.

19
Keith flies to London to make the video for 'Sex Drive'.

21-22
The Stones shoot a promo-video for 'Sex Drive' at Twickenham Studios with Julien Temple once again directing.

30
Mick attends a Lenny Kravitz concert at the Zenith in Paris and duets on 'No Expectations'.

JUNE
Date: The Charlie Watts Quintet: Blue Note, New York City (3).

1
Ron celebrates his 44th birthday in Ireland.

2
Charlie flies to New York and checks into the Mark Hotel on 72nd Street. It is his 50th birthday and he celebrates by having a quiet dinner with the men in his band.

4
Bill holds a party at his restaurant, Sticky Fingers, to celebrate its second anniversary. His latest girlfriend, Charlotte Walden, is at his side.

6
Charlie appears on ABC-TV's *Good Morning America* show for an interview and a number with his quintet. At 1pm he does an autograph session at the Rizzoli Bookshop to promote *From One Charlie*.

7
Charlie dines at Keith and Patti's house in New York.

8
Charlie flies to London from New York.

10
Ron sees Billy Connolly play the Hammersmith Odeon.

13
Ron is at the 20th anniversary party for the Hard Rock Café in London.

14
Ron, Jo and Jerry Hall are at a party given by Desmond Guinness at Leixlip castle in Dublin.

17
Ron is at the Limelight, London, for the launch party for John McEnroe and Pat Cash's new CD.

18
Ron opens an exhibition of work by cancer patients at the Royal Marsden Hospital.

19 - 20
Charlie and Shirley have a brief holiday in Germany.

20
Bill appears on London's TV-AM talk show.

21
Bill and Charlotte Walden attend the premier of the film *Naked Gun 2½*.

Pianist Johnnie Johnson's solo album 'Johnnie B. Bad' is released on Elektra featuring Keith on two tracks.

23
Mick watches cricket at Lords, meets his parents and Jade at the Imperial War Museum then takes them to see the new house he's bought: Downe House, a Georgian mansion on Richmond Hill has six reception rooms, Adam ceilings, a gym, a Jacuzzi and a nursery. Bay windows overlook the Thames and box hedges keep the rose garden in place. It cost £2,200,000.

Bill and Ron jam in a tent after the charity cricket match at Blenheim Palace gets rained off.

25
Mick and Jerry attend the opening night of *Tosca* at Earls Court, London.

AUGUST
4
Ron arrives in Ireland to prepare artwork for a show to tour Japanese galleries in September.

SEPTEMBER
Dates: The Charlie Watts Quintet: Spiral Hall, Tokyo, Japan (15-17).

John Lee Hooker's album, 'Mr. Lucky' is released featuring Keith on one track.

7
The Stones concert film, *At The Max* is premièred at the Toronto Film Festival.

18
Mick is in attendance at a book launch at Spencer House, London.

Charlie is the host at a "bow tie contest" at Spiral Hall, Tokyo.

20
Ron and Jo attend the première of the film *The Commitments* in Dublin.

Charlie takes part in a signing session of his book and CD set *From One Charlie* at Tokyo's Virgin Megastore.

21
Charlie flies to London from Japan.

26
Mick attends a post-concert party for Dave Stewart of Eurythmics.

Ron flies to Tokyo for a five city tour of his artwork beginning at Art Collection House in Tokyo.

30
Ron takes the bullet train to Kobe where his paintings open at Seiden Hall.

Left: Mick with daughter Karis.

OCTOBER
Dates: The Charlie Watts Quintet: Ronnie Scott's, Birmingham (28-31).

1
Ron arrives in Kyoto to show his paintings.

2
Ron shows his paintings in Kyoto.

4
Ron flies to Fukuoka where his work is on display at the Bayside Palace.

8
Ron flies to London.

14
Keith flies to Seville, Spain, from

New York and checks into the Tryp Colon Hotel to attend the Guitar Legends Show, a five day festival featuring 30 guitarists. He sees Bo Diddley play that night.

15
Keith begins rehearsals for the Guitar Legend Show to be held in La Cartuja Auditorium.

17
Keith plays before 6,000 people at the Guitar Legends Show, introduced to the audience by Bob Dylan. He and Dylan jammed on Joe Turner's 'Shake Rattle and Roll'.

18
Mick and Jerry attend the private view of Francesco Clemente's *Three*

Worlds exhibition at the Royal Academy of Arts, London.

Keith flies into London from Seville.

19
Sections of Keith's performance at the *Guitar Legends Show* is shown on pay-as-you-view cable TV in the USA.

Keith, Ron and Jo attend the bar mitzvah for Greg Morris, the son of drummer Simon Kirke of Bad Company.

28
Mick answers questions in both French and English at the press launch of the film *At The Max* held at La Geode in Paris.

31
The Charlie Watts Quintet records at Ronnie Scott's, Birmingham, on the Fleetwood Mobile for future release.

Bill holds a charity masquerade party at his restaurant, Sticky Fingers, in aid of the Royal Marsden Hospital.

NOVEMBER
Date: The Charlie Watts Quintet: Ronnie Scott's, Birmingham (1-2).

1
The Charlie Watts Quintet records at Ronnie Scott's, Birmingham, on the Fleetwood Mobile for future release. Ron and Jo Wood, Robert Plant and Jack Bruce all attend the show. Charlie walks to the gig each day from the Birmingham Hyatt Hotel.

18
Keith flies to London from New York.

19
The Stones sign a three album deal with Virgin Records for £25,000,000 which also gives Virgin distribution rights to the back catalogue of all Rolling Stones Records product. Richard Branson says, "I first saw the group as an 18-year-old in Hyde Park..." The deal is made at the London office of Prince Rupert Loewenstein after which Branson makes an announcement, "The Stones are the greatest rock'n'roll band and I am honoured they have chosen Virgin." Mick, Keith, Ron and their wives go to dinner with Richard Branson at Mossimann's restaurant where the celebrations continue until 4am. Four months later Branson sells Virgin Records to Thorn-EMI.

20
Keith flies to New York from London.

21
Keith attends a press conference in New York to promote the film *At The Max*. He avoids discussing the details of the Stones' new record deal.

25
Keith attends a memorial for Bill Graham at the Beacon Theater, New York.

26
'Keith Richards & The Expensive Winos Live At The Hollywood Palladium, December 15, 1988' is released by Virgin Records as CD VUS 45. Produced by Keith Richards, Steve Jordan and Don Smith, it features material from Keith's solo album, plus a couple of Stones' favourites, 'Happy' and 'Time Is On My Side'. The X-Pensive Winos are: Keith on guitar and vocals; Waddy

Wachtel on guitar and vocals; Steve Jordan on drums, bass and vocals; Charley Drayton on drums and vocals; Ivan Neville on keyboards and vocals; Sarah Dash on background vocals; and Bobby Keys on saxophone.

Keith: "One of the reasons I put this out was because there's so much crap around these days. If you really wanted to get upset about bootlegs, it would drive you mad, but my attitude is that, in a way, bootlegs are another indication that people like what you do. But people kept coming up to me, telling me they had bought this concert for seventy-five dollars, and all it was was a load of shit with the Winos screaming faintly in the background. I'm very happy with it. It has a flow. I like the atmosphere on it, and I love Sarah Dash singing 'Time Is On My Side', which is the best version I've ever heard."

DECEMBER
9
Keith takes live telephone calls from fans on ABC Radio's *Rockline* show.

13-18
Charlie stays with Ron at his house in Ireland, recording tracks for Ron's solo album.

20
Keith and Patti host a party at their place outside New York.

21
Keith attends a charity screening of the concert film *At The Max* held at the Maritime Center in Norwalk, Connecticut in aid of the Fairfield County Fund For Environmental Education.

1992

JANUARY

Press reports claim that Bill Wyman has left The Rolling Stones.

12
Jerry Hall gives birth to Georgia May at the Portland Hospital, London, a private clinic patronised by the Royal family. Mick was present at the birth.

14
Mick flies to Los Angeles to attend the premier of *Freejack*.

15
The Stones press office refuses to comment on the fact that Bill Wyman will not sign the band's new £25,000,000 contract with Virgin Records saying only that "Bill Wyman has made no decision as to his future with The Rolling Stones." However, in the February issue of *Vanity Fair*, Mick speaks as though Bill has already gone, "It's a terrible thing. I don't know how I'm going to live with it. I think Bill's kind of had enough of it really. I don't know, he seemed alright on the last tour. He's got enough money and I suppose he feels he's done it. We haven't really talked about it, but I don't think I'd be out of order saying that I doubt we'd actually get someone new in the band who'd be a permanent Rolling Stone. We'd make a record, do a tour and see how it works over a two-year period."

Keith inducts the late Leo Fender into the Rock'n'Roll Hall of Fame at a ceremony held at the Waldorf Astoria in New York. After fooling around and pretending to read from the menu instead of his speech, Keith says that Fender's "true stroke of genius was not his inventing the electric guitar, but inventing the amplifier to go with it... He gave us the weapons..."

16
Mick attends the premier of *Freejack* at Mann's Chinese Theater. Afterwards he and David Bowie go to the Asylum club. He stays in Los Angeles another week, jamming in the S.I.R. studio and partying with Jack Nicholson.

FEBRUARY
12
Mick appears at a press conference to announce National Music Day, an idea he first suggested to Arts Minister Tim Renton in the Nubian Room of the British Museum, and which was taken up by his successor David Mellor, the Arts Council, Equity and the National Union of Musicians.

14
The Stones' concert film, *At The Max* directed by Julien Temple is premièred in Britain at the Bradford National Museum of Film and Photography, the only place in Britain with a screen big enough to take the giant IMAX format which requires an 80 foot high screen. Bradford's screen is 52 feet by 64 feet but could be used. The film, which features footage from five shows on the Steel Wheels / Urban Jungle tour, will play in Bradford until July. Even in the States there are only 15 cinemas capable of showing it.

16
Mick arrives at Narita Airport, Tokyo, to promote the film *Freejack*. Despite the fact that he has toured the country in 1988 and 1990, the Japanese refuse to allow him entry. He spends 38 hours in the Rest House Hotel at the airport while Japanese bureaucrats study the details of a 22 year old drug conviction.

17
The Japanese decide that Mick Jagger is not a threat to the security of the State and allow him into their country. The London *Times* sarcastically headlines, "Japan Relents And Allows Family Man, 48, To Enter." Mick checks into the Okura Hotel.

18
Mick holds a 40 minute press conference at the Sohgetuo Hall to promote the film and does TV and press interviews.

19
Mick parties at the Lexington Queen club with Axl from Guns n'Roses in the Roppongi district.

20
Mick flies to Phuket, Thailand, where he stays at the Amanpuri Hotel and is frequently seen in the company of a teenage girl. Jerry Hall later complains to the *Daily Mail*, "I confronted him and asked who he was with in Thailand... A man is supposed to be with his woman when she's just had a baby."

22
Keith flies into New York after a two week vacation in Antigua with his father, Bert.

23
Mick flies to Los Angeles.

29
Mick and guitarist Jimmy Rip attend a concert by Lixx Array at the Whiskey in Los Angeles.

MARCH
10
Ron and Jo arrive in Los Angeles to mix Ron's solo album.

13
Ron attends Ian McLagan's set at the Coconut Teaser club and joins him on stage for a few numbers.

Keith holds a party for Patti at Metropolis in New York.

18
Keith flies into San Rafael, California, with The X-pensive Winos after weeks of rehearsals in New York. He begins recording immediately at The Site studio. The Site combines all the comforts of a hotel, with bedrooms, restaurant facilities and a basketball court. Keith works through the night for two weeks.

23
Ron again joins Ian McLagan on stage, this time at The Mint in Los Angeles.

27
Ron completes the mixing of his solo album.

28
Ron reveals his new solo album, 'Slide On This', to a couple of dozen friends at A&M Records. Phil Spector, Ian McLagan, Ginger Baker, Herbie Hancock and Spencer Davis are among the guests.

31
Ron and Jo fly to Antigua from Los Angles.

APRIL
2
Keith flies to New York from San Rafael, California.

26
Ron and Jo fly to London from Antigua.

MAY
Dates: The Charlie Watts Quintet: The Canecao, Rio de Janeiro, Brazil (4); five shows at the Palladium, São Paolo (dates unknown); Teatro Da Reitoria, Puerto Allegre (15).

4
Mick and Jerry attend *Slip Of The Tongue* at the Shaftesbury Theatre, London, and afterwards visit its star, John Malkovich.

at the Bel Air Hotel, and the reception afterwards at Graham's sculpture studio in Venice, California.

24

Mick flies to the East Coast to attend his daughter Karis's graduation ceremony at Yale. Mick and Jerry visit with Karis's mother, Marsha Hunt.

25

Mick and Jerry are guests at Keith's Memorial Day barbecue before flying back to Los Angeles to continue work on his solo album.

28

Keith attends John Mooney's set at Tramp's, New York.

JUNE

2

Mick spotted dining with friends at the Hollywood Cantina.

15

Mick flies to London.

22

Mick and Jerry attend a party for Prince at Tramp in London.

24

Georgia May, Mick and Jerry's six month old daughter, is christened at St. Andrew's Church in Ham, Surrey. Charlie is named as her Godfather. Afterwards Mick and Jerry see Prince play Earls Court.

25

Ron and snooker player Jimmy White attend Wimbledon and see John McEnroe beat Pat Cash.

28

National Music Day is celebrated by 1,500 scheduled events across the nation. Mick appears at an open air session on Clapham Common, but doesn't perform. Later Mick, Ron and Charlie headline a "Celebration of the Blues" evening at Hammersmith Odeon, playing first individually, then together.

JULY

Dates: The Charlie Watts Quintet: Theater of the Living Arts, Philadelphia, Pennsylvania (12); The Blue Note, New York City (14-19); Park West, Chicago, Illinois (21); Hollywood Palace, Los Angeles, California (23); Royce Hall, University of California, Los Angeles (25).

Willy and The Poorboys: Hotel Tolysand, Holmstad, Sweden (28-31).

2

Mick's daughter Jade gives birth to a daughter Assisi. The father is her fellow art student Piers Jackson. Mick visits her in hospital and says he is "delighted". That evening, Mick throws a party for Jerry's birthday at their house in Richmond. The party has a Moroccan theme and is held in a large marquee in the garden. Ron, Charlie and Billy Connolly all arrive dressed as Arabs.

5 - 6

Ron tapes a promo-video in Dublin for his next solo single, 'Show Me'.

13

Charlie and his quintet arrive at the Hard Rock Café in New York to celebrate the opening of their tour and donate an autographed drum skin to the restaurant's rock memorabilia collection.

Above: Mick and Jerry. Below left: Ron with snooker star Jimmy White at Planet Hollywood. Below, right: Charlie at the Hard Rock Café in New York.

18

Charlie slips on a newly polished floor at his home and fractures his left elbow, causing the cancellation of a May 20-30 tour of Germany.

Mick joins The Red Devils on stage at the King Kong Club, Los Angeles.

19

Charlie releases his latest solo album, 'A Tribute To Charlie Parker, With Strings' by the Charlie Watts Quintet on Continuum 19201-2.

Recorded at Ronnie Scott's, Birmingham on October 31 and November 1, 1991 it features Peter King on alto saxophone, Gerard Presencer on trumpet, Brian Lemon on piano, David Green on acoustic bass and Charlie on drums.

21

Ron, Jo and the children attend the premier of *Wayne's World* in London.

23

Mick attends the wedding of Anjelica Huston and Robert Graham

14
Charlie and his trumpeter, Gerard Presencer, drop in on Keith at the studio at 2am.

16
The Charlie Watts Quintet arrive at the David Letterman Show, ready to perform, but Letterman's organisation insist that their house band, led by Paul Shaffer, accompany them. Charlie insists that this will ruin the song's arrangement and since Letterman will not back down, they leave without playing.

22
The Charlie Watts Quintet appear on the Los Angeles TV show: the *Dennis Miller Show*, talking and playing "Loverman".

26
Jerry throws a party for Mick's birthday in London at the recently opened 41 Beak Street Club in Soho.

28
28 - 1 AUGUST
Bill's ad hoc group, Willy and The Poorboys, play five nights at the Hotel Tolysand, Halmstad, Sweden, with Andy Fairweather-Low

on guitar, Gary Brooker on vocals and keyboard and Bill on bass.

29
Mick flies to Los Angeles where, according to press gossip, he is visiting one of the many women he is seen with in night-clubs around the world.

AUGUST
Dates: Willy and The Poorboys: Hotel Tolysand, Halmstad, Sweden (1).

3
Ron hosts a press party at Tatou in New York to plug his new album. Keith arrives to give moral support for half an hour before returning to Studio 900.

4
Ron appears on the *Howard Stern* radio show at 9:30am.

8
Mick is among the guests at a party at Rick Rubin's house in Los Angeles when the police break it up after neighbours complain about the noise.

10
Ron Wood's solo single 'Show

Me' from his forthcoming solo album 'Slide On This' released on Continuum 12210 / 2.

Ron appears on the Rockline radio phone-in show to plug his new single.

14
Ron visits Ian McLagan at Sonora Recording Studio in Los Angeles and sings on a vocal track for an upcoming Who tribute album.

16
Bill organises a charity cricket match at Penshurst Place, Kent, in aid of the Royal Marsden Hospital.

18
Ron visits ex-Face Rod Stewart in Los Angeles.

22
Mick and Jerry are spotted dining at Mansion on Turtle Creek in Dallas, Texas. They are staying at Jerry's ranch in Mesquite, Texas.

SEPTEMBER
5
Mick plays cricket in Los Angeles.

16

Ron plays at the Bob Dylan Tribute concert at Madison Square Garden.

18 - 26

Ron rehearsing his band at S.I.R. studios, New York, ready for his solo tour.

19

Keith appears live on the US radio phone-in show *Rockline*. That night, Keith visits Ron at the S.I.R. studio where he is rehearsing.

20

Keith's second studio album 'Main Offender' is released on Virgin Records CD VUS 59.

Produced by Keith, Steve Jordan and Waddy Wachtel, it features Keith on vocals and guitars with Waddy Wachtel, Steve Jordan, Charlie Drayton, Ivan Neville, Sarah Dash, Bernard Fowler and Babi Floyd. The core of these musicians constitutes X-Pensive Winos.

Keith holds a record signing session at Tower Records on Broadway to promote the new album. Almost 3,000 line up to meet him and a discreet bribe to the doorman was the only way to get in. Art dealer Stellan Holm found that $20 was the going rate and got a guitar signed.

26

Keith and Ron attend a book launch at Tower Books for the Bill Graham autobiography. After dining at Il Cantanori, Keith invites Ron to watch him rehearse The X-Pensive Winos.

28

Ron tapes a segment for the

David Letterman Show before going to Connecticut for a warm up gig at the Sting Club in New Brighton.

30

Keith does an interview with WNEW-FM's Scott Muni live from the Hard Rock Café, New York.

31

Bill holds a charity Hallowe'en party at his restaurant and raises £6,000 for the Royal Marsden Hospital.

NOVEMBER

Dates : Keith and his X-Pensive Winos: Velez Sarsfield Stadium, Buenos Aires, Argentina (7); K.B.Hall, Copenhagen, Denmark (27); Sportshalle, Cologne, Germany (29).

Ron Wood's 'Slide On This' tour: Electric Lady, New York City (2); The Roxy, Atlanta, Georgia (4); Jannus Landing, St. Petersburg, Florida (6); Cameo Theater, Miami, Florida (7); Tipitina's, New Orleans, Louisiana (10); The Tower Theater, Houston, Texas (11); The Terrace, Austin, Texas (13); The Agora, Dallas, Texas (14); The Rhythm Café, San Diego, California (16); Hollywood Palace, Los Angeles, California (18); The Rhythm Café, Santa Ana, California (19); Warfield Theater, San Francisco, California (21); Parker's, Seattle, Washington (23); The Commodore, Vancouver, Canada (24); The Vic, Chicago, Illinois (27); The Ritz, Detroit, Michigan (28); Concert Hall, Toronto, Canada (30).

2

Keith and his band arrive in Buenos Aires and check into the Sheraton. They rehearse in a discothèque for several days.

6

Keith finishes work on his solo album at Studio 900 in New York.

8

'Slide On This', Ron Wood's latest solo album, is released on Continuum 19210-2. (CD). Produced by Bernard Fowler and Ron Wood, it features Ron on vocals, guitars, acoustic bass and has contributions from Charlie Watts, Simon Kirke, Chuck Leavell, Joe Elliott, The Edge, Ian McLagan, members of The Hothouse Flowers and Ron's pal, and top snooker player, Jimmy 'Whirlwind' White, who is credited with special overdub on 'Like It'.

Keith masters his new solo album in New York.

9

Mick presents Van Halen with the Best Video Of The Year award at the MTV awards ceremony held at the Pauley Pavilion, Los Angeles. It was shown live by satellite in 150 countries.

OCTOBER

Dates: Ron Wood's 'Slide On This' tour: The Sting, New Brighton, Connecticut (28); Toad's Place, New Haven, Connecticut (30); The Ritz, New York (31).

Mick is back in London, recording his third solo album at Olympic Studios in Barnes.

1

Mick and Jerry fly to an undisclosed destination for a "second honeymoon".

9 - 10

Keith shoots a promo-video for 'Wicked As It Seems' in a shabby part of Los Angeles. Props include a three legged dog and several genuine winos who wander by.

10

Mick and Jerry attend the Chelsea Arts Ball at the Royal Albert Hall, London.

12

Keith flies to New York from Los Angeles.

13

Keith flies to Paris for five days of press for his new album.

15

Ron and Jo arrive in New York and check into Loew's Hotel.

Ron tapes a segment for the *Later With Bob Costas* talk show for NBC-TV. That evening, Ron performs live to an invited audience of about 75 people at the Electric Lady Studio on 8th Street, broadcast live on WNEW-FM in New York.

7
Keith and The X-Pensive Winos play to a sell-out audience of 45,000 in Buenos Aires.

9
Keith flies back to New York for two weeks of rehearsals with The X-Pensive Winos.

12
Keith and Patti attend *Rolling Stone* Magazine's 25th anniversary celebrations at the Four Seasons restaurant, New York.

17
Ron does a record signing session at Tower Records on Sunset, Hollywood.

19
Ron appears on the *Arsenio Hall Show* in Los Angeles.

21
Van Morrison joins Ron on stage at his concert at the Warfield Theater, San Francisco.

DECEMBER
Dates: Ron Wood's 'Slide On This' tour: La Brique, Montreal, Canada (1); The Avalon, Boston, Massachusetts (3); Chestnut Cabaret, Philadelphia, Pennsylvania (5).

Keith and his X-Pensive Winos: The Marquee, London (2); The Ahoy, Rotterdam, Netherlands (4); The Zenith, Paris, France (7); Zeleste, Barcelona, Spain (9-10); The Aqualung, Madrid, Spain (13-14); Town & Country Club, London, (17-18), The Academy, New York (31).

2
Keith plays a surprise date with The X-Pensive Winos at London's Marquee Club on Charing Cross Road. Mick and his brother Chris are in the audience but leave early because fans hassle Mick.

4
Mick and Jerry attend a charity event at the Intercontinental Hotel, London, organised by cricket star Imran Khan in aid of cancer research.

10-11
Mick spends two days at the Pump Rooms, Leamington Spa, filming the video for his new single 'Sweet Thing' with director Julien Temple. Mick says, "Course I love making videos. I just love being up all night dancing in the middle of a freezing empty swimming pool in an English market town in the middle of winter." In the middle of filming a local band playing in the building

blew the power supply, just as Mick was dancing with a group of nude girls whose bodies had been painted to resemble swimming pool tiles. "The poor girls were freezing for about ten minutes," says Mick, "I had a coat so I did my best to keep them all warm... by dancing."

17
Keith talks about his drug addiction to a reporter from *Kerrang!* magazine: "I never felt I was jeopardising future operations. Maybe I was testing myself... Fame is a brain-rotting thing. It can take over sane guys, and suddenly they're gone like a fucking meteor! You can be in the Stones and live in that bubble but look what happens - Bill Wyman and Mandy! Maybe the dope was my way of keeping my feet, uh, in the air! I can't say on the ground! To me being famous is the task. It's what I gotta put up with in order to do what I wanna do."

19
Keith checks out of the Carlton Tower and flies back to New York.

25
Mick, Jerry and their family spend Christmas in Mustique.

28
Keith tapes a concert with The X-Pensive Winos at WTTW-TV's studio in Chicago for their show *Center Stage*.

31
Keith and The X-Pensive Winos play The Academy, New York City. He brings in the New Year with "Time Is On My Side".

1993

JANUARY
Dates: Keith and The X-Pensive Winos tour: The Arena, Seattle, Washington (17); The Orpheum, Vancouver, Canada (19); Civic Center, San Francisco, California (21); Universal Amphitheater, Los Angeles, California (23); Golden Hall, San Diego, California (26); American West, Phoenix, Arizona (28); Auditorium Theater, Denver, Colorado (30).

Ron Wood's solo tour: Koseinenkinkakan, Osaka, Japan (10); Sun Palace, Fukuoka, Japan (11); Aichi 'kinakakan, Nagoya, Japan (13); Budokan, Tokyo, Japan (14).

Keith on stage at his X-Pensive Winos band gig at the Beacon Theater, New York.

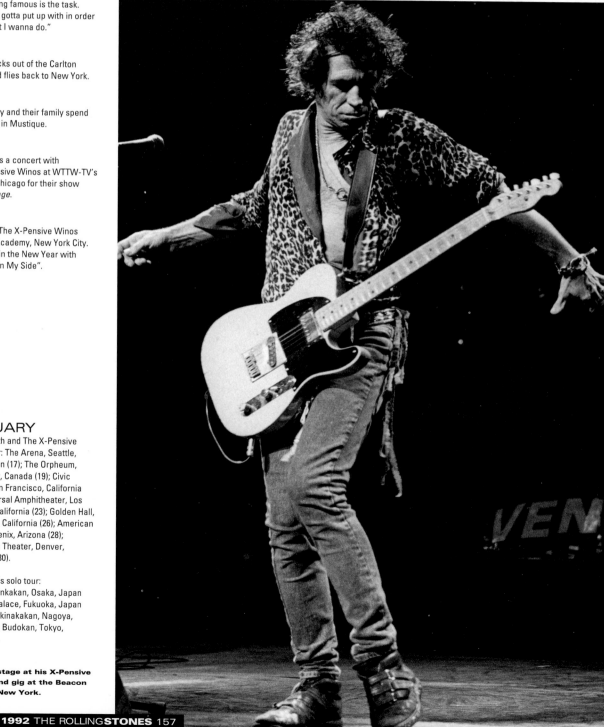

6

Bill officially leaves The Rolling Stones. On the *London Tonight* news programme, Bill tells viewers: "I really don't want to do it anymore. I have many special memories, it's been wonderful. But I thought the last two tours with them were the best we have ever done, so I was quite happy to stop after that... When I joined this band, we thought we would last two or three years with a bit of luck and come out with a few shillings in our pocket. Now here I am, 30 years later, and I haven't done any of the other important things in life. I have a very successful restaurant. I'm working on a new book. I've just released a solo album. I do archaeology in an amateurish way. And I have a private life to deal with, as well."

Mick responded, "I don't think it will faze us that much. We'll miss Bill, but we'll get someone good, a good dancer."

11

After his Sun Palace concert, Ron spent the evening at a karaoke bar called Tremoille, singing along with The Platters' 'Only You'.

14

After two weeks of rehearsal at S.I.R. studio in New York, Keith and The X-Pensive Winos fly to Seattle to begin their tour.

15

Ron attends a show of his paintings at Shibuya-Beam, in Tokyo, then catches the Guns n'Roses concert at the Tokyo Dome. He joins the band on stage for Dylan's 'Knocking On Heaven's Door'.

17

The X-Pensive Winos open their tour with a line-up change: bass player Charley Drayton has prior commitments and is replaced by Jerome Smith. The rest of the line-up is the same: Waddy Wachtel on guitar; Steve Jordan on drums; Ivan Neville on keyboards; Sarah Dash and Babi Floyd on vocals; Bobby Keys on saxophone.

22

Keith does a record signing session at Tower Records, Los Angeles.

23

The video for 'Sweet Thing', Mick's new single, is given its British TV première on ITV's *Video Chart Show*.

25

Mick releases 'Sweet Thing' / 'Wandering Spirit' on Atlantic Records.

26

Ron releases 'Somebody Else'.

30

Mick sighted with supermodel Elle McPherson at Club USA in New York.

FEBRUARY

Dates: Keith and The X-Pensive Winos tour: Wilkins Auditorium, Minneapolis, Minnesota (2); Aragon Ballroom, Chicago, Illinois (4); Massey Hall, Toronto, Canada (6); Fox Theater, Detroit, Michigan (8); Constitution Hall, Washington, D.C. (10); Orpheum Theater, Boston, Massachusetts (12-14); Beacon Theater, New York (19-20, 22-24).

Mick Jagger solo: Webster Hall, New York City (9).

2

Many radio stations, including K-ROCK in New York and KLOS in Los Angeles, run the syndicated programme *The World Première of Mick Jagger's Wandering Spirit*.

4

Mick tapes promo spots for *Saturday Night Live* at NBC and does a brief walk-on for the NBC-TV *David Letterman show*, aired that night.

5

Ron takes part in Rod Stewart's edition of MTV's *Unplugged*, playing on 13 of his songs. The event was videoed before an audience of 400 people at Universal Studios in Los Angeles.

6

Mick appears on the TV talk show *Saturday Night Live* in the States.

8

Mick's solo album, 'Wandering Spirit', is released on East West Records in the States and on Atlantic in Europe. He recorded a number of tracks in England and France before flying to Los Angeles to work with producer Rick Rubin. Mick: "We were in a pretty funky studio that looked like the end of the '60s- Ocean Way, which doesn't change. The guy who owns it is a complete nut for the late '60s or early '70s, so all the equipment is this big, old stuff. I couldn't work out quite where I was. I did often think I was making a throwback record. I didn't consciously want to make an album of 1972, or whatever. I don't think that in the end it sounds like it, but there are nods to that."

Mick told Robin Eggar, "My producer Rick Rubin never goes to his office and does all his business from his car, a 1976 Rolls Royce.

We recorded in a very seedy area of Hollywood, a soup kitchen on one corner, a transvestite pick up on the other. Rick and I would always go and listen to mixes in his Rolls parked in the street. We couldn't decide which version of 'Sweet Thing' to choose so all the local bums surrounded the car and gave us their opinion - not always politely - of what they liked best. I still think they were right."

9

The video of Mick's *Sweet Thing* is premièred on MTV.

After playing Webster Hall to an invited audience of press and corporate people, Mick goes on to the end of tour party (one gig only) at Tatou.

16

Ron and Rod Stewart appear at The Faces reunion at the *British Music Awards* at Alexander Palace. Rod sings 'Stay With Me' with Ron on guitar and ex-Stone Bill Wyman on bass.

19

Keith sets up X-Pensive Winos headquarters at the Mayflower for the week they are in New York.

25

Keith flies to St. Barts for a vacation.

MARCH

The story breaks that Patsy Smith, 46, the mother of Bill's ex-wife Mandy, is to marry Bill's son Stephen, 30, which would make Bill not only the father-in-law of his former mother-in-law but also the step-grandfather of his former wife.

Mick and Keith get together to work on songs for a new album, the Stones' first without Bill Wyman.

2

Keith's set taped for the TV show *Center Stage* is transmitted across the USA.

APRIL
14

Ron's appearance on Rod Stewart's edition of MTV's *Unplugged* is shown.

20

Mick and Keith arrive in Barbados to work on material for the Stones' next album. They met at JFK airport and flew down together.

21

Bill marries Californian fashion designer Suzanne Accosta in St. Paul de Vence, in the South of France. The ceremony begins in the 16th century dungeon of the village Registry Office and continues at the 13th century church of the Conversion of St. Paul where they receive a blessing from Anglican priest Keith Anderson. The reception, for just 42 guests, is at the nearby Colombe d'Or hotel and restaurant. None of the Stones attend. They are all recording in Bermuda. Bill is 56, Suzanne is 33.

27

Ron and Rod Stewart fly into New York.

29

Ron and Rod Stewart are interviewed on NBC-TVs the *David Letterman Show*.

30

Charlie joins Mick and Keith in Barbados to lay down some tracks for their new album.

MAY
1

Ron, Jo, Rod Stewart and his wife Rachel fly to Louisville to attend the Kentucky Derby where they back the winner, Sea Hero, at 12 to 1.

3

Ron and Rod appear on the live radio talk show *Rockline* in New York.

5

Ron, Jo, Rod and Rachel take Concorde back to London.

12

Ron and Rod Stewart take a Lear jet to Nice to appear at the World Music Awards in Monte Carlo where Ron presents Rod with a Lifetime Achievement Award at the Sporting Club. They fly back to London directly after the ceremony.

17

Ron and Jo take their children to the opening of the Planet Hollywood restaurant in London.

21

Ron appears in a promo-video for Pete Townshend, pretending to be a member of Townshend's band on the song 'English Boy'.

23

Ron appears on the *Aspel & Co* TV show in London, backing Jerry Lee Lewis live on 'Great Balls Of Fire' and 'Whole Lotta Shakin' Goin' On'.

24

Rod Stewart, Unplugged... and Seated is released featuring Ron Wood. It is the recording of the MTV programme in which Ron joined Rod for a very friendly reunion.

30

Ron joins Guns n'Roses on stage at the Milton Keynes Bowl to jam on their version of 'Honky Tonk Woman'.

JUNE
1

Ron celebrates his 46th birthday with a few drinks at Cook's Café in Dublin.

2

Keith and Mick are inducted into the Songwriters Hall of Fame at a ceremony held at the Sheraton Hotel in New York. Mick is in London so Keith represents them both and says a few words to the assembled guests: "There was really only one song ever written. That was by Adam and Eve. We just do the variations..."

11

Ron Wood joins Rod Stewart on *Michael Aspel's TV chat show. The pair duet on 'Have I Told You Lately That I Love You'.

JULY
16

Mick holds his 50th birthday party ten days early at Walpole House, a neo-Gothic mansion in Twickenham. 300 of rock'n'roll's élite dance until dawn dressed as characters from the French Revolution: Jerry Hall as Marie Antoinette and Marie Helvin as a shepherdess. Walpole House is used as a summer language school, and a group of French students were only given a few hours notice to move their own party to a separate house in the grounds. One student, Karine Bruyant said, "It would have been nice if they had invited the French students to come and sing the National Anthem for them, they're singing it very badly."

Left: Bill with Suzanne Accosta.

POSTSCRIPT

As this book went to press, there was talk that the Stones had signed a new sponsorship deal with the Italian fashion house Benetton, who would underwrite the cost of their forthcoming world tour, presumably in the summer of 1994.

In the autumn of 1993 Mick, Keith and Charlie spent time at Ron Wood's farmhouse near Dublin rehearsing new material, with Keith and Ronnie alternating on bass now that Bill had finally hung up his rock'n'roll shoes and become a restaurateur, author and photographer. The new material was due to be recorded in Trinidad during December, probably with Don Was in the producer's chair.

In November Mick Jagger formally announced that with Bill's departure from the Stones they would become a "four-piece" band with a "cacophony of bass players". In the studio, at least, the bass chores can be shared between Keith and Ron, but others named as potential "guest bassists" include ex-Miles Davis bass man Darryl Jones and Living Colour's Doug Wimbish.

With the band set to tour the stadiums of the world once again in 1994, this could, indeed, be the last time.